Effective Coding Skill Development in Education

Fatih Yaman
https://orcid.org/0000-0002-7425-1369
Kırşehir Ahi Evran University, Turkey

Nihal Dulkadir Yaman
Kırşehir Ahi Evran University, Turkey

IGI Global
Scientific Publishing
Publishing Tomorrow's Research Today

Vice President of Editorial Melissa Wagner
Director of Acquisitions Mikaela Felty
Director of Book Development Jocelynn Hessler
Production Manager Mike Brehm
Cover Design Jose Rosado

Published in the United States of America by
IGI Global Scientific Publishing
701 East Chocolate Avenue
Hershey, PA, 17033, USA
Tel: 717-533-8845 | Fax: 717-533-7115
Website: https://www.igi-global.com E-mail: cust@igi-global.com

Library of Congress Cataloging-in-Publication Data

Names: Yaman, Fatih, 1984- editor | Yaman, Nihal Dulkadir, 1986- editor
Title: Effective coding skill development in education / edited by Fatih Yaman, Nihal Dulkadir Yaman.
Description: Hershey, PA : IGI Global Scientific Publishing, 2026. | Includes bibliographical references and index. | Summary: "This book aims to increase the knowledge and skills of university students by introducing them to the opportunities offered by technology in education"-- Provided by publisher.
Identifiers: LCCN 2025020212 (print) | LCCN 2025020213 (ebook) | ISBN 9798337326603 h/c | ISBN 9798337326610 s/c | ISBN 9798337326627 ebook
Subjects: LCSH: Computer science--Study and teaching (Higher) | Computer programming--Study and teaching (Higher) | Artificial intelligence--Study and teaching (Higher) | Computer-assisted instruction.
Classification: LCC QA76.27 .E297 2026 (print) | LCC QA76.27 (ebook)
LC record available at https://lccn.loc.gov/2025020212
LC ebook record available at https://lccn.loc.gov/2025020213

British Cataloguing in Publication Data
A Cataloguing in Publication record for this book is available from the British Library.

Table of Contents

Detailed Table of Contents

teacher competence, curriculum integration, and adaptation to technological change are presented along with suggested solutions. Research shows that coding education not only develops technical skills but also fosters future-oriented competencies such as creativity, critical thinking, and collaborative problem-solving.

This section analyzes coding education challenges through Cognitive Load Theory (CLT), which identifies working memory limitations in processing complex coding concepts. We examine three load types: intrinsic (task complexity), extraneous (poor instructional design), and germane (schema construction). CLT-based solutions include sequenced instruction, worked examples, and multimodal learning to optimize cognitive load distribution. Findings demonstrate these strategies improve knowledge retention and problem-solving transfer. The research highlights educators' role as cognitive designers and emphasizes adaptive scaffolding for diverse learners. By implementing CLT principles, coding education can become more effective and inclusive while reducing cognitive overload.

Coding education has become integral to preparing learners for the digital age. However, persistent challenges—ranging from inadequate foundational knowledge to teacher training gaps—compromise the effectiveness of coding programs worldwide. This chapter analyzes common barriers that students and educators face, while proposing evidence-based strategies to mitigate these issues. Drawing on research between 2015 and 2024, the authors highlight the necessity of scaffolded curricula, collaborative learning models, professional development opportunities, and inclusive pedagogies. By examining multiple interventions, the chapter underscores how coding education can evolve into a dynamic, accessible, and engaging discipline that equips learners with essential problem-solving skills. The overarching goal is to guide education stakeholders in designing and implementing coding programs that not only address short-term learning objectives but also foster long-term digital literacy and career readiness.

This chapter presents how an inquiry-based approach in teaching computational thinking (CT) can be embedded in teacher education. Informed by the expectancy-value theory, it provides strategies to help preservice teachers (PSTs) develop interest in CT, recognize its relevance to content and pedagogy, and build competence with it. Furthermore, the chapter describes various learning units that use 2D, 3D, robotics technologies as well as an AI extension to illustrate how to promote students' CT in an inquiry format. Varying difficulty levels of coding and personalization opportunities are also included for more effective implementation of the activities while the suggested timeline can be useful to help interested teacher education faculty plan their curricula. The implementation of the described activities aims to assist PSTs in preparing their future pupils to think computationally.

This chapter introduces eduMathStatAI, a developing R package designed to enhance mathematics and statistics education by integrating coding and digital tools into teaching. Currently, it provides structured lesson module examples and customized functions that enable teachers to incorporate computational thinking into their instruction. Focusing on sustainable, non-formal teacher training, the chapter highlights strategies that ensure accessibility for educators with varying programming experience. By emphasizing scalable, modular, and open-access resources, eduMathStatAI aims to foster equitable digital transformation and align with international recommendations for inclusive STEM education. The chapter offers a practical guide for gradually expanding the toolkit and integrating coding into curriculum-aligned instruction while supporting sustainable development.

The integration of programming and coding into education and research has gained prominence. These skills are viewed as both core technical competencies and tools for

Preface

In today's technology-driven world, coding has become an essential skill, not only for careers in computer science but also as a foundation tool for critical thinking across all disciplines. As education systems strive to help students in this digital age, the development of coding skills has become increasingly important. Integrating coding into educational curricula and projects can help empower students to become creators rather than consumers of technology. By using computational thinking and innovation, it can equip learners with skills for future success.

Effective Coding Skill Development in Education examines strategies and approaches for developing strong coding skills in educational settings, from fundamental concepts to advanced problem-solving techniques. It highlights practical frameworks, teaching methodologies, and curriculum innovations that prepare students for success in an increasingly digital and technology-focused world. Carefully selected book chapters by the editorial team on topics such as coding skills, education, and computer science will enable teachers, educators, teacher candidates, academics, students, instructional designers, curriculum developers, and administrators to better integrate coding skills education into schools.

ORGANIZATION OF THE BOOK

Chapter 1: The Essentials of Coding Education

The Essentials of Coding Education" explores the foundational principles and effective methodologies for teaching programming in the digital age. As computational thinking becomes a critical skill across disciplines, this paper highlights key strategies for fostering problem-solving abilities, logical reasoning, and creativity through coding. It examines the importance of hands-on learning, project-based approaches, and adaptive instruction tailored to diverse learners. Additionally, the discussion addresses common challenges in coding education, such as engagement barriers and varying skill levels, while proposing evidence-based solutions. By integrating pedagogical best practices with emerging technologies, this work underscores the transformative potential of coding education in preparing students for future careers. Ultimately, the paper advocates for inclusive, accessible, and student-centered coding instruction to cultivate a generation of proficient and innovative thinkers.

Chapter 2: Coding Education Why And How?

This section discusses why coding education is necessary, its contribution to learning processes, and its relationship with different disciplines. It emphasizes that coding education supports cognitive development from an early age and can be effectively implemented with age-appropriate content, methods, and tools. The selection criteria for popular programming languages and their roles in education are detailed. The educational value of languages such as Scratch, Python, and Java is explained with examples. In addition, the platforms and tools used in coding education are examined in four main categories, and the importance of practical and gamified learning approaches is emphasized. At the end of the section, common challenges such as teacher competence, curriculum integration, and adaptation to technological change are presented along with suggested solutions. Research shows that coding education not only develops technical skills but also fosters future-oriented competencies such as creativity, critical thinking, and collaborative problem-solving.

Chapter 3: Common Challenges in Coding Education: A Cognitive Load Theory Perspective

This section analyzes coding education challenges through Cognitive Load Theory (CLT), which identifies working memory limitations in processing complex coding concepts. We examine three load types: intrinsic (task complexity), extraneous (poor instructional design), and germane (schema construction). CLT-based solutions include sequenced instruction, worked examples, and multimodal learning to optimize cognitive load distribution. Findings demonstrate these strategies improve knowledge retention and problem-solving transfer. The research highlights educators' role as cognitive designers and emphasizes adaptive scaffolding for diverse learners. By implementing CLT principles, coding education can become more effective and inclusive while reducing cognitive overload.

Chapter 4: Common Challenges in Coding Education and Proposed Solutions - A Theoretical-Framework Approach

Coding education has become integral to preparing learners for the digital age. However, persistent challenges—ranging from inadequate foundational knowledge to teacher training gaps—compromise the effectiveness of coding programs worldwide. This chapter analyzes common barriers that students and educators face, while proposing evidence-based strategies to mitigate these issues. Drawing on research between 2015 and 2024, the authors highlight the necessity of scaffolded curricula, collaborative learning models, professional development opportunities, and inclusive pedagogies. By examining multiple interventions, the chapter underscores how coding education can evolve into a dynamic, accessible, and engaging discipline that equips learners with essential problem-solving skills. The overarching goal is to guide education stakeholders in designing and implementing coding programs that not only address short-term learning objectives but also foster long-term digital literacy and career readiness.

Chapter 5: An Inquiry-based Computational Thinking Approach in Teacher Education: Inquiry CT in Teacher Education

This chapter presents how an inquiry-based approach in teaching computational thinking (CT) can be embedded in teacher education. Informed by the expectancy-value theory, it provides strategies to help preservice teachers (PSTs) develop interest in CT, recognize its relevance to content and pedagogy, and build competence with it. Furthermore, the chapter describes various learning units that use 2D, 3D, robotics technologies as well as an AI extension to illustrate how to promote students' CT in an inquiry format. Varying difficulty levels of coding and personalization opportunities are also included for more effective implementation of the activities while the suggested timeline can be useful to help interested teacher education faculty plan their curricula. The implementation of the described activities aims to assist PSTs in preparing their future pupils to think computationally.

Chapter 6: eduMathStatAI: Enhancing Mathematics and Statistics Education through Coding and Digital Tools

This chapter introduces eduMathStatAI, a developing R package designed to enhance mathematics and statistics education by integrating coding and digital tools into teaching. Currently, it provides structured lesson module examples and customized functions that enable teachers to incorporate computational thinking into their instruction. Focusing on sustainable, non-formal teacher training, the chapter highlights strategies that ensure accessibility for educators with varying programming experience. By emphasizing scalable, modular, and open-access resources, eduMathStatAI aims to foster equitable digital transformation and align with international recommendations for inclusive STEM education. The chapter offers a practical guide for gradually expanding the toolkit and integrating coding into curriculum-aligned instruction while supporting sustainable development.

Chapter 7: Educational Neuroscience of Programming: Cognitive and Neural Perspectives

The integration of programming and coding into education and research has gained prominence. These skills are viewed as both core technical competencies and tools for enhancing cognitive development. This chapter reviews research from neuroscience, education, and cognitive psychology to examine the cognitive and neural processes involved in programming. The chapter examines how programming fosters critical skills like problem-solving, creative thinking, and critical analysis, alongside its demands on analytical intelligence and metacognitive abilities. It delves into the neural mechanisms involved, highlighting the activation of various brain regions responsible for working memory, language processing, and executive control. The chapter highlights neuroplastic changes in gray matter volume and neural efficiency, showcasing how the brain adapts to programming learning across ages. It also explores the cognitive effects of coding education, emphasizing its integration into curricula and its impact on cognitive development through an interdisciplinary research approach.

Chapter 8: Technology in Education for People with Disabilities: Coding for Inclusion and Accessible Learning Design

This chapter examines how coding and artificial intelligence (AI) can advance inclusive education for learners with disabilities. Focusing on a real-time American Sign Language (ASL) recognition system, it demonstrates how assistive coding innovations enhance classroom communication and participation. The system, developed using MediaPipe and Convolutional Neural Networks (CNNs), translates hand gestures into text, enabling equitable interaction between hearing and non-hearing students. Beyond technical development, the chapter highlights pedagogical integration, offering practical guidance for classroom implementation and emphasizing teacher and student perspectives. Ethical issues such as data privacy, fairness, and accessibility are also addressed. By linking coding skill development with inclusive teaching practices, the chapter underscores the potential of AI-driven technologies to create equitable and engaging learning environments for all students.

Chapter 9: Navigating Skill Development and Ethical Challenges in Coding Education with Generative AI

The rise of generative AI tools like ChatGPT and GitHub Copilot is transforming computer science education by changing how students learn to code and how instructors design curricula and assess learning. These tools offer real-time feedback, code generation, and debugging assistance, making programming more accessible and efficient. However, this shift raises concerns about overreliance on automation, erosion of foundational skills, and ethical issues around authorship and academic integrity. This chapter explores the educational and moral implications of using generative AI in programming instruction. Based on interviews with students across computer science programs and professional programmers, the paper examines how these tools affect learning outcomes, engagement, and skill development. While students appreciate AI support, educators note reduced critical thinking and understanding of core concepts. Many learners struggle to explain AI-generated code, revealing a gap between task completion and proper comprehension.

Chapter 1
The Essentials of Coding Education

Milan Sahoo
https://orcid.org/0009-0007-0619-3682
Brainware University, India

Aditya Saha
https://orcid.org/0009-0004-1783-8587
Brainware University, India

Ranjan Banerjee
https://orcid.org/0009-0003-1950-7530
Brainware University, India

Misha Samanta
https://orcid.org/0009-0000-6037-2760
Brainware University, India

Malay Maity
https://orcid.org/0009-0001-9173-6763
Brainware University, India

Debesh Das
https://orcid.org/0009-0009-0287-4995
Brainware University, India

Salankara Sarkar
https://orcid.org/0009-0005-0123-3724
Brainware University, India

ABSTRACT

The Essentials of Coding Education" explores the foundational principles and effective methodologies for teaching programming in the digital age. As computational thinking becomes a critical skill across disciplines, this paper highlights key strategies for fostering problem-solving abilities, logical reasoning, and creativity through coding. It examines the importance of hands-on learning, project-based approaches, and adaptive instruction tailored to diverse learners. Additionally, the discussion addresses common challenges in coding education, such as engagement barriers and varying skill levels, while proposing evidence-based solutions. By integrating pedagogical best practices with emerging technologies, this work underscores the transformative potential of coding education in preparing students

DOI: 10.4018/979-8-3373-2660-3.ch001

for future careers. Ultimately, the paper advocates for inclusive, accessible, and student-centered coding instruction to cultivate a generation of proficient and innovative thinkers.

INTRODUCTION

Coding is no longer just a technical skill—it is a fundamental literacy in the digital age. As technology reshapes every aspect of modern life, the ability to understand and create with code has become as essential as reading and mathematics. Coding education fosters problem-solving, logical reasoning, and creativity, equipping learners with skills that extend far beyond computer science. Whether for career success, academic growth, or personal innovation, mastering coding unlocks opportunities in an increasingly tech-driven world.

FOUNDATIONAL CONCEPTS & PEDAGOGY:

Effective pedagogy arises from a deep understanding and seamless integration of foundational concepts. Learning theories, such as constructivism and cognitivism, inform how we design instruction, moving beyond rote memorization to active knowledge construction and meaningful information processing. Developmental psychology guides us in tailoring instruction to meet the diverse cognitive, social, and emotional needs of learners, particularly through differentiated approaches. Embracing diversity and inclusion through culturally responsive teaching ensures all students feel valued and engaged, fostering a sense of belonging. Assessment, when used formatively, becomes a powerful tool for learning, providing actionable feedback that drives student growth. Ethical considerations underpin all pedagogical decisions, creating a safe and supportive learning community where students feel respected and empowered. Ultimately, successful teaching relies on the dynamic interplay of these foundational concepts, creating a responsive and adaptable learning environment that prioritizes student engagement and success.

1. Why Code? The Importance and Evolution of Coding Education:

Coding is now a fundamental skill, not just for tech careers but for navigating our digital world. It teaches problem-solving, logical thinking, and creativity—skills valuable in any field.

Originally limited to computer science, coding education now starts early in schools worldwide, preparing students for a tech-driven future. From healthcare to finance, coding literacy opens doors to opportunities and empowers people to shape technology, not just use it.

Key Reasons to Learn Coding:

- Develops critical thinking & problem-solving
- Essential for future job markets
- Enables innovation across all industries
- Builds adaptability in a fast-changing digital world

Coding isn't just about programming—it's about learning how to think and create in the 21st century.

2. Computational Thinking: The Core Skill of Coding Education:

In today's technology-driven world, computational thinking has emerged as a fundamental cognitive skill that transcends traditional programming education. This problem-solving methodology, which forms the core of coding instruction, equips learners with transferable abilities applicable across disciplines and daily life.

Understanding Computational Thinking

At its essence, computational thinking involves four key processes:

1. **Decomposition** - Breaking complex problems into smaller, manageable parts
2. **Pattern Recognition** - Identifying similarities and trends within problems
3. **Abstraction** - Focusing on relevant details while ignoring irrelevant information
4. **Algorithm Design** - Creating step-by-step solutions that can be automated

These cognitive strategies mirror how computer scientists approach challenges, but their value extends far beyond writing code.(Papert, 1980) Research indicates that students who develop computational thinking skills demonstrate improved performance in mathematics, science, and even language arts.

Educational Applications

Modern curricula increasingly emphasize computational thinking as early as elementary school. Tools like Scratch and Blockly introduce these concepts through visual programming, allowing young learners to grasp abstract ideas through tangible projects. As students progress, these foundational skills support more advanced programming in Python, Java, or C++.

Real-World Relevance

The applications of computational thinking span numerous fields:

1. Healthcare - Analyzing Patient Data Patterns for Diagnosis

In healthcare, analyzing patient data patterns plays a crucial role in improving diagnosis accuracy. By leveraging machine learning and big data analytics, medical professionals can identify trends in symptoms, genetic predispositions, and treatment outcomes. Predictive models help detect diseases like cancer and diabetes at early stages, enhancing patient survival rates. Additionally, electronic health records (EHRs) streamline data sharing among doctors, reducing diagnostic errors. AI-powered tools also assist in personalized medicine, where treatments are tailored based on individual patient data, improving overall healthcare efficiency.

2. Business - Optimizing Logistics and Supply Chains

Businesses rely on data-driven strategies to optimize logistics and supply chain operations. Advanced analytics help track inventory levels, predict demand fluctuations, and identify cost-effective shipping routes. Machine learning algorithms improve warehouse automation, reducing delays and minimizing human error. Real-time tracking systems enhance transparency, allowing companies to respond swiftly to disruptions. By optimizing supply chains, businesses reduce operational costs, improve delivery times, and enhance customer satisfaction, giving them a competitive edge in the market.

3. Engineering - Designing Efficient Systems and Structures

Engineering benefits greatly from computational tools that enhance system and structural design. Simulation software allows engineers to test prototypes virtually, reducing material waste and development costs. Finite element analysis (FEA) and computational fluid dynamics (CFD) help optimize designs for durability, energy efficiency, and safety. In civil engineering, AI assists in smart city planning by analyzing traffic patterns and environmental impacts. By integrating data-driven approaches, engineers create innovative, sustainable solutions that meet modern infrastructure demands.

4. Everyday Life - Organizing Personal Tasks and Decision-Making

Data-driven decision-making has become integral to everyday life. Smartphone apps analyze personal habits to improve time management, fitness, and financial planning. AI-powered virtual assistants schedule tasks, set reminders, and provide recommendations based on user preferences. Wearable devices track health metrics, encouraging better lifestyle choices. Additionally, personalized algorithms in e-commerce and entertainment platforms enhance user experiences by suggesting relevant products and content. These tools empower individuals to make informed decisions efficiently.

Assessment and Measurement

Educators employ various methods to evaluate computational thinking:

- Project-based assessments
- Problem-solving scenarios
- Debugging challenges
- Algorithm design tasks

These approaches measure not just technical ability, but more importantly, the underlying cognitive processes.

Future Directions

As artificial intelligence and automation reshape the workforce, computational thinking will become increasingly vital. Educational systems worldwide are recognizing this shift, with many countries integrating these concepts into national standards. The challenge lies in developing effective pedagogical approaches that make these abstract concepts accessible to all learners.

3. Learning Theories and Coding Pedagogy: Effective Teaching Strategies:

The field of coding education has evolved significantly, moving beyond traditional lecture-based instruction to embrace pedagogical approaches grounded in cognitive science and learning theories. Effective coding instruction today integrates constructivist principles, social learning theory, and cognitive load management to create engaging, sustainable learning experiences. This discussion explores how modern coding pedagogy applies these theoretical frameworks to develop computational thinking and programming skills across diverse learner populations.

Constructivist Approaches in Coding Education

Constructivism forms the backbone of contemporary coding instruction, emphasizing knowledge construction through active experience. This approach manifests in several key strategies:

Programming education has evolved significantly, moving away from rote memorization to more interactive and practical approaches. Three key methodologies—Project-Based Learning (PBL), Scaffolded Challenges, and Discovery Learning—have proven highly effective in helping learners grasp coding concepts while maintaining engagement and motivation.

1. Project-Based Learning (PBL)

PBL immerses students in real-world programming tasks, such as developing apps, games, or websites, rather than abstract exercises. This approach provides immediate context, making learning more meaningful. For instance, instead of simply studying Python syntax, a student might build a text-based adventure game, applying variables, loops, and functions in a practical setting.

The benefits of PBL include:

- Increased motivation – Learners see tangible results, reinforcing their progress.
- Better retention – Applying concepts in projects strengthens understanding.
- Problem-solving skills – Debugging and refining projects teach critical thinking.

Educators can enhance PBL by incorporating collaborative projects, where students work in teams to simulate real development environments.

2. Scaffolded Challenges

A structured learning path is essential for preventing frustration and ensuring steady progress. Scaffolding involves starting with simple concepts (e.g., block-based programming in Scratch) before advancing to text-based languages like Python or JavaScript (Resnick, 2017).

Key aspects of scaffolding include:

- Gradual complexity – Each lesson builds on prior knowledge while introducing new challenges.
- Reduced cognitive load – Breaking concepts into manageable steps prevents overwhelm.

- Adaptive learning – Adjusting difficulty based on student progress keeps them engaged.

For example, a beginner might first create animations in Scratch, then transition to Python for basic scripting, and eventually develop full-fledged applications. This step-by-step approach builds confidence and competence.

3. Discovery Learning

Modern programming education emphasizes guided discovery, where learners experiment with code snippets to deduce patterns and logic. This method mirrors how professional developers learn new frameworks—through trial, error, and exploration.(Guzdial, 2015)

Advantages of discovery learning include:

- Active engagement – Students take ownership of their learning by testing hypotheses.
- Deeper understanding – Figuring out how code works leads to stronger retention.
- Adaptability – Encourages self-reliance when encountering unfamiliar problems.

Interactive platforms like Codecademy and freeCodeCamp use this approach, allowing learners to modify code and see instant results. Instructors can facilitate discovery by providing open-ended challenges with minimal initial guidance, prompting students to think critically.

Social Learning Applications

Vygotsky's social development theory finds practical application in coding education through:

1. Pair Programming

Modeled after industry practices, this collaborative approach pairs learners as "driver" and "navigator." Research shows it improves code quality, reduces frustration, and develops communication skills essential for tech careers.

2. Community Coding

Platforms like GitHub Classroom facilitate social learning through code sharing, peer review, and open-source contributions. These mirror real-world development workflows while fostering professional networking (Kafai & Burke, 2014).

3. Competitive Learning

Hackathons and coding competitions leverage social motivation through team challenges and public demonstrations. These events build confidence and showcase applied skills.

Cognitive Load Management

Cognitive load theory informs critical instructional design choices:

1. Visual Programming First

Tools like Scratch or Blockly reduce initial cognitive load by eliminating syntax errors, allowing focus on algorithmic thinking. Studies show students transitioning from visual to text-based languages demonstrate better problem-solving skills.

2. Worked Examples with Fading

Instruction begins with fully worked examples, gradually removing steps as competency increases. This "fading" technique helps learners internalize problem-solving patterns.

3. Error-Based Learning

Purposeful debugging exercises train students to interpret error messages and develop systematic troubleshooting approaches—a critical professional skill (Wing, 2006).

Emerging Instructional Strategies

1. Adaptive Learning Systems

AI-driven platforms now customize problem sets based on individual progress, providing optimal challenge levels. These systems identify conceptual gaps and serve targeted exercises.

2. Gamification Elements

Badge systems, experience points, and leaderboards increase engagement, particularly for younger learners. However, effective implementation balances competition with collaborative elements(Grover & Pea, 2013).

3. Contextualized Learning

Teaching coding through discipline-specific applications (e.g., data analysis for social studies) increases relevance and motivation for non-CS majors.

Assessment Innovations

Moving beyond traditional exams, modern coding assessment emphasizes:

1. Process Over Product

Evaluating problem-solving approaches and debugging strategies rather than just final output.

2. Portfolio Assessments

Longitudinal collections demonstrating skill progression through varied projects.

3. Reflective Practices

Journals or viva voce exams where students explain their code decisions.

Implementation Challenges

Despite these advances, barriers remain:

1. Teacher Preparedness

Many educators lack dual expertise in pedagogy and programming, necessitating specialized professional development.

2. Resource Disparities

Schools in under-resourced areas often lack hardware, software, or reliable internet for modern coding instruction.

3. Curriculum Integration

Balancing coding instruction with existing curricular demands requires careful planning.

Future Directions
The field continues evolving with:

1. Immersive Technologies

VR/AR coding environments providing tangible, 3D programming experiences.

2. Neuroscience Applications

Brain-based research informing optimal learning sequences and retention strategies.
3. Global Competency Frameworks
Standardized computational thinking progressions across education systems.

4. Choosing the Right Language and Tools: A Guide for Educators

Selecting the appropriate programming language and development tools is one of the most critical decisions in coding education. This choice significantly impacts student engagement, learning outcomes, and future career readiness. With the rapid evolution of technology and diverse learner needs, educators must carefully evaluate multiple factors when designing their coding curriculum. This guide provides a detailed framework to help teachers make informed decisions about programming languages and tools based on educational objectives, student demographics, and available resources(Brennan et, al., 2012).

Section 1: Foundational Considerations

1. Age and Developmental Stage

The cognitive abilities and motor skills of learners vary significantly across age groups. For early learners (ages 5-9), visual programming interfaces like ScratchJr or Blockly provide an ideal introduction through drag-and-drop blocks that eliminate syntax errors. These tools focus on developing logical thinking without the frustration of typing code.

For middle school students (ages 10-13), transitional environments like regular Scratch or Alice offer more complexity while maintaining visual elements. These allow students to create animations and simple games while gradually introducing programming concepts like loops and conditionals.

High school students (ages 14+) can handle text-based languages like Python or JavaScript. Python's clean syntax and versatility make it excellent for beginners, while JavaScript's immediate visual feedback through browser output keeps students engaged. At this stage, students can also begin using professional tools like Visual Studio Code to gain industry-relevant experience.

2. Learning Objectives

The choice of language should align with specific educational goals. If the primary objective is developing computational thinking, languages with simple syntax like Python or block-based environments work best. For career-focused programs, consider languages dominant in local industries - Java for Android development in tech hubs, or C# for game development programs.

Cross-curricular applications might favor Python for data analysis in math and science classes, or JavaScript for digital art projects. Creative expression goals may lead to choosing Processing for visual arts or Sonic Pi for music-oriented coding(Maloney, et al.,2010).

3. Available Resources

Real-world constraints significantly impact language selection. Schools with limited hardware may need to prioritize web-based tools like Trinket or Replit that run in browsers. Institutions with Raspberry Pi kits can leverage Python for physical computing. Budget considerations often make open-source options like Python or Scratch preferable to commercial solutions.

Teacher expertise is another crucial factor. Schools should balance adopting modern technologies with the professional development needs of their faculty. Starting with more accessible languages allows teachers to build confidence before tackling more complex options.

Section 2: Language Comparison

1. Beginner-Friendly Options

Python remains the gold standard for introductory text-based programming due to its readable syntax and gentle learning curve. Its extensive standard library allows students to create meaningful projects early, from simple games to data visualizations. The language's popularity in scientific computing and AI also makes it relevant for advanced students.

JavaScript offers the advantage of immediate visual feedback through browser output, which helps maintain student motivation. However, its loose typing and asynchronous nature can introduce conceptual challenges for beginners. Tools like p5.js provide a more structured approach to learning JavaScript through creative coding.

Swift Playgrounds on iPad provides an engaging, interactive environment for learning programming concepts through puzzle-like challenges. Its tight integration with Apple's ecosystem makes it particularly valuable in schools with iPad programs, though it's less versatile than Python for general programming education (Denning, 2017).

2. Languages

For mobile development pathways, Java (for Android) and Swift (for iOS) offer professional relevance but come with steeper learning curves. Kotlin presents a more modern alternative to Java for Android development with cleaner syntax.

Game development programs often use C# with Unity, providing students with industry-standard tools while maintaining relative accessibility. The visual nature of game creation helps maintain engagement, though the complexity of game engines may require careful scaffolding.

In data science programs, R and Python compete for dominance. R's statistical focus makes it powerful for advanced analysis, while Python's general-purpose nature provides more flexibility. Jupyter Notebooks serve as an excellent environment for teaching data science concepts in either language.

3. Emerging Contenders

Go (Golang) has gained attention for its simplicity and performance in backend development. Its clean syntax and built-in concurrency support make it interesting for advanced high school courses, though its ecosystem isn't as education-focused as Python's.

Rust offers memory safety guarantees that make it valuable for systems programming education, potentially serving as a more modern alternative to C++. However, its complexity likely makes it suitable only for advanced high school or college-level courses.

Julia's performance and simplicity position it as a strong contender for scientific computing education, though its ecosystem is still maturing. Schools with a strong focus on computational mathematics might consider it for advanced students.

Section 3: Development Environments

1. Block-Based Environments

Scratch remains the most popular introductory environment, with its colorful interface and extensive community sharing features. Educators can find countless shared projects to use as teaching examples. The recent Scratch 3.0 update improved touchscreen compatibility and added new extension capabilities.

App Inventor provides a similar block-based approach but focused on creating functional Android apps. Students can immediately test their creations on mobile devices, which provides strong motivation. The environment simplifies complex mobile development concepts while still teaching fundamental programming logic.

Microsoft's MakeCode platform offers block programming for various hardware platforms including micro:bit and Adafruit boards. This is particularly valuable for schools incorporating physical computing into their curriculum, as students can transition seamlessly from blocks to JavaScript or Python.

2. Lightweight Editors

Thonny stands out as an ideal Python IDE for beginners, with its simple interface and built-in debugger that visualizes variable states. It eliminates much of the complexity found in professional IDEs while still teaching proper programming workflows.

Repl.it provides a cloud-based solution that works across devices and operating systems. Its collaborative features allow for real-time pair programming, and it supports numerous languages from Python to C++. The classroom management features make it particularly useful for teachers.

CodePen serves as an excellent sandbox for front-end web development. Students can immediately see the results of their HTML, CSS, and JavaScript code, with the platform handling all the setup complexities. The social features allow for easy sharing of student work.

3. Professional-Grade Tools

Visual Studio Code has become the editor of choice for many professional developers and works well in educational settings. Its extensive extension marketplace allows customization for different languages and frameworks. The built-in terminal and version control integration provide exposure to professional workflows.

IntelliJ IDEA (Community Edition) offers a free, powerful environment for teaching Java and Kotlin. Its intelligent code completion and refactoring tools help students learn industry best practices, though the interface may initially overwhelm beginners.

Jupyter Notebooks provide an interactive environment particularly suited for data science and scientific computing. The notebook format allows mixing code, visualizations, and explanatory text, making it excellent for project-based learning and documentation of student work.

Section 4: Implementation Strategies

1. Progressive Skill Development

A spiral curriculum approach works well for coding education. In the first year, focus on fundamental concepts using visual programming tools. Students learn sequencing, loops, and conditionals without struggling with syntax.

In the second year, transition to text-based languages while maintaining focus on core concepts. At this stage, students can begin working on larger projects and learn basic debugging techniques. Simple game development or interactive stories work well to maintain engagement.

By the third year, students should be ready for more advanced paradigms like object-oriented programming or functional concepts. This is when specialized languages or frameworks can be introduced based on student interests and program goals.

2. Cross-Platform Considerations

Web-based solutions offer maximum flexibility, allowing students to work across different devices and locations. However, they depend on reliable internet access, which may not be available in all educational settings.

Installed software provides more consistent performance and offline access but requires IT support for installation and updates. Schools need to consider their device management capabilities when choosing these solutions.

Mobile compatibility has become increasingly important as many students primarily access technology through smartphones and tablets. Environments like Repl.it or CodePen that offer mobile-friendly interfaces can help bridge the digital divide.

3. Assessment Integration

Automated testing tools like unittest in Python or Jest for JavaScript can be introduced to teach students about test-driven development. These help objectively evaluate student code while reinforcing good programming practices.

Version control systems like GitHub Classroom provide structure for managing student assignments and tracking progress over time. They also expose students to professional collaboration workflows.

Project rubrics should evaluate not just working code but also design decisions, documentation quality, and problem-solving processes. Portfolio assessments allow students to showcase their best work and demonstrate growth over time.

Section 5: Overcoming Common Challenges

1. Resource Limitations

Open-source solutions like Python, Scratch, and VS Code eliminate licensing costs. Many cloud-based platforms offer free educational tiers sufficient for classroom use.

Schools can implement BYOD (Bring Your Own Device) policies supplemented by loaner devices for students who need them. This approach works particularly well with web-based development environments.

Partnerships with local tech companies can provide access to professional tools and expertise. Many software vendors offer significant educational discounts or free classroom licenses.

2. Teacher Training

Professional development should focus on both technical skills and pedagogical approaches. Many organizations offer specialized training for computer science teachers, including Code.org and the Computer Science Teachers Association.

Peer learning communities, both within schools and through online platforms, help teachers share resources and strategies. Local meetups or online forums can provide ongoing support.

Vendor certification programs, while sometimes costly, can give teachers confidence in specific technologies and may qualify schools for additional resources or recognition.

3. Curriculum Alignment

Mapping coding instruction to established standards like CSTA or NGSS helps integrate it into existing school frameworks. This demonstrates the subject's academic value to administrators and parents.

Interdisciplinary projects show coding's relevance across subjects. A history class might create interactive timelines using JavaScript, while a science class could use Python for data analysis.

Maintaining connections with local industries ensures the curriculum remains relevant to regional job markets. Advisory boards with industry professionals can provide valuable input on language and tool selection.

Assessment and Evaluation in Coding Education: Measuring Progress and Understanding

Assessment and evaluation in coding education focus on measuring both technical skills and conceptual understanding. Formative methods like code reviews and debugging exercises provide ongoing feedback, while summative assessments such as projects and exams evaluate final outcomes. Tools range from automated grading platforms to peer reviews and project-based evaluations, which test problem-solving and creativity. Challenges include balancing syntax accuracy with deeper comprehension and accommodating different learning paces. Innovations like AI-driven analytics and competency-based models are reshaping how progress is tracked, emphasizing mastery over memorization. Ultimately, effective coding education requires diverse assessment strategies to foster both skill development and computational thinking.

1. The Importance of Assessment in Coding Education

Evaluating coding skills presents unique challenges compared to traditional subjects. Where mathematics or history assessments might focus on factual recall, coding requires assessing cognitive processes – how students approach problems, structure solutions, and adapt to errors. Research indicates that effective coding assessment should measure three key dimensions:

Conceptual Understanding (e.g., recognizing when to use a loop versus conditional statement)

Practical Implementation (translating concepts into functional code)

Problem-Solving Approach (debugging strategies, algorithm design)

A 2022 study by the Computer Science Teachers Association (CSTA) found that programs combining all three assessment dimensions saw 42% higher student retention in advanced CS courses compared to those relying solely on output-based grading.

2. Formative vs. Summative Assessment Strategies

Formative Techniques in Practice

Peer Code Reviews have emerged as particularly effective when structured properly. In a Massachusetts Institute of Technology (MIT) implementation:

1. Students submit draft code 72 hours before deadline
2. Peers evaluate using a 5-point rubric covering:

- Variable naming conventions
- Function modularity
- Comment clarity

3. Authors receive feedback before final submission

This approach reduced common syntax errors by 37% while improving code documentation quality.

Debugging Think-Alouds provide valuable process insights. Educators at Stanford's CS Education group recommend:

- Providing intentionally flawed code samples
- Recording students' verbal problem-solving narration
- Analyzing hesitation points to identify conceptual gaps

Summative Benchmarking

The Advanced Placement Computer Science Principles exam demonstrates evolving best practices:

- 30% portfolio assessment (create → analyze → refine cycle)
- 20% performance tasks (time-constrained problem-solving)
- 50% conceptual understanding (multiple-choice)

This balance helps prevent "trial-and-error coders" from advancing without deeper comprehension.

3. Project-Based Assessment Design

Effective project rubrics should evaluate multiple competency levels:

Basic Proficiency

- Code executes without runtime errors
- Meets specified functional requirements

Intermediate Mastery

- Includes exception handling
- Demonstrates algorithm efficiency awareness

Advanced Excellence

- Implements optimization techniques
- Shows creative extension beyond requirements

A University of California study found that adding a "Code Evolution" component – requiring students to document and justify iterative changes – improved final project quality by 28%.

4. Addressing Assessment Challenges

AI and Plagiarism Detection

Current tools have significant limitations:

- Standard plagiarism detectors fail with code (90%+ false positives on basic constructs)
- New approaches like Berkeley's CodeMR analyze:
    - Variable naming patterns
    - Structural similarity
    - Comment style consistency

However, the most effective deterrent remains **oral defense components**, where students explain their code line-by-line.

Differentiation Strategies

Tiered assessment frameworks help accommodate varied skill levels:

Table 1. Differentiation Strategies

Level	**Task Example**	**Evaluation Focus**
Foundation	Fix pre-written code	Syntax recognition
Application	Complete partial solutions	Logic implementation
Mastery	Design original system	Architecture planning

5. Emerging Research Directions

Recent neuroeducation studies using fMRI reveal:

- Successful debuggers show distinct prefrontal cortex activation patterns
- Pattern recognition development follows measurable stages
- Stress responses differ between syntax vs. logic errors

These findings suggest future assessments may incorporate:

- Biometric response analysis
- Cognitive load measurement
- Adaptive difficulty scaling

Implementation Recommendations

1. Adopt Process Portfolios
    - Collect code drafts with revision notes
    - Include planning documents and flowcharts
    - Require reflection on failure points
2. Utilize Two-Stage Exams
    - Individual coding test (45 minutes)
    - Immediate group revision session (30 minutes)
    - Assess both independent and collaborative skills
3. Implement Longitudinal Tracking
    - Map error type frequency over time
    - Identify persistent misconception patterns
    - Adjust instruction based on cohort analytics

PRACTICAL IMPLEMENTATION & CURRICULUM

The practical implementation of coding education relies on a well-structured curriculum that balances theory with hands-on experience. Courses should integrate real-world projects, such as app development or algorithm challenges, to reinforce learning. A modular approach allows students to progress from basic syntax to complex problem-solving at their own pace. Incorporating collaborative tools like GitHub or pair programming fosters teamwork and code review skills. Additionally, adaptive learning platforms can personalize content based on student performance. To ensure relevance, curricula must align with industry trends, including AI, cybersecurity, and data science. Regular updates and feedback loops with educators and professionals help maintain an effective, dynamic learning framework.

Table 2. Practical implementation

Feature	Commonality	Differentiation
Fundamental Concepts	Similar explanations of basic programming principles.	Unique examples, analogies, and teaching methodologies.
Algorithms & Data Structures	Standard implementations of common algorithms.	Application of algorithms to novel problems, optimization techniques.
Programming Languages	Shared syntax and core library usage.	Custom libraries, framework development, and unique project structures.
Practical Implementation	Similar project types (e.g., web apps).	Original project ideas, innovative features, and personalized user experiences.
Curriculum Design	Standard topics covered.	Unique teaching styles, project based learning, and emphasis on real world problem solving.

In today's digitally-driven world, coding education has transitioned from a specialized skill to a fundamental literacy. The practical implementation of coding curricula requires careful consideration of pedagogical approaches, technological advancements, and industry needs. This comprehensive discussion explores the key components of an effective coding curriculum, implementation strategies, assessment methods, and solutions to common challenges in coding education (Sentence & Csizmadia, 2017).

Core Components of a Coding Curriculum

1. Foundational Programming Concepts

A strong coding curriculum must begin with fundamental concepts that form the building blocks of computational thinking:

- **Basic Syntax and Logic:** Variables, data types, operators, and control structures (loops, conditionals)
- **Functions and Modular Programming:** Understanding parameters, return values, and code organization
- **Memory Management:** Stack vs heap, pointers (in languages like C/C++), and garbage collection

These fundamentals should be taught using beginner-friendly languages like Python or JavaScript before introducing more complex paradigms.

2. Data Structures and Algorithms

The curriculum should progressively introduce:

- **Linear Structures:** Arrays, linked lists, stacks, and queues
- **Non-linear Structures:** Trees, graphs, and hash tables
- **Algorithmic Techniques:** Recursion, sorting (quick sort, merge sort), searching (binary search), and complexity analysis

Practical implementation should include visualizations and interactive coding platforms to enhance understanding.

3. Software Development Methodologies

Modern coding education must include:

- **Version Control Systems:** Git workflows and collaborative development using GitHub
- **Testing Frameworks:** Unit testing, integration testing, and test-driven development
- **Debugging Techniques:** Using debuggers, logging, and systematic error diagnosis

Curriculum Design and Progression

1. Beginner Level (First 3-6 Months)

Focus areas:

- Basic programming constructs
- Simple problem-solving
- Introduction to computational thinking

Sample projects:

- Number guessing games
- Basic calculator applications
- Simple text-based adventures

2. Intermediate Level (6-12 Months)

Key topics:

- Object-oriented programming
- Basic data structures
- Web development fundamentals

Hands-on activities:

- Building personal websites
- Creating weather apps using APIs
- Developing simple database applications

3. Advanced Level (12+ Months)

Specialization options:

- Full-stack web development
- Mobile app development
- Data science fundamentals
- Game development

Capstone projects:

- E-commerce platforms
- Machine learning models
- Multiplayer game development

Effective Teaching Methodologies

1. Project-Based Learning

Implementation strategies:

- **Scaffolded Projects:** Gradually increasing complexity
- **Real-world Applications:** Solving community or industry problems
- **Portfolio Development:** Creating tangible work products

2. Collaborative Learning Environments

Best practices:

- Pair programming sessions

- Code review processes
- Hackathons and coding competitions
- Open-source contributions

3. Differentiated Instruction

Adaptations for diverse learners:

- Visual programming for beginners (Scratch, Blockly)
- Multiple difficulty levels for coding challenges
- Personalized learning paths based on student interests

Assessment and Feedback Mechanisms

1. Formative Assessments

Continuous evaluation methods:

- Weekly coding challenges
- Mini-projects with rubrics
- Peer code reviews
- Automated testing systems

2. Summative Assessments

Comprehensive evaluations:

- Final projects with demonstrations
- Technical interviews
- Coding certification exams
- Portfolio assessments

3. Feedback Systems

Effective approaches:

- Automated feedback from coding platforms
- Instructor code reviews
- Peer feedback sessions
- Industry mentor evaluations

Technology Integration

1. Coding Platforms and Tools

Essential resources:

- Online IDEs (Replit, CodePen)
- Learning platforms (Codecademy, freeCodeCamp)
- Competitive coding sites (LeetCode, HackerRank)

2. Classroom Technologies

Implementation tools:

- Version control systems for education
- Classroom management software
- Automated grading systems
- Virtual coding environments

Industry Alignment and Career Preparation

3. Current Technology Stacks

Curriculum should cover:

- Web development frameworks (React, Angular, Vue)
- Backend technologies (Node.js, Django, Spring Boot)
- Database systems (MySQL, MongoDB, PostgreSQL)
- Cloud computing basics (AWS, Azure, GCP)

4. Professional Skills Development

Critical competencies:

- Technical documentation
- Agile development practices
- Software development life cycle
- Interview preparation strategies

5. Work-Based Learning

Implementation models:

- Internship programs
- Industry-sponsored projects
- Guest lectures from professionals
- Company site visits

Challenges and Solutions

1. Keeping Curriculum Current

Solutions:

- Regular industry advisory board meetings
- Modular curriculum design for easy updates
- Faculty professional development programs

2. Student Engagement and Retention

Strategies:

- Gamification elements (badges, leaderboards)
- Project-based learning with real-world relevance
- Early success experiences to build confidence

3. Resource Constraints

Approaches:

- Open educational resources
- Cloud-based development environments
- Community partnerships for equipment and mentorship

4. Assessment at Scale

Innovative solutions:

- Automated code evaluation
- Peer assessment systems
- AI-assisted grading tools

- Portfolio-based evaluations

Future Directions in Coding Education

1. Emerging Technologies

Integration of:

- Artificial intelligence and machine learning
- Blockchain development
- Internet of Things (IoT) programming
- Quantum computing concepts

2. Personalized Learning

Advancements in:

- Adaptive learning platforms
- AI-powered coding tutors
- Competency-based progression
- Micro-credentialing systems

3. Global Collaboration

Opportunities for:

- International coding projects
- Cross-cultural development teams
- Global hackathons and competitions
- Open-source community participation

The practical implementation of coding curricula requires a dynamic, student-centered approach that balances foundational knowledge with real-world application. By incorporating project-based learning, industry-aligned technologies, and robust assessment methods, educators can create programs that prepare students for successful careers in technology. Continuous adaptation to technological advancements and industry needs ensures that coding education remains relevant and effective in our rapidly evolving digital landscape.

The future of coding education lies in creating accessible, engaging, and practical learning experiences that develop not just coding skills, but also computational thinking, problem-solving abilities, and professional competencies. Through thoughtful curriculum design and innovative teaching methods, we can empower the next generation of developers and technologists to shape our digital future.

CURRICULUM DESIGN: BUILDING A PROGRESSIVE CODING EDUCATION PATHWAY

To equip learners with the necessary competencies, educators must design a structured, progressive coding curriculum that evolves with students' growing expertise. A well-structured pathway ensures that learners transition smoothly from basic concepts to advanced programming, fostering problem-solving skills and computational thinking.

Table 3. Building a Progressive Coding Education Pathway

Aspect	Traditional Approach	Progressive Pathway
Structure	Linear, theory-heavy	Modular, skill-based milestones
Tools Used	Textbook exercises, limited practice	Interactive platforms (Scratch, GitHub)
Learner Engagement	Passive (lectures)	Active (projects, hackathons)
Outcome Focus	Exam scores	Portfolio, real-world problem-solving
Flexibility	Rigid syllabus	Adapts to learner pace/industry trends

Importance of Progressive Learning

- Coding education should follow a **scaffolded approach** (simple → complex).
- Prevents cognitive overload and builds confidence.

Stages of a Coding Curriculum

- **Beginner:** Focus on logic (block coding, basic Python).
- **Intermediate:** Problem-solving (web/app development).
- **Advanced:** Specialization (OOP, AI/ML basics).
- **Real-World Prep:** Collaboration (Git, Agile, hackathons).

Pedagogical Strategies

- **Project-Based Learning (PBL):** Reinforces concepts through hands-on tasks.
- **Gamification:** Motivates learners via challenges (e.g., coding puzzles).
- **Peer Review:** Encourages collaborative improvement.

Assessment & Adaptation

- Use **adaptive quizzes, debugging tasks, and portfolios** to track progress.
- Update curriculum based on **industry trends** (e.g., AI tools).

EXPANDING HORIZONS & INCLUSIVITY IN CODING EDUCATION

The field of coding education is rapidly evolving, driven by technological advancements and a growing recognition of the need for inclusivity and ethical responsibility. As digital literacy becomes essential in nearly every profession, educators and policymakers must ensure that coding education is accessible, engaging, and socially impactful. This article explores key themes in modern coding education, including ethical coding practices, inclusivity, hands-on learning with robotics, emerging technologies, and the importance of community-building. By addressing these areas, we can create a more equitable and innovative future for tech education.

1. Coding for Social Good: Developing Ethical and Responsible Coders

The Power of Code in Addressing Social Issues

Coding is more than just a technical skill—it is a tool for social change. From developing apps that improve healthcare access to creating algorithms that combat climate change, programmers have the power to address pressing global challenges. Initiatives like **"Code for Good"** hackathons encourage students to build solutions for nonprofits, while open-source projects allow coders to contribute to humanitarian causes.

Teaching Ethics in Technology

As technology increasingly influences society, ethical considerations in coding are crucial. Students must learn about:

- **Data Privacy & Security** – Understanding how to protect user information.
- **Algorithmic Bias** – Recognizing and mitigating biases in AI and machine learning models.
- **Digital Equity** – Ensuring technology serves all communities fairly.

By integrating ethics into coding curricula, educators can nurture a generation of responsible technologists who prioritize social impact over profit.

2. Inclusivity and Accessibility in Coding Education: Reaching All Learners

Breaking Down Barriers in Tech Education

Historically, coding education has been dominated by certain demographics, leaving women, minorities, and individuals with disabilities underrepresented. To create a more inclusive tech industry, we must:

- **Offer Multilingual Resources** – Providing coding lessons in multiple languages to support non-native English speakers.
- **Use Adaptive Learning Tools** – Customizing lessons for students with different learning styles and abilities.
- **Promote STEM for Girls & Underrepresented Groups** – Encouraging early exposure through coding camps and mentorship programs.

Assistive Technologies in Coding

Students with disabilities should have equal opportunities to learn coding. Tools like:

- **Screen readers** for visually impaired learners.
- **Voice-controlled coding platforms** for those with motor disabilities.
- **Simplified coding interfaces** (e.g., block-based programming like Scratch) for neurodiverse students.

By making coding education more accessible, we empower a diverse range of future innovators (Korkmaz et al., 2017).

3. The Role of Robotics and Physical Computing in Coding Education

Making Coding Tangible and Engaging

Many students struggle with abstract coding concepts. Robotics and physical computing (using devices like **Arduino, Raspberry Pi, and LEGO Mindstorms**) bridge this gap by allowing learners to see their code come to life. Benefits include:

- **Hands-on Learning** – Students build and program real devices, reinforcing coding principles.
- **Problem-Solving Skills** – Debugging a robot or sensor requires critical thinking.
- **Interdisciplinary Learning** – Combines coding with engineering, physics, and design.

Applications in Classrooms

Schools are increasingly adopting robotics programs to make STEM more interactive. Competitions like **FIRST Robotics** inspire teamwork and creativity, while classroom projects (e.g., building weather sensors or automated plant-watering systems) demonstrate real-world coding applications.

4. The Future of Coding Education: Trends and Emerging Technologies

How AI and Machine Learning Are Changing Coding Education

Artificial Intelligence (AI) is revolutionizing how coding is taught:

- **AI-Powered Tutors** – Personalized learning assistants (like GitHub Copilot) help students debug code in real time.
- **Automated Grading Systems** – AI can provide instant feedback on coding assignments.
- **Low-Code/No-Code Platforms** – Tools like **Bubble and AppSheet** allow beginners to build apps without deep programming knowledge.

Other Emerging Trends

- **Virtual Reality (VR) Coding Labs** – Immersive environments where students can practice coding in 3D.
- **Blockchain & Web3 Development** – Growing demand for decentralized app (DApp) developers.
- **Quantum Computing Basics** – Preparing students for next-gen computing paradigms.

Educators must adapt curricula to include these technologies, ensuring students are future-ready.

5. Building a Coding Community: Collaboration and Support

Why Community Matters in Coding

Learning to code can be challenging, but a strong support network makes a difference. Benefits of coding communities include:

- **Peer Learning** – Students help each other troubleshoot problems.
- **Mentorship Opportunities** – Experienced coders guide beginners.
- **Networking & Career Growth** – Connecting with professionals opens job opportunities.

How to Foster a Coding Community

- **Coding Clubs & Hackathons** – Schools and organizations should host regular coding events.
- **Online Platforms** – Encouraging participation in **GitHub, Stack Overflow, and CodePen**.
- **Open-Source Contributions** – Students gain experience by collaborating on real-world projects.

A strong coding community keeps learners motivated and accelerates skill development.

THE ESSENTIALS OF CODING EDUCATION

In today's rapidly evolving digital landscape, coding education has emerged as a fundamental pillar of modern learning, equipping individuals with the skills necessary to navigate and shape the technological future. The ability to understand

and write code is no longer confined to computer scientists and software engineers; it has become a vital literacy for professionals across diverse fields, from healthcare to finance, and even the arts. As the demand for digital proficiency grows, the essentials of coding education have taken center stage, ensuring that learners of all ages and backgrounds can harness the power of programming to solve problems, innovate, and thrive in an increasingly interconnected world.

At its core, coding education is about more than just teaching syntax or memorizing commands; it fosters critical thinking, creativity, and problem-solving skills that are applicable far beyond the computer screen. Learning to code encourages a structured approach to breaking down complex challenges into manageable components, a methodology that proves invaluable in both personal and professional contexts. Whether designing a simple website, developing a mobile application, or analyzing large datasets, the principles of coding empower individuals to approach tasks methodically and with confidence. The transformative potential of coding education lies in its ability to democratize access to technology, enabling people from all walks of life to participate in the digital economy and contribute meaningfully to technological advancements.

One of the key essentials of coding education is its emphasis on hands-on, experiential learning. Unlike traditional subjects that may rely heavily on theoretical instruction, coding thrives in an environment where learners actively engage with the material through practice and experimentation. Writing code, debugging errors, and refining algorithms in real-time provide immediate feedback, reinforcing concepts and building resilience in the face of challenges. This iterative process not only deepens understanding but also cultivates a growth mindset, where mistakes are viewed as opportunities for learning rather than setbacks. By integrating project-based learning, coding education ensures that students can apply their knowledge to real-world scenarios, making the learning process both relevant and rewarding.

Another critical aspect of coding education is its adaptability to different learning styles and paces. With the proliferation of online resources, interactive platforms, and coding bootcamps, individuals can tailor their learning experiences to suit their unique needs and goals. Beginners can start with visual programming languages like Scratch, which simplify coding concepts through drag-and-drop interfaces, while more advanced learners may delve into languages such as Python, Java, or C++ for greater complexity and versatility. The flexibility of coding education allows it to be accessible to children in elementary school, university students, career changers, and even retirees seeking to acquire new skills. This inclusivity underscores the universal relevance of coding as a tool for empowerment and lifelong learning.

Collaboration and community also play a vital role in the essentials of coding education. Programming is rarely a solitary endeavor; it thrives in environments where individuals can share ideas, seek feedback, and work together to solve problems. Coding communities, hackathons, and open-source projects provide platforms for learners to connect with peers and mentors, fostering a culture of knowledge exchange and mutual support. These collaborative experiences not only enhance technical skills but also nurture soft skills such as communication, teamwork, and adaptability—qualities that are increasingly valued in the modern workforce. By engaging with a global network of coders, learners gain exposure to diverse perspectives and innovative approaches, enriching their overall educational journey.

As technology continues to reshape industries and redefine job markets, the importance of coding education cannot be overstated. Governments, educational institutions, and private organizations worldwide are recognizing the need to integrate coding into curricula and workforce development programs. Initiatives aimed at bridging the digital divide, such as providing coding workshops in underserved communities or offering scholarships for underrepresented groups, are helping to create a more inclusive and equitable tech landscape. The essentials of coding education extend beyond technical proficiency; they encompass a vision of a future where everyone has the opportunity to participate in and benefit from the digital revolution.

Ultimately, coding education is a gateway to unlocking human potential in the 21st century. It equips individuals with the tools to innovate, adapt, and contribute to a world driven by technology. By embracing the essentials of coding education—hands-on learning, adaptability, collaboration, and accessibility—we can prepare current and future generations to meet the challenges and opportunities of an ever-changing digital era. Whether aspiring to become a software developer, enhance one's career prospects, or simply gain a deeper understanding of the technology shaping our lives, coding education offers a pathway to empowerment and endless possibilities. The journey of learning to code is not just about mastering a skill; it is about embracing a mindset of curiosity, resilience, and lifelong growth.

Figure 1. Process of learning

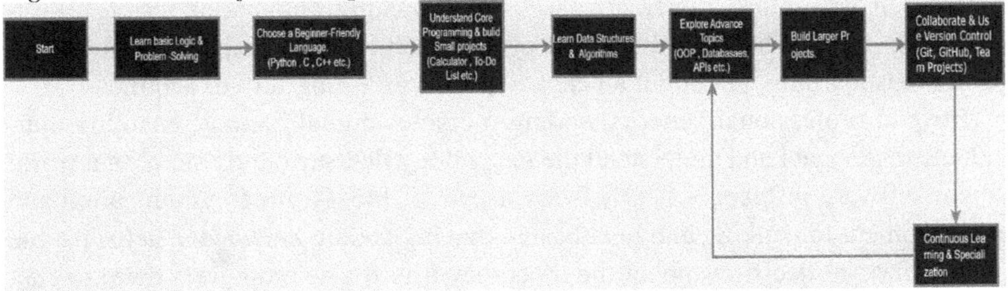

Importance of Coding Skills

In the modern digital era, coding skills have become as essential as reading and writing. The ability to understand and create software is no longer limited to computer scientists; it is now a valuable asset across various industries, from healthcare and finance to education and entertainment. As technology continues to shape the way we live and work, coding skills empower individuals to innovate, solve problems, and stay competitive in an increasingly tech-driven world.

One of the most significant advantages of learning to code is the enhancement of problem-solving abilities. Programming teaches logical thinking and structured reasoning, enabling individuals to break down complex challenges into smaller, manageable steps. This analytical mindset is beneficial not only in software development but also in everyday decision-making and professional problem-solving across different fields. Whether optimizing business processes, automating repetitive tasks, or developing new digital solutions, coding skills provide a framework for efficient and creative problem-solving.

Another key benefit of coding is its role in career advancement. The demand for professionals with programming knowledge continues to rise, with many high-paying jobs requiring at least a basic understanding of coding. Even in non-technical roles, familiarity with programming can set candidates apart, as businesses increasingly rely on digital tools and data-driven strategies. Learning to code opens doors to diverse career opportunities, from software engineering and data analysis to digital marketing and cybersecurity. Moreover, coding skills enable individuals to adapt to technological changes, ensuring long-term employability in a rapidly evolving job market.

Coding also fosters creativity and innovation. Unlike the misconception that programming is rigid and monotonous, it is a highly creative discipline that allows individuals to build websites, apps, games, and other digital solutions from scratch. With coding, people can turn their ideas into reality, whether developing a mobile application, designing an interactive website, or creating automation scripts to simplify daily tasks. This creative aspect of coding encourages experimentation and continuous learning, making it an engaging and rewarding skill to acquire.

Beyond professional benefits, coding promotes digital literacy, enabling individuals to navigate and understand the technology that surrounds them. In a world where software influences nearly every aspect of life—from communication and entertainment to banking and healthcare—having coding knowledge helps people make informed decisions about the tools they use. It also empowers them to customize technology to their needs, rather than relying solely on pre-built solutions.

Finally, coding skills contribute to societal progress by addressing real-world challenges. From developing sustainable technologies to improving healthcare systems, programmers play a crucial role in creating solutions that benefit communities worldwide. By learning to code, individuals can contribute to open-source projects, participate in tech-driven social initiatives, and help bridge the digital divide by making technology more accessible.

Starting with the Basics

Learning to code can feel overwhelming at first, but like any new skill, it becomes manageable when broken down into fundamental concepts. The key to success lies in starting with the basics—understanding core principles before moving on to complex topics. This foundational approach not only builds confidence but also ensures a solid grasp of programming logic that applies across all languages and technologies.

The first step in coding is choosing a beginner-friendly programming language. Languages like Python, JavaScript, or Scratch are often recommended for newcomers because of their simple syntax and readability. Python, for example, uses plain English-like commands, making it easier to focus on problem-solving rather than memorizing complicated rules. Starting with such languages allows beginners to quickly see results, keeping them motivated as they progress.

Once a language is selected, the next essential concept is understanding basic programming structures. These include variables (containers for storing data), data types (such as numbers, strings, and booleans), and operators (symbols that perform operations on data). Grasping these elements helps learners write simple programs, like a calculator or a text-based game. From there, they can explore control structures—such as loops and conditional statements—which enable programs to make decisions and repeat tasks efficiently.

Another critical aspect of early coding education is learning how to debug. Errors are inevitable, but beginners who embrace them as part of the learning process develop resilience and problem-solving skills. Simple debugging techniques, like checking for typos or using print statements to track program flow, can demystify why a program isn't working as expected. Over time, these practices build a mindset of patience and attention to detail.

Finally, hands-on practice is irreplaceable. Starting with small projects—such as a to-do list app or a basic website—reinforces theoretical knowledge and fosters creativity. Online coding platforms, tutorials, and interactive exercises provide structured ways to apply concepts in real time. By mastering the basics through consistent practice, beginners lay a strong foundation for tackling more advanced topics in the future.

In summary, starting with the basics of coding involves selecting an accessible language, learning core programming concepts, embracing debugging, and applying knowledge through practical projects. This approach ensures a smooth and rewarding entry into the world of programming, setting the stage for continuous growth and innovation.

Choosing the Right Programming Language

Selecting an appropriate programming language is one of the most important decisions for beginners and experienced developers alike. With hundreds of languages available, each designed for specific purposes, the choice can significantly impact learning efficiency, project success, and career opportunities. Understanding key factors such as purpose, learning curve, community support, and industry demand can help guide this decision effectively.

The first consideration when choosing a programming language should be the intended application. Different languages excel in different domains, making it essential to align the choice with project goals. For web development, JavaScript remains indispensable due to its universal browser support and robust frameworks like React and Node.js. Python, known for its simplicity and versatility, is widely used in data science, artificial intelligence, and scripting. For mobile app development, Swift (for iOS) and Kotlin (for Android) are the preferred choices, while game developers often turn to C# with Unity or C++ for high-performance engines. System programming and operating systems frequently rely on languages like C and Rust for their efficiency and low-level control. By identifying the primary use case, learners can narrow down options to languages that best suit their objectives.

Another critical factor is the learning curve, especially for beginners. Some languages prioritize readability and simplicity, making them more accessible to newcomers. Python, for example, uses clean syntax and emphasizes code readability, allowing beginners to focus on problem-solving rather than complex syntax rules. Ruby and JavaScript also offer relatively gentle learning curves, with immediate feedback through interactive environments. In contrast, languages like C++ or Java, while powerful, come with steeper learning curves due to their strict syntax rules and memory management requirements. Beginners should weigh their patience and long-term goals against the initial difficulty to choose a language that balances approachability with future growth potential.

Community support and resources play a vital role in the learning process. A language with a large, active community ensures access to extensive documentation, tutorials, forums, and open-source projects. Python and JavaScript boast some of the largest developer communities, offering countless free resources for troubleshooting and skill enhancement. Languages like Go and Rust, though newer, have rapidly growing communities that provide modern tools and collaborative opportunities. Strong community backing not only accelerates learning but also helps developers stay updated with industry trends and best practices. Industry demand and career prospects should also influence the decision. Researching job market trends can reveal which languages are most sought after in specific fields. For instance, JavaScript and Python consistently rank high in job postings due to their widespread use in web development and data science. Java remains a staple in enterprise environments, while languages like SQL are essential for database management. Emerging fields like blockchain development favor Solidity, and machine learning heavily relies on Python and R. By aligning language choice with career aspirations, learners can position themselves for better job opportunities and professional growth.

Long-term viability is another consideration. While it's tempting to chase the latest trends, opting for a language with enduring relevance ensures skills remain valuable over time. Established languages like Python, JavaScript, and Java have demonstrated longevity and continuous evolution. However, newer languages like Kotlin (for Android) or Swift (for iOS) have gained rapid adoption due to industry backing and modern features. Evaluating a language's ecosystem—including frameworks, libraries, and corporate support—can provide insight into its staying power. Experimentation is key to making an informed decision. Many developers start with one language only to discover another better aligns with their interests or strengths. Trying out multiple languages through small projects or online courses can help identify personal preferences in terms of syntax, workflow, and problem-solving approaches. Platforms like Codecademy, freeCodeCamp, and LeetCode offer interactive environments to explore different languages without extensive setup.

In conclusion, choosing the right programming language depends on a combination of factors, including project goals, learning difficulty, community support, job market trends, and long-term relevance. Beginners should start with languages that match their immediate needs while remaining open to exploring others as their skills advance. By making an informed choice, developers can build a strong foundation, enhance their career prospects, and adapt to the ever-evolving tech landscape with confidence. The ideal language is not just about popularity—it's about finding the right tool for the task at hand and enjoying the journey of learning and creation.

Core Programming Concepts

Programming, at its heart, is about solving problems through logical thinking and structured approaches. Whether you're building a simple website or developing complex artificial intelligence systems, certain fundamental concepts form the backbone of all programming. Mastering these core principles provides a solid foundation that applies across all languages and technologies, enabling you to transition between different programming environments with confidence.

- **Variables and Data Types**

Every program works with data, and variables are the containers that store this information. A variable is essentially a named reference to a value that can change during program execution. Understanding different data types is crucial because each type serves specific purposes. Common primitive data types include integers (whole numbers), floating-point numbers (decimals), booleans (true/false values), and strings (text). More complex data structures like arrays, lists, and dictionaries allow programmers to organize and manipulate collections of data efficiently.

- **Control Structures**

Control structures dictate the flow of a program, determining which instructions execute under what conditions. The two primary categories are conditional statements and loops.

- **Conditional statements (if, else, switch)** allow programs to make decisions
- **Loops (for, while, do-while)** enable repetitive tasks without redundant code. A loop could process thousands of records in a database or animate a sequence in a game.

These structures introduce logic into programs, making them dynamic and responsive rather than linear and static.

- **Functions and Modularity**

Functions (also called methods or procedures) are reusable blocks of code that perform specific tasks. They help avoid repetition, improve readability, and make programs easier to debug and maintain. A well-designed function takes inputs (parameters), processes them, and returns an output. For instance, a function might calculate the average of a list of numbers or validate a user's password.

Modularity—breaking a program into smaller, independent functions—is a key principle in software development. It promotes code reusability and collaboration, as different team members can work on separate functions simultaneously.

- **Error Handling and Debugging**

Even experienced programmers write code that doesn't work as expected initially. Debugging—identifying and fixing errors—is an essential skill. Common errors include syntax mistakes (typos), logical errors (incorrect calculations), and runtime errors (problems that occur during execution, like dividing by zero).

Modern programming languages provide tools like exception handling (`try-catch` blocks) to manage errors gracefully. For example, if a program tries to open a missing file, proper error handling can display a user-friendly message instead of crashing.

- o **Object-Oriented Programming (OOP)**

OOP is a paradigm that organizes code into "objects," which bundle data (attributes) and behaviors (methods) into self-contained units. Key OOP concepts include:

- **Classes and Objects**: A class is a blueprint (e.g., a "Car" class), while an object is an instance of that class (e.g., a specific car like a Tesla Model 3).
- **Encapsulation:** Restricting direct access to an object's data to prevent unintended modifications.
- **Inheritance:** Creating new classes based on existing ones to reuse code (e.g., an "ElectricCar" class inheriting from "Car").
- **Polymorphism**: Allowing objects of different classes to be treated as objects of a common superclass.

OOP is widely used in languages like Java, Python, and C# because it mirrors real-world relationships and simplifies complex systems (Israel et al.,2015).

- o **Algorithms and Efficiency**

An algorithm is a step-by-step procedure for solving a problem, such as sorting a list or finding the shortest path on a map. Writing efficient algorithms is critical—especially for applications handling large datasets—because inefficient code can slow down programs or consume excessive memory.

Concepts like **time complexity** (how runtime grows with input size) and **space complexity** (memory usage) help evaluate an algorithm's performance. For example, a search algorithm might be "O(n)" (time increases linearly with input) or "O(log n)" (much faster for large inputs).

- o **Data Structures**

Choosing the right data structure—a way to organize and store data—can dramatically impact a program's performance. Common structures include:

- **Arrays/Lists**: Ordered collections, ideal for indexed access.
- **Stacks and Queues**: Manage data in Last-In-First-Out (LIFO) or First-In-First-Out (FIFO) order.

- **Hash Tables**: Enable fast lookups by mapping keys to values.
- **Trees and Graphs**: Represent hierarchical or networked data, like folders on a computer or social media connections.

Each structure has trade-offs; for instance, hash tables provide speedy lookups but use more memory.

Core programming concepts are universal, transcending specific languages or frameworks. By mastering variables, control structures, functions, OOP, algorithms, and data structures, you develop a toolkit to tackle diverse challenges in software development. These fundamentals not only make learning new technologies easier but also empower you to write cleaner, more efficient, and maintainable code. Whether you're a beginner or an experienced developer revisiting the basics, a strong grasp of these principles is the key to becoming a proficient programmer.

CONCLUSION

Coding education has evolved from a specialized technical skill into a fundamental literacy that empowers individuals to navigate and shape our increasingly digital world. In an era where technology permeates every aspect of modern life—from communication and commerce to healthcare and entertainment—understanding the language of computers is no longer optional but essential. Coding education provides far more than vocational training for future programmers; it cultivates critical cognitive skills such as logical reasoning, systematic problem-solving, and creative innovation that are valuable across all professions and disciplines. The ability to break down complex challenges into manageable components, identify patterns, and develop structured solutions—core aspects of computational thinking—prepares learners to tackle problems in fields ranging from scientific research to business strategy and social innovation.

The pedagogical approach to coding education has also undergone significant transformation, shifting from rote memorization of syntax to more engaging, project-based learning that emphasizes real-world applications. Modern coding curricula recognize that students learn best by doing—whether through developing mobile apps, analyzing datasets, or programming robotics—and that failure and iteration are integral parts of the learning process. This hands-on methodology not only builds technical proficiency but also fosters resilience, adaptability, and confidence in tackling unfamiliar challenges. Furthermore, the integration of coding with other subjects demonstrates its interdisciplinary value, showing students how programming intersects with art, music, biology, and social sciences, thereby broadening its appeal and relevance.

Despite its growing importance, coding education still faces significant barriers to universal access, including socioeconomic disparities in technology resources, uneven teacher training, and persistent stereotypes that discourage diverse participation in computer science. Addressing these challenges requires concerted efforts from governments, educational institutions, and the tech industry to provide equitable access to quality instruction, modern tools, and inspiring role models. Initiatives like community coding clubs, online learning platforms, and corporate-sponsored education programs have shown promise in democratizing access to programming knowledge. Additionally, the rise of artificial intelligence in education presents both opportunities and challenges, as AI-powered coding assistants can provide personalized learning support while requiring educators to emphasize deeper conceptual understanding over reliance on automated tools.

Looking ahead, coding education must continue evolving to prepare learners for a future where digital fluency will be as fundamental as reading and writing. Emerging trends like quantum computing, blockchain technologies, and the Internet of Things will create new dimensions of digital literacy to explore. However, the core mission remains unchanged: to equip individuals with the skills and mindset to be active creators in the digital landscape rather than passive consumers. In doing so, coding education serves as a powerful equalizer and engine of opportunity, fostering innovation, economic mobility, and informed citizenship. As we stand at the threshold of unprecedented technological advancement, investing in comprehensive, inclusive, and forward-thinking coding education is not just an educational priority but a societal imperative—one that will determine our collective capacity to harness technology for human progress and solve the complex challenges of our time.

REFERENCES

Brennan, K., & Resnick, M. (2012). New frameworks for studying and assessing the development of computational thinking. Paper presented at the annual meeting of the American Educational Research Association, Vancouver, BC, Canada. https://scratched.gse.harvard.edu/ct/files/AERA2012.pdf

Denning, P. J. (2017). Remaining trouble spots with computational thinking. *Communications of the ACM*, *60*(6), 33–39. DOI: 10.1145/2998438

Grover, S., & Pea, R. (2013). Computational thinking in K–12: A review of the state of the field. *Educational Researcher*, *42*(1), 38–43. DOI: 10.3102/0013189X12463051

Guzdial, M. (2015). *Learner-centered design of computing education: Research on computing for everyone*. Morgan & Claypool Publishers., DOI: 10.2200/S00684ED1V01Y201511HCI033

Israel, M., Pearson, J. N., Tapia, T., Wherfel, Q. M., & Reese, G. (2015). Supporting all learners in school-wide computational thinking: A cross-case qualitative analysis. *Teaching Exceptional Children*, *47*(6), 308–316. DOI: 10.1177/0040059915579868

Kafai, Y. B., & Burke, Q. (2014). *Connected code: Why children need to learn programming*. MIT Press. DOI: 10.7551/mitpress/9992.001.0001

Korkmaz, Ö., Çakir, R., & Özden, M. Y. (2017). A validity and reliability study of the Computational Thinking Scales (CTS). *Computers in Human Behavior*, *72*, 558–569. DOI: 10.1016/j.chb.2017.01.005

Maloney, J., Resnick, M., Rusk, N., Silverman, B., & Eastmond, E. (2010). The Scratch programming language and environment. *ACM Transactions on Computing Education*, *10*(4), 16. Advance online publication. DOI: 10.1145/1868358.1868363

Papert, S. (1980). *Mindstorms: Children, computers, and powerful ideas*. Basic Books.

Resnick, M. (2017). *Lifelong kindergarten: Cultivating creativity through projects, passion, peers, and play*. MIT Press. DOI: 10.7551/mitpress/11017.001.0001

Sentance, S., & Csizmadia, A. (2017). Computing in the curriculum: Challenges and strategies from a teacher's perspective. *Education and Information Technologies*, *22*(2), 469–495. DOI: 10.1007/s10639-016-9482-0

Wing, J. M. (2006). Computational thinking. *Communications of the ACM*, *49*(3), 33–35. DOI: 10.1145/1118178.1118215

Chapter 2
Coding Education:
Why and How?

İsmail Tonbuloğlu
https://orcid.org/0000-0001-7059-9125
Marmara University, Turkey

ABSTRACT

This section discusses why coding education is necessary, its contribution to learning processes, and its relationship with different disciplines. It emphasizes that coding education supports cognitive development from an early age and can be effectively implemented with age-appropriate content, methods, and tools. The selection criteria for popular programming languages and their roles in education are detailed. The educational value of languages such as Scratch, Python, and Java is explained with examples. In addition, the platforms and tools used in coding education are examined in four main categories, and the importance of practical and gamified learning approaches is emphasized. At the end of the section, common challenges such as teacher competence, curriculum integration, and adaptation to technological change are presented along with suggested solutions. Research shows that coding education not only develops technical skills but also fosters future-oriented competencies such as creativity, critical thinking, and collaborative problem-solving.

INTRODUCTION

In this section the formulation of why Coding Education is necessary will be conducted through existing literature. It will examine and build on different aspects such as the contribution of Coding Education to learning processes and its interdisciplinary relations. Also, the importance of Coding Education relevance for present and future needs will be clarified. The appropriateness of age groups concerning

DOI: 10.4018/979-8-3373-2660-3.ch002

method, application, content, and other factors regarding Coding Education will be discussed. This section will also include important teaching languages that are used during coding education processes as well as the concepts to be considered when selecting these languages. Furthermore, an overview of instruments and platforms that may be utilized in Coding Education will be provided. Finally, the chapter will discuss encountered challenges in coding education processes alongside possible solutions.

The teaching and learning of programming languages and computational thinking is Coding Education. It equips learners with the skills necessary to shape a digitalized world hands-on, along with algorithmic problem solving methods. It includes practical coding sessions alongside the relevant theoretical knowledge known as didactic programming (Kapucu & Batu, 2022). In addition to didactic programming, supplemental collaborative tools greatly improve real-time interactive coding sessions and broaden the scope of learning (Paiva et al., 2020). A well-rounded EdTech program cultivates children's cognitive development in tandem with technical proficiencies because it prepares them for potential careers where they would engineer technology products instead of just writing code (Ari et al., 2022).

New research in computer science indicates that Coding Education not only cultivates specific mental skills like problem solving and critical thinking, but also enhances motivation and engagement from students. As an illustration, Güleryüz (2023) notes the positive impacts of robotics and coding integration into STEM on learners' attitudes towards focus and learning, particularly among those who struggle with attention and concentration during traditional lessons. Another study emphasizes the fact that coding can yield cognitive benefits due to overlap between coding and creative or mathematical problem solving (Scherer et al., 2021). The merging of different disciplines within education is made possible through innovative online platforms which enable real-time interaction (Zhang & Li, 2023). Through the systematic application of real-world scenarios, Coding Education offers a framework that helps students prepare for future challenges shaped by technology (Hudin, 2023).

IMPORTANCE AND FUTURE IMPACTS OF CODING

In education, the importance of coding is increasingly recognized concerning future employability prospects and advancement in technology. In this context, coding serves the dual purpose of providing students with vital problem-solving competencies alongside fostering creativity and logical reasoning in a world brimming with automation and artificial intelligence (Hudin, 2023). Also, given the projections depicting an increasing need for programming skills among diverse professionals, the introduction of writing coding instruction at school is expected to equip learners with relevant skills to enable them compete favorably in the global technological marketplace (Almadhun et al., 2024; Almadhun et al., 2019).

With the advancement of technology in various sectors, Coding Education is becoming more important. In addition to computer science, programming skills are essential in industries like healthcare, finance, and education. This underscores the need for thorough and timely coding education that integrates problem solving and nurtures students' imagination, logical reasoning, critical thinking, and judgment skills. Numerous studies show that teaching coding fosters a healthy disposition toward technology among learners while boosting motivation and self-efficacy. Kapucu and Batu (2022) reported that coding instruction benefits students' verbal creativity and overall attitude toward technology, illustrating that its advantages are not limited to computer science education alone. Scherer et al. (2021) also support this by explaining how the ability to code goes beyond a technical skill; it enables one to grasp computational thinking necessary for solving problems in today's intricate working environments.

Coding has immense importance for Education, a fact that has come to be known only recently. For starters, children get inspired to learn computer science and related technologies when they witness the practical application of programming and robotics (Ragusa & Leung, 2023). Monteiro et al (2021) also supports this by stating that coding literacy drives educational literacy. Evidence suggests that with the infusion of coding into the frameworks and creative and critical thinking skills in subjects, students acquire requisite knowledge along with programming skills for their innovative future careers. Creativity in coding is key towards student involvement as well as problem solving. Ferrari and Pelizzari (2023) point out how relentlessly pushing to mix creative endeavors with coding results in risk-taking and imaginative thought along with their focus on providing kids opportunities instead of limited tasks controlled by adults. Flynn et al., 2023 add stronger math by emphasizing active collaborative problem solving reinforces computational participation that has become somewhat indispensable in our economy today strengthens these further.

Another study states that alongside learning to code, students can develop additional educational outcomes such as problem solving in mathematics, advanced critical thinking, social interaction, self-management skills, academic proficiency, and many others. The work of Popat & Starkey (2019) highlights the importance of coding education's instructional design owing to its potential to nurture skills through coding education.

Acquiring coding skills aids students in attaining abilities that go beyond the realm of programming. When students are supported to engage creatively with coding, they acquire technical competencies alongside a multitude of thinking skills necessary for overcoming workforce challenges due to automation and AI. Integrating coding enhances the curriculum serves to give far greater core competencies required during critical employment opportunities later on in life. Besides nurturing creativity along with problem solving, education in coding applies to all aspects of life and equips learners for an evolving technologically advanced world which is highly innovative. Schools and colleges that integrate coding as part of core learning can place their graduates many steps ahead of their peers. The ability to program makes learning easier and more innovative by giving one the power to shape things in a world dominated by technology. The knowledge obtained via teaching coding can be leveraged in various practical fields such as website creation, cybersecurity, mobile application development, or even artificial intelligence.

CODING EDUCATION IN DIFFERENT AGE GROUPS

Because modern coding education is geared towards young learners, teaching forms which promote computational thinking must vary with age. Even for preschoolers, early exposure to coding concepts is possible; they can learn basic problem-solving and creativity through gaming at their cognitive level (Demir, 2021). In middle school and high school, more advanced programming languages and projects will better prepare learners for post-secondary studies and careers in the tech field (Deniz & Korucu, 2023). The curriculum along with the pedagogy will determine the range of skills acquired through learning to code (Popat & Starkey, 2019). Thus, accurate methods, techniques, tools or even a structured curriculum must be designed around the learner group in question when delivering coding education. Clearly defined age divisions alongside appropriate tailored content ensure relevant coding education.

The importance of coding education continues to grow as it now corresponds with the development milestones and age-appropriate interests of learners. It can begin in preschool with simple games that solve problems and make use of imaginative play, creativity, and self-directed exploration. In early childhood education centers, experiment-based learning as a dominant form of work can enhance cognitive skill development (Kapyk et al., 2024). During this period, the goal is to develop computational thinking alongside advanced problem-solving skills which concrete physical methodologies will achieve most effectively. Computerized coding lessons may either stand alone or be woven into other subjects just as easily as offline coding activities do. Furthermore, some researchers have integrated storytelling and literacy sessions with coding at the preschool level (Uğraş et al., 2025).

In middle school, the teaching of coding becomes formalized at an academic level combining advanced programming languages industry standards with frameworks taught in school. For instance, Minecraft coding projects have been shown to support middle grade students' computational thinking skills (Kutay & Öner, 2022). Moreover, block-based coding has a significant impact on shaping students' perspectives towards coding positively and connects engagement with learning results (Totan & Korucu, 2023). They help students develop robust problem-solving skills that are necessary in this technological era.

With high school syllabuses increasingly centered on Python or Java programming and software engineering, many consider these fields to be the focus of advanced study. Students are also intellectually prepared by teaching them project management in addition to coding, which as they learn, helps facilitate its application at an international level. A good example is NASA where they incorporate project management into their coding programs so that learners can appreciate technology's application across different disciplines (Delle-Vergini et al., 2023)

POPULAR PROGRAMMING LANGUAGES AND SELECTION

The impact of the widely-used programming languages taught at school on students' competencies in this age is undeniable. It would also be pertinent to mention that their use, along with other block-based Scratch-like languages which help cultivate the most basic programming skills indecipherable without a proper syntax, aids junior students greatly (Bachiller et al., 2020). Such tutors improve learner motivation at different ages by working based on previously gained knowledge and fixed goals. Having said that, teaching coding through more advanced programming languages ought to follow first offering learners closely structured criteria merged with real-world applicability and psychology heuristic hands-on learning tools aligned with cutting-edge technological developments. While doing so educators must apply techniques allowing constant reassessment aimed within changing classrooms defined by active educational systems.

Multidimensional considerations such as application opportunities, ease of mastering them, their popularity or community support tend to refine didactic value closer associated with effectiveness.

Picking the right programming languages for teaching coding is crucial in a setting overwhelmed by competing technologies. The popularity and selection of certain languages is determined by the set objectives, intended learners, and their relevance to the field. Below are some key programming languages commonly used in educational settings along with the rationale for their choice based on recent literature:

Scratch

Type: Block-based

Use Case: Encourages algorithmic thinking; makes learning fun through media and story-driven projects (Resnick et al., 2020)

Age Level: Elementary – Middle School

Scratch serves as a gaming animation and game creation platform that utilizes coding which assists in critical thinking, functions like a programming language with the potential to create games and animations through computational concepts (Yıldız & Çengel, 2022; Park & Shin, 2019). It is beneficial for teachers reaching out to their students since it broadens their horizon towards coding (Yıldız & Çengel, 2022).

Blockly

Type: Block-based

Use Case: Eases transition to text-based coding; eliminates syntax errors (Montoya et al., 2017)

Age Level: Elementary – Middle School

Blockly is another programming language with strong focus towards primary –n middle school children. Its major strength lies in simplifying the transition from visual to traditional text-based coding, effectively reducing syntax errors that often hinder novice programmers (Rousouliotis et al., 2023; Glas et al., 2023) . Apart from robotics, it also enclosed cyber security within its scope of learning making users have the interest tackling multiple fields at once. As an open source tool, it continues to evolve with community support while still being accessible for teachers and students (Bieg et al., 2022).

Python

Type: High-level text-based

Use Case: General-purpose with simple syntax; widely used in data science and AI (Guo et al., 2020)

Age Level: Middle School – High School – Adult

Due to its direct and clear syntax, Python is regarded as one of the most accessible programming languages for teaching basic programming skills (Moumoutzis et al., 2021). It also supports libraries which improve data science and machine learning. Furthermore, community support improves data science and machine learning (Moumoutzis et al., 2021). Python's tediousness enhances its usefulness in reading materials with a high degree importance for learners, since it allows active engagement with text through rubrics or guided exercises (Sun et al., 2019; Andonov, 2019).

JavaScript

Type: Web-oriented text-based

Use Case: Provides immediate browser-based visual feedback; essential for web development (Karim & Cragg, 2016)

Age Level: High School – University

Due to its dominance in web development, JavaScript is indispensable for students interested in full-stack development. As suggested by Naveed(2021), seeing results from JavaScript code is very important for motivating learners. JavaScript's frameworks React and Node.js boost prospects in software development further expanding employment opportunities (Sun et al., 2019).

Java

Type: Object-oriented text-based

Use Case: Included in AP curricula; teaches software engineering principles (Altadmri & Brown, 2015)

Age Level: High School – Adult

Concerned over its complexity for beginners fails to overshadow Java's popularity as a mandatory element in curricula owing to being prevalent in the business world and adaptable across different systems. It helps construct a solid understanding of foundational concepts taught at the school level essential for workings of enterprises (Naveed, 2021).

C++

Type: System-level text-based

Use Case: Used to teach memory management and algorithmic thinking (Salikhov et al., 2018)

Age Level: High School – Adult

Despite facing criticism for its steep learning curve, C++ serves as an invaluable tool for teaching low-level programming concepts, memory management, and string handling. It is particularly important in the field of computer science education because it is used in high-performing applications such as game development and systems programming. These factors enable a student to transition to complex languages (Naveed, 2021; Kaszab & Cserép, 2023).

Logo

Type: Graphical text-based

Use Case: Effective for teaching geometry and loops (Papert & Harel, 2016)

Age Level: Elementary – Middle School

Logo is a pedagogical language meant for teaching programming along with computational thinking. It is primarily focused on engaging students which philosophically sets them up to control a turtle which forms drawings which aids them to solve problems systematically (Messer et al., 2018). Brady emphasizes that Logo encourages young children to deconstruct and analyze intricate problems while nurturing critical thought and imagination (Brady, 2021).

Alice

Type: 3D visual programming
Use Case: Suitable for animation-based learning and event-driven programming (Cooper et al., 2017)
Age Level: Middle School – High School

Alice is targeted toward middle school learners to teach Computer Science using storytelling and animation through an innovative 3D Programming environment. The complexity of coding is mitigated by its drag-and-drop interface that textual coding would replace making accessibility easier for novices (Batiha et al., 2022). Alice's impact extends beyond coding itself, fostering creativity, critical thinking, problem solving all within captivating contexts. Moreover it greatly enhances attitude and performance relative to text-based environments (Al-Tahat, 2019; Morán et al., 2019).

R

Type: Text-based for data analysis
Use Case: A powerful tool for data visualization and statistical analysis (Wickham & Grolemund, 2017)
Age Level: High School – Adult

With regard to data science and statistics, R enables efficient data management and complex statistical modeling so helps students acquire relevant skills needed for quantitative analyst professions alongside offering robust packages tailored for scholarly investigation alongside practical industry tasks aiding pupils eyeing data-oriented jobs (Foughali, 2023).

Ruby

Type: High-level text-based
Use Case: Easy to learn with clean syntax; supports rapid application development (Ford & Parnell, 2016)
Age Level: High School – Adult

Ruby prioritizes productivity and is well-known due to its web application development framework: Ruby on Rails. Its modules, packages, and timeless classic elegant syntax help reduce the burden experienced by novices which aids in grasping foundational principles minimizing overhead (Fraser et al., 2021). Foughali (2023) notes that streamlining support-seeking processes improves user satisfaction making Ruby's student-friendly community philosophy appealing.

Swift

Type: Modern text-based

Use Case: Designed for iOS development; interactive with Playground environment (Apple Education, 2020)

Age Level: Middle School – High School – Adult

Apple-backed Swift is widely taught because it facilitates iOS app development, capturing interest from students keen on owning mobile applications during their studies (Foughali, 2023).

Tynker

Type: Block + text-based

Use Case: Offers gamified instruction and various STEM applications (Grover et al., 2021)

Age Level: Elementary – Middle School

Tynker serves as a coding platform for children and utilizes a unique game-based approach to learning programming. Its modular design motivates inventive problem-solving, enabling self-expression through the development of games and animations. Its ease-of-use combined with powerful features makes it one of the best coding education platforms for young children.

PHP

Type: Web server language

Use Case: Teaches dynamic website development; provides simple server-side logic (Welling & Thomson, 2017)

Age Level: High School – Adult

PHP (Hypertext Preprocessor) serves as a powerful, server-side scripting language with an outsized popularity amongst web developers due to its specialized applications on websites and web applications. One of PHP's main advantages is its ease of use and rapid development capabilities. Popular frameworks like CodeIgniter and Laravel foster increased productivity by providing reusable components based on the MVC architecture (Maulana et al., 2023). With a modular design, PHP not only simplifies complex function deployment but also improves long-term maintainability. Coupled with extensive documentation, strong community support makes it easy for beginners, furthering cross-platform compatibility which allows apps to be run on multiple operating systems. Its continuous community-based improvements bolster security against ongoing vulnerabilities enhancing resilience; thus making PHP trusted at all scales (Niarman et al., 2023).

Kodu

Type: Graphical game programming language
Use Case: Teaches basic 3D world design and event-driven logic (Microsoft, 2014)
Age Level: Elementary – Middle School

One of its key advantages is the interface's design, as it allows children to construct interactive games without any programming training. This real-time responsiveness fosters creativity and curiosity among learners (Lindberg et al., 2018). Kodu also focuses on developing critical thinking by resolving puzzles associated with characters and game operations logically (Choleva et al., 2022). Moreover, Kodu promotes computational thinking by guiding learners through systematic problem-solving in a playful context while integrating storytelling and imagination (Choleva et al., 2022). In conclusion, Kodu provides a well-balanced environment for enjoyable and effective learning which makes it suitable for all students from kindergarten to grade twelve.

App Inventor

Type: Block-based mobile development
Use Case: Enables easy development of Android apps (MIT, 2018)
Age Level: Middle School – High School

App Inventor is an agile visual programming system tailored to suit the needs of absolute beginners. Students can easily use Android phones because one of the main features of the platform is the drag-and-drop construction of applications (Pérez-Jorge & Martínez-Murciano, 2022). The tasks were used to explain how people can use them to generate engaging learning solutions (Park & Shin, 2019). Furthermore, Ndebele and Mazhindu (2023) argue that App Inventor fosters project-based learning as it enables students to solve various real-life problems through creative application development. With these attributes, App Inventor serves as a powerful application for not just K-12 learners, but higher education institutions focused on teaching programming in a hands-on manner(Patton et al., 2019).

Arduino (C/C++)

Type: Physical computing
Use Case: Enables coding with physical outputs for robotics and IoT projects (Salikhov et al., 2018)
Age Level: Middle School – High School – Adult

Arduino is an electronic platform which is open-source; thus, its integration of hardware and software makes it a very useful tool in engineering, robotics and education at all levels. One of its key strengths is accessibility: the Arduino IDE uses a simplified version of C/C++, allowing users to quickly write and upload code to microcontroller boards without requiring deep programming knowledge (Morais & Araújo, 2022). Because of this simplicity, educators are able to teach students programming and circuit design through al hands-on methods that stimulate innovative thinking (Morais & Araújo, 2022). In addition, the wide range of sensors and components within Arduino's ecosystem supports applications like data logging or environmental monitoring (Beddows & Mallon, 2018). Students and professionals understand the value of Arduino as an educational resource, especially in developing multi-faceted projects.

HTML/CSS

Type: Web markup/style language
Use Case: Teaches web structure and design (W3C, 2019)
Age Level: Middle School – High School

Individuals beginning their careers in web development must know that building and designing websites involves two integral skills: Hypertext Markup Language (HTML) and Cascading Style Sheets (CSS). These two technologies have a remarkable strength—they can be utilized by all aspiring students. With both CSS and HTML, even learners without considerable programming skill sets can design functional websites. That is because CSS enhances aesthetics while HTML aids in structuring content (Amandha et al., 2024). Students are attracted to these tools because their basic principles allow learners to grasp concepts quickly and through tangible experiences, enabling practical web project implementation (Fakhri et al., 2023). In addition to this, mastery of HTML and CSS guarantees immediate industry readiness as the skills are universally applicable which greatly enhances employability potential while providing room for mastering more complex frameworks or languages later on (Fakhri et al., 2023).

MicroPython

Type: Python-based embedded language

Use Case: Enables physical computing with devices like Micro:bit and ESP32 (BBC, 2021)

Age Level: Middle School – High School

Aimed at beginners and experts alike, MicroPython serves as a stripped down version of Python tailored for use with microcontrollers, making it perfect within the IoT ecosystem. A significant advantage is that it can operate on low-power, resource-constrained devices with no compromise to functionality, offering a convenient programming environment (Marevac et al., 2025). For these reasons, MicroPython Is appropriate for teaching purposes, especially as more educators seek to incorporate programming and robotics into STEM subjects (Rodríguez-Ponce & Mota-Muñoz, 2020). Staacks et al. (2025) notes that MicroPython's simple syntax and rich library support accelerate prototyping and development. This enables learners and hobbyists to build electronics projects ranging from rudimentary ones to sophisticated IoT systems. By providing a powerful means of programming devices and electronics, MicroPython aids learners tremendously bridging the gap between theoretical concepts and practical work.

C# (C-Sharp)

Type: Object-oriented text-based language

Use Case: Enables game and Windows application development, especially with Unity (Microsoft, 2020)

Age Level: High School – Adult

C# (C-Sharp), developed by Microsoft, is an example of a versatile and powerful programming language. Its prominence stems from its capability in software development for web, desktop, and mobile interfaces all at once. One key benefit includes precision-type error checking during compilation which enhances software reliability making enterprise solutions based on C# exceptionally appealing (Huang et al., 2022). Moreover .EXT frameworks have rich libraries that allow developers to create high-performance applications with less code which makes them very efficient (Méri et al., 2021). As stated by Werner and Olanow (2021), C# supports both object-oriented and functional programming paradigms, making it easier for large teams to write maintainable and readable code. Professionals in complex systems whether new or experienced still find C# an added advantage because of the broad application scope the language has along with a powerful developer community.

Flutter

Type: Mobile-oriented text-based framework

Use Case: Enables development of modern mobile apps (Google, 2021)

Age Level: High School – Adult

One of the Google products, Flutter, is one of the leader frameworks in mobile apps development as it aids creators dealing with both iOS and Android applications from a single code base. Its standout feature is its unique architecture that removes the need for platform-specific bridges, significantly reducing development time and complexity—offering up to 50% time savings compared to other cross-platform technologies (Rajput et al., 2023). Comprehensive functionality paired with flawless performance delivers an exceptional user experience (Ameen & Mohammed, 2022). It also offers a set of stylish customizable widgets enabling smooth interface construction therefore appealing to UI/UX designers. Also, in view of Hassan (2022), increased developer productivity due to instant visibility on changes made to codes through "hot reload" makes Flutter more lovable (Hassan, 2022). The cross-platform efficiency and aesthetics of Flutter made it a fork favorite for mobile-focused companies and even freelancers.

SQL

Type: Query language

Use Case: Widely used for database querying and data analysis (Kaszab & Cserép, 2023)

Age Level: High School – Adult

In business and data administration, Structured Query Language (SQL) has its own benefits as well. Its one of the strongest assets to have in any enterprise environment that works with structured data is its compatibility with relational database management systems (RDBMS), as noted by Pina et al. 2022. For companies dealing with massive datasets, SQL's structure for executing complicated queries comes in handy because it was built to work on heavily loaded datasets. And because the various database systems employs similar architecture, there is ease in switching or mulitasking between systems, thus lowering the need to train when new systems are introduced (Hatami & Wolcott, 2020). In this age where data security is essential (Gao & Contreras, 2023), having an SQL based databases is a preferred solution due to their excellent controls for integrity, confidentiality, protection and access restrictions concerning sensitive information. Even more so powerful considering how cloud computing today integrates with the rest of modern technology powered by IoT(Oliveira et al., 2021; Telukdarie et al., 2023). There is no doubt that sql holds dominace over other tools concerning data management due to how easy they can be integrated with advanced technologies putting them at an advantage regardless of user experience level.

The appropriateness of programming languages for teaching coding centers on their ease of learning, usefulness in the job market, and compatibility with industry expectations. For this reason, educators need to pay attention to these issues and implement a curriculum that aims at multi-language exposure to provide comprehensive computer science training.

TOOLS AND PLATFORMS USED IN CODING EDUCATION

As in other subjects, teaching aids are used to achieve the objectives set for students in coding education. There is a strong focus on using technology to boost both interest and ease of access. Sites such as Scratch and Code.org have beginner-friendly settings which allow students to learn the fundamental ideas of coding through block-based programming which is fun and interactive. Advanced tools like GitHub enable student programmers to participate in collaborative works through project sharing along with code revision practices giving them an opportunity to practice and improve their coding skills aided by peer criticism and community feedback. A range of tools designed specifically for different levels of learners in coding education have emerged over time, along with basic programming language software and advanced evaluation methods. The use of these aids not only meets diverse learner needs but also facilitates cross-learner collaboration while fostering essential technical competencies, resulting in a well-rounded approach to teaching coding.

These tools can be systematically categorized into four main groups: Development Environments and Programming Languages, Assessment and Evaluation Platforms, Robotics and Hands-on Learning Platforms, and Interactive and Gamified Learning Tools. Each category plays a distinct role in developing coding competencies and shaping instructional methods. This classification is supported by various empirical studies and educational approaches.

Development Environments and Programming Languages

This section covers the solutions and resources where learners can create, assess, and troubleshoot code. Integrated Development Environments (IDEs) Like Visual Studio and PyCharm offer modern conveniences like text illumination, debugging, and managing multiple projects at a time. In education, languages such as Python and Java which are easy to read are commonly preferred because of their extensive use (Kado, 2022; Simon et al., 2024). Scratch and Blockly are also educational programming tools within this group. They enable very early-stage learners to write programs using visual blocks rather than the conventional string-based syntax through beginner's stub programs. Younger learners who need greater engagement while grasping fundamental programming concepts greatly benefit from learning using Scratch's block-based programming approach (Bachiller et al., 2020; Tsikalakis et al., 2023). Moreover, GitHub is more than just a code repository. It equips learners with collaboration skills through version control which enable them to work on group projects seamlessly (Farah et al., 2022; Indriasari et al., 2020).

Assessment and Evaluation Platforms

All such tools serve a vital purpose when it comes to appraisal regarding students coding skills mastery benchmarks as well as understanding basic principles taught in class. A case in point is AABC which combines practical tests alongside theory to evaluate essential coding skills comprehensive in the Arduino environment (Tselegkaridis et al., 2025). Just like Hyperstyle, other automated code review services give immediate evaluations of the submitted work using preset criteria. Students learn from the mistakes and successes of their peers during GitHub-based peer code reviews (Farah et al., 2022; Indriasari et al., 2020). Generative AI powered tools such as GitHub Copilot assist learners in more advanced tasks by providing instantaneous guidance and critique, which makes learning simpler and more efficient (Avramovic et al., 2024; Simon et al., 2024).

Robotics and Hands-on Learning Platforms

LEGO robotics help students with practical programming skills and strengthen cascade concepts learned in theory. Embedded programming is a hands-on activity when students utilize Python with LEGO sets (Lee & Yi, 2021). Moreover, Valls et al. demonstrated that the integration of robotics into project based learning greatly enhances computation thinking skills among learners (Valls et al., 2022). With robotics education, students can apply theoretical knowledge to real life situations and through experimentation, hone various skills while problem solving.

Interactive and Gamified Learning Tools

This section focuses on the significance of motivation and engagement in the context of coding education. Game-based learning tools foster computational thinking, problem-solving skills, and student interest in the subjects (Zhang et al., 2022; Marín et al., 2018). These platforms promote enjoyment while learning through competition by utilizing gamification techniques like scoring systems and challenges. Additionally, students can pursue self-directed projects via methods such as project-based learning, which fosters broader practical application of coding skills

(Arendes et al., 2024; Mecca et al., 2021). These platforms facilitate collaborative and creative approaches to learning. The COVID-19 pandemic underscored the need for technology-integrated learning solutions—and resilient educational practices—exemplified by the flexibility offered through these tools (Zhang et al., 2022).

COMMON CHALLENGES AND SOLUTIONS IN CODING EDUCATION

Common barriers within coding education include learners' relative inexperience with foundational programming skills, coding conceptualization errors, and bridges between theory and practice. Remedies to these concerns include employing project-based learning, teaching younger students foundational concepts using Scratch's visual programming capabilities, coupled with tailored support strategies like personalized tutoring or peer mentoring (Ericson et al., 2023; Indriasari et al., 2020). Integration of collaborative platforms, such as GitHub, improves students' understanding of coding difficulties through group projects and peer assessments (Zagalsky et al., 2015).

At the school level, integration of coding is still limited by socio-educational factors, notably the attitudes held by faculty, particularly teachers and principals towards the discipline and their openness to change traditional approaches to teaching and learning (Wong et al., 2015). Pair programming is an example of a different approach which positively affects coding fluency; originality and creativity have been reported in middle schoolers as well (Seo & Kim, 2016). The quality of programming assignments also greatly benefits from automated or semi-automated grading. In addition to improving efficiency for instructors, these systems provide feedback on many errors that students tend to be blind to (Kaszab & Cserép, 2023).

The challenges and proposed solutions in coding education can be classified based on existing academic literature into six main categories: **Teacher Competence**, **Curriculum Integration**, **Student Engagement**, **Access to Resources**, **Assessment Issues**, and **Technological Change**.

Teacher Competence

Challenge:

Effective coding education in primary and secondary schools faces mounting challenges such as a lack of teacher training in this field. Instructional quality suffers when educators lack computer science training (Kadar et al., 2021).

Solution:

Teachers need to engage with workshops supplemented with online certification courses that are available (Farah et al., 2022). Moreover, the formation of mentorship circles and professional development communities can help foster knowledge-sharing among teachers and encourage greater specialization in this area (Farah et al., 2022).

Curriculum Integration

Challenge:

In educational institutions, coding is often viewed as an extracurricular activity. This classification prevents it from being acknowledged as a key subject, which reduces its academic value (Chen et al., 2022).

Solution:

Rather, coding activities should be incorporated into math, science, and visual arts classes. This integration not only fulfills curricular requirements but also enables students to work on projects that are truly impactful (Chen et al., 2022).

Student Engagement

Challenge:

Many students consider coding to be abstract and extremely challenging, greatly reducing their motivation and participation levels (Kamarudin et al., 2022).

Solution:

Through the application of competition and enjoyment, gated learning frameworks capture students' attention and interest (Kamarudin et al., 2022). Engagement can also be enhanced through project-based learning where students create applications or find solutions to social issues. Learning becomes more enjoyable when collaborative methods—such as pair programming—are employed (Allsop, 2019).

Access to Resources

Challenge:

Students with limited financial means often lack access to fundamental resources like computers or the internet. The persistent lack of access most students face across the globe continues to hamper learning for all students (Kadar et al., 2021).

Solution:

Support from public institutions and NGOs should be directed towards hardware and infrastructure gaps (Tiwari & Fahrudin, 2024). Streamed coding lessons with minimal hardware requirements coupled with "unplugged" activities conducted offline can promote equitable access to learning for all students (Tiwari & Fahrudin, 2024).

Assessment Issues

Challenge:

Evaluation of coding competencies particularly within loose and imaginative frameworks can be very subjective, thus inconsistent (Ramadani et al., 2023).

Solution:

The use of automated assessment systems helps benchmark and accelerate evaluative workflows (Farah et al., 2022). Agile creation of comprehensive scoring guides structured around detailed per-task processes enhances clarity. Active participation within the classroom can also be heightened by reflexive peer evaluation (Ramadani et al., 2023).

Technological Change

Challenge:

Keeping pace in class with new programming languages and software tools is a challenge for both educators and learners due to their rapidly changing nature (Hudin, 2023).

Solution:

When tackling the latter focus on sustainable problem solving in algorithmic thinking is more effective than specific technologies. Relevance is maintained through wide-use languages like Python and elective modules on emerging technologies offered (Farah et al., 2022).

Addressing hurdles posed by teaching coding will require concerted efforts by teachers, school leaders, and educational policy makers. This will enable a more equitable, available, and impactful ecosystem for learning to code.

REFERENCES

Al-Tahat, K. S. (2019). The impact of a 3d visual programming tool on students' performance and attitude in computer programming. *Journal of Cases on Information Technology*, *21*(1), 52–64. DOI: 10.4018/JCIT.2019010104

Allsop, Y. (2019). Assessing computational thinking process using a multiple evaluation approach. *International Journal of Child-Computer Interaction*, *19*, 30–55. DOI: 10.1016/j.ijcci.2018.10.004

Almadhun, S., Swese, R. F., Ali, A., Nasef, A. A., Alasoud, A., & Rmis, A. (2024). Programming education in focus: Investigating and analyzing the present state in libyan primary and secondary schools. *Humanitarian and Natural Sciences Journal*, *5*(1). Advance online publication. DOI: 10.53796/hnsj51/39

Almadhun, S., Toycan, M., & Adalıer, A. (2019). Vb2algo: An educational reverse engineering tool to enhance high school students' learning capacities in programming. *Revista de Cercetare si Interventie Sociala*, *67*, 67–87. DOI: 10.33788/rcis.67.5

Altadmri, A., & Brown, N. C. C. (2015). 37 million lines of code: Identifying common student mistakes in novice programs. *Proceedings of the 46th ACM Technical Symposium on Computer Science Education*, 278–283. https://doi.org/DOI: 10.1145/2676723.2677258

Amandha, S., Dani, R., Hierdawati, T., Armandito, A., & Rahmat, B. (2024). Workshop pengenalan web dan css dasar pada mahasiswa universitas muhammadiyah jambi. *KREATIF: Jurnal Pengabdian Masyarakat Nusantara*, *4*(1), 65–71. DOI: 10.55606/kreatif.v4i1.2842

Ameen, S. Y., & Mohammed, D. Y. (2022). Developing cross-platform library using flutter. *European Journal of Engineering and Technology Research*, *7*(2), 18–21. DOI: 10.24018/ejeng.2022.7.2.2740

Andonov, F. (2019). Comparative analysis of python with other programming languages. *Yearbook Telecommunications*, *6*, 1–15. DOI: 10.33919/YTelecomm.19.6.1

Apple Education. (2020). *Everyone Can Code Curriculum*. Apple Inc.

Arendes, K., Kerkhoff, S. N., & Adhikari, B. (2024). Engaging students to learn coding in the ai era with emphasis on the process. *Edukasiana: Jurnal Inovasi Pendidikan*, *3*(2), 257–268. DOI: 10.56916/ejip.v3i2.728

Ari, F., Arslan-Ari, I., & Vasconcelos, L. (2022). Early childhood preservice teachers' perceptions of computer science, gender stereotypes, and coding in early childhood education. *TechTrends*, *66*(3), 539–546. DOI: 10.1007/s11528-022-00725-w

Avramovic, S., Avramovic, I., & Wojtusiak, J. (2024). Exploring the impact of github copilot on health informatics education. *Applied Clinical Informatics*, *15*(05), 1121–1129. DOI: 10.1055/a-2414-7790

Bachiller, P., Barbecho, I., Calderita, L. V., Bustos, P., & Manso, L. J. (2020). Learnblock: A robot-agnostic educational programming tool. *IEEE Access : Practical Innovations, Open Solutions*, *8*, 30012–30026. DOI: 10.1109/ACCESS.2020.2972410

Batiha, Q. A., Ashaari, N. S., Aini, N., & Mohd, N. (2022). Adoption of visual programming environments in programming learning. *International Journal on Advanced Science, Engineering and Information Technology*, *12*(5), 1921–1930. DOI: 10.18517/ijaseit.12.5.15500

BBC. (2021). *MicroPython and BBC micro:bit – Getting Started Guide.* https://microbit.org

Beddows, P. A., & Mallon, E. K. (2018). Cave pearl data logger: A flexible arduino-based logging platform for long-term monitoring in harsh environments. *Sensors (Basel)*, *18*(2), 530. DOI: 10.3390/s18020530

Bieg, T., Schmoigl-Tonis, M., Sturm, N., Nativel, C., & Sackl, A. (2022). Enabling cross-domain robot programming by end-users: the robxtask platform. 2022 *IEEE Symposium on Visual Languages and Human-Centric Computing* (VL/HCC). https://doi.org/DOI: 10.1109/VL/HCC53370.2022.9833136

Brady, C. (2021). Patches as an expressive medium for exploratory multi-agent modelling. *British Journal of Educational Technology*, *52*(3), 1024–1042. DOI: 10.1111/bjet.13087

Chen, C., Jong, M. S., & Tsai, C. (2022). A comparison of in-service teachers' conceptions of barriers to mobile technology-integrated instruction and technology-integrated instruction. *Australasian Journal of Educational Technology*, •••, 35–50. DOI: 10.14742/ajet.7299

Choleva, V., Stagakis, S., Choleva, E., & Patrikakis, C. Z. (2022). Integrating the 4cs into creating games by visual programming and project based learning. *European Conference on Games Based Learning, 16*(1), 147-154. https://doi.org/DOI: 10.34190/ecgbl.16.1.694

Cooper, S., Dann, W., & Pausch, R. (2017). *Learning to Program with Alice* (3rd ed.). Pearson.

Delle-Vergini, S., Eacersall, D., Dann, C., Ally, M., & Chakraborty, S. (2023). Teaching project management to primary school children: A scoping review. *Australian Educational Researcher*, *51*(4), 1035–1062. DOI: 10.1007/s13384-023-00627-7

Demir, B. E. (2021). *Okulöncesi eğitimde kodlama, robotik ve bilişimsel düşünme: magne-board'un gelişimi*. European Journal of Science and Technology., DOI: 10.31590/ejosat.842483

Deniz, T., & Korucu, A. T. (2023). The effect of coding education designed with different visual *programs on academic success and attitudes and self-efficiencies of secondary school students. Journal of Teacher Education and Lifelong Learning*, *5*(1), 307–323. DOI: 10.51535/tell.1279547

Ericson, B., Pearce, J. L., Rodger, S. H., Csizmadia, A., Garcia, R., Gutiérrez, F. J., & Bernuy, A. Z. (2023). Conducting multi-institutional studies of parsons problems. *Proceedings of the 2023 Conference on Innovation and Technology in Computer Science Education* v. 2. https://doi.org/DOI: 10.1145/3587103.3594211

Fakhri, M. M., Fardan, M., Leo, M. A., Wulandari, W., & Hawari, M. D. (2023). Peningkatan kompetensi front end web programming: pelatihan bahasa pemrograman html dan css bagi mahasiswa. *Jurnal Sipakatau: Inovasi Pengabdian Masyarakat*, 35-45. https://doi.org/DOI: 10.61220/jsipakatau.v1i1.235

Farah, J. C., Spaenlehauer, B., Rodríguez-Triana, M. J., Ingram, S., & Gillet, D. (2022). Toward code review notebooks. *2022 International Conference on Advanced Learning Technologies (ICALT)*, 209-211. https://doi.org/DOI: 10.1109/ICALT55010.2022.00068

Ferrari, S., & Pelizzari, F. (2023). *Coding and creativity: reflections and design proposals. Pedagogy*. Learning, and Creativity., DOI: 10.5772/intechopen.109971

Flynn, D., Hughes, J., & Robb, J. (2023). Improving Mathematics Learning Through Computational Participation. *Journal of Educational Informatics*, *4*(1). Advance online publication. DOI: 10.51357/jei.v4i1.214

Ford, M., & Parnell, J. (2016). Teaching Ruby in the secondary school curriculum. *Journal of Computers in Education*, *4*(1), 15–29. DOI: 10.1007/s40692-015-0043-5

Foughali, M. (2023). Some thoughts on teaching introductory programming and the first language dilemma (discussion paper)., 1-8. https://doi.org/DOI: 10.1145/3631802.3631812

Fraser, G., Heuer, U., Körber, N., Obermüller, F., & Wasmeier, E. (2021). Litterbox: a linter for scratch programs.. https://doi.org/DOI: 10.1109/ICSE-SEET52601.2021.00028

Gao, M., & Contreras, A. (2023). *A structured note-taking program to aid in data retention and promote organization using mobile devices as a medium*. Signal Image Processing and Multimedia., DOI: 10.5121/csit.2023.130923

Glas, M., Vielberth, M., Reittinger, T., Böhm, F., & Pernul, G. (2023). Improving cybersecurity skill development through visual programming. *Information and Computer Security*, *31*(3), 316–330. DOI: 10.1108/ICS-11-2022-0170

Google. (2021). *Flutter & Dart Documentation*. https://flutter.dev

Grover, S., Basu, S., & Schank, P. (2021). Scaling computational thinking through Tynker: A case study of a widely used platform. *Computers & Education*, *164*, 104121. DOI: 10.1016/j.compedu.2021.104121

Güleryüz, H. (2023). Attitudes of secondary school students towards robotics and coding in stem education with tinkercad. *Bayburt Eğitim Fakültesi Dergisi*, *18*(38), 471–485. DOI: 10.35675/befdergi.1270169

Guo, P. J., Watson, C., & Li, X. (2020). Python usage in introductory computer science courses. *ACM Inroads*, *11*(1), 28–33. DOI: 10.1145/3375880

Hassan, A. M. (2022). The design and implementation of a libyan salary mobile application using flutter. *Al-Mukhtar Journal of Sciences*, *37*(3), 251–260. DOI: 10.54172/mjsc.v37i3.802

Hatami, Z., & Wolcott, P. (2020). Understanding students' identification and use of patterns while writing sql queries. *Proceedings of the 21st Annual Conference on Information Technology Education*, 20-25. https://doi.org/DOI: 10.1145/3368308.3415367

Huang, C., Hung, H., Jaw, F., & Young, Y. (2022). Comparison of the wii balance board system and foam posturography system in assessing postural balance. *Ear and Hearing*, *43*(6), 1800–1806. DOI: 10.1097/AUD.0000000000001242

Hudin, S. S. (2023). A systematic review of the challenges in teaching programming for primary schools' students. *Online Journal for TVET Practitioners*, *8*(1). Advance online publication. DOI: 10.30880/ojtp.2023.08.01.008

Indriasari, T. D., Luxton-Reilly, A., & Denny, P. (2020). A review of peer code review in higher education. *ACM Transactions on Computing Education*, *20*(3), 1–25. DOI: 10.1145/3403935

Kadar, R., Wahab, N. A., Othman, J., Shamsuddin, M., & Mahlan, S. B. (2021). A study of difficulties in teaching and learning programming: A systematic literature review. *International Journal of Academic Research in Progressive Education and Development, 10*(3). Advance online publication. DOI: 10.6007/IJARPED/v10-i3/11100

Kado, K. (2022). Teaching and learning the fundamental of calculus through python-based coding. *International Journal of Didactical Studies*. https://doi.org/ DOI: 10.33902/IJODS.202215006

Kamarudin, N. A. B., Ikram, R. R. R., Azman, F. N. B., Ahmad, S. S. S., & Zainuddin, D. B. (2022). A study of the effects of short-term ai coding course with gamification elements on students' cognitive mental health. *TEM Journal,* 1854-1862. https://doi.org/DOI: 10.18421/tem114-53

Kapucu, M. S., & Batu, A. (2022). Analysis of studies on coding education: A meta synthesis study. *The Eurasia Proceedings of Educational and Social Sciences, 24*, 1–16. DOI: 10.55549/epess.1179319

Kapyk, I., Kolesnik, K., Kryvosheya, T., Pakhalchuk, N., & Pokhyla, S. (2024). Trends of implementation of research-experimental activities in preschool educational institutions of ukraine in today's conditions. *Society Integration Education. Proceedings of the International Scientific Conference*, 2, 16-26. https://doi.org/ DOI: 10.17770/sie2024vol2.7890

Karim, M., & Cragg, C. (2016). Web development pedagogy with JavaScript. *Education and Information Technologies, 21*(3), 679–697. DOI: 10.1007/s10639-014-9344-4

Kaszab, P., & Cserép, M. (2023). Detecting programming flaws in student submissions with static source code analysis. *Studia Universitatis Babes-Bolyai. Informatica, 68*(1), 37–54. DOI: 10.24193/subbi.2023.1.03

Kutay, E., & Öner, D. (2022). Coding with minecraft: The development of middle school students' computational thinking. *ACM Transactions on Computing Education, 22*(2), 1–19. DOI: 10.1145/3471573

Lee, S., & Yi, S. (2021). A development of an embedded programming education platform using Python and LEGO NXT. *Journal of Engineering Education Research, 24*(1), 45–53. DOI: 10.18108/jeer.2021.24.1.45

Lindberg, R. S. N., Laine, T. H., & Haaranen, L. (2018). Gamifying programming education in k-12: A review of programming curricula in seven countries and programming games. *British Journal of Educational Technology*, *50*(4), 1979–1995. DOI: 10.1111/bjet.12685

Marevac, E., Kadušić, E., Živić, N., Buzađija, N., & Lemeš, S. (2025). Framework design for the dynamic reconfiguration of iot-enabled embedded systems and "on-the-fly" code execution. *Future Internet*, *17*(1), 23. DOI: 10.3390/fi17010023

Marín, B., Frez, J., Cruz-Lemus, J. A., & Genero, M. (2018). An empirical investigation on the benefits of gamification in programming courses. *ACM Transactions on Computing Education*, *19*(1), 1–22. DOI: 10.1145/3231709

Maulana, T. S., Setyawan, H., & Asroni, A. (2023). Web-based data information system for students and teachers at al-qur'an education parks in kasihan, bantul. *Emerging Information Science and Technology*, *2*(1), 24–29. DOI: 10.18196/eist.v2i1.16870

Mecca, G., Santoro, D., Sileno, N., & Veltri, E. (2021). Diogene-ct: Tools and methodologies for teaching and learning coding. *International Journal of Educational Technology in Higher Education*, *18*(1), 12. Advance online publication. DOI: 10.1186/s41239-021-00246-1

Méri, L., Gaál, L., Bartók, J., Gažák, M., Gera, M., Jurašek, M., & Келемен, M. (2021). Improved radar composites and enhanced value of meteorological radar data using different quality indices. *Sustainability (Basel)*, *13*(9), 5285. DOI: 10.3390/su13095285

Messer, D., Thomas, L., Holliman, A., & Kucirkova, N. (2018). Evaluating the effectiveness of an educational programming intervention on children's mathematics skills, spatial awareness and working memory. *Education and Information Technologies*, *23*(6), 2879–2888. DOI: 10.1007/s10639-018-9747-x

Microsoft. (2014). *Kodu Game Lab Documentation*. https://www.kodugamelab.com

Microsoft. (2020). *C# Programming Guide*. https://docs.microsoft.com/en-us/dotnet/csharp/

MIT. (2018). *MIT App Inventor – Beginner Tutorials*. Massachusetts Institute of Technology. https://appinventor.mit.edu

Monteiro, A. F., Miranda-Pinto, M. S., & Osório, A. J. (2021). Coding as literacy in preschool: A case study. *Education Sciences*, *11*(5), 198. DOI: 10.3390/educsci11050198

Montoya, J., Hernández, J., & Reyes, R. (2017). Blockly-based environments in early programming education. *International Journal of Advanced Computer Science*, *8*(10), 209–215.

Morais, C., & Araújo, J. L. (2022). An alternative experimental procedure to determine the solubility of potassium nitrate in water with automatic data acquisition using arduino for secondary school: Development and validation with pre-service chemistry teachers. *Journal of Chemical Education*, *100*(2), 774–781. DOI: 10.1021/acs.jchemed.2c00615

Morán, J. A. C., Rodas-Silva, J., & Morales, M. G. V. (2019). El uso del software alice como herramienta para el aprendizaje de programación: una revisión de literatura. Proceedings of the 17th LACCEI International Multi-Conference for Engineering, Education, and Technology: "Industry, Innovation. https://doi.org/DOI: 10.18687/LACCEI2019.1.1.161

Moumoutzis, N., Xanthaki, C., Perrakis, S., Manousakas, M., & Pavlova, L. (2021). Promoting python code clubs in greece: A teacher training program and a case study. *Digital Presentation and Preservation of Cultural and Scientific Heritage*, *11*, 187–202. DOI: 10.55630/dipp.2021.11.16

Naveed, M. (2021). Comparison of c++ and java in implementing introductory programming algorithms. *Quaid-E-Awam University Research Journal of Engineering Science & Technology*, *19*(1), 95–103. DOI: 10.52584/QRJ.1901.14

Ndebele, M., & Mazhindu, A. N. (2023). Design and implementation of an android gis data collection application for students with non-programming experience using the mit app inventor: A case study on a tick data collection app. *Intelligent Information Management*, *15*(01), 11–23. DOI: 10.4236/iim.2023.151002

Niarman, A., Iswandi, I., & Candri, A. K. (2023). Comparative analysis of php frameworks for development of academic information system using load and stress testing. [IJSECS]. *International Journal Software Engineering and Computer Science*, *3*(3), 424–436. DOI: 10.35870/ijsecs.v3i3.1850

Oliveira, V. F. d., Pessoa, M. A. O., Junqueira, F., & Miyagi, P. E. (2021). Sql and nosql databases in the context of industry 4.0. https://doi.org/DOI: 10.20944/preprints202111.0019.v1

Paiva, J. C., Leal, J. P., & Queirós, R. (2020). Fostering programming practice through games. *Information (Basel)*, *11*(11), 498. DOI: 10.3390/info11110498

Papert, S., & Harel, I. (2016). *Constructionism: Research Reports and Essays, 1985–1990* (Reprint ed.). Routledge. https://doi.org/DOI: 10.4324/9781315045398

Park, Y., & Shin, Y. (2019). Comparing the effectiveness of scratch and app inventor with regard to learning computational thinking concepts. *Electronics (Basel)*, *8*(11), 1269. DOI: 10.3390/electronics8111269

Patton, E. W., Tissenbaum, M. B., & Harunani, F. (2019). Mit app inventor: objectives, design, and development. *Computational Thinking Education,* 31-49. https://doi.org/DOI: 10.1007/978-981-13-6528-7_3

Pérez-Jorge, D., & Martínez-Murciano, M. C. (2022). Gamification with scratch or app inventor in higher education: A systematic review. *Future Internet*, *14*(12), 374. DOI: 10.3390/fi14120374

Pina, E., Sá, F., & Bernardino, J. (2022). Newsql databases assessment: Cockroachdb, mariadb xpand, and voltdb. *Future Internet*, *15*(1), 10. DOI: 10.3390/fi15010010

Popat, S., & Starkey, L. (2019). Learning to code or coding to learn? A systematic review. *Computers & Education*, *128*, 365–376. DOI: 10.1016/j.compedu.2018.10.005

Ragusa, G., & Leung, L. Y. (2023). The impact of early robotics education on students' understanding of coding, robotics design, and interest in computing careers. *Sensors (Basel)*, *23*(23), 9335. DOI: 10.3390/s23239335

Rajput, K. K., Siddiqui, I. F., Saddar, S., Hussain, H., Ayaz, U., & Ruk, S. A. (2023). Mobile apps development: Towards incorporating regional and national languages in flutter app. *Sukkur IBA Journal of Emerging Technologies*, *6*(1), 44–53. DOI: 10.30537/sjet.v6i1.1192

Ramadani, N. I., Surganingsih, M., & Rafee, N. N. B. M. (2023). Cultivating independent character in students at the cendekia berseri school in makassar city. *TEMATIK: Jurnal Pemikiran Dan Penelitian Pendidikan Anak Usia Dini*, *9*(2), 100. DOI: 10.26858/tematik.v9i2.54728

Resnick, M., Maloney, J., Monroy-Hernández, A., Rusk, N., Eastmond, E., Brennan, K., & Kafai, Y. (2020). Scratch: Programming for all. *Communications of the ACM*, *63*(11), 28–30. DOI: 10.1145/3424000

Rodríguez-Ponce, R., & Mota-Muñoz, F. G. (2020). Microcontroller-based direct torque control servodrive. *Journal of Robotics*, *2020*, 1–11. DOI: 10.1155/2020/9152494

Rousouliotis, M., Vasileiou, M., Manos, N., & Kavallieratou, E. (2023). Employing an underwater vehicle in education as a learning tool for python programming. *Computer Applications in Engineering Education*, *32*(1), e22693. Advance online publication. DOI: 10.1002/cae.22693

Salikhov, K. M., Zaslavskiy, D. A., & Balabanov, D. (2018). C++ in robotics education. *IEEE Global Engineering Education Conference (EDUCON)*, 1079–1082. https://doi.org/DOI: 10.1109/EDUCON.2018.8363335

Scherer, R., Siddiq, F., & Sánchez-Scherer, B. (2021). Some evidence on the cognitive benefits of learning to code. *Frontiers in Psychology*, *12*, 559424. Advance online publication. DOI: 10.3389/fpsyg.2021.559424

Seo, Y. H., & Kim, J. H. (2016). Analyzing the effects of coding education through pair programming for the computational thinking and creativity of elementary school students. *Indian Journal of Science and Technology*, *9*(46), 1–5. DOI: 10.17485/ijst/2016/v9i46/107837

Simon, S., Coelho, R., Marfisi-Schottman, I., & Pea, R. (2024). Generative ai tools in an undergraduate computer science program. Proceedings of the 18th International Conference of the Learning Sciences - ICLS 2024. https://doi.org/DOI: 10.22318/icls2024.271910

Staacks, S., Dorsel, D., Krampe, A., Hagedorn, M., Leier, E., Heinke, H., & Stampfer, C. (2025). Bluetooth sensors in phyphox with arduino and micropython: Paving the way from an idea to an experiment for teachers and learners. *Physics Education*, *60*(3), 035014. DOI: 10.1088/1361-6552/adbf5f

Sun, Q., Wu, J., Rong, W., & Liu, W. (2019). Formative assessment of programming language learning based on peer code review: Implementation and experience report. *Tsinghua Science and Technology*, *24*(4), 423–434. DOI: 10.26599/TST.2018.9010109

Telukdarie, A., Munsamy, M., Katsumbe, T., Maphisa, X., & Philbin, S. P. (2023). Industry 4.0 technological advancement in the food and beverage manufacturing industry in south africa—Bibliometric analysis via natural language processing. *Information (Basel)*, *14*(8), 454. DOI: 10.3390/info14080454

Tiwari, S. P., & Fahrudin, A. (2024). *Evolving school dynamics and emerging technologies in education: critical success factors*. SciFormat Publishing Books., DOI: 10.69635/978-1-0690482-0-2

Totan, H. N., & Korucu, A. T. (2023). The effect of block based coding education on the students' attitudes about the secondary school students' computational learning skills and coding learning: Blocky sample. *Participatory Educational Research*, *10*(1), 443–461. DOI: 10.17275/per.23.24.10.1

Tselegkaridis, S., Sapounidis, T., Tokatlidis, C., Rapti, S., & Papakostas, D. (2025). Aabc: A tool for assessing arduino basic coding skills. *Computer Applications in Engineering Education, 33*(3), e70029. Advance online publication. DOI: 10.1002/cae.70029

Tsikalakis, G., Neofotistou, E., Kontogiannakis, E., Pau, A., Caglayan, E. M., Fernandez-Canez, R., ... & Perez-Accino, M. (2023). Sustainable development as an education tool for primary school students through scratch code. E3S Web of Conferences, 436, 06007. https://doi.org/DOI: 10.1051/e3sconf/202343606007

Uğraş, M., Güneş, H., Uğraş, H., Papadakis, S., & Kalogiannakis, M. (2025). Coding activities in early childhood: A systematic review. *International Journal of Technology Enhanced Learning, 17*(1), 45–80. DOI: 10.1504/IJTEL.2025.143512

Valls, J., Fonseca, D., Redondo, E., & Navarro, I. (2022). Impact of educational robotics on computational thinking through project-based learning activities. *Education and Information Technologies, 27*(1), 947–968. DOI: 10.1007/s10639-021-10644-2

W3C. (2019). *HTML & CSS Standards*. World Wide Web Consortium. https://www.w3.org

Welling, L., & Thomson, L. (2017). *PHP and MySQL Web Development* (5th ed.). Addison-Wesley.

Werner, M. H., & Olanow, C. W. (2021). Parkinson's disease modification through abl kinase inhibition: An opportunity. *Movement Disorders, 37*(1), 6–15. DOI: 10.1002/mds.28858

Wickham, H., & Grolemund, G. (2017). *R for Data Science: Import, Tidy, Transform, Visualize, and Model Data*. O'Reilly Media. https://r4ds.hadley.nz

Wong, G. K., Cheung, H. Y., Ching, E. C., & Huen, J. M. (2015). *School perceptions of coding education in K-12: A large scale quantitative study to inform innovative practices. In 2015 IEEE international conference on teaching, Assessment, and learning for engineering (TALE)*. IEEE.

Yıldız, E., & Çengel, M. (2022). An experimental study in determining basic robotic coding skills of pre-school students with intellectual disabilities. *International Journal of Interactive Mobile Technologies (Ijim), 16*(23), 84–98. DOI: 10.3991/ijim.v16i23.36077

Zagalsky, A., Feliciano, J., Storey, M., Zhao, Y., & Wang, W. (2015). The emergence of github as a collaborative platform for education. *Proceedings of the 18th ACM Conference on Computer Supported Cooperative Work & Social Computing,* 1906-1917. https://doi.org/DOI: 10.1145/2675133.2675284

Zhang, D., & Li, A. (2023). *A smart interactive and collaborative online coding platform for programming education using machine learning and web socket*. Software Engineering and Applications., DOI: 10.5121/csit.2023.131703

Zhang, S., Wong, G. K. W., & Chan, P. C. F. (2022). Playing coding games to learn computational thinking: What motivates students to use this tool at home? *Education and Information Technologies*, *28*(1), 193–216. DOI: 10.1007/s10639-022-11181-7

KEY TERMS AND DEFINITIONS

Algorithmic Thinking: The capacity to define specific problems with detailed methodical processes resolve them sequentially; at earliest stages during formal education on coding its importance is already vital.

Automated Assessment Systems: University developed evaluation technologies that use artificial intelligence analyze students' codes and provide instant marking feedback improving reliability and effectiveness during evaluation.

Block-Based Programming: An introductory level programming model where coding tasks are framed as blocks that can be clicked together for sequential action, ideal for novices (e.g., Scratch, Blockly).

Computational Thinking: A mental process which entails breaking down and resolving problems through systematic step-by-step procedures; it is essential in the teaching of programming.

IDE (Integrated Development Environment): Integrated Development Environment, a software application which enables programmers to write their computer programs, compile them and run debugging in a single interface (e.g., Visual Studio, PyCharm).

Pair Programming: A type of learning-centric software engineering collaboration where two students share a single workstation for increased learning and inventive work.

Programming Languages: A selected medium appropriate would be age and proficiency benchmarks for equipping learners with relevant skills in developing programs software (e.g., Scratch, Python, Java).

Unplugged Activities: Approaches intended to teach principles related to coding without the use of computers or digital devices through hands-on or paper activities.

Visual Programming Language: One of such programming languages is Alice or Kodu where users can program by joining visual elements instead of using text therefore easing the learning process.

Chapter 3
Common Challenges in Coding Education: A Cognitive Load Theory Perspective

Fırat Hayyam Sabuncu
https://orcid.org/0000-0002-6324-9386
Ege University, Turkey

Onur Dönmez
https://orcid.org/0000-0001-5200-1468
Ege University, Turkey

ABSTRACT

This section analyzes coding education challenges through Cognitive Load Theory (CLT), which identifies working memory limitations in processing complex coding concepts. We examine three load types: intrinsic (task complexity), extraneous (poor instructional design), and germane (schema construction). CLT-based solutions include sequenced instruction, worked examples, and multimodal learning to optimize cognitive load distribution. Findings demonstrate these strategies improve knowledge retention and problem-solving transfer. The research highlights educators' role as cognitive designers and emphasizes adaptive scaffolding for diverse learners. By implementing CLT principles, coding education can become more effective and inclusive while reducing cognitive overload.

DOI: 10.4018/979-8-3373-2660-3.ch003

INTRODUCTION

Coding (more broadly programming) is the process of writing instructions in a programming language that a computer can understand and execute. It involves translating human logic into algorithms which are precise, step-by-step commands to create software, apps, websites, games, and more. Coding has been a key competency in the current digital age, empowering learners with problem-solving skills, logical reasoning, and computation skills (Cakir et al., 2021; Garcia et al., 2022; Wing, 2006). Recognizing its importance, educational institutions and online platforms worldwide have increasingly integrated computer science and coding into curricula to prepare learners for a rapidly evolving, technology-driven future (Garcia et al., 2022; Hu, 2024; Oyetade et al., 2025).

At this point, it is helpful to clarify a terminological distinction that is often blurred in both educational discourse and everyday usage. Within the realm of professional business, coding and programming are conceptually similar yet not synonymous. While they are often used interchangeably in informal settings, they differ in scope (Girardin & Courtney, 2023; "indeed", 2025). Coding typically refers to the act of writing code in a programming language, with an emphasis on syntax (Menon, 2025). In contrast, programming encompasses the entire software development process, including problem-solving, design, testing, and optimization (Felleisen et al., 2018). Thus, coding is a part of programming, not its entirety (see Figure 1). Although the distinction is significant in technical contexts, it is often overlooked in popular or educational discourse (Corradini et al., 2018). Given the interchangeable use of the terms in educational discourse, this section includes studies that employ either or both coding and programming for terminological inclusivity and comprehensiveness purposes.

Figure 1. The Conceptual Relationship Between Programming and Coding

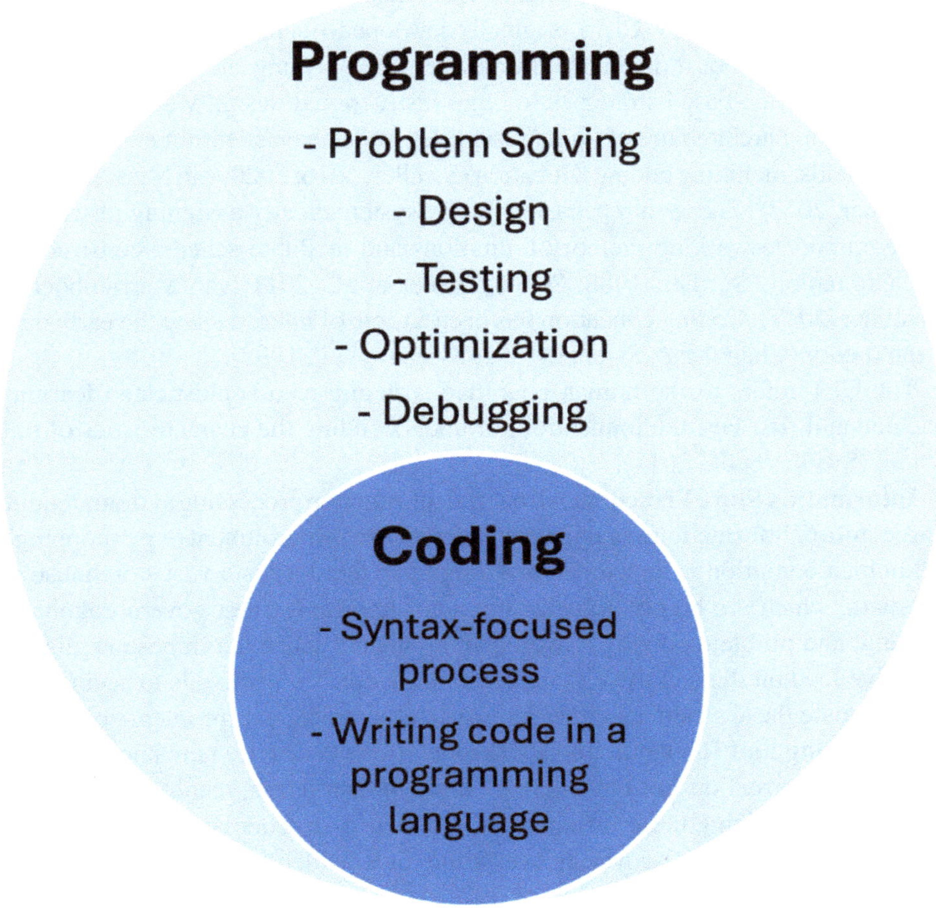

Despite its growing prominence, coding education faces a range of pedagogical and infrastructural challenges that hinder effective teaching and learning. These include disparities in technological access (OECD, 2021), varying levels of educator preparedness (OECD, 2024), learner engagement difficulties (Fan et al., 2025; Zhang et al., 2025) and -most critically- the substantial cognitive demands imposed on novice learners (Huang et al., 2025; Zhang et al., 2025; Yao & Lin, 2025).

Learning to code often requires learners to simultaneously process unfamiliar syntax, abstract algorithmic concepts, and complex problem-solving strategies. These demands can easily exceed the limitations of working memory, resulting in cognitive overload which hinders learning and problem solving (Paas & van Merriënboer, 2020; Sweller et al., 2019; Sweller et al., 2011). Consequently, the efficacy of coding instruction depends not only on curricular content but also on how it is structured to mitigate excessive cognitive demands (Kirschner et al., 2006).

Cognitive Load Theory (CLT), originally developed to support learning in complex domains, offers a robust theoretical framework for analyzing such challenges. CLT provides evidence-based strategies to align instructional design with the inherent limitations and architecture of human cognition and enhance learning efficiency in various fields, including coding education (Sweller, 2016; 2020; van Merriënboer & Kirschner, 2017). The theory achieves this by systematically designing instruction to accommodate working memory limitations and facilitate schema construction and automation (Sweller, 1988; 2016; Sweller et al., 2011; van Merriënboer & Kirschner, 2017). Coding education has been a topic of interest since the early days of the theory (Chandler & Sweller, 1992; Sweller et al., 1998).

The CLT refers to the human cognitive structure as a sophisticated learning machine and first lays the foundation for understanding the characteristics of this system (Sweller et al., 2011):

Information Store Principle: All natural information processing systems require a large store of information to navigate the surrounding environment (e.g., shopping), and human cognition is no exception. Long-term memory is a vast storehouse of schemata, which are highly organized units of knowledge that govern cognition, learning, and problem-solving. Given that automated schemata impose negligible cognitive load on the cognitive system, the individual's objective is to accumulate and automate these schemata either by instruction, practice or problem-solving.

Borrowing and Reorganizing Principle: Humans acquire new knowledge by borrowing information from others (e.g., through instruction, reading, or observation) and reorganizing these information into their own schemata. This process is far more efficient than discovering everything independently and helps reduce the cognitive load during learning.

Randomness as Genesis Principle: New knowledge is created through problem-solving or trial and error when relevant schemata do not exist and borrowing is not an option. In such cases, learners must randomly or experimentally generate solutions, a process that is cognitively demanding and less efficient than learning through guidance.

Narrow Limits of Change Principle: Working memory (WM) is involved in schema construction and problem-solving. However, WM capacity is limited both temporally and spatially. Therefore, learning and problem solving must occur in small, manageable steps. Otherwise, the cognitive resources will be overwhelmed by the imposed cognitive load, and no learning or problem-solving will occur.

Environmental Organizing and Linking Principle: Once schemata are accumulated in the long-term memory, it can be used to organize and interpret new incoming information from the environment. This stored knowledge helps learners recognize patterns, make connections, and efficiently process complex tasks by linking new data to existing schemata. In essence, prior knowledge facilitates interpretation of the environment and incoming information.

Figure 2. A Simplified Model of the Cognitive Architecture

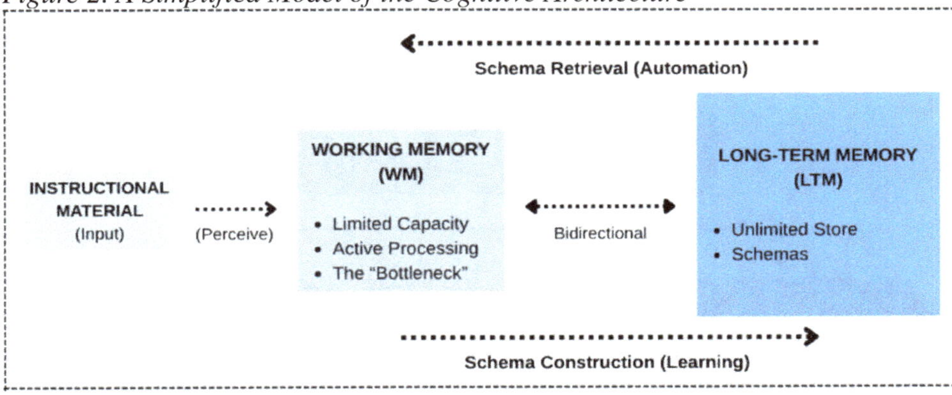

This characterization posits that WM is the bottleneck of human learning and functioning (see Figure 2). WM can hold about seven pieces of information, but can only process about four at a time (Baddeley, 1986, 1992; Cowan, 2001). Furthermore, this information can only be retained for up to 30 seconds unless it is actively maintained (Cowan, 1988; Peterson & Peterson, 1959). These limitations imply that learning complex or unfamiliar material is challenging without automated schemata or effective instruction. CLT emphasizes optimizing WM use by adhering to the aforementioned characterization of the human cognitive architecture (Sweller et al., 2019; Sweller, 2024).

CLT identifies three types of cognitive load sources: intrinsic cognitive load (ICL) (stemming from the inherent complexity of coding concepts), extraneous cognitive load (ECL) (imposed by suboptimal instructional design), and germane cognitive load (GCL) (the mental effort directed toward meaningful learning and problem solving) (Sweller, 2010; Sweller et al., 1998; van Merriënboer & Sweller, 2005). Coding has an inherently high ICL due to several factors, including the necessary prior knowledge, problem-solving skills, and technical abilities. First, coders must understand programming (e.g., loops) and data (e.g., primitive and abstract) structures. Second, coders must apply abstract algorithms to problem contexts (e.g., sorting a list of users). Lastly, coding requires technical abilities, such as navigating development environments, debugging, compiling, testing, and running programs. Figure 3 visually summarizes these specific components of cognitive load within the context of coding education.

Figure 3. Components of Cognitive Load in Coding Education

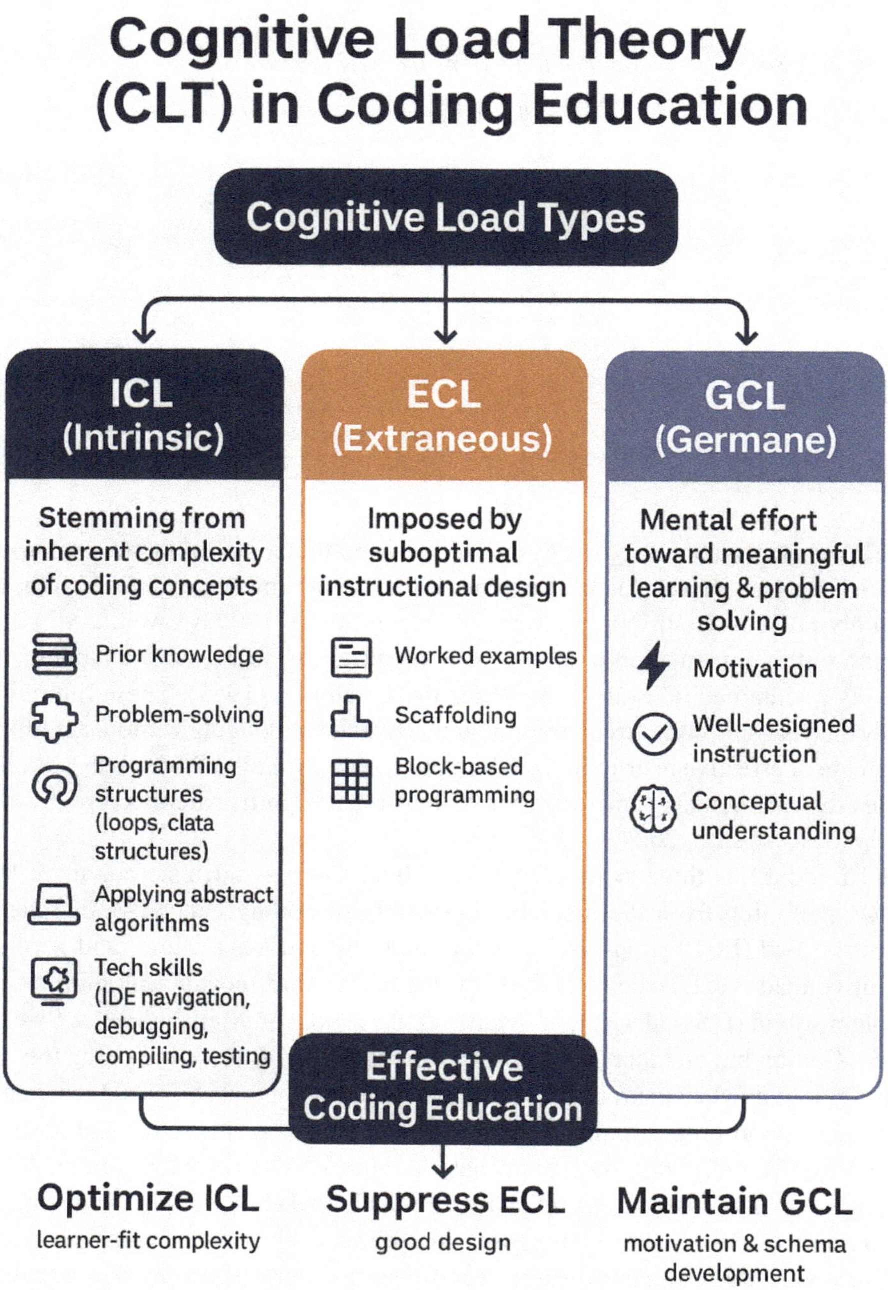

In order to achieve effective coding education through the lens of the CLT, the following elements must be considered: 1) Optimised release of ICL with respect to learner characteristics, 2) Suppression of ECL through optimal instructional design, and 3) Maintenance of GCL through induced learner motivation. Figure 4 illustrates the dynamic interaction of these load types, showing how suppressing ECL (Scenario 2) frees up limited cognitive capacity for GCL, whereas poor design (Scenario 1) leads to cognitive overload.

Figure 4. The Effect of Instructional Design on Load Allocation within Limited Cognitive Capacity

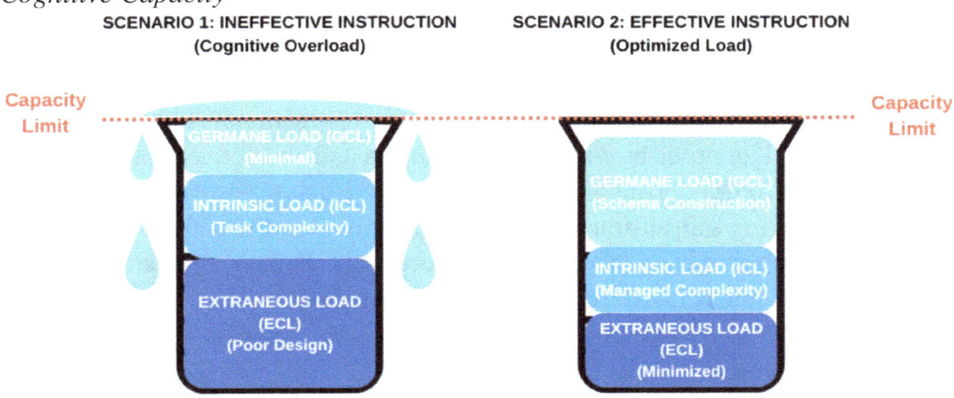

Note. *This model illustrates how limited working memory capacity is allocated under two instructional scenarios. Ineffective design (Scenario 1) creates high extraneous load (ECL), leaving no cognitive resources for germane load (GCL), resulting in cognitive overload. Effective design (Scenario 2) minimizes ECL, freeing up working memory capacity to manage intrinsic load (ICL) and—critically—to foster germane load (GCL) for schema construction and deep learning.*

This conceptualisation is supported by empirical studies which demonstrated that excessive intrinsic and extraneous loads hinder novice coders, whereas well-designed instruction enhances germane load, which in turn fosters deeper conceptual understanding (Morrison et al., 2014; Sweller, 2020; 2024). Instructional strategies such as worked examples (Beege et al., 2021; Chen, Kalyuga, & Sweller, 2015; Muldner et al., 2022; Sozio et al., 2024), scaffolding (Jung et al., 2024; Shin et al., 2025; Stachel et al., 2013), and block-based implementations (Gao et al., 2025; Huang et al., 2025; Zhang & Rutherford, 2024) can be employed to reduce extraneous load and enhance germane processing (Chandler & Sweller, 1992; Huang et al., 2025; van Merriënboer & Sweller, 2005).

CLT is a theory of how human brains learn and store knowledge. Dylan Wiliam has described CLT as 'the single most important thing for teachers to know'. This section adopts the framework of CLT to explore common challenges in coding education and to propose evidence-based instructional strategies aimed at improving learning outcomes. By aligning pedagogical design with cognitive principles, educators can create more effective and accessible coding instruction that meets the diverse needs of learners. Rather than focusing on specific programming languages or code examples, we emphasize universal cognitive mechanisms that affect learning across all coding contexts.

MANAGİNG INTRİNSİC COGNİTİVE LOAD (ICL): NAVİGATİNG CONCEPTUAL COMPLEXİTY AND TRANSİTİONS

Introduction

In coding education, one of the most persistent instructional challenges lies in managing the ICL imposed by conceptually complex and interactive content. As students transition from understanding basic coding constructs to developing functional systems or engaging with abstract paradigms such as object-oriented or event-driven coding, the number of elements they must process simultaneously increases. This section explores how ICL—defined by the complexity and interactivity of elements that must be processed together—can be effectively managed using principles from CLT and evidence-based instructional effects.

Understanding ICL in Coding Contexts

ICL arises from the inherent complexity of the material and is determined by the degree of element interactivity (Sweller et al., 2019). In coding, even introductory tasks like writing a simple if-else statement can involve multiple interacting elements: logical conditions, syntax rules, indentation, and control flow expectations. As learners progress, these interactions escalate—looping structures, lexical scopes, function scopes, recursion, and asynchronous execution all require simultaneous coordination of increasingly interrelated knowledge.

Importantly, element interactivity is not an objective property of the material alone but is relative to the learner's prior knowledge. Novices must consider multiple new elements when interpreting a loop, whereas experts address this phenomenon with a single cognitive chunk retrieved from long-term memory.

Instructional Effects for Managing ICL

In the foundational review by Sweller et al. (2019), a total of sixteen instructional effects related to CLT are described. While this section focuses primarily on ICL, several effects that traditionally address extraneous or germane load are also highly relevant in managing conceptual complexity and transitions in coding education. For example, worked examples that mitigate the ICL are useful for novices, but they may become a source of ECL for experts. Therefore, rather than matching the effects with individual cognitive load resources, we elaborated on each effect within the relevant cognitive load source scopes. In the following sections, we explore both well-known and less commonly emphasized effects, highlighting their significance for instructional design in coding contexts.

Although ICL stems from the essential complexity of learning tasks and cannot be reduced without simplifying the content, instructional design can effectively manage it by supporting learners through well-sequenced instruction, transitional scaffolding, and structured practice. By aligning instructional support with learners' evolving expertise and cognitive capacity, educators can help students engage with challenging content without exceeding WM limitations. The following cognitive load effects offer specific, evidence-based strategies to achieve this goal:

1. Element Interactivity Effect

This effect, articulated by Sweller (1994), highlights how learning is influenced by the number of elements that must be processed simultaneously. When information is highly interdependent (i.e., high element interactivity), ICL increases. The effect is central to understanding how different instructional methods influence the mental effort required of learners, especially when content complexity cannot be reduced.

Challenge: Coding involves many highly interactive elements. Novices must coordinate syntax, semantics, and control flow, which may overload WM.

Solution: Sequence content from low to high element interactivity. Begin with simple, linear code before introducing nested or concurrent structures. Increase complexity only after prior elements are mastered.

2. Worked Example Effect

First identified by Sweller and Cooper (1985), this effect demonstrates that learners perform better when they study worked-out examples rather than solving problems independently. Worked examples reduce extraneous cognitive load by removing the burden of problem solving, allowing learners to focus on understanding problem structures and developing schemas. This effect shows that learners benefit from studying fully solved problems rather than solving them from scratch. It reduces extraneous load and fosters schema construction.

Challenge: Learners expend cognitive resources on surface-level problem solving, leaving little capacity for understanding the underlying structure of solutions.

Solution: Provide worked examples of complete solutions. Use annotations to highlight each step and its rationale. Encourage students to study the relationship between problem states and applied operations.

3. Completion Problem Effect

Introduced by van Merriënboer and Krammer (1987), this effect describes the benefits of providing learners with partially worked solutions that they must complete. It combines the guidance of worked examples with the active engagement of problem solving, thereby supporting schema construction while managing cognitive demands. This effect refers to the use of partially worked-out problems. It encourages active engagement while limiting cognitive overload compared to open-ended problem solving.

Challenge: Fully worked examples may not always prompt deep engagement or active construction.

Solution: Use partially completed problems that learners must finish. These "completion tasks" maintain structure but require active problem solving, supporting schema construction without overloading memory.

4. Guidance-Fading Effect

Described by Renkl and Atkinson (2003), this effect underscores the importance of gradually removing instructional support as learners gain expertise. It ensures that cognitive load remains aligned with learners' growing capabilities and promotes autonomy and adaptive problem-solving.

Challenge: Prolonged use of scaffolds can hinder the development of independence and adaptability in learners.

Solution: Gradually reduce instructional support as learners gain expertise. Move from worked examples to completion tasks to open-ended coding activities.

5. Variability Effect

Paas and van Merriënboer (1994) found that exposing learners to a variety of problem contexts can enhance transfer and generalization. While variability increases ICL, it encourages learners to focus on deep structures and develop flexible knowledge representations. exposing learners to a wide range of task conditions fosters transfer and deeper learning. Although it increases ICL, variability supports schema abstraction when managed well.

Challenge: Learning from repetitive, similar tasks may not prepare learners for applying knowledge to novel or diverse problems.

Solution: Introduce variability across practice tasks (e.g., different data types, use cases, or problem constraints). This helps learners abstract key principles, supporting far transfer and adaptive expertise.

6. Isolated Elements Effect

As described by Pollock et al. (2002), this effect suggests that learners benefit when complex content is first presented in separate, simpler parts. By isolating elements initially, instructors help students manage WM load and build individual schemas before integrating them into more complex structures. This effect suggests that teaching complex materials in isolated parts before integrating them can reduce WM load during early stages of learning.

Challenge: Presenting all interacting components of a program at once can overwhelm WM.

Solution: Teach interacting elements in isolation first. Once each is understood, integrate them into more complex tasks. For example, teach conditions, booleans and scopes separately before combining them into a loop structure.

7. Expertise Reversal Effect

Kalyuga et al. (2003) demonstrated that instructional methods effective for novices can become counterproductive for more experienced learners. As expertise increases, learners benefit more from problem-solving activities rather than guided instruction, due to reduced element interactivity and increased ability to process complex material independently. instructional methods effective for novices—such as worked examples—can become inefficient or detrimental as learners gain expertise.

Challenge: Instructional strategies that benefit novices (e.g., worked examples, completion problems) may bore or hinder experts, reducing learning efficiency.

Solution: Adapt instruction to learners' expertise levels. Use formative assessments to determine when to shift from guided learning to autonomous practice and challenge-based learning.

8. Split-Attention Effect

Identified by Tarmizi and Sweller (1988), this effect occurs when learners must divide their attention between multiple, physically or temporally separated sources of related information. Such split-attention increases extraneous cognitive load and hinders schema acquisition. It is especially relevant in coding when students must constantly look back and forth between code and its explanation, or documentation and implementation steps.

Challenge: When learners must mentally integrate physically separated but related information (e.g., code and explanation), cognitive load increases.

Solution: Integrate sources of information spatially or temporally. Place annotations next to code, or use tools that highlight corresponding explanation lines while the learner reads code.

9. Redundancy Effect

Also from Chandler and Sweller (1991), the redundancy effect states that providing learners with information that duplicates what they already have can cause unnecessary processing, adding extraneous load. In coding, this occurs when learners are given verbal narration that repeats what's already written on the screen, or when identical code examples are repeated across different contexts with no added instructional value.

Challenge: Repeating identical information in different formats (e.g., reading code aloud while also displaying it) can create unnecessary processing.

Solution: Eliminate redundant explanations. Use one clear and concise representation unless each version adds unique value.

10. Modality Effect

The modality effect, proposed by Mousavi et al. (1995), suggests that WM capacity can be expanded by distributing information across different sensory modalities—typically visual and auditory. For example, instead of displaying both text and code visually, pairing visuals with spoken instructions can reduce overload and enhance comprehension.

Challenge: Presenting all instructional content in a single modality (e.g., all written text) can overload that channel.

Solution: Use spoken explanations to accompany visual materials (e.g., narrated walkthroughs of code). This distributes cognitive processing across channels. Using both auditory and visual channels for instruction (rather than only one) can expand WM capacity.

11. Segmentation Effect

Spanjers et al. (2011) describe the segmentation effect as the benefit of breaking down complex content into smaller, meaningful units or steps. This technique gives learners time to process and consolidate information before moving to the next segment, which is particularly helpful in video tutorials, algorithm visualizations, or step-by-step problem explanations.

Challenge: Large or uninterrupted blocks of content can overwhelm learners' WM.

Solution: Segment lessons into short, focused chunks. In coding education, this might involve breaking a long algorithm explanation into separate steps with pauses and checkpoints.

12. Transient Information Effect

This effect, discussed by Leahy and Sweller (2011), highlights the difficulty learners experience when processing non-permanent information—such as spoken dialogue or rapidly disappearing animations. In coding, this may apply to live coding demonstrations or lectures where the code scrolls out of view before students can fully understand it.

Challenge: When learners cannot review transient instructional content, understanding and retention suffer.

Solution: Provide persistent support, such as transcripts of spoken explanations or replayable screencasts. Avoid relying solely on temporary displays of critical information.

13. Imagination Effect

The imagination effect, identified by Cooper et al. (2001), refers to the benefit of mentally simulating a procedure or process after studying it. This technique enhances schema automation and strengthens memory consolidation. In coding, learners who mentally rehearse the logic and flow of a function often internalize it more effectively than those who passively reread it.

Challenge: Passive review may not fully engage deeper learning processes.

Solution: Encourage learners to mentally rehearse or visualize code execution after observing examples. For example, ask them to predict output or describe step-by-step flow in their own words.

14. Self-Management Effect

Discussed by de Roodenrys et al. (2012), the self-management effect emphasizes learners' ability to regulate their own cognitive load by applying metacognitive strategies. These strategies include self-monitoring, time management, and knowing when to seek help—all of which are essential in self-paced coding environments or during debugging tasks.

Challenge: Learners may not know how to regulate effort or identify when they are cognitively overloaded.

Solution: Teach metacognitive strategies, such as pausing to summarize, identifying confusion, or revisiting simpler examples.

15. Collective Working Memory Effect

Kirschner et al. (2009) introduced this effect to show that learning in groups allows for shared cognitive resources. By distributing element interactivity among multiple learners, collaborative tasks such as pair coding can reduce the load on any one individual while improving problem solving and retention.

Challenge: Individual learners may struggle to process complex problems alone.

Solution: Use pair coding or collaborative debugging to distribute cognitive demands among students.

16. Human Movement Effect

According to Paas and Sweller (2012), the human movement effect refers to the positive impact of observing meaningful gestures and actions during learning. This effect is grounded in embodied cognition and the activation of mirror neurons. In coding education, watching an instructor type, gesture to the screen, or use a cursor to highlight active areas helps students associate verbal explanations with visual-spatial changes.

Challenge: Static visuals or text may not sufficiently demonstrate coding processes.

Solution: Use videos or animations with instructor gestures or cursor movements that align with code changes to aid understanding.

Strategic Transitions Between Cognitive Complexity Levels

Effective coding instruction requires scaffolding learners through three key cognitive phases (van Merriënboer & Kirschner, 2017):

1. **Declarative Knowledge** ("What is a loop?")
2. **Procedural Fluency** ("How do I use loops?")
3. **Strategic Control** ("When/why should I use a loop?")

These transitions demand careful management of ICL through CLT-aligned strategies:

Table 1. CLT Strategies for Cognitive Phase Transitions

Cognitive Phase	Primary Challenge	CLT Effects to Apply	Instructional Strategy	Example
Declarative Knowledge	High element interactivity	• Isolated elements effect	Teach concepts in isolation using *non-interactive* examples	Introduce if statements before combining with loops
		• Modality effect	Use dual-channel presentations (visual code + auditory explanations)	Annotated video explaining Python syntax rules
Procedural Fluency	Integrating multiple elements	• Completion problem effect	Provide partial solutions for learners to finish	Half-written loop structures to complete
		• Worked example effect	Show fully annotated code with line-by-line explanations	Commented sorting algorithm with self-explanation prompts
Strategic Control	Adaptive application of knowledge	• Variability effect	Present diverse problem contexts to reinforce transfer	Use loops for: 1) number sequences 2) string processing 3) file operations
		• Expertise reversal effect	Fade scaffolding as competence grows	Shift from guided practice to open-ended projects

Example: Loop Concept Across Instructional Strategies

The loop concept can be introduced gradually using CLT-aligned instructional strategies (see Figure 5). As learners progress from novice to more expert-like states, instructional support is faded and element interactivity is managed accordingly. The examples below show how the same concept—looping—can be adapted using worked examples, completion tasks, self-explanation, and more open-ended, collaborative or imaginative challenges.

Figure 5. Conceptual ordering of Cognitive Load Effects (Dönmez, 2022)

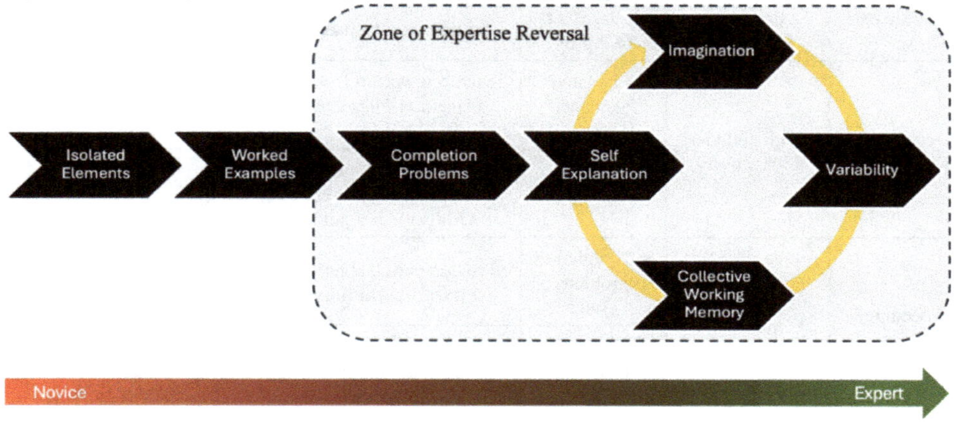

1. Worked Example (Novice)

```
for i in range(1, 6):
print(i)
```

Explanation: This loop prints numbers from 1 to 5. 'range(1, 6)' generates numbers 1 through 5.

2. Completion Problem (Guided Practice)

```
for i in range(___):
print(i)
```

Explanation: Learner completes the range to print numbers from 10 to 15. (e.g., range(10, 16))

3. Self-Explanation (Intermediate)

```
for i in range(5, 10):
print(i)
```

Explanation: Prompt: What values will be printed? Why does it stop before 10?

4. Expert Engagement (Variability, Imagination, or Collaboration)

Task: Work with a peer to write a loop that processes a list of scores and prints only the passing ones.

Then, mentally simulate how the loop would behave with different datasets.

Explanation: This task integrates variability (different data sets), imagination (mental simulation), and collective working memory (peer collaboration) to deepen schema construction and adaptive problem-solving.

Table 2. Managing ICL in Coding: Summary of Effects and Strategies

Effect Name	Challenge	Solution Strategy
Element Interactivity	Coding involves many highly interactive elements.	Sequence content from low to high element interactivity.
Worked Example	Learners expend cognitive resources on surface-level problem solving.	Provide complete worked examples with annotations.
Completion Problem	Fully worked examples may not prompt deep engagement.	Use partially completed problems that learners must finish.
Guidance Fading	Prolonged scaffolds hinder independent learning.	Gradually reduce instructional support as learners gain expertise.
Variability	Repetitive tasks limit transfer of learning.	Introduce variation in problem types and conditions.
Isolated Elements	Complex content overwhelms working memory.	Teach elements in isolation before integration.
Expertise Reversal	Novice strategies become ineffective for experts.	Adapt instruction based on learners' expertise level.
Split-Attention	Learners must integrate information from separate sources.	Integrate related information spatially or temporally.
Redundancy	Redundant information causes unnecessary processing.	Avoid duplicating identical information across modalities.
Modality	Single-channel instruction overloads processing.	Distribute content across visual and auditory channels.
Segmentation	Long content blocks overwhelm working memory.	Break content into meaningful chunks or steps.
Transient Information	Fleeting information can't be reviewed.	Use persistent formats like transcripts or replays.
Imagination	Passive review limits deeper processing.	Encourage mental rehearsal and prediction.
Self Management	Learners may not manage cognitive load effectively.	Teach metacognitive strategies for load regulation.
Collective Working Memory	Individual learners struggle with complex tasks.	Encourage collaborative learning to share load.
Human Movement	Static visuals may not convey the process effectively.	Use instructional videos with gestures or motion cues.

Conclusion

ICL is an unavoidable aspect of learning to code, especially as learners progress toward more complex and abstract tasks. The complexity of coding content—such as nested control structures, functional abstractions, and algorithmic logic—often requires the simultaneous coordination of multiple interactive elements. These demands can quickly exceed the limits of learners' WM, especially among novices.

However, by applying instructional effects grounded in CLT—such as the worked example effect, the guidance-fading effect, and the element interactivity effect—educators can design instruction that systematically reduces unnecessary burden and enhances meaningful processing. These effects offer a principled approach to sequencing complexity, managing transitions, and matching instructional support to learner expertise levels.

Moreover, complementary effects like the modality, segmentation, and collective WM effects help ensure that instructional delivery matches the cognitive architecture of learners. When integrated thoughtfully into coding instruction, these design principles not only support short-term understanding but also promote long-term schema development and transfer.

Ultimately, managing ICL is not about diluting the richness of coding tasks, but about optimizing the pathway through which learners can progressively master conceptual complexity. With a theory-informed instructional design, we can build environments where learners are challenged—not overwhelmed—and where cognitive effort leads to meaningful and enduring learning outcomes.—particularly those addressing high element interactivity and transitions—educators can design experiences that maximize schema acquisition while minimizing overload. The goal is not to simplify content, but to strategically sequence, scaffold, and support learners as they navigate conceptual complexity in coding education.

REDUCING EXTRANEOUS COGNITIVE LOAD (ECL): ADDRESSING INSTRUCTIONAL DESIGN, TECHNOLOGICAL BARRIERS, AND DEBUGGING CHALLENGES

Note on Terminology and Effects

The instructional effects discussed in this title—such as the split-attention effect, redundancy effect, and modality effect—have been introduced and defined in Managing Intrinsic Cognitive Load (ICL): Navigating Conceptual Complexity and Transitions. Each effect was presented alongside its theoretical origin and key empirical sources. Therefore, in the current section, we focus on the practical application of these effects to reduce extraneous cognitive load in coding instruction. The aim is to highlight context-specific challenges and design-based solutions without repeating foundational definitions.

ECL arises from the way information is presented and the instructional procedures imposed on learners, rather than the complexity inherent in the learning task itself. In coding education, ECL often manifests in the form of disjointed interfaces, inconsistent terminology, redundant instructional formats, or poor sequencing of debugging tasks. Reducing this type of load is essential because it competes directly with WM resources that could otherwise support intrinsic processing and learning.

To alleviate these burdens, several evidence-based instructional effects provide practical design strategies.

1. Split-Attention Effect

Challenge: When learners must mentally integrate spatially or temporally separated but related sources of information, their cognitive resources are consumed by coordination rather than comprehension.

Solution: Embed code explanations within code editors, use synchronized narration with demonstrations, and eliminate layout separation between related instructional elements.

2. Redundancy Effect

Challenge: Presenting the same information across multiple formats—such as onscreen code and its verbatim narration—can cause unnecessary load.

Solution: Avoid repeating identical information. Instead, use complementary modes, such as combining visuals with conceptual summaries or providing one mode at a time.

3. Modality Effect

Challenge: Using only one sensory modality (e.g., all visual) overloads a single cognitive channel.

Solution: Deliver spoken explanations with visual code. Pair diagrams or interfaces with oral explanations rather than redundant text.

4. Transient Information Effect

Challenge: Learners struggle to retain fleeting, transient content like spoken code walkthroughs or auto-scrolling animations.

Solution: Use persistent displays, captions, replayable videos, or step-by-step screen interactions that allow learners to pause and review content.

5. Segmentation Effect

Challenge: Long, uninterrupted explanations can overwhelm WM.
Solution: Break down explanations or demonstrations into coherent segments with clear boundaries and learner-controlled pacing.

6. Self-Management Effect

Challenge: Learners often do not recognize when they are overloaded or how to manage complex instructions.
Solution: Train learners in metacognitive strategies, such as pausing, summarizing, identifying confusion, and restructuring materials for personal use.

7. Self-Explanation Effect

Challenge: Even well-designed materials may not foster active understanding without learner-initiated reflection.
Solution: Incorporate prompts asking learners to explain their reasoning, trace execution steps, or justify debugging decisions.

8. Collective Working Memory Effect

Challenge: Debugging large or unfamiliar codebases alone can overload WM.
Solution: Promote pair or group coding. Have learners articulate and distribute tasks collaboratively to reduce individual cognitive demands.

Table 3. Reducing ECL in Coding: Summary of Effects and Strategies

Effect Name	Challenge	Solution Strategy
Split-Attention	Mentally integrating separated but related sources of information.	Physically or temporally integrate related materials (e.g., code and explanation side-by-side).
Redundancy	Presenting duplicated information across modalities.	Eliminate unnecessary repetitions; use complementary formats.
Modality	Overloading a single sensory modality (e.g., all visual).	Distribute information across auditory and visual channels.

continued on following page

Table 3. Continued

Effect Name	Challenge	Solution Strategy
Transient Information	Loss of fleeting instructional content such as spoken instructions.	Provide persistent resources like transcripts or replayable videos.
Segmentation	Overload from long, uninterrupted instruction.	Break content into short, coherent, learner-paced segments.
Self-Management	Learners may not detect or manage cognitive overload.	Teach metacognitive strategies for regulating effort.
Self-Explanation	Learners passively consume content without reflection.	Encourage learners to explain code logic and decisions.
Collective Working Memory	High individual load during complex debugging or projects.	Use pair or group coding to distribute cognitive demands.

Conclusion

ECL is not a feature of the learning content itself but of the way that content is structured and delivered. As such, it is within the educator's control to design environments that minimize unnecessary processing. By applying effects such as split-attention, redundancy, modality, segmentation, and transient information, instructors can optimize information delivery. Meanwhile, self-management, collective memory, and self-explanation effects support learners' ability to engage with and regulate their own cognitive load.

In coding education—where complex syntax, abstract logic, and layered debugging environments already impose high intrinsic load—reducing ECL is not optional; it is foundational. Clear design, interactive supports, and learner-aware pacing are critical. When extraneous barriers are removed, cognitive resources can be redirected toward meaningful code comprehension, schema development, and coding fluency.

ENHANCING GERMANE COGNITIVE LOAD (GCL): PROMOTING ENGAGEMENT, MOTIVATION, AND PROBLEM-SOLVING SKILLS

While intrinsic and extraneous cognitive loads must be managed or minimized, GCL should be actively encouraged. GCL represents the WM resources allocated to genuine learning processes such as schema construction, abstraction, and automation. According to Sweller et al. (2019), GCL is not an additional category of load in the overall total but a redistribution of cognitive effort toward intrinsic aspects of learning when extraneous load is reduced.

However, learners will only invest cognitive effort into schema acquisition if they are sufficiently engaged, motivated, and able to connect with the learning content. In coding education, disengagement often stems from low perceived task relevance, anxiety caused by debugging failures, and sociocultural barriers—particularly for underrepresented learners such as women and students from marginalized communities. Instructional designs aimed at enhancing GCL must therefore foster interest, relevance, and metacognitive engagement, while remaining sensitive to the overall WM capacity.

Cognitive Load Effects for Enhancing GCL

Several cognitive load effects support the enhancement of germane processing in coding education:

1. Self-Explanation Effect

Challenge: Learners passively engage with materials, failing to construct meaningful schemas.

Solution: Use self-explanation prompts during or after worked examples, asking learners to explain why certain coding decisions are made or to verbalize control flow logic.

2. Imagination Effect

Challenge: Learners focus on superficial repetition rather than mentally simulating processes, especially when they possess sufficient prior knowledge.

Solution: Encourage students to mentally rehearse the flow of a function or algorithm before running the code. Use brief pauses in instruction to support this reflection.

3. Self-Management Effect

Challenge: Students lack awareness of cognitive overload or how to manage it during complex tasks.

Solution: Teach metacognitive strategies such as chunking problems, using pseudocode before implementation, or pausing to summarize key operations.

4. Variability Effect

Challenge: Learners become dependent on repetitive practice and fail to generalize their understanding.

Solution: Provide diverse examples of the same programming principle applied in varied contexts—e.g., looping over arrays, files, or user input.

5. Completion Problem Effect

Challenge: Fully worked examples may reduce active engagement and hinder knowledge construction.

Solution: Present partially completed code that learners must complete, allowing them to actively apply structures with moderate guidance.

6. Guidance-Fading Effect

Challenge: Excessive instructional support can restrict learner independence and long-term retention.

Solution: Gradually fade support by transitioning from full examples to completion tasks, then to open-ended coding challenges.

7. Collective Working Memory Effect

Challenge: Individual learners may struggle to process complex programming tasks on their own.

Solution: Promote collaborative coding environments (e.g., pair coding or shared debugging tasks) to distribute cognitive demands.

Table 4. Enhancing GCL in Coding: Summary of Effects and Strategies

Effect Name	Challenge	Solution Strategy
Self-Explanation	Learners may not deeply engage with examples.	Prompt learners to explain reasoning behind code steps.
Imagination	Novices struggle to mentally simulate complex processes.	Encourage visualization of code execution after examples.
Self-Management	Learners may not recognize or manage overload.	Teach metacognitive strategies for monitoring and control.
Variability	Exposure to novel problems increases initial cognitive load.	Provide diverse practice tasks with gradual complexity.
Completion Problem	Fully open tasks may overwhelm beginners.	Use partially completed code to scaffold problem solving.

continued on following page

Table 4. Continued

Effect Name	Challenge	Solution Strategy
Guidance-Fading	Over-scaffolding reduces autonomy for advanced learners.	Gradually reduce guidance as expertise increases.
Collective Working Memory	Individual learners may be overloaded by complex tasks.	Encourage collaborative coding and role-sharing.

Conclusion

Enhancing GCL involves more than just reducing distractions—it requires creating the conditions for deep, effortful learning to flourish. By using strategies like the self-explanation effect, completion problem effect, and guidance-fading effect, instructors can cultivate learner investment in schema acquisition and promote transfer. Importantly, cognitive effort will only be sustained if learners perceive the content as relevant, challenging, and meaningful.

Supporting GCL in coding education thus entails a dual focus: one on instructional effects that foster structured learning, and the other on affective-motivational supports that promote belonging and persistence. When these design elements align with learners' evolving expertise, motivation, and identity, the result is not only more efficient learning—but more empowered learners.

Motivational Design Principles: Supporting GCL through Engagement and Belonging

While CLT primarily focuses on the architecture of human cognition and instructional design, it is increasingly recognized that learners' motivation, sense of belonging, and task involvement play a critical role in their willingness to invest cognitive effort in schema construction. These motivational factors do not constitute additional cognitive load effects per se, but they act as enablers of GCL—determining whether learners will allocate mental resources to productive learning.

In coding education, especially, students may disengage due to perceived irrelevance, stereotype threat, lack of role models, or a disconnect between the learning content and their lived experiences. Without intentional design, even well-structured materials may fail to activate GCL because students simply do not see the value or accessibility of the task.

The following motivational design principles offer guidance for enhancing GCL through learner-centered engagement:

1. Promote Perceived Relevance

Rationale: Learners are more likely to invest in problem solving and schema construction when they believe the task has personal, social, or career relevance.

Application in Coding: Frame coding assignments around real-world applications (e.g., accessibility, sustainability, health tech). Connect tasks to students' interests, cultural contexts, or future aspirations.

2. Design for Autonomy and Choice

Rationale: According to Self-Determination Theory, learners are more motivated when they experience autonomy.

Application in Coding: Allow students to select between projects (e.g., game design vs. data analysis), or choose tools and languages that align with their goals. Autonomy fosters agency, which increases germane engagement.

3. Support Belonging and Representation

Rationale: Learners who see themselves reflected in the curriculum—and feel socially accepted in the classroom—are more likely to persist and engage.

Application in Coding: Include diverse role models in teaching materials, showcase inclusive tech projects, and use collaborative structures that affirm all voices. For underrepresented learners, this helps overcome identity-related barriers to engagement.

4. Foster Productive Struggle

Rationale: Tasks that are too easy do not stimulate learning, while those that are too difficult may discourage effort. Well-calibrated challenges can promote GCL by encouraging sustained attention and self-regulation.

Application in Coding: Provide tiered challenges, adaptive difficulty levels, or scaffolding that fades as competence grows. Encourage a growth mindset by framing errors as part of learning, especially during debugging.

5. Create Goal-Oriented, Feedback-Rich Environments

Rationale: Clear goals and timely, informative feedback support learners in monitoring progress and adjusting strategies, which in turn reinforces meaningful cognitive effort.

Application in Coding: Use rubrics, checklists, and formative feedback loops in coding tasks. Highlight partial success and guide students toward refining their solutions.

6. Gamify Without Overloading

Rationale: Gamification can increase engagement, but poorly designed systems may introduce ECL.

Application in Coding: Use lightweight gamified elements—such as badges, progress bars, or friendly competitions—to enhance motivation, but avoid complex interfaces or irrelevant challenges that distract from core learning.

Table 5. Motivational Design Principles for Supporting GCL in Coding Education

Principle	Theoretical Rationale	Application in Coding Education
Enhance Perceived Relevance	Learners invest more cognitive effort when tasks align with personal, social, or career goals.	Frame coding tasks around real-world applications (e.g., health tech, sustainability); connect to students' cultural backgrounds or aspirations.
Support Autonomy & Choice	Self-Determination Theory: Autonomy increases intrinsic motivation and cognitive engagement.	Allow students to choose projects (e.g., game dev vs. data analysis) or select programming tools/languages aligned with their goals.
Foster Belonging & Representation	Identity safety and role-model visibility reduce stereotype threat and increase persistence.	Highlight diverse tech role models; use inclusive case studies; structure collaborative learning to validate all voices.
Design for Productive Struggle	Optimal challenge (Vygotsky's ZPD) sustains engagement without overwhelming cognitive capacity.	Implement tiered challenges, adaptive scaffolding, and growth-mindset feedback (e.g., debugging as learning).
Provide Goal-Oriented Feedback	Clear goals and formative feedback help learners regulate effort and refine schemas.	Use rubrics, iterative feedback cycles, and progress checklists; emphasize incremental improvements.
Gamify Strategically	Gamification boosts engagement but must avoid ECL.	Use lightweight mechanics (badges, progress bars) without distracting from core learning objectives.

Conclusion

Motivational design principles complement CLT by addressing the why of cognitive effort. While instructional effects like the self-explanation or completion problem effects shape how learners process information, motivational supports influence whether they will engage deeply enough to benefit from those effects. Especially in coding education, where abstract logic meets identity and confidence, designing for relevance, belonging, and challenge is not optional—it is foundational.

When motivation and instructional design align, learners are more likely to persist, reflect, and engage in the kinds of meaningful activity that lead to robust, transferable coding knowledge.

SUPPORTING EDUCATORS: ENHANCING PEDAGOGICAL PREPAREDNESS AND RESOURCE ACCESS

Teachers are not merely conveyors of content; they are cognitive designers whose instructional decisions shape the load imposed on learners. A lack of pedagogical preparation in coding instruction can inadvertently increase both intrinsic and extraneous cognitive load—especially when abstract or interactive coding concepts are introduced without consideration for sequencing, prior knowledge, or cognitive capacity.

The following challenges and solutions outline how educator training and systemic support can reduce cognitive overload and optimize instructional effectiveness:

Challenge 1: Unstructured Instruction Increases ICL

Teachers unfamiliar with coding pedagogy may introduce complex coding concepts (e.g., recursion, object-oriented design) without appropriate sequencing, overwhelming novice learners' WM.

Solution: Teacher training should emphasize sequencing based on element interactivity. Educators should begin with simpler, isolated concepts and progressively integrate more complex structures. Use of worked examples, isolated elements and completion problems should be modeled in teacher development programs.

Challenge 2: Ineffective Scaffolding Elevates ECL

Rigid, tool-centric tutorials or disconnected instructional materials can lead to split attention, redundancy, or transient information overload.

Solution: Equip teachers with strategies to reduce ECL. These include:

- Integrating explanations directly within code environments
- Breaking lessons into segmented, learner-paced chunks
- Using audio-visual combinations rather than redundant text-based instruction.

Challenge 3: Over-Scaffolding Reduces GCL

Instructors may avoid open-ended tasks or problem solving out of concern for student difficulty, leading to underdeveloped schemas and low GCL.

Solution: Promote the guidance-fading effect and completion problem effect in teacher training. Teachers should learn when and how to remove scaffolds, introduce variability, and support self-explanation.

Challenge 4: Resource Scarcity Increases Teacher Cognitive Load

In under-resourced schools, teachers may lack instructional materials, planning time, or peer collaboration, leading to cognitive overload that negatively impacts instructional quality.

Solution: Institutions should provide:

- Ready-to-use, CLT-informed coding lesson plans
- Access to coding pedagogy workshops and professional learning communities
- Time-efficient templates and collaborative planning time.

Challenge 5: Teachers Lack a Cognitive Design Mindset

Teachers are often trained in tools and content, but not in managing cognitive load in their instructional design.

Solution: Reframe teacher professional development to position educators as cognitive designers. Programs should include foundational CLT knowledge, instructional effects, and case-based coding pedagogy applications.

Table 6. Supporting Educators: Optimizing Teaching Practices with CLT

Challenge	Solution Strategy
Unstructured instruction increases intrinsic load.	Train teachers to sequence content based on element interactivity using isolated elements and worked examples.
Ineffective scaffolding elevates extraneous load.	Promote integrated materials, segmented lessons, and multimodal instruction to reduce unnecessary processing.
Over-scaffolding reduces germane load.	Encourage the use of guidance-fading, completion problems, and variability to foster productive struggle.
Resource scarcity increases teacher cognitive load.	Provide access to CLT-aligned lesson plans, pedagogy workshops, and collaborative planning tools.
Teachers lack a cognitive design mindset.	Offer professional development on CLT principles and their application to coding instruction.

Conclusion

Instructional quality in coding education depends not only on curriculum and tools, but also on the pedagogical fluency of teachers. When teachers understand how to regulate cognitive load—through sequencing, scaffolding, and learner-centered design—they can create environments where students are challenged but not overwhelmed. Building such capacity is not optional; it is essential to equitable, effective coding instruction.

DISCUSSION

Cognitive Load Theory as a Design Framework for Coding Education

The integration of CLT into coding education offers a compelling framework for addressing the unique cognitive challenges that students face in this domain. As learners navigate syntax, abstraction, logic, and debugging—often simultaneously—unregulated cognitive demands can quickly exceed their WM capacity. CLT provides a principled approach to instructional design that not only mitigates overload but strategically directs learners' mental effort toward meaningful schema construction.

This section outlined how instructional effects derived from CLT can be used to:

- Manage ICL through sequencing, isolating elements, and structuring conceptual transitions.
- Reduce ECL by eliminating avoidable barriers like split attention, redundancy, and transient information.
- Foster GCL via self-explanation, guided problem solving, and challenge-based engagement.
- Equip educators with pedagogical strategies and resources that allow them to act as cognitive designers.
- Incorporate motivational principles that enable learners—especially those from underrepresented groups—to meaningfully engage with coding content.

While these strategies are theoretically grounded, their practical implementation presents both opportunities and challenges. For example, applying the guidance-fading effect requires teachers to have deep insight into students' evolving expertise levels—a task complicated by large class sizes or limited assessment data. Similarly, fostering self-management and self-explanation depends not only on instructional design but also on learners' metacognitive maturity.

Moreover, CLT-based interventions must be adapted to diverse educational contexts. What works in a well-equipped computer science lab may not translate directly to under-resourced schools with limited internet access or minimal teacher training. This raises questions about equity, scalability, and contextual adaptation—topics that warrant further empirical research.

At the same time, framing coding instruction through the lens of cognitive load invites a shift in mindset: from delivering content to designing learning experiences. It positions the teacher not just as a guide but as an architect of cognitive activity, capable of shaping not only what is learned but how it is processed and retained.

Limitations in Current Research

While this section outlines a theoretically grounded and practically relevant framework for applying CLT in programming education, it is important to acknowledge limitations in how CLT has been used in computing education research to date.

First, as Duran et al. (2022) highlight, CLT is often referenced superficially in computing education literature. Many studies cite the theory without clearly specifying which version of CLT they are using (e.g., classical vs. revised formulations), and few operationalize cognitive load components in meaningful or measurable ways. This weakens the connection between theory and instructional practice.

Second, empirical studies that attempt to measure intrinsic, extraneous, and germane cognitive load separately are still rare in the field. Most rely on unidimensional self-report tools that do not differentiate between types of load, limiting the validity of findings. This points to a broader methodological gap in the rigorous application and testing of CLT-based interventions in programming education (Duran et al., 2022). Although some researchers have developed multi-dimensional instruments to separately assess intrinsic, extraneous, and germane cognitive load (e.g., Dönmez et al., 2022; Leppink et al., 2013; Klepsch et al., 2017), such tools remain underutilized in computing education contexts.

These critiques suggest the need for more nuanced, theory-aligned empirical research in coding education—studies that not only draw on CLT conceptually, but also measure its constructs with precision.

Implications and Future Directions

1. Teacher Training: Professional development should embed CLT principles, helping educators recognize cognitive bottlenecks and apply instructional effects with flexibility.
2. Curriculum Design: Coding curricula should be designed with an awareness of element interactivity, segmenting, and fading techniques.
3. Technology Integration: Digital learning platforms can be evaluated and optimized through CLT criteria—for example, minimizing transient information or offering scaffolded practice environments.

4. Research Agenda: More empirical studies are needed to explore how specific CLT effects interact with student background, motivation, and prior knowledge in coding contexts.

By combining CLT with pedagogical sensitivity and practical design, educators can foster not only competence but confidence in learners of coding. CLT is not a prescriptive method but a lens—one that empowers us to align instruction with how the mind works and how learners grow.

REFERENCES

Baddeley, A. (1992). Working memory. *Science, 255*(5044), 556–559. DOI: 10.1126/science.1736359

Baddeley, A. D. (1986). *Working memory*. Oxford University Press.

Beege, M., Schneider, S., Nebel, S., Zimm, J., Windisch, S., & Rey, G. D. (2021). Learning programming from erroneous worked-examples. Which type of error is beneficial for learning? *Learning and Instruction*, *75*, 101497. Advance online publication. DOI: 10.1016/j.learninstruc.2021.101497

Cakir, R., Korkmaz, Ö., İdil, Ö., & Uğur Erdoğmuş, F. (2021). The effect of robotic coding education on preschoolers' problem solving and creative thinking skills. *Thinking Skills and Creativity*, *40*, 100812. Advance online publication. DOI: 10.1016/j.tsc.2021.100812

Chandler, P., & Sweller, J. (1991). Cognitive load theory and the format of instruction. *Cognition and Instruction*, *8*(4), 293–332. DOI: 10.1207/s1532690xci0804_2

Chandler, P., & Sweller, J. (1992). The Split-Attention Effect as a Factor in the Design of Instruction. *The British Journal of Educational Psychology*, *62*(2), 233–246. DOI: 10.1111/j.2044-8279.1992.tb01017.x

Chen, O., Kalyuga, S., & Sweller, J. (2015). The worked example effect, the generation effect, and element interactivity. *Journal of Educational Psychology*, *107*(3), 689–704. DOI: 10.1037/edu0000018

Cooper, G., Tindall-Ford, S., Chandler, P., & Sweller, J. (2001). Learning by imagining. *Journal of Experimental Psychology. Applied*, *7*(1), 68–82. DOI: 10.1037/1076-898X.7.1.68

Corradini, I., Lodi, M., & Nardelli, E. (2018). An investigation of Italian primary school teachers' view on coding and programming. In Pozdniakov, S., & Dagienė, V. (Eds.), *Informatics in schools: Fundamentals of computer science and software engineering* (pp. 18–30). Springer., DOI: 10.1007/978-3-030-02750-6_18

Cowan, N. (1988). Evolving conceptions of memory storage, selective attention, and their mutual constraints within the human information-processing system. *Psychological Bulletin*, *104*(2), 163–191. DOI: 10.1037/0033-2909.104.2.163

Cowan, N. (2001). The magical number 4 in short-term memory: A reconsideration of mental storage capacity. *Behavioral and Brain Sciences*, *24*(1), 87–114. DOI: 10.1017/S0140525X01003922

Dönmez, O. (2022). A Cognitive Load Perspective to Instructional Design for Online Learning. In Durak, G., & Çankaya, S. (Eds.), *Handbook of Research on Managing and Designing Online Courses in Synchronous and Asynchronous Environments* (pp. 380–403). IGI Global Scientific Publishing., DOI: 10.4018/978-1-7998-8701-0.ch019

Dönmez, O., Akbulut, Y., Telli, E., Kaptan, M., Özdemir, İ. H., & Erdem, M. (2022). In search of a measure to address different sources of cognitive load in computer-based learning environments. *Education and Information Technologies*, *27*(7), 10013–10034. DOI: 10.1007/s10639-022-11035-2

Duran, R., Zavgorodniaia, A., & Sorva, J. (2022). Cognitive load theory in computing education research: A Review. *ACM Transactions on Computing Education*, *22*(4), 1–27. DOI: 10.1145/3483843

Fan, G., Liu, D., Zhang, R., & Pan, L. (2025). The impact of AI-assisted pair programming on student motivation, programming anxiety, collaborative learning, and programming performance: A comparative study with traditional pair programming and individual approaches. *International Journal of STEM Education*, *12*(16), 16. Advance online publication. DOI: 10.1186/s40594-025-00537-3

Felleisen, M., Findler, R. B., Flatt, M., & Krishnamurthi, S. (2018). *How to Design Programs: An Introduction to Programming and Computing* (2nd ed.). MIT Press.

Gao, X., Yang, Y., Du, Y., & Sun, D. (2025). Effect of mind mapping-based scaffolding on elementary students' computational thinking in block-based programming. *Journal of Educational Computing Research*, *63*(1), 236–271. DOI: 10.1177/07356331241303067

Garcia, F. W. S., Oliveira, S. R. B., & Carvalho, E. C. (2022). A second experimental study the application of a teaching plan for the algorithms subject in an undergraduate course in computing using active methodologies. *Informatics in Education*, *22*(2), 233–255. DOI: 10.15388/infedu.2023.12

Girardin, M., & Courtney, E. (2023, December 5). *Coding vs. programming: What's the difference?* Forage. https://www.theforage.com/blog/skills/coding-vs-programming

Hu, L. (2024). Programming and 21st century skill development in K-12 schools: A multidimensional meta-analysis. *Journal of Computer Assisted Learning*, *40*(2), 610–636. DOI: 10.1111/jcal.12904

Huang, A. Y. Q., Lin, C.-Y., Su, S.-Y., & Yang, S. J. H. (2025). The impact of GenAI-enabled coding hints on students' programming performance and cognitive load in an SRL-based Python course. *British Journal of Educational Technology*, *00*(5), 1–31. DOI: 10.1111/bjet.13589 indeed. (2025, March 28). *Understanding the difference between coding vs. programming*. indeed. https://ca.indeed.com/career-advice/career-development/coding-vs-programming

Jung, J., Shin, Y., Chung, H., & Fanguy, M. (2024). The effects of pre-training types on cognitive load, self-efficacy, and problem-solving in computer programming. *Journal of Computing in Higher Education*. Advance online publication. DOI: 10.1007/s12528-024-09407-3

Kalyuga, S., Ayres, P., Chandler, P., & Sweller, J. (2003). The expertise reversal effect. *Educational Psychologist*, *38*(1), 23–31. DOI: 10.1207/S15326985EP3801_4

Kirschner, F., Paas, F., & Kirschner, P. A. (2009). A cognitive load approach to collaborative learning: United brains for complex tasks. *Educational Psychology Review*, *21*(1), 31–42. DOI: 10.1007/s10648-008-9095-2

Kirschner, P. A., Sweller, J., & Clark, R. E. (2006). Why Minimal Guidance During Instruction Does Not Work: An Analysis of the Failure of Constructivist, Discovery, Problem-Based, Experiential, and Inquiry-Based Teaching. *Educational Psychologist*, *41*(2), 75–86. DOI: 10.1207/s15326985ep4102_1

Klepsch, M., Schmitz, F., & Seufert, T. (2017). Development and validation of two instruments measuring intrinsic, extraneous, and germane cognitive load. *Frontiers in Psychology*, *8*, 1997. DOI: 10.3389/fpsyg.2017.01997

Leahy, W., & Sweller, J. (2011). Cognitive load theory, modality of presentation and the transient information effect. *Applied Cognitive Psychology*, *25*(6), 943–951. DOI: 10.1002/acp.1787

Leppink, J., Paas, F., Van der Vleuten, C. P. M., Van Gog, T., & Van Merriënboer, J. J. G. (2013). Development of an instrument for measuring different types of cognitive load. *Behavior Research Methods*, *45*(4), 1058–1072. DOI: 10.3758/s13428-013-0334-1

Menon, K. (2025, June 9). *Difference between coding and programming*. simplilearn. https://www.simplilearn.com/tutorials/c-tutorial/coding-vs-progrmming

Morrison, B. B., Dorn, B., & Guzdial, M. (2014). Measuring cognitive load in introductory CS: Adaptation of an instrument. *In Proceedings of the 10th Annual Conference on International Computing Education Research (ICER '14)* (p. 131–138). Association for Computing Machinery. https://doi.org/DOI: 10.1145/2632320.2632348

Mousavi, S. Y., Low, R., & Sweller, J. (1995). Reducing cognitive load by mixing auditory and visual presentation modes. *Journal of Educational Psychology*, *87*(2), 319–334. DOI: 10.1037/0022-0663.87.2.319

Muldner, K., Jennings, J., & Chiarelli, V. (2022). A review of worked examples in programming activities. *ACM Transactions on Computing Education*, *23*(1), 1–35. DOI: 10.1145/3560266

OECD. (2021). *OECD Digital Education Outlook 2021: Pushing the frontiers with artificial intelligence, blockchain and robots*. OECD Publishing., DOI: 10.1787/589b283f-

OECD. (2024). *Education Policy Outlook 2024: Reshaping teaching into a thriving profession from ABCs to AI*. OECD Publishing., DOI: 10.1787/dd5140e4-

Oyetade, K., Zuva, T., & Harmse, A. (2025). Integrating industry 4.0 technologies into IT education. *Cogent Education*, *12*(1), 2479195. Advance online publication. DOI: 10.1080/2331186X.2025.2479195

Paas, F., & Sweller, J. (2012). An evolutionary upgrade of cognitive load theory: Using the human motor system and collaboration to support the learning of complex cognitive tasks. *Educational Psychology Review*, *24*(1), 27–45. DOI: 10.1007/s10648-011-9179-2

Paas, F., & van Merriënboer, J. J. G. (1994). Variability of worked examples and transfer of geometrical problem-solving skills: A cognitive-load approach. *Journal of Educational Psychology*, *86*(1), 122–133. DOI: 10.1037/0022-0663.86.1.122

Paas, F., & van Merriënboer, J. J. G. (2020). Cognitive load theory: Methods to manage working memory load in the learning of complex tasks. *Current Directions in Psychological Science*, *29*(4), 394–398. DOI: 10.1177/0963721420922183

Peterson, L., & Peterson, M. J. (1959). Short-term retention of individual verbal items. *Journal of Experimental Psychology*, *58*(3), 193–198. DOI: 10.1037/h0049234

Pollock, E., Chandler, P., & Sweller, J. (2002). Assimilating complex information. *Learning and Instruction*, *12*(1), 61–86. DOI: 10.1016/S0959-4752(01)00016-0

Renkl, A., & Atkinson, R. K. (2003). Structuring the transition from example study to problem solving in cognitive skill acquisition: A cognitive load perspective. *Educational Psychologist*, *38*(1), 15–22. DOI: 10.1207/S15326985EP3801_3

Roodenrys, K., Agostinho, S., Roodenrys, S., & Chandler, P. (2012). Managing one's own cognitive load when evidence of split attention is present. *Applied Cognitive Psychology*, *26*(6), 878–886. DOI: 10.1002/acp.2889

Shin, Y., Jung, J., Choi, S., & Jung, B. (2025). The influence of scaffolding for computational thinking on cognitive load and problem-solving skills in collaborative programming. *Education and Information Technologies*, *30*(1), 583–606. DOI: 10.1007/s10639-024-13104-0

Sozio, G., Agostinho, S., Tindall-Ford, S., & Paas, F. (2024). Enhancing teaching strategies through cognitive load theory: Process vs. product worked examples. *Education Sciences*, *14*(8), 813. DOI: 10.3390/educsci14080813

Spanjers, I. A. E., Wouters, P., van Gog, T., & van Merriënboer, J. J. G. (2011). An expertise reversal effect of segmentation in learning from animated worked-out examples. *Computers in Human Behavior*, *27*(1), 46–52. DOI: 10.1016/j.chb.2010.05.011

Stachel, J., Marghitu, D., Brahim, T. B., Sims, R., Reynolds, L., & Czelusniak, V. (2013). Managing cognitive load in introductory programming courses: A cognitive aware scaffolding tool. *Journal of Integrated Design & Process Science*, *17*(1), 37–54. DOI: 10.3233/jid-2013-0004

Sweller, J. (1988). Cognitive load during problem solving: Effects on learning. *Cognitive Science*, *12*(2), 257–285. DOI: 10.1207/s15516709cog1202_4

Sweller, J. (1994). Cognitive load theory, learning difficulty, and instructional design. *Learning and Instruction*, *4*(4), 295–312. DOI: 10.1016/0959-4752(94)90003-5

Sweller, J. (2010). Element interactivity and intrinsic, extraneous and germane cognitive load. *Educational Psychology Review*, *22*(2), 123–138. DOI: 10.1007/s10648-010-9128-5

Sweller, J. (2016). Working memory, long-term memory, and instructional design. *Journal of Applied Research in Memory and Cognition*, *5*(4), 360–367. DOI: 10.1016/j.jarmac.2015.12.002

Sweller, J. (2020). Cognitive load theory and educational technology. *Educational Technology Research and Development*, *68*(1), 1–16. DOI: 10.1007/s11423-019-09701-3

Sweller, J. (2024). Cognitive load theory and individual differences. *Learning and Individual Differences*, *110*, 102423. Advance online publication. DOI: 10.1016/j.lindif.2024.102423

Sweller, J., Ayres, P., & Kalyuga, S. (2011). *Cognitive load theory*. Springer New York., DOI: 10.1007/978-1-4419-8126-4

Sweller, J., & Cooper, G. A. (1985). The use of worked examples as a substitute for problem solving in learning algebra. *Cognition and Instruction*, *2*(1), 59–89. DOI: 10.1207/s1532690xci0201_3

Sweller, J., van Merriënboer, J. J. G., & Paas, F. (1998). Cognitive architecture and instructional design. *Educational Psychology Review*, *10*(3), 251–296. DOI: 10.1023/A:1022193728205

Sweller, J., van Merriënboer, J. J. G., & Paas, F. (2019). Cognitive architecture and instructional design: 20 years later. *Educational Psychology Review*, *31*(2), 261–292. DOI: 10.1007/s10648-019-09465-5

Tarmizi, R., & Sweller, J. (1988). Guidance during mathematical problem solving. *Journal of Educational Psychology*, *80*(4), 424–436. DOI: 10.1037/0022-0663.80.4.424

van Merriënboer, J. J. G., & Kirschner, P. A. (2017). *Ten steps to complex learning: A systematic approach to four-component instructional design* (3rd ed.). Routledge., DOI: 10.4324/9781315113210

van Merriënboer, J. J. G., & Krammer, H. P. M. (1987). Instructional strategies and tactics for the design of introductory computer programming courses in high school. *Instructional Science*, *16*(3), 251–285. DOI: 10.1007/BF00120253

van Merriënboer, J. J. G., & Sweller, J. (2005). Cognitive load theory and complex learning: Recent developments and future directions. *Educational Psychology Review*, *17*(2), 147–177. DOI: 10.1007/s10648-005-3951-0

Wing, J. M. (2006). Computational thinking. *Communications of the ACM*, *49*(3), 33–35. DOI: 10.1145/1118178.1118215

Yao, D., & Lin, J. (2025). Cognitive enhancement through competency-based programming education: A 12-year longitudinal study. *Education and Information Technologies*, *30*(14), 20347–20383. Advance online publication. DOI: 10.1007/s10639-025-13582-w

Zhang, I., Jia, Y. R., Cheng, X. A., Son, J. Y., & Stigler, J. W. (2025). Empowering novice programmers: Redesigning documentation for effective informal learning. *Journal of Educational Computing Research*, *63*(3), 695–727. DOI: 10.1177/07356331241311505

Zhang, Y., & Rutherford, T. (2024). Scaffolding expertise: Evaluating scaffolds for block-based coding among experts and novices. In *ISAIE '24: Proceedings of the 2024 International Symposium on Artificial Intelligence for Education* (pp. 277-282). Association for Computing Machinery. https://doi.org/DOI: 10.1145/3700297.3700345

Chapter 4
Common Challenges in Coding Education and Proposed Solutions:
A Theoretical-Framework Approach

Satwik Jambula
https://orcid.org/0009-0002-7184-8319
Jawaharlal Nehru Technological University, India

ABSTRACT

Coding education has become integral to preparing learners for the digital age. However, persistent challenges—ranging from inadequate foundational knowledge to teacher training gaps—compromise the effectiveness of coding programs worldwide. This chapter analyzes common barriers that students and educators face, while proposing evidence-based strategies to mitigate these issues. Drawing on research between 2015 and 2024, the authors highlight the necessity of scaffolded curricula, collaborative learning models, professional development opportunities, and inclusive pedagogies. By examining multiple interventions, the chapter underscores how coding education can evolve into a dynamic, accessible, and engaging discipline that equips learners with essential problem-solving skills. The overarching goal is to guide education stakeholders in designing and implementing coding programs that not only address short-term learning objectives but also foster long-term digital literacy and career readiness.

DOI: 10.4018/979-8-3373-2660-3.ch004

INTRODUCTION: THE GLOBAL IMPERATIVE FOR CODING LITERACY

In the rapidly evolving landscape of the 21st century, coding has transitioned from a niche skill to a fundamental form of literacy, widely recognized as essential for future career success and informed global citizenship (Grover & Pea, 2013). The proliferation of digital technologies across all sectors of society has underscored the critical importance of computational thinking and programming proficiency (Wing, 2006). Over the past decade, a concerted global effort has emerged, with governments and educational institutions increasingly acknowledging computer science (CS) and programming skills as core competencies for navigating and contributing to the digital economy (Bocconi et al., 2022). This recognition is supported by research indicating that students engaged in coding education often exhibit improved performance across various academic subjects, demonstrate enhanced problem-solving capabilities, and are more likely to pursue higher education opportunities (Çiftçi & Bildiren, 2020).

The momentum behind integrating coding and computational thinking into school curricula is undeniable. High-profile initiatives, such as the widely popular Hour of Code and the development of comprehensive Computational Thinking curricula, have played a pivotal role in raising public awareness and introducing millions of young learners to the foundational principles of programming (Phillips & Brooks, 2017). Concurrently, policymakers worldwide have introduced national strategies designed to ensure students acquire coding skills early in their educational journey, thereby aiming to cultivate a workforce capable of adapting to the swift demands of technological change (Bocconi et al., 2022).

This global impetus is distinctly observable across both secondary (K-12) and tertiary (higher) education sectors. As of the early 2020s, a significant number of countries have formally integrated computer science into their mandatory educational frameworks. However, the extent and depth of this implementation vary considerably based on regional and economic contexts. A comprehensive analysis by the Brookings Institution highlights a pronounced disparity: no low-income countries have yet succeeded in implementing nationwide computer science education, in stark contrast to over 20% of high-income countries that now mandate computer science instruction in both primary and secondary grades (Brookings Institution, 2021). This data suggests that economically advantaged nations are spearheading formal coding education, while developing countries are still in the nascent stages of building the requisite infrastructure and policy frameworks.

Beyond purely economic considerations, the rationale for widespread coding education is multifaceted, encompassing a range of significant policy goals. These objectives include augmenting national competitiveness in the technology sector, mitigating the pervasive shortages of skilled Information and Communication Technology (ICT) workers, and fostering greater equity in access to high-wage employment opportunities (Bocconi et al., 2022). For instance, Japan's recent coding mandate was explicitly articulated as a workforce development strategy, designed to fill the high-tech worker shortfall and enable the nation to maintain its pace with global innovation (Ministry of Education, Culture, Sports, Science and Technology, 2020). Beginning in 2020, Japan systematically introduced mandatory programming classes from the 5th grade through high school, ensuring that every student gains continuous coding experience throughout their formative years.

Similarly, the European Union's educational agenda has consistently positioned coding and broader digital skills as critical literacies (Bocconi et al., 2022). The EU's Digital Education Action Plan (2021-2027) actively encourages member states to integrate computer science and computational thinking across primary and secondary education, providing financial backing for curriculum development resources and essential teacher training initiatives. International bodies such as UNESCO and the World Economic Forum have also emerged as strong advocates for coding in schools, frequently emphasizing its role in cultivating creativity, enhancing problem-solving capabilities, and generating economic opportunities in an increasingly technology-driven global landscape. In essence, a broad consensus has coalesced: integrating coding skills into educational systems is not merely about achieving computer literacy; it is fundamentally about empowering the next generation to engage fully and meaningfully in an ever-more digital world.

NATIONAL STRATEGIES AND POLICIES FOR CODING IN SCHOOLS

Governments across the globe have embarked on ambitious policy initiatives to introduce or significantly expand coding education, predominantly at the secondary level (middle and high school), with a growing trend toward integration at the primary level as well. These national strategies, while diverse in their scope and methodologies, uniformly aim to provide students with substantive exposure to programming and computational thinking. The subsequent sections synthesize several real-world case studies and policy developments from the period of 2018-2024, illuminating various implementation models and their respective outcomes.

United States: "CS for All" and State-Level Mandates

In the United States, the advancement of coding skill development within the K-12 education system has been a collaborative effort, driven by a combination of federal vision and decisive state-level policy actions. The launch of the "Computer Science for All" initiative by the Obama Administration in 2016 marked a significant federal commitment to broadening access to CS education nationwide (Google & Gallup, 2016). While the U.S. education system operates without a centralized national curriculum, with educational standards primarily determined at the state level, the federal government, in conjunction with private partners such as technology companies and nonprofit organizations, channeled investments into curriculum development and teacher training grants, notably through the National Science Foundation.

These advocacy efforts and strategic investments have yielded substantial results, with the majority of U.S. states adopting policies that either recognize or mandate computer science education in high schools. By 2022, all 50 states had implemented at least some form of policy supporting CS education, such as allowing computer science courses to count toward high school graduation requirements, while many states established ambitious targets or mandates for offering CS in every school (Code.org, 2023). This decentralized yet widespread policy uptake has spurred remarkable growth in student participation. For instance, the percentage of U.S. high schools providing foundational computer science courses surged to nearly 58% in 2023, a considerable increase from just 35% in 2018 (Code.org, 2023).

A particularly influential program in secondary education is the College Board's AP Computer Science Principles (AP CSP) course, which debuted in 2016 with support from the National Science Foundation, specifically designed to broaden participation in computing (College Board, 2020). AP CSP offers an accessible and interdisciplinary introduction to the core concepts of coding and computational thinking. Its impact on student enrollment has been profound. In 2021, over 116,000 students took the AP CSP exam, representing more than double the enrollment observed in the course's inaugural year (College Board, 2021). Critically, the introduction of AP CSP has significantly diversified the demographic composition of computing students. Schools that implemented this course have reported substantial increases in the enrollment of female, Black, and Latino students in their computer science classes (Code.org, 2023). Specifically, the number of AP computer science exams taken by Black or Hispanic students experienced a 2.5-fold increase after AP CSP's introduction, marking an impressive 380% rise from the baseline (College Board, 2021).

The U.S. experience serves as a compelling demonstration of how strategic policy support and innovative curriculum design can profoundly influence student outcomes. Research conducted by Code.org and other organizations consistently indicates that exposing high school students to computer science yields long-term benefits: individuals who take an AP CS course are considerably more likely to pursue a major in computer science or related fields in college (Code.org, 2023).

This effect is particularly pronounced for Black and Hispanic students who took AP CS in high school, as they are 7-8 times more likely to pursue CS degrees compared to their peers without such exposure.

Despite this progress, significant challenges persist in ensuring equitable access to CS education. Rural and low-income urban schools continue to be less likely to offer coding courses, and disparities in participation based on race and gender remain (Code.org, 2023). Addressing these gaps has been a central focus for organizations like Code.org, which actively partners with school districts to provide curriculum resources and teacher professional development, often supported by state grants or philanthropic funding. As of 2023, Code.org reports that its signature Hour of Code campaign—frequently serving as educators' initial foray into integrating CS into the classroom—has reached students in over 180 countries and accumulated more than a billion hours of coding activities globally (Phillips & Brooks, 2017). This immense engagement is effectively generating widespread demand for more comprehensive CS offerings within schools across the nation.

England (UK): National Computing Curriculum and Teacher Training

England has implemented one of the most comprehensive reforms in coding education globally, notably by making Computer Science a mandatory subject from primary through secondary school. In 2014, England introduced a new national curriculum that fundamentally transformed previous "ICT" classes, which largely focused on basic computer literacy (Department for Education, 2014). The new rigorous Computing curriculum emphasizes programming, algorithms, and computational thinking for all students beginning from Key Stage 1 (ages 5-6). The curriculum's objectives are ambitious: by the conclusion of primary school (age 11), students are expected to be proficient in writing simple programs utilizing sequences, loops, and conditionals; by age 14, they should confidently employ at least two programming languages to solve problems. While this policy positioned England as a pioneer in mandating coding education for all age groups, its implementation also unveiled significant challenges.

Early assessments of England's computing curriculum revealed mixed outcomes. On one hand, the policy unequivocally signaled that coding is a core skill, stimulating the development of new curriculum resources (e.g., textbooks, programming tools tailored for children) and leading to increased enrollment in computer science courses at the upper-secondary level (GCSE and A-Level Computer Science). The number of students taking the GCSE Computer Science exam surged from a few thousand in 2014 to over 70,000 by 2020 as the subject scaled nationwide (McDonald, 2019).

However, studies also indicated that many schools struggled to meet the curriculum requirements, particularly in the initial years. The Royal Society reported a 33% decline in the total hours of computing instruction delivered to students aged 11-18 between 2013 and 2018, suggesting a significant gap between the intended curriculum and actual classroom practice (Royal Society, 2017). A primary reason for this was that a substantial proportion of existing ICT teachers lacked the necessary background and confidence to teach rigorous computer science content. Indeed, a survey revealed that only 25% of computing teachers possessed a degree in CS or a related field, and more than half reported low confidence in delivering the new material (Sentance & Csizmadia, 2017). Consequently, many teachers either minimized or entirely omitted the programming aspects of the curriculum, reverting to more familiar ICT topics. This deficit in teacher capacity severely limited the initial effectiveness of the reform in many schools.

In response to these challenges, the UK government strategically shifted its focus, investing heavily in teacher training and support initiatives. In late 2018, England's Department for Education announced an £84 million (approximately $110 million USD) funding allocation to establish the National Centre for Computing Education (NCCE). The NCCE, a collaborative consortium comprising the Raspberry Pi Foundation, British Computer Society, and other key organizations, was tasked with enhancing teacher skills through professional development programs, developing comprehensive classroom resources, and providing ongoing support to schools in curriculum delivery (Raspberry Pi Foundation, 2021). By 2020, the NCCE had engaged over 29,000 educators and delivered intensive training to approximately 1,300 new "GCSE-level" computer science teachers (Computer Weekly, 2020). These teachers participated in a rigorous Computer Science Accelerator program, which included extensive coursework and a certification exam designed to ensure their proficiency in teaching programming fundamentals effectively. The impact of these efforts has been highly promising: among teachers who completed the training, 90% reported a marked increase in their confidence to teach CS, and 70% indicated that the training boosted their enthusiasm for computing education (Computer Weekly, 2020). Crucially, over half of these teachers observed a subsequent increase in student enrollment in CS classes at their respective schools, suggesting a positive ripple effect where better-prepared teachers attract greater student interest.

England's experience powerfully underscores the critical importance of coupling curriculum mandates with robust teacher capacity-building efforts. While it required several years to establish comprehensive support structures, England now possesses all key policy components: a clearly defined curriculum, extensive in-service training programs, established pre-service training pathways (with universities now offering Computing specializations for trainee teachers), dedicated resource hubs, and ongoing pedagogical research. A Brookings analysis of CS education policies recognizes England as "the only country to have taken all seven key policy actions" identified for successful computing education implementation: curriculum standards, mandatory status, in-service teacher training, pre-service training, a specialized support center, dedicated funding, and ICT infrastructure (Brookings Institution, 2021). This holistic approach, despite its inherent complexities, positions England as a leading case study, offering valuable lessons for other nations.

One significant lesson is the indispensable need for sustained government investment. It took England four years following the curriculum launch to inject substantial funding into teacher training, after initial evidence revealed that many teachers rejected the mandated curriculum due to a lack of comfort with coding content (Sentance & Csizmadia, 2017). With the NCCE now fully operational, England has considerably enhanced teacher preparedness, a development anticipated to translate into stronger student outcomes in the coming years. Persistent challenges include addressing the enduring gender gap—computer science enrollment at the upper-secondary level remains approximately 80% male—and ensuring that all schools, not merely early adopters, fully implement the curriculum (McDonald, 2019). Nevertheless, England's policy initiative stands as one of the boldest national endeavors to transform "coding for all" into a tangible reality.

European Perspectives: Finland, Italy, and Others

Several other European nations have also played a pioneering role in coding education, each adopting distinct and innovative strategies:

Finland: Finland pioneered integrating coding into its national curriculum in 2016, embedding it within mathematics, craft, and ICT courses instead of as a separate subject (Bocconi et al., 2022). This cross-curricular, creative approach, using tools like robots, was initially well-received but varied in implementation due to teacher training and enthusiasm. Finland's model inspired Estonia and Sweden to also incorporate coding into their curricula by 2020.

Italy: Italy's "Programma il Futuro" initiative, a public-private partnership with Code.org, began in 2014 as an opt-in coding program for schools. It saw rapid teacher and student engagement, reaching three million students and 35,000 teachers. This success led Italy to formally mandate computational thinking in primary schools in 2016. By utilizing Code.org resources, Italy became a leading nation in its usage and a "powerhouse of computer science teaching" in Europe (Bocconi et al., 2022). This demonstrates how voluntary programs can drive significant interest and pave the way for policy changes.

Poland and France: Poland successfully piloted "Coding Masters," training teachers in Scratch, and integrated coding into its national curriculum from grade 1 by 2017 (Bocconi et al., 2022). France initially offered optional high school programming, then mandated computing in middle school and a CS stream in high school by 2020. France also created Pix, an online digital skills platform with coding exercises. French evaluations showed inconsistent primary implementation and a need for further teacher training.

Germany: Germany's federated education system leads to varying coding education policies across states. Some states made CS courses compulsory in lower secondary schools around 2018-2020, while others offer it as an elective. National initiatives aim to teach coding, particularly to girls, and fund CS teaching research (Bocconi et al., 2022). However, the lack of a unified mandate results in uneven coding education distribution. Although CS has been taught in some regions for decades, there's a push to modernize and universally require it to align with international trends.

European Union Initiatives: The European Union actively supports coding education through campaigns like EU Code Week, which reached over 72,000 events and 4 million participants in 2021, many K-12 students (Bocconi et al., 2022). The EU also supports projects like "Coding for All" and funds initiatives such as "Informatics for All."

Asia-Pacific: Mandatory Coding in East Asia

Many countries within the Asia-Pacific region have similarly taken strategic steps to embed coding into their educational systems, often driven by the goal of fostering innovation-led economies. South Korea and Japan stand out as two prominent examples, both having recently made programming a mandatory component of their national curricula.

South Korea: South Korea mandated coding instruction in schools starting in 2018, requiring programming courses in middle schools and annual software education for elementary and high school students (Bocconi et al., 2022). The goal was to improve problem-solving and develop tech talent, prompting curriculum updates and teacher training. Despite initial challenges with unprepared teachers and resources, the government and private sector supported the implementation. By 2021, significant teacher training had occurred, and student interest and programming skills improved. This shows that mandatory coding requires substantial preparation but can quickly enhance coding literacy with strong policy support.

Japan: Japan mandated coding education for all students from elementary to high school, starting in 2020 (Ministry of Education, Culture, Sports, Science and Technology, 2020). The age-appropriate curriculum progresses from basic programming in math for 5th graders to computer science theory in high school, addressing an IT professional shortage and aiming to boost software innovation. Initial challenges included teacher inexperience and curriculum burden. The goal is to introduce students to programming basics and generate interest, with ongoing teacher training and support. The policy emphasizes the importance of coding and ensures continuous exposure, which is crucial for sustained student interest. Long-term success relies on continued support and curriculum adjustments.

Other nations in the Asia-Pacific region are also making significant strides. Singapore, renowned for its strong STEM education, has integrated computational thinking into primary science and mathematics classes and provides coding enrichment through its "Code for Fun" program in all elementary schools, although it is not a strictly mandatory subject (Bocconi et al., 2022). China has adopted a different trajectory, experiencing tremendous growth in extracurricular coding programs, with some provinces incorporating programming into their high school curricula or examinations (Yang, 2018). For instance, certain provinces in China have begun including programming problems in the university entrance exam (Gaokao) or offer special CS elective tests, which has incentivized more schools to teach coding. The Chinese government has also launched nationwide youth coding competitions and invested in online judge systems to automate coding skill assessment in schools. While not yet a uniform national requirement, these developments reflect China's recognition of coding as a critical skill. Across Asia, a common underlying theme is that governments are simultaneously aiming to foster innovation and creativity through coding education while addressing the immediate and future need for a tech-skilled labor force.

IMPACTS ON STUDENT LEARNING OUTCOMES

A central inquiry for educators and policymakers revolves around whether these widespread coding education initiatives are indeed leading to measurable improvements in student learning and overall development. A growing body of research and program evaluations conducted between 2018 and 2024 consistently indicates several positive outcomes from well-implemented coding programs, spanning both academic performance and the cultivation of essential 21st-century skills. This section outlines key findings related to student outcomes.

Improved Problem-Solving and Cognitive Skills

Numerous studies have demonstrated that engaging in coding activities can significantly enhance students' general cognitive abilities (Acar & Dikkartın Övez, 2022; Aksu & Durak, 2019; Lye & Koh, 2014; Yılmaz & İzmirli, 2023). For example, an experimental study conducted in Europe reported that primary school children who participated in weekly coding activities exhibited significantly greater gains in executive functions, such as planning and inhibitory control, when compared to a control group without coding exposure (Arfe et al., 2019). Following a semester of programming lessons that utilized age-appropriate, game-like coding tasks, these children showed substantial improvement in tasks requiring planning and self-regulation. This finding aligns with the intrinsic nature of coding, which inherently exercises logical reasoning and systematic problem-solving skills (Çam & Kıyıcı, 2022; Durak, 2014).

Even at the secondary level, educators frequently observe that students who actively engage in coding projects become more proficient at deconstructing complex problems into smaller, more manageable components—a highly transferable problem-solving strategy (Popat & Starkey, 2019). Research explicitly indicates that coding in the classroom is linked to improved problem solving and analytical reasoning, noting that students who achieve coding mastery tend to display a natural aptitude for hypothesizing, experimenting, and iteratively refining solutions (Denning & Tedre, 2019). In essence, coding functions as a form of "brain training" that strengthens critical thinking capabilities (Grover & Pea, 2013).

Higher Achievement in Math and Science

Emerging evidence suggests a positive spillover effect between coding education and performance in other STEM subjects, particularly mathematics and science. Computational thinking concepts acquired through programming, such as sequencing, logical operations, and the use of variables, reinforce foundational mathematical thinking (Weintrop et al., 2016). A study involving middle school students participating in a robotics coding program revealed that they not only developed specific CS skills but also demonstrated improved achievement in their mathematics classes (Çam & Kıyıcı, 2022; Kunduracıoğlu, 2018). This outcome is hypothesized to be a result of the hands-on practice with algorithms, which solidified their understanding of abstract mathematical concepts. Similarly, research indicates that high school students who undertake computer science courses tend to perform better in college-level mathematics and science courses (Code.org, 2023). While further research is necessary to fully establish causality, these correlations are encouraging educators to actively integrate coding projects with mathematics and science curricula. Examples include using coding to simulate scientific experiments or to visualize complex geometric concepts.

Increased Interest and Engagement in STEM

One of the most consistently reported outcomes of introducing coding into education is a notable boost in student engagement and enthusiasm for technology.

Surveys conducted after initiatives such as Hour of Code events and brief coding workshops indicate that even a single exposure can significantly increase students' interest in computer science and their self-efficacy—their belief in their own ability to succeed in CS (Phillips & Brooks, 2017). This positive impact is particularly evident among female students and those from traditionally underrepresented groups, who frequently report more favorable attitudes toward coding after participating in even short, enjoyable coding activities. For instance, a survey involving thousands of students who participated in an Hour of Code event found that girls' interest in pursuing CS doubled in the immediate aftermath of the event (Phillips & Brooks, 2017). Engaging, context-based coding projects, such as creating animations, designing games, or controlling robots, appear to effectively demystify programming and make it a more enjoyable learning experience. Teachers frequently observe that coding projects effectively tap into students' creativity and can particularly excite those who may not excel in traditional academic subjects.

In numerous case studies, once a coding curriculum or club is introduced, schools consistently report growing enrollment in these courses year over year, suggesting that initial cohorts of students spread positive word-of-mouth about the experience. This phenomenon is not limited to elective courses; schools that integrate coding as a regular part of their curriculum often report improved overall student engagement. Educational authorities have observed that some students who were otherwise disengaged in school "came alive" during digital technologies lessons, exhibiting persistence and collaborative skills in coding activities that they had not displayed elsewhere (Gerritsen, 2019).

Pathways to Computer Science Degrees and Careers

A significant long-term outcome of secondary coding education is its influence on students' trajectories into higher education and ultimately into the technology workforce. While the full extent of these impacts is still becoming measurable, early indicators are highly promising. In the U.S., the expansion of high school CS courses, such as AP CSP, has correlated with a record number of students choosing computer science as their major in college, including many who might not have considered it previously (Code.org, 2023). Universities are reporting unprecedented enrollments in introductory programming courses, not only from declared CS majors but also from students across a wide range of disciplines, signaling that more incoming students possess prior coding experience and interest.

This trend of burgeoning CS enrollments is a global phenomenon: universities in diverse countries have noted a surge in demand for CS and IT courses, partly attributable to the exposure students received from coding in secondary school or through online platforms. From a policy perspective, this is a highly desirable outcome, as these programs aim to broaden the pipeline into STEM fields. Furthermore, it has significant equity implications: widening participation in school coding means that a more diverse group of students are empowered to pursue high-paying careers in technology. Early data demonstrates that a student who takes just one AP CS class in high school is significantly more likely to major in CS, and this effect is particularly strong for underrepresented minorities (Code.org, 2023). In summary, effective coding programs at the secondary level can ignite a passion that extends into tertiary education choices, thereby directly influencing the future composition of the workforce.

Student Project Outcomes and Competitions

Another tangible measure of impact is observed through the quality of student-created projects and their success in competitive environments. Many coding initiatives culminate in student-developed projects—ranging from a simple animated story created in Scratch by a middle schooler to a more complex application or game engineered by a high school student. Educators frequently express admiration for the speed with which students can progress from having no prior knowledge to constructing something tangible and functional. Hackathons, coding Olympiads, and robotics competitions have proliferated at the school level, providing invaluable venues for students to apply and further hone their coding skills (Çam & Kıyıcı, 2022).

Countries that are early adopters of national coding programs have reported increased student participation in international programming contests since implementing their initiatives, suggesting improvements in both competency and confidence. In the U.S., the attendance at high school hackathons and the volume of submissions to youth coding challenges have consistently grown year after year, reflecting a broadening base of students capable of transforming ideas into functional software.

It is crucial to acknowledge that not all outcomes have been uniformly positive. Some studies caution that the quality of implementation significantly influences the benefits derived: students only realize these advantages if coding is taught in a meaningful, hands-on, inquiry-based, and appropriately scaffolded manner, rather than through rote code copying (Popat & Starkey, 2019). There have been instances where poorly executed coding classes, characterized by unprepared teachers or overly abstract lessons, led to student frustration or a disinterest in computer science. For example, an evaluation in England found that in some schools where the new computing curriculum was delivered superficially due to teacher discomfort, students reported boredom or confusion, resulting in a subsequent decline in enrollments for optional CS courses in those schools (Sentance & Csizmadia, 2017). Therefore, the positive outcomes discussed above are predicated on the assumption that teachers receive adequate support and resources to teach coding effectively.

When implemented correctly, the existing evidence strongly suggests that coding education can significantly enhance students' analytical skills, academic interests, and future opportunities.

TEACHER PREPAREDNESS AND PROFESSIONAL DEVELOPMENT

The successful large-scale implementation of coding education in both secondary and tertiary institutions fundamentally depends on one crucial factor: teacher preparedness. Virtually every case study and policy report from recent years consistently underscores the challenge of ensuring that teachers possess the requisite confidence, content knowledge, and pedagogical skills to effectively deliver coding instruction (Adıgüzel et al., 2023; Çoban & Göğebakan Yıldız, 2025; Yadav et al., 2017). A significant proportion of instructors currently in the workforce did not receive programming education during their own schooling or teacher training programs, necessitating substantial large-scale upskilling or reskilling efforts. This section examines various strategies and programs designed to improve teacher readiness for coding instruction, along with their documented outcomes.

In-Service Training Programs

As evidenced by the England case study, dedicated professional development (PD) programs serve as a cornerstone of successful coding education implementation (Computer Weekly, 2020). Governments and educational organizations globally have established a diverse array of in-service training models. These include intensive short workshops (e.g., summer coding bootcamps for teachers), comprehensive long-term blended courses, flexible online training modules, and peer-led communities of practice (Yadav et al., 2017).

The National Centre for Computing Education (NCCE) in England stands as a leading example, having successfully trained over 1,300 teachers to become certified computing instructors within a two-year period (Computer Weekly, 2020). Evaluations of the NCCE's Computer Science Accelerator program demonstrate significant benefits for participating teachers—90% reported feeling more confident in teaching coding after program completion (Computer Weekly, 2020). Furthermore, a follow-up study revealed that more than half of these trained teachers observed increased student enrollment in CS classes, indicating that a confident teacher can inspire greater student interest in the subject (Raspberry Pi Foundation, 2021).

Research on teacher professional development in computational thinking has emphasized the importance of sustained, practice-based learning experiences (Mumcu et al., 2025). Teachers' value beliefs about computer science and programming must be understood when designing professional development programs, as these beliefs significantly influence their willingness and ability to integrate computational thinking into their teaching practice (Mumcu et al., 2025). Studies have shown that teachers who participate in comprehensive professional development not only gain technical skills but also develop greater self-efficacy for teaching programming concepts.

In the United States, nonprofit-led professional development has played a pivotal role. Code.org, for instance, offers multi-day workshops and year-long support to K-12 teachers adopting its CS curriculum (Code.org, 2023). As of 2021, Code.org had equipped over 100,000 teachers, many without prior CS backgrounds, to teach courses such as CS Discoveries (for middle school) and CS Principles. These workshops not only focus on content acquisition (e.g., learning Scratch, Python, JavaScript) but also emphasize equity-focused teaching strategies designed to engage diverse classrooms (Goode et al., 2014). The Computer Science Teachers Association (CSTA) in the U.S. has also cultivated a robust network of regional chapters that facilitate monthly meetups and the sharing of best practices, resources that teachers find invaluable for their continuous professional growth (Computer Science Teachers Association, 2021).

Internationally, countries like Australia and New Zealand have allocated substantial funding for teacher PD as integral components of their curriculum rollouts. Despite these considerable efforts, surveys frequently indicate that a significant percentage of teachers still feel underprepared. For example, even two years after New Zealand's curriculum change, only 35% of schools reported that their teachers and leaders were knowledgeable about the new content and ready to teach it (Gerritsen, 2019). This highlights the critical necessity for PD to be continuous and to commence well in advance of curriculum changes taking effect.

Pre-Service Teacher Education

To ensure the long-term sustainability of coding education, some regions are strategically embedding coding instruction into pre-service teacher training programs—that is, within university education degrees and teacher certification pathways. The Brookings policy study identified the establishment of pre-service CS education programs as one of seven crucial actions for countries implementing computing curricula (Brookings Institution, 2021). England and several Scandinavian countries have begun requiring new primary school teachers to learn how to teach computing as part of their training, and similarly, secondary teacher candidates in science or mathematics disciplines are now expected to gain exposure to computing pedagogy (Department for Education, 2014). In the United States, a growing number of universities are offering CS education concentrations or dual-certification programs, allowing, for instance, a mathematics education major to also become certified to teach computer science (Yadav et al., 2017).

However, globally, this area remains in development, with progress often being slow due to a lack of faculty expertise in CS education within many teacher training institutions. A promising development is the proliferation of online courses and open educational resources specifically tailored for pre-service teachers. By integrating CS teaching methodologies into pre-service programs, countries can progressively build a workforce where new teachers entering schools are already equipped to teach coding, thereby significantly reducing the subsequent retraining burden.

Teacher Communities and Support Networks

Given the rapid and continuous evolution of technology, teachers derive substantial benefits from peer support and shared resources. Several initiatives are specifically designed to foster and build communities of practice among educators (Yadav et al., 2017). Research has documented networks that enable teachers to discuss programming tasks and collectively troubleshoot classroom issues, which in turn enhanced teachers' self-efficacy. In various countries, governments in collaboration with university partners have established regional programs where experienced lead teachers mentor their peers on effectively integrating coding into existing subject areas. These community-based approaches often help teachers feel less isolated in overcoming challenges.

Nonprofit organizations also play a crucial role in providing support. The Raspberry Pi Foundation, a key leader of the NCCE, manages an online community where educators can share research-based practices and innovative coding activities (Raspberry Pi Foundation, 2021). All these diverse support structures collectively aim to empower teachers, transitioning them from a mindset of uncertainty to a confident conviction that they have the network and tools to succeed.

Overcoming Teacher Anxiety and Misconceptions

A significant hurdle in widespread coding education is the psychological barrier experienced by teachers who do not perceive themselves as "tech-savvy" (Sentance & Csizmadia, 2017). Studies have consistently found that intensive yet approachable professional development can effectively shift these mindsets. For example, a teacher survey conducted in the UK revealed that prior to training, over 50% of teachers did not feel fully capable of teaching coding concepts (Sentance & Csizmadia, 2017).

After completing training and teaching for a year, that percentage dropped dramatically, with many reporting that teaching coding was, in fact, enjoyable.

Key strategies to mitigate teacher anxiety include the initial use of block-based languages and "unplugged" activities, allowing teachers (and students) to grasp fundamental concepts without being bogged down by syntax (Lye & Koh, 2014). Once confidence is built with visual programming environments like Scratch, teachers often find the transition to text-based languages considerably easier. The availability of user-friendly curriculum materials is equally vital. In England, comprehensive curriculum packages provide ready-made lesson slides, code examples, and even assessment rubrics for every grade level, which teachers have praised as a "safety net" when they are unsure how to explain a concept (Raspberry Pi Foundation, 2021). Similarly, Code.org's curriculum offers meticulously scripted lesson plans that new CS teachers can closely follow until they gain more experience (Code.org, 2023). These resources collectively alleviate the pressure on teachers to be coding experts from day one. Another effective approach has been co-teaching or partnering novice CS teachers with more experienced colleagues or industry volunteers.

Despite the notable progress, teacher preparedness remains an ongoing global challenge. The New Zealand case is illustrative: in 2019, education authorities issued a warning that many schools were unprepared for the new digital technologies curriculum because too many schools did not have sufficient understanding, knowledge and skills to implement it (Gerritsen, 2019). This assessment prompted an acceleration of training efforts. The clear conclusion derived from these experiences is that investing in teachers is an indispensable requirement for effective coding skill development. Countries that strategically pair their student-focused initiatives with robust teacher development programs and ongoing support communities consistently observe far better uptake and more positive outcomes (Brookings Institution, 2021).

INNOVATIVE APPROACHES AND TOOLS IN CODING EDUCATION

The pedagogical methodologies and technological tools employed in coding education significantly influence the effectiveness of student learning and the sustained level of their engagement. Educators have demonstrated considerable creativity in deploying a diverse array of approaches—ranging from intuitive visual programming environments for beginners to comprehensive project-based learning frameworks and flexible blended online modules—all aimed at making coding accessible and enjoyable. This section highlights several pedagogical strategies and tools that have proven effective in secondary and early tertiary education, supported by concrete case examples.

Block-Based Programming for Novices

One of the most revolutionary innovations for introducing coding, particularly to beginners, has been the development of block-based coding environments such as Scratch, Snap!, and Blockly. These platforms empower students to construct programs by dragging and dropping puzzle-piece shaped blocks that visually represent fundamental code constructs like loops, conditionals, and variables, thereby eliminating the need for precise text-based syntax (Lye & Koh, 2014). Block-based languages effectively remove initial syntax barriers, allowing novices to concentrate on logical flow, problem-solving, and creative expression.

Millions of secondary students worldwide gain their initial exposure to programming through Scratch, frequently within a dedicated computing class or integrated into subjects like art or science. Educators have found that even at the high school level, a brief introduction using Scratch can effectively demystify programming concepts before students transition to text-based languages (Grover & Pea, 2018). Scratch's design, developed by MIT, is widely lauded for its user-friendliness: each colorful block represents a chunk of real code, which means students are learning real coding concepts when they work in Scratch. Students can create animated stories, interactive games, or complex simulations, providing immediate visual feedback and a strong sense of accomplishment.

Block-based coding is not exclusively for the youngest learners; it is also widely employed in secondary introductory courses. For instance, Code.org's CS Discoveries curriculum for middle school predominantly utilizes Blockly-based puzzles before transitioning students to JavaScript (Code.org, 2023). Research indicates that the use of block tools can significantly enhance students' confidence and overall interest in programming (Lye & Koh, 2014). A study comparing block-based versus text-based instruction found that middle school students who initiated their learning with blocks performed better on subsequent programming tasks and were less likely to withdraw from a CS course. Consequently, numerous countries have integrated Scratch or similar tools into their official curriculum resources. For example, France's middle school computing module recommends Scratch as the initial programming language, and Japan has provided elementary teachers with Scratch-like tools to teach foundational concepts (Bocconi et al., 2022). These intuitive tools are also bridging the knowledge gap for teachers, allowing even educators with no prior coding background to quickly learn and often enjoy using block platforms.

Transition to Text-Based Programming

Following initial exposure through block-based environments, secondary education programs typically guide students toward text-based programming languages—

most commonly Python, JavaScript, or Java—which offer greater power and closer alignment with real-world development practices (Robins et al., 2003). Python, in particular, has become a favored choice in education due to its highly readable syntax and remarkable versatility, applicable across a spectrum from simple scripts to complex data science projects. Many high school curricula, such as the AP Computer Science Principles and England's GCSE Computing, now incorporate Python for teaching core programming concepts like loops, functions, and data structures (College Board, 2020; Department for Education, 2014).

An effective pedagogical practice for this transition is to make it gradual. Some curricula, for instance, adopt a hybrid approach where students might use a block-based interface that can also display the equivalent Python code, helping them make the conceptual connection (Grover & Pea, 2018). When introducing text-based coding, educators often prioritize small, meaningful projects over repetitive syntax drills. A beginner-level Python exercise might involve something relatable, such as analyzing class survey data or coding a simple game.

Text-based coding in classrooms is increasingly facilitated by sophisticated online programming environments. Many schools utilize web-based Integrated Development Environments (IDEs) or interactive notebooks that allow students to code on inexpensive Chromebooks without complex software installations. The emergence of in-browser coding platforms has been a transformative development, enabling students to write and execute Python or JavaScript code on virtually any device, while providing teachers with the ability to view student code and offer real-time feedback (Code.org, 2023). This capability is particularly advantageous in resource-constrained educational settings where access to fully configured development environments on every computer may be limited. Furthermore, online IDEs often support automated grading and instantaneous feedback mechanisms. Teachers can assign coding problems, and the platform can automatically verify the output, which significantly helps in managing large class sizes and provides students with immediate corrections, thereby accelerating the learning process.

Project-Based and Inquiry Learning

Project-based learning (PBL) is highly effective for cultivating comprehensive coding skills beyond mere syntax knowledge (Popat & Starkey, 2019). Instead of prescriptive exercises, students conceptualize, design, code, test, and refine projects, mirroring real-world tasks. For example, assignments like "Create an interactive quiz program" or "Simulate an ecosystem with animated animals" compel students to apply their knowledge and learn autonomously. PBL consistently increases student motivation and enhances the transfer of learned skills. Research demonstrates that project-based approaches enable students to develop deeper understanding of programming concepts while simultaneously building problem-solving and creative thinking skills (Grover & Pea, 2013).

Despite its benefits, scaling PBL presents challenges. It often requires smaller student-to-teacher ratios, ample time, and sufficient resources like hardware and devices. Not all schools can provide a fully equipped makerspace. Thus, many schools adopt a blended model, combining structured lessons with focused mini-projects. A semester-long course might include three shorter projects (2-3 weeks each) interspersed with guided lessons, ensuring students gain creative experience without overburdening teachers or disrupting the timetable (Yadav et al., 2016).

Robotics and Physical Computing

Integrating robotics kits or microcontrollers (such as Arduino, micro:bit, or Raspberry Pi) has proven to be an exceptionally effective strategy for engaging students who might find purely screen-based coding too abstract (Çam & Kıyıcı, 2022). In secondary education, robotics programs—utilizing kits like LEGO Mindstorms, VEX, or more affordable DIY robot platforms—teach coding by allowing students to write programs that control robot movement, navigate mazes, or interact with various sensors. Research consistently demonstrates that robotics can enhance computational thinking skills and concurrently appeal to a broader spectrum of learners, as it directly connects coding with tangible, physical outcomes (Çam & Kıyıcı, 2022). A study found that middle school students who participated in a robotic coding course exhibited significant improvements in their computational thinking skills and reported higher self-efficacy compared to a control group. Many national curricula explicitly mention robotics; for instance, Israel's high school CS curriculum permits a robotics project as a capstone, and Australia's Digital Technologies curriculum encourages the use of micro:bit devices for programming tasks (Bocconi et al., 2022).

A notable advantage of physical computing is its inherent promotion of teamwork; students frequently collaborate in pairs or small groups on robotics projects. This mirrors collaborative coding practices prevalent in industry, such as pair programming, and concurrently builds crucial communication skills. Furthermore, there are substantial cross-curricular benefits: a robotics project might seamlessly integrate coding with physics (e.g., interpreting sensor data), mathematics (e.g., calculating trajectories), and even art (e.g., designing the robot's aesthetic or performance routine) (Weintrop et al., 2016). The primary caveats are cost and the need for specialized teacher training—not all schools can afford class sets of robots, and teachers may require specific training to manage hardware components. Some education systems mitigate these challenges by establishing lending libraries of equipment or forging partnerships with local technology hubs to share resources.

Blended Learning and Online Resources

Blended learning, which integrates traditional classroom instruction with online resources, has become a prevalent method in coding education (Yadav et al., 2016). The "flipped classroom" model is often used, where students engage with instructional videos or tutorials at home, and class time is dedicated to hands-on practice with teacher coaching. This model has shown promise, with studies indicating higher student achievement and satisfaction due to immediate assistance during in-class sessions.

Online platforms have revolutionized self-paced learning, offering interactive coding lessons through websites that provide immediate feedback and visualization, enhancing student engagement, especially in remote environments (Code.org, 2023). The rise of Massive Open Online Courses (MOOCs) and university-industry partnerships further expands learning opportunities. These developments have blurred the lines between formal and informal education and created a continuous spectrum of coding learning (Grover & Pea, 2018).

Contextualized and Culturally Relevant Curriculum

Connecting coding projects to students' personal lives and interests significantly enhances effective coding skill development (Goode et al., 2014). This includes creating applications to address local issues, analyzing relevant data, or integrating arts and music, such as generating musical compositions through code. Initiatives demonstrate success by framing coding as social impact projects, resonating particularly with those initially less inclined towards computers.

Several case studies show deeper student engagement when coding is viewed as a tool for expression or community assistance. Designing curricula relevant to student interests, like games, apps, and data narratives, and being inclusive of diverse cultures fosters "culturally responsive computing," emphasizing interactive, student-centered, and real-world-oriented approaches beyond rote syntax learning (Goode et al., 2014).

INTEGRATION OF CODING SKILLS IN TERTIARY EDUCATION

While a significant portion of policy attention has historically concentrated on K-12 education, the tertiary education sector—comprising colleges, universities, and vocational institutes—has simultaneously and actively developed strategies to enhance coding skills for a broader student demographic. The overarching objective at the tertiary level is twofold: first, to better equip computer science majors with industry-relevant skills, thereby strengthening the pipeline of qualified software developers, engineers, and scientists; and second, to ensure that non-CS majors also acquire a foundational level of coding competency that is increasingly essential within their respective fields. This section delves into how universities and colleges worldwide are adapting their curricula, launching novel programs, and leveraging governmental or industry support to promote coding proficiency among their students.

Expansion of Computer Science and Related Programs

Globally, universities have witnessed an extraordinary surge in enrollment in computer science courses over the last decade. This heightened demand has prompted a significant expansion of CS departments, the creation of entirely new academic programs (e.g., specialized majors in Data Science, Artificial Intelligence, or Cybersecurity, all with substantial coding components), and the emergence of innovative interdisciplinary programs (such as computational biology or digital humanities). Many governments, recognizing the pervasive skills gap in the technology workforce, have provided incentives or direct funding to expand CS capacity within higher education (Bocconi et al., 2022).

The direct consequence of these efforts is that a far greater proportion of tertiary students now undertake at least one coding course. In the U.S., data indicates that the number of computer science majors more than doubled between 2013 and 2019, and while there has been a slight plateau, CS remains among the most frequently chosen majors (Code.org, 2023). This surge in popularity has presented some growing pains, such as increased class sizes and waitlists for popular CS courses. However, universities are actively adapting by recruiting more faculty, utilizing large-scale online course formats, and integrating undergraduate teaching assistants to support instruction effectively.

Introductory Course Reforms

A critical area of focus in tertiary education has been the reform of CS1/CS2 (introductory programming) courses, with the aim of improving student retention and success, especially in light of the increasingly diverse student body enrolling in these courses (Robins et al., 2003). Research-driven pedagogies, including pair programming, peer instruction, and flipped classrooms, have been widely implemented. Studies have shown that peer instruction with interactive questioning in CS1 courses can lead to significant increases in pass rates, particularly benefiting female students who reported feeling more included in class discussions. Pair programming, where two students share a single computer and alternate between writing code and navigating the solution, has also demonstrated positive effects on student performance and persistence in CS courses (Robins et al., 2003).

Furthermore, many universities have strategically shifted the content of their initial programming courses away from exclusively abstract programming concepts (e.g., merely coding mathematical formulas) toward more contextual and engaging topics that appeal to a wider audience (Grover & Pea, 2018). The AP Computer Science Principles framework, with its emphasis on creativity, data analysis, and societal impacts, has also influenced university course design (College Board, 2020). Some colleges have developed new, non-major-friendly courses such as "Introduction to Computing and Data Analysis" to teach basic Python within the context of data science, making them accessible to students across any major. These courses frequently satisfy general education requirements, thereby ensuring that even students in the arts or humanities graduate with some foundational coding experience.

Blended and Online Learning in Higher Education

Tertiary institutions have broadly adopted blended learning methodologies for coding education, a natural fit given the abundance of online resources available (Yadav et al., 2016). Beyond the integration of MOOCs, universities are investing in automated grading systems, dedicated online forums, and interactive e-textbooks. The global COVID-19 pandemic (2020-2021) significantly accelerated the acceptance and implementation of online course delivery; consequently, many programming courses now continue to incorporate recorded lectures or fully online sections, providing students with greater flexibility to learn coding at their own pace. However, universities also recognized the sustained importance of in-person interaction for tackling complex problem-solving scenarios. The prevailing trend is now a hybrid model: foundational content and coding exercises are completed online, supplemented by essential in-person lab sessions or tutoring for more in-depth guidance and support.

Additionally, some universities are forging partnerships with industry bootcamps or certification programs to complement their formal academic curricula. For instance, a university might facilitate student access to an external coding bootcamp during the summer to reinforce practical skills, such as web development frameworks, that may not be extensively covered in traditional academic courses. Governments have occasionally supported these collaborations to enhance graduate employability (Bocconi et al., 2022).

Incorporating Coding Across Disciplines

A pivotal development in tertiary education is the increasing integration of coding into non-computer science fields, driven by the pervasive recognition that data and automation are now integral to virtually all disciplines (Weintrop et al., 2016). Many science and engineering programs have introduced mandatory programming courses (e.g., an "Introduction to Python for Engineers" or "Programming for Chemists" course). Business schools are incorporating Python for business analytics; psychology departments are introducing R programming for statistical analysis; and even journalism programs are now teaching HTML/JavaScript for web media skills. The overarching aim is to produce graduates in every field who possess at least the ability to write simple scripts or comprehend code relevant to their specific domain.

Some institutions have gone further, instituting a requirement for all undergraduates to take a general computational thinking course (Grover & Pea, 2013). These institutional policy decisions underscore the evolving perception of coding as an integral component of a well-rounded education, rather than merely a specialized skill for computer scientists.

Centres of Excellence and Research in CS Education

With increased interest in computer science education, universities and governments have established research centers to improve coding teaching methodologies (Brookings Institution, 2021). Organizations like the National Centre for Computing Education (NCCE) in England and the National Science Foundation (NSF) in the U.S. fund projects to innovate teaching methods (Raspberry Pi Foundation, 2021). This research refines approaches in both secondary and tertiary education, making learning coding more accessible.

A major challenge is balancing academic preparation with industry needs, which evolve quickly. Universities offer electives or practicums to teach in-demand skills like mobile development or cloud computing, sometimes with government support (Bocconi et al., 2022). Tertiary education benefits from better-prepared students from secondary schools and must further develop these skills. The synergy between levels is crucial; increased high school CS readiness requires universities to offer more advanced courses, creating a positive feedback loop for a digitally skilled society (Code.org, 2023).

LESSONS LEARNED AND FUTURE DIRECTIONS

The collective experiences garnered from coding education initiatives across the globe offer invaluable lessons on how to effectively foster coding skills at both the secondary and tertiary levels. While specific contexts and national characteristics vary, successful initiatives frequently share common elements and recurrent challenges. This section summarizes these critical insights.

Key Lessons Learned

1. **Early and Universal Exposure:** Early, universally accessible coding education is key (Brookings Institution, 2021). Countries with primary/lower secondary coding see more advanced computer science participation. Early, playful exposure demystifies coding and builds interest (Phillips & Brooks, 2017). Mandatory coding in the core curriculum ensures equitable access and reaches all demographics, avoiding self-selection by underrepresented groups. Creating demand and making coding mandatory is essential for equitable access and skill development (Brookings Institution, 2021).
2. **Invest in Teachers and Teacher Training:** Consistent, high-quality teacher training is crucial for effective policy implementation (Mumcu et al., 2025). One-time workshops are inadequate; continuous development, accessible materials, mentorship, and recognition are necessary (Yadav et al., 2017). Formal certifications or endorsements, especially in computer science, professionalize teaching roles. National centers or networks effectively coordinate professional development and facilitate the sharing of best practices (Computer Weekly, 2020; Raspberry Pi Foundation, 2021).
3. **Public-Private Partnerships:** Successful coding education programs thrive on strong collaborations between governments, nonprofits like Code.org and Raspberry Pi Foundation, and industry partners (Code.org, 2023; Raspberry Pi Foundation, 2021). Nonprofits provide curricula and training, while industry offers resources and real-world insights. These partnerships accelerate implementation and keep curricula updated. Educational systems benefit greatly from collaboration to scale and enhance coding education programs (Brookings Institution, 2021).
4. **Curriculum Integration and Flexibility:** A debate exists on whether coding should be a separate subject or integrated into the curriculum. A hybrid approach is emerging: dedicated CS classes alongside cross-curricular projects (Weintrop et al., 2016). Integration shows coding's versatility, but too much flexibility can lead to avoidance. Clear, compulsory coding outcomes are needed (Bocconi et al., 2022). A blended model—core CS with integrated projects—appears best, fostering a strong computing culture.
5. **Student-Centered and Culturally Relevant Pedagogy:** Student-centered, hands-on, and creative coding activities drive engagement better than lectures (Goode et al., 2014). Interactive approaches like pair programming and gamified tutorials are more effective (Lye & Koh, 2014). Culturally relevant, localized content, including translations, significantly boosts engagement by using local examples and reducing language barriers.

6. **Continuous Monitoring and Adaptation:** Continuous evaluation and system flexibility are vital in education (Brookings Institution, 2021). Adjust strategies based on outcomes, like adding targeted teacher training or support programs. Policymakers use data on student enrollment, demographics, achievement, and career paths to secure funding and identify effective approaches (Code.org, 2023).

Future Directions

Coding skill development in education is evolving to include AI/ML concepts, mirroring society's AI growth. Nations are integrating AI education into curricula (Bocconi et al., 2022). Increased inclusivity, particularly for students with disabilities via adaptive tools, is prioritized. Global collaboration drives open-source resources to ensure equitable access (Raspberry Pi Foundation, 2021). Developing coding skills requires supportive policies, trained teachers, engaging curricula with tools, and inclusion. Case studies show these elements foster programming skills, analytical thinking, creativity, and opportunities (Brookings Institution, 2021; Code.org, 2023). Continuous refinement is necessary with technological evolution, but significant progress from 2018-2024 is promising. Coding is established in education, creating opportunities globally.

REFERENCES

Acar, İ. G., & Övez, F. D. (2022). The effect of block-based game development activities on the geometry achievement, computational thinking skills and opinions of seventh-grade students. *Journal of Educational Technology and Online Learning*, *5*(4), 1106–1121. DOI: 10.31681/jetol.1151170

Adıgüzel, S., Eryılmaz, S., Gencer, T., & Göksu, H. (2023). Coding activities in IT courses through the lenses of IT teachers. *Journal of Educational Technology and Online Learning*, *6*(2), 384–402. DOI: 10.31681/jetol.1219963

Aksu, F. N., & Durak, G. (2019). Robotics in Education: Examining Information Technology Teachers' Views. *Journal of Education and e-learning Research*, *6*(4), 162–168. DOI: 10.20448/journal.509.2019.64.162.168

Arfe, B., Vardanega, T., Montuori, C., & Lavanga, M. (2019). Coding in primary grades boosts children's executive functions. *Frontiers in Psychology*, *10*, 2713. Advance online publication. DOI: 10.3389/fpsyg.2019.02713

Bocconi, S., Chioccariello, A., Kampylis, P., Dagienė, V., Wastiau, P., Engelhardt, K., Earp, J., Horvath, M. A., Jasutė, E., Malagoli, C., Masiulionytė-Dagienė, V., & Stupurienė, G. (2022). *Reviewing computational thinking in compulsory education*. Publications Office of the European Union., DOI: 10.2760/126955

Brookings Institution. (2021). *Building skills for life: How to expand and improve computer science education around the world*. Center for Universal Education at Brookings. https://www.brookings.edu/articles/building-skills-for-life/

Çam, E., & Kıyıcı, M. (2022). The impact of robotics assisted programming education on academic success, problem solving skills and motivation. *Journal of Educational Technology and Online Learning*, *5*(1), 47–65. DOI: 10.31681/jetol.1028825

Çiftçi, S., & Bildiren, A. (2020). The effect of coding courses on the cognitive abilities and problem-solving skills of preschool children. *Computer Science Education*, *30*(1), 3–21. DOI: 10.1080/08993408.2019.1696169

Çoban, D., & Yıldız, D. G. (2025). An evaluation of the 10th grade robotic coding curriculum (2020) within a participant oriented curriculum evaluation approach. *Journal of Educational Technology and Online Learning*, *8*(2), 226–250. DOI: 10.31681/jetol.1568614

Code.org. (2023). *State of computer science education: Illuminating disparities*. https://advocacy.code.org/stateofcs

College Board. (2020). *AP computer science principles course and exam description.* https://apcentral.collegeboard.org/courses/ap-computer-science-principles

College Board. (2021). *AP program participation and performance data 2021.* https://research.collegeboard.org/programs/ap/data

Computer Science Teachers Association. (2021). *CSTA K-12 computer science standards* (Revised 2017). https://www.csteachers.org/page/standards

Computer Weekly. (2020, November 12). More than 1,300 teachers are trained by the National Centre for Computing Education. https://www.computerweekly.com/news/252492701/

Denning, P. J., & Tedre, M. (2019). *Computational thinking*. MIT Press. DOI: 10.7551/mitpress/11740.001.0001

Department for Education. (2014). *National curriculum in England: Computing programmes of study*. UK Government. https://www.gov.uk/government/publications/national-curriculum-in-england-computing-programmes-of-study

Durak, G. (2014). The Effects of a Distance Education Programming Language Course on Student Performance/Uzaktan Eğitimle Verilen Programlama Dilleri Dersinin Öğrenen Başarısı Üzerine Etkisi. *Eğitimde Kuram ve Uygulama, 10*(1), 202–219.

Gerritsen, J. (2019, November 27). New NZ digital curriculum set for 2020, are schools ready? *RNZ News*. https://www.rnz.co.nz/news/national/404558/new-nz-digital-curriculum-set-for-2020-are-schools-ready

Goode, J., Chapman, G., & Margolis, J. (2014). Beyond curriculum: The Exploring Computer Science program. *ACM Inroads, 3*(2), 47–53. DOI: 10.1145/2189835.2189851

Google & Gallup. (2016). *Trends in the state of computer science in U.S. K-12 schools*. https://services.google.com/fh/files/misc/trends-in-the-state-of-computer-science-report.pdf

Grover, S., & Pea, R. (2013). Computational thinking in K-12: A review of the state of the field. *Educational Researcher, 42*(1), 38–43. DOI: 10.3102/0013189X12463051

Grover, S., & Pea, R. (2018). Computational thinking: A competency whose time has come. In Sentance, S., Barendsen, E., & Schulte, C. (Eds.), *Computer science education: Perspectives on teaching and learning in school* (pp. 19–38). Bloomsbury Academic. DOI: 10.5040/9781350057142.ch-003

Kunduracıoğlu, İ. (2018). Examining the interface of lego mindstorms ev3 robot programming. *Journal of Educational Technology and Online Learning, 1*(1), 28–46. DOI: 10.31681/jetol.372826

Lye, S. Y., & Koh, J. H. L. (2014). Review on teaching and learning of computational thinking through programming: What is next for K-12? *Computers in Human Behavior, 41*, 51–61. DOI: 10.1016/j.chb.2014.09.012

McDonald, C. (2019). *England: Computer science GCSE, AS, and A levels*. British Computer Society. https://www.bcs.org/

Ministry of Education. Culture, Sports, Science and Technology. (2020). *Programming education in elementary schools*. Government of Japan. https://www.mext.go.jp/

Mumcu, F. K., Andic, B., Maricic, M., Tejera, M., & Lavicza, Z. (2025). Unpacking teachers' value beliefs about computational thinking and programming. *Journal of Educational Technology and Online Learning, 8*(1), 41–63. DOI: 10.31681/jetol.1497284

Phillips, R., & Brooks, B. (2017). *The Hour of Code: Impact on attitudes towards and self-efficacy with computer science*. Code.org. https://code.org/about

Popat, S., & Starkey, L. (2019). Learning to code or coding to learn? A systematic review. *Computers & Education, 128*, 365–376. DOI: 10.1016/j.compedu.2018.10.005

Raspberry Pi Foundation. (2021, March 15). Computer science education is a global challenge [Blog post]. https://www.raspberrypi.org/blog/

Robins, A., Rountree, J., & Rountree, N. (2003). Learning and teaching programming: A review and discussion. *Computer Science Education, 13*(2), 137–172. DOI: 10.1076/csed.13.2.137.14200

Royal Society. (2017). *After the reboot: Computing education in UK schools*. https://royalsociety.org/topics-policy/projects/computing-in-schools/report/

Sentance, S., & Csizmadia, A. (2017). Computing in the curriculum: Challenges and strategies from a teacher's perspective. *Education and Information Technologies, 22*(2), 469–495. DOI: 10.1007/s10639-016-9482-0

Weintrop, D., Beheshti, E., Horn, M., Orton, K., Jona, K., Trouille, L., & Wilensky, U. (2016). Defining computational thinking for mathematics and science classrooms. *Journal of Science Education and Technology, 25*(1), 127–147. DOI: 10.1007/s10956-015-9581-5

Wing, J. M. (2006). Computational thinking. *Communications of the ACM, 49*(3), 33–35. DOI: 10.1145/1118178.1118215

Yadav, A., Hong, H., & Stephenson, C. (2016). Computational thinking for all: Pedagogical approaches to embedding 21st century problem solving in K-12 classrooms. *TechTrends*, *60*(6), 565–568. DOI: 10.1007/s11528-016-0087-7

Yadav, A., Stephenson, C., & Hong, H. (2017). Computational thinking for teacher education. *Communications of the ACM*, *60*(4), 55–62. DOI: 10.1145/2994591

Yang, S. (2018). Investigation of programming education in China's primary and secondary schools. *Education and Information Technologies*, *23*(5), 2005–2021. DOI: 10.1007/s10639-018-9750-x

Yılmaz, T., & İzmirli, S. (2023). Effect of unplugged and plugged coding activities on secondary school students' computational thinking skills. *Journal of Educational Technology and Online Learning*, *6*(4), 1180–1193. DOI: 10.31681/jetol.1375335

Chapter 5

An Inquiry-Based Computational Thinking Approach in Teacher Education

Ugur Kale
https://orcid.org/0000-0003-2286-5251
Indiana University, USA

Kyungbin Kwon
Indiana University, USA

Gamze Ozogul
https://orcid.org/0000-0002-8044-9021
Indiana University, USA

Juhyun Park
https://orcid.org/0009-0001-4899-7415
Indiana University, USA

ABSTRACT

This chapter presents how an inquiry-based approach in teaching computational thinking (CT) can be embedded in teacher education. Informed by the expectancy-value theory, it provides strategies to help preservice teachers (PSTs) develop interest in CT, recognize its relevance to content and pedagogy, and build competence with it. Furthermore, the chapter describes various learning units that use 2D, 3D, robotics technologies as well as an AI extension to illustrate how to promote students' CT in an inquiry format. Varying difficulty levels of coding and personalization opportunities are also included for more effective implementation of the activities while the

DOI: 10.4018/979-8-3373-2660-3.ch005

suggested timeline can be useful to help interested teacher education faculty plan their curricula. The implementation of the described activities aims to assist PSTs in preparing their future pupils to think computationally.

INTRODUCTION

As an effective approach to solving problems via the techniques adapted from the computer science field (Wing, 2008), computational thinking (CT) has gained the interest among researchers and practitioners in education (Kale et al., 2018). The focus on CT in education reflects the recognized need for preparing students for a technology driven society and the increasing number of computer science (CS) education initiates (Code.org, CSTA, ECEP Alliance, 2024). The importance of CT is even amplified further in the presence of AI-powered technologies. A deeper understanding of how such technologies function is considered fundamental to their meaningful use, which also necessitates thinking computationally (Dohn et al., 2022; Hsu & Chen, 2024).

Given the value of CT, preparing PSTs to teach it is essential to future students' ability to think computationally. Nonetheless, opportunities to expose PSTs to CT are limited (Code.org, CSTA, ECEP Alliance, 2024), and much of the existing literature focuses primarily on what CT is and how it can be integrated into disciplinary instruction, rather than on why PSTs choose to engage with CT or how their motivation shapes implementation. Prior framework such as the Brennan and Resnick (2012) model of CT dimensions, the Weintrop et al. (2016) taxonomy of CT practices, and V. Barr and Stephenson's (2011) cross-disciplinary CT framework offer rich descriptions of CT's components, but they tend to lack a motivational or affective lens for understanding teacher engagement. Consequently, there remains a need to connect motivation theories with pedagogical approaches that effectively prepare PSTs to teach CT with confidence and purpose.

Informed by the expectancy–value theory (Wigfield & Eccles, 2000; Wigfield et al., 2008), this chapter responds to this gap by emphasizing PSTs' interest, perceived value, and competence as drivers of CT engagement and usage. It integrates inquiry-based pedagogy, specifically, the 5E instructional model (Bybee, 2015) with CT practices to show how data-rich, inquiry-oriented experiences can strengthen both cognitive and motivational outcomes. The chapter therefore contributes to the literature by:

1. Bridging expectancy–value theory with CT pedagogy, addressing the underexplored motivational dimension of CT in teacher education;

2. Proposing an inquiry-based CT framework that operationalizes motivation through data practices, 2D/3D environments, robotics, and AI applications; and
3. Offering a replicable implementation model with scaffolded activities and a semester-long structure to guide teacher-education faculty.

In doing so, this chapter situates CT not only as a set of cognitive skills but as a motivational and pedagogical process essential to developing teachers and students who can think computationally in an era shaped by AI.

WHAT IS COMPUTATIONAL THINKING?

CT has been considered as an effective approach to solving problems through using computer science methodologies (Bocconi et al., 2016; Kale et al., 2018; Nouri et al., 2020; Wing, 2008; Yadav et al., 2017). As discussed in the earlier section, the importance of CT is also amplified in the presence of AI technologies. Through creating and presenting solutions to given situations, thinking computationally can engage students consciously in making artifacts (e.g., design systems) in situated environments (Harel & Papert, 1991). In particular, CT starts with being confronted by problems, the solution of which involves decomposition, pattern recognition, abstraction, algorithm & automation, and analysis (D. Barr et al., 2011; Grover & Pea, 2013; Wing, 2008), closely mirroring the components of the problem-solving process (Mayer & Wittrock, 2006; OECD, 2003, 2013, 2015) as outlined in Table 1.

Table 1. Comparison of Problem Solving and Computational Thinking

Computational thinking		**Problem solving**	
Define and understand problems	**Confrontation**	**Understand & represent**	Understand a situation, information, main features
Logically organize, decompose and analyze	**Decomposition**	**Plan & Monitor**	Identify constraints, parts, variables, relations
Identify pattern	**Pattern recognition**		
Represent & formulate problem through abstractions	**Abstraction**		Represent alternatives, relations, functions
Automate solutions through algorithmic thinking	**Algorithm/ Automation**	**Execute**	Carry out planned operations
Analyze possible solutions Test/debug/troubleshoot	**Analysis**	**Self-regulate**	Check & reflect on the decision, analysis & design, diagnosis/ solution
Analyze the appropriateness of the abstractions made			

CT's problem-solving nature (Voogt et al., 2015) coupled with the importance of problem-solving in learning underscore the significance of CT even further. This is also because opportunities that entail students' CT naturally attract the interest of researchers and educators who focus on problem-solving (Kale et al., 2018).

Further, the CT has been predominantly approached as a cognitive outcome in the recent K-12 initiatives (Kafai & Proctor, 2021). While such portrayal of CT emphasizes its cognitive construct, CT is more than solving computing-related problems, but rather a broader approach that can be applied to problem-solving in various contexts (Tsarava et al., 2022). Despite its commonly perceived applicability to STEM fields, CT is beyond a subject-specific skill (Tagare, 2024). For instance, a rather critical perspective of CT has emphasized self-expression, connection, and questioning (Kafai & Proctor, 2021; Brennan & Resnick, 2012) and been also been considered as a potential way to engage learners in the social, economic, political challenges of the world that directly impact them (Kafai et al., 2019; Kafai & Proctor, 2021; Tissenbaum et al., 2019). Limited examples include the development of apps around social justice issues (Vakil, 2014), interactive map of gentrification (Lee & Soep, 2016), and environmental awareness (Tissenbaum et al., 2019), as well as storytelling projects for political resistance (Aghasaleh et al., 2019).

VALUE OF CT IN THE AGE OF AI

Given CT's multifaceted role as both a problem-solving approach and a broader cognitive and creative capacity, it is important to consider how its educational value continues to evolve amid the growing influence of artificial intelligence (AI). AI has significantly impacted education, fundamentally transforming how students learn and how teachers instruct. AI-powered technologies now enable personalized learning by identifying learner's strengths and gaps (Lee et al., 2019), provide intelligent tutoring systems (Walkington & Bernacki, 2019), and support automatic scoring and formative assessment (Zhu et al., 2020). Given such potentials, the use of AI systems such as Generative AI (GenAI) technologies have also been more recently explored with regards to supporting students' CT. For instance, in one study, undergraduate students using ChatGPT during a programming course had developed significantly higher levels of CT, motivation, and programming self-efficacy (Yilmaz & Yilmaz, 2023). In another study (Hsu & Hsu, 2025), using a GenAI tool when coding tasks helped sixth graders develop CT such as algorithmic thinking while their CT concept development did not benefit from the GenAI too.

Likewise, the importance of CT for AI use has also been explored. Dohn et al. (2022) found a significant positive relationship between CT and AI literacy, indicating that individuals with advanced CT skills are better equipped to understand and apply AI technologies. Similarly, Hsu and Chen (2024) demonstrated that students with strong CT abilities more readily comprehend and engage with AI concepts, underscoring the necessity of integrating CT into education in the era of AI.

Further, among the various AI technologies, machine learning (ML) stands out as a "scientific method on steroids" (Domingos, 2015), allowing computers to learn from data and make decisions autonomously (Popenici & Kerr, 2017). The operation of ML closely parallels the core processes of computational thinking (CT): both involve breaking down complex problems, recognizing patterns, formulating procedures, and generating solutions—whether in machines or in humans. This strong connection means that fostering CT is essential for understanding and effectively utilizing AI, particularly ML, in educational contexts.

BRIDGING CT AND COMPUTER SCIENCE IN TEACHER EDUCATION

As discussed in the previous section, CT serves as a foundational capacity for understanding and engaging with technologies such as artificial intelligence (AI). Because CT underpins many of the problem-solving and analytical processes at the heart of computer science (CS), strengthening CS education represents an essential avenue for fostering CT development in schools.

The recognized urgency of preparing students for a society driven by AI and computing technology prompted many states in the US to adopt computer science (CS) education policies and requirements. Despite the increased number of CS courses, millions of students still lack access to CS education as many schools need to have qualified CS teachers (Code.org, CSTA, ECEP Alliance, 2024) and CS teaching positions are among the top three teaching positions with the highest vacancy rates in the public school systems (National Center for Education Statistics, 2023). While in-service teacher professional development is helpful, they will fall short of meeting the demand for CS courses. Thus, preparing PSTs to teach CS education is critical to the supply of newly qualified CS teachers, given the number of teacher candidates completing such programs has a direct relationship to the availability of teachers (National Center for Education Statistics, 2023). Yet, less than half of the states have initiatives that focus on PSTs and only a few of them require CS or CT exposure (Code.org, CSTA, ECEP Alliance, 2024).

Although a few universities offered undergraduate CS education licensure programs (Ozogul et al., 2018), they are not attracting an adequate number of PSTs. There is minimal impetus for them to take additional coursework while all they need is take a praxis test. Due to low enrollment, for instance, the CS licensure program in universities may get on hiatus. Without quality pathways infused with CT and CS concepts, PSTs' preparation for teaching CS can be impeded, significantly lowering the quality of future CS and CT education.

A MOTIVATIONAL FRAMEWORK FOR PSTS' CT: EXPECTANCY-VALUE THEORY

While the expansion of CS education highlights the structural need for qualified teachers, fostering preservice teachers' engagement with CT also requires attention to their motivational and affective factors. Beyond providing content knowledge and technical preparation, teacher education programs must help PSTs develop the confidence, interest, and perceived value necessary to implement CT in their future classrooms. As the content knowledge is essential to quality teaching, the understanding of CT, a foundational skill for CS, is critical to PSTs' future practices with CS education. Luckily, the growing number of new initiatives investigating CT as the foundational skill for PSTs' CS education efforts signals the possible spread of CT to teacher education (e.g., Adler et al., 2023; Breslyn & McGinnis, 2019; Jaipal-Jamani & Angeli, 2017; Kaya et al., 2020; McGinnis et al., 2020; Pewkam & Chamrat, 2022; Suters, 2021; Yun & Crippen, 2024). As a technological innovation, the successful implementation of CT, however, depends, to an extent, on (a) the expected degree of successful use in lessons and (b) the perceived usefulness and relevance to teaching and learning CT. This assertion reflects the perspective of the expectancy-value theory, which posits that our willingness to start or the effort we put into an activity (future performance) depends on how much we expect to be able to complete it successfully (competence) and how much we value and are interested in the activity (utility and interest) (Brophy, 2008, 2010; Wigfield & Eccles, 2000; Wigfield et al., 2008;).

Expectations for success are beliefs about people's evaluations of their competence and how well they can perform an upcoming task, impacting their future performance and interest (Wigfield & Eccles, 2000). Likewise, interest can play a key role in performance. It is considered to consist of triggered situational interest, maintained situational interest, and personal interest. The triggered situational interest, is generally elicited by environmental factors, and can impact one's re-engagement with a given task or content. If triggered interest is sustained overtime, it can turn into maintained situational interest – a more persistent psychological state. At this point, finding the given task meaningful helps deepen one's interest while their increasing knowledge and the value they place on it resulting from repeated completion of the task can make their interest more personal. Utility value, another concept that has also been observed to predict performance, is the degree to which a task is perceived as relevant for aspects of one's life (e.g., occupation

(Hulleman et al., 2010). Such constructs have also been found to play an important role in teacher education. For example, a recent systematic review of studies conducted on PSTs' CT development (Dong et al., 2024) identified self-efficacy and attitudes as the most critical factors, while enhanced CT was also seen as essential for strengthening their confidence and informing their future CT-related teaching practices. In sum, fostering preservice teachers' motivation to use CT requires not only building their confidence and interest but also helping them see its practical relevance to what and how they teach. The next section highlights how CT can be meaningfully connected to both disciplinary content and pedagogy, establishing a foundation for its effective integration into classroom practice.

LINKING CT TO TEACHING PRACTICE

Connecting CT to Disciplinary Content

A key step in helping PSTs perceive CT as relevant to their teaching is demonstrating how it intersects with core disciplinary content. One influential framework mapping CT practices across subject areas was proposed by V. Barr and Stephenson (2011), offering valuable guidance for CT-focused teacher education initiatives. Yet, most of such efforts tend to focus on mathematics and sciences, due, in part, to the similarities between CT and the thinking practices in these fields (Rich et al., 2019). Furthermore, the initiatives integrating CT in these fields still seem to be limited. For instance, according to a review of studies examining the use of a visual programming tool (Zhang & Nouri, 2019), only 9% of the studies focused on mathematics and 4% dealt with science while the majority were about computer science only.

The limited number of studies may speak to the difficulties in applying CT in the disciplinary classroom context. To clarify the meaning of CT specific to mathematics and science, Weintrop et al. (2016) developed a taxonomy with four main categories — (1) Data Practices (e.g., collect, create, analyze), (2) Modeling and Simulation Practices (e.g., use, assess, design, and construct), (3) Computational Problem Solving Practices (e.g., abstracting and debugging), and (4) Systems Thinking Practices (e.g., understanding relationships within a system). Although the practices look distinct, they are not mutually exclusive, and the last two categories reflect rather a problem-solving process that can be engaged simultaneously with the practices. For instance, learners may analyze data (Data Practices) or construct models (Modeling and Simulation Practices) as they try solutions to a given problem (Computational Problem-Solving Practices) that may involve understanding the relationship among multiple factors (Systems Thinking Practices). Thus, differentiating (1) Data and (2)

Modeling and Simulation as CT practices from (3) Computational Problem Solving and (4) Systems Thinking as CT processes, which can be engaged via the practices, is a more accurate and simplified approach to classifying CT (See Figure 1).

Figure 1. Earlier and Proposed Classification of Computational Thinking

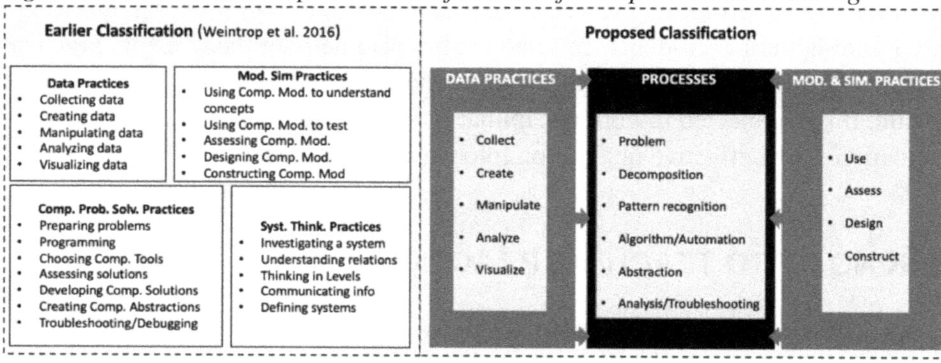

Connecting CT to Pedagogy

Beyond content integration, PSTs must also learn how CT aligns with effective pedagogical strategies. Teaching CT is not only about applying computational tools but also about adopting strategies such as inquiry-oriented methods that naturally elicit CT processes such as data collection, pattern recognition, and abstraction. Data practices, in particular, offer a powerful link between CT and inquiry-based learning. These practices are an essential component of CT, and engaging students in them (e.g., collect and analyze data) elicits their core CT processes (e.g., identify patterns) and supports the development of their empirical skills needed for solving CS problems (Braught et al., 2004). While algorithmic thinking and problem solving have been central to CT initiatives, the data involving such practices has been advocated to be its new pillar (Palop et al., 2025), reflecting the growing importance of understanding the data-driven nature of our societal activities. These practices are also a key aspect of inquiry-based pedagogy, which emphasizes problem-solving, discipline-specific reasoning and collaborative investigation (Hmelo-Silver et al., 2007) where students can use data to answer their questions, test their hypotheses, and explore patterns. Given that the data practices are at the intersection of these approaches (See Figure 2) and that inquiry-based pedagogy is high applicable to a wide-range of curricular subjects such as science, mathematics, and humanities (Aghazadeh, 2020; Blessinger & Carfora, 2014; Preston et al., 2015), perceiving

CT relevant to data practices can better help PSTs recognize its pedagogical connection to teaching.

Figure 2. Data Practices at the intersection of Inquiry-based Learning and Computational Thinking

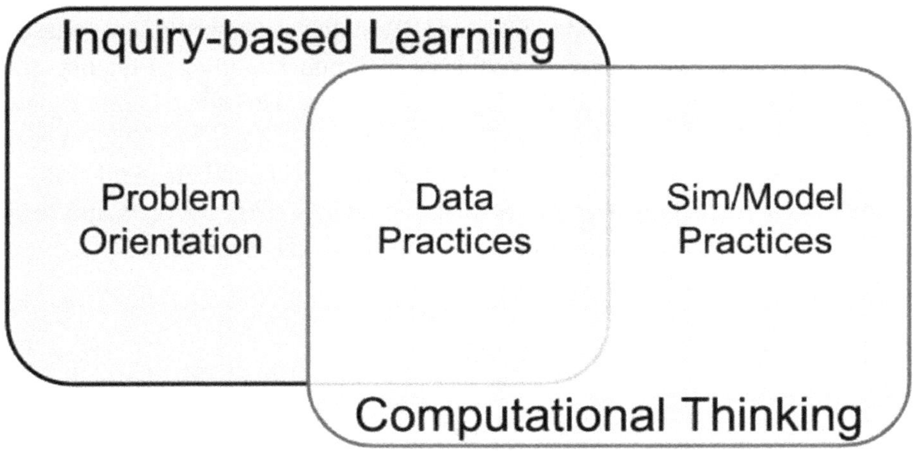

Seeing CT relevant to data practices can increase PSTs' motivation to use CT. As observed in our earlier studies (Kale & Wang, 2025), for instance, designing and teaching CT-infused lessons promoting data practices increased PSTs' interest, perception of CT's utility value to a significantly greater extent than teaching lessons with no emphasis on data.

Connecting to An Inquiry-Based Framework: The 5E Model

Among various inquiry-based approaches, the 5E model (Bybee, 2015), widely used and researched in teacher education (Kazempour et al., 2020), provides a particularly useful structure for embedding CT in teacher education. Its sequential phases, including Engage, Explore, Explain, Elaborate, and Evaluate, mirror the iterative, data-driven reasoning central to CT. The focus of the Engage phase is to promote learners' curiosity and interest in the topic while helping them make connections to what they already know about it. During the Explore phase, learners are given opportunities to design and conduct investigations about the topic while they are guided to explain and share their understanding from such experiences in the Explain phase. The focus of the Explain phase is not for teachers to provide the explanation, but rather to allow the learners to explain their observations. Learners also broaden their newly gained understanding by applying it onto new issues or aspects of the topic in the Elaborate phase. This phase may also resemble the Explore phase but differs in that learners build on and use their newly gained understanding to investigate a new aspect of the topic. During the Evaluation phase, which can occur concurrently with any previous phases, learners are engaged in self-evaluation while teachers monitor their progress and assess their understanding. As observed in our earlier studies (Kale et al., 2024), the 5E model structured PSTs' to lessons focusing on science, which may also enhance their understanding of inquiry-based instruction (Hanuscin & Lee, 2008). The 5E model has also been recently explored in connection with CT. For instance, a recent study (Fang et al., 2025) revealed that the model benefited elementary school students' CT mathematical skills. As an inquiry-based teaching framework that encourages data practices and fosters students' CT, the 5E model represents a strong fit for CT instruction.

DEVELOPING CT COMPETENCE

While connecting CT to both disciplinary content and pedagogy helps PSTs recognize its relevance to teaching, sustained engagement also depends on how competent they feel in applying it. Strengthening this sense of efficacy requires opportunities for meaningful, scaffolded, and motivating practice. Drawing on findings from our prior implementations of CT activities (Kale & Wang, 2025), this section presents two complementary approaches for supporting PSTs' CT competence:

(a) providing coding experiences with varying levels of difficulty, and
(b) incorporating immersive platforms, robotics, and personalized learning tasks.

Scaffolding Competence through Varying Levels of Difficulty

Our earlier research (Kale & Wang, 2025) revealed that PSTs' initial enthusiasm for CT can decline when activities feel overly complex or when they perceive their skills as insufficient. This pattern reflects a common motivational dynamic: individuals tend to disengage from tasks they expect to perform poorly on, even when they recognize their value (Eccles & Wigfield, 2002).

To counter this, in the context of PSTs learning CT via coding activities, simplified tasks may be useful. Working on easy coding tasks may contribute to their competence while it may also help maintain their initial interest and positive perception of CT's value and relevance. However, a simplified activity entailing easy coding may minimize the opportunities to be engaged in the Abstraction process – one the most important components of CT (Cetin & Dubinsky, 2017; Kramer, 2007; Wing,

2014) and essential to effective algorithms (Wing, 2014). Thus, a balanced strategy that involves both easy and difficult levels of coding may be necessary. Such an approach may start with easier activities during which the skills for basic coding tasks can be acquired, which then can support the development of advanced skills that are needed for more complex coding tasks at a later stage of the learning activity.

Enhancing Competence through Immersion, Robotics, and Personalization

Beyond scaffolding task complexity, competence can also be strengthened through learning environments that are immersive, interactive, and personally meaningful. Our observations of PSTs learning CT indicated that the use of Minecraft Education with its more immersive nature in 3D interface was conducive for PSTs to develop models and simulations than the use of Scratch in the course activities (Kale & Wang, 2025). Specifically, PSTs CT lessons promoted the practice of "Use Computational Models to Understand Concepts" to a greater extent when they practiced with Minecraft Education instead of Scratch. Likewise, robotics, which have been explored for CT (Ioannou & Makridou, 2018), can afford more tangible representations and the interactions of real physical objects, providing PSTs to a diversified and concrete practice opportunity with CT (Angeli & Valanides, 2020; Kazakoff et al., 2013).

More specifically, immersive embodied learning experiences that engage students in bodily movements—such as navigating physical or virtual grids, performing programmed actions, or gesturing to express sequences—have been shown to significantly enhance conceptual understanding and problem-solving in computational thinking (CT) education (Kwon et al., 2024, 2025). By mapping CT concepts like sequencing and loops onto physical actions, students not only gain deeper comprehension but also improve their ability to transfer knowledge to new modalities such as robot programming tasks (Kwon et al., 2024). Studies also indicate that embodied interactions help reduce cognitive load, foster spatial reasoning, and support the development of abstract thinking through concrete sensorimotor experiences, especially in early elementary learners (Kwon et al., 2025).

Lastly, the degree to which a given coding task can be personalized and offer autonomy may impact motivation and competence. While predetermined tasks allowed PSTs to practice various coding concepts such as loops, conditionals, events, and variables, such tasks did not cultivate the level of ownership (Kale & Wang, 2025), which may be necessary to active and creative learning experiences (Cocieru et al., 2021; Crook, 2009; Gonzalez-Maldonado et al., 2022). Creating open-ended and free-choice programming tasks, in fact, has been observed to promote creativity and engagement, which can consequently lead to quality artifacts and development of CT concepts (Grover et al., 2018). Thus, providing PSTs with more personalized coding tasks where they can choose, plan, draw, and develop their own projects with varying levels of coding difficulties and engaging them in immersive platforms and robotics will be critical elements of opportunities supporting their competence with CT. By combining immersive, embodied, and personalized learning experiences with scaffolding across different levels of task difficulty, teacher education programs can create powerful environments that cultivate both competence and confidence in CT.

PUTTING IT ALTOGETHER: AN INQUIRY-BASED CT

To bring together the ideas discussed so far, this section illustrates how an inquiry-based CT pedagogy can be implemented through a sequence of interconnected learning units. The example focuses on the theme of food growth and sustainability, which is considered an approach to increase food scarcity, a worldwide issue, providing a rich inquiry allowing for data practices. It starts with a description of a seed germination experiment followed by the use and design of a 2D simulation via Scratch that will mimic the observed outcomes of the experiment while also describing the impact of pollination and its simulation. Next will be another simulation but in a 3D modality via Minecraft Education and MakeCode where the seed planting and pollination will also be modeled. Finally via a robotic system (MatataLab Coding and Vincibot), similar tasks will be completed including planting and pollination. The graphical representations including the figures and tables are original works generated by the authors in order to exemplify and illustrate the activities and to clarify the concepts and explanations provided in the text.

Seed Germination Experiment

Temporal, spatial, and socio-economic factors act as barriers to obtaining adequate and nutritional food (Wilson et al., 2018). Community gardens and active participation in gardening have been considered one of the means to increase local food production (Furness & Gallaher, 2018). An example learning activity that can be designed and taught by PSTs focuses on engaging students in using basic gardening techniques and employing inquiry skills with the following guiding questions: “We cannot harvest cucumbers in our region until early Summer. Can we germinate the seeds earlier in our classroom? What will be the most ideal condition to germinate them when considering the heat, light, and kinds of seeds?” Having discussed the guiding questions, students are guided to work in four groups to sow cucumber seeds in a hydrated putting mix inside plug trays, each of which has 36 cells. To examine the impact of heat and light on germination rates, each group’s tray has a different set up representing one of 4 possible variations—Group 1: The tray has no heat mat and is exposed to normal daylight during the day (NH and NL), Group 2: The tray has no heat mat (NH) but is exposed an extra light source (YL)- an LED grow light placed over it, Group 3: The tray is placed on a heat mat (YH) and is exposed to normal daylight (NL), and Group 4: The tray is placed on a heat mat (YH) and is exposed an extra light source (YL)- an LED grow light placed over it. To determine the germination rates, groups observe the trays everyday for a week, count the total number of seeds that have germinated, and compare them for identifying any patterns associated with each group (See figure 3).

Figure 3. Seeds Germinating in Four Conditions

A more challenging level of this activity would guide students to use the total number of seeds that germinated, then to key them in Excel or GoogleSheet to construct scatter plots and trendlines with the right function displaying the number of seeds that germinated each day. They compare the scatter plots side by side and discuss the differences of each condition. The PST helps students generate one graph displaying the trendlines for comparisons while an equation representing the relationship between the day and percentages is also added (See Figure 4).

Figure 4. Trendline Regarding Total Number of Seeds Germinated by a Given Day in Each Condition

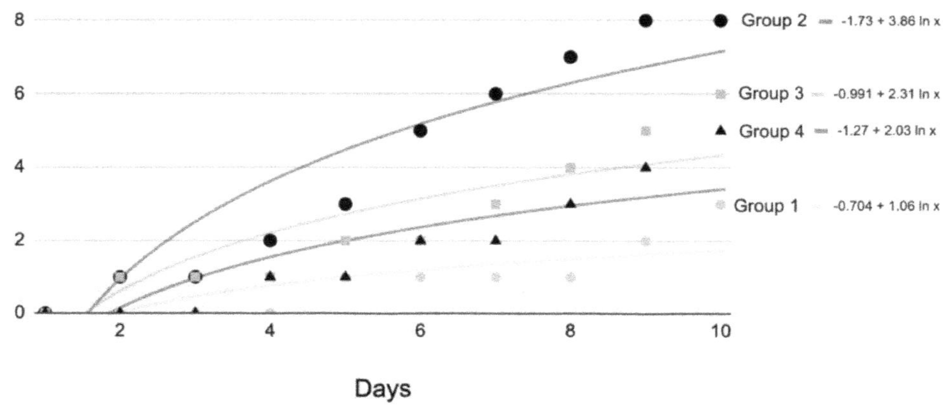

Then, the PST guides students regarding how to use the equation to predict the outcome for a given day beyond the observation period. Table 2 below outlines the tasks, inquiry stages, CT practices & processes engaged.

Table 2. Learning Tasks, Inquiry Stage, and CT Practices / Processes Engaged in Investigation

Dif. Level	**Task**	**Inquiry**		**Computational Thinking**	
	Planting	5E Stages	Data Practice	Sim/Mod Practice	Process
Low	Carry out investigation on conditions impacting germination and identify patterns within the observation period	-Engage -Explore -Explain	-Collect data -Analyze data		-Pattern Recog.
High	Carry out investigation on conditions impacting germination and predict trends beyond the observation period	-Engage -Explore -Explain -Elaborate	-Collect data -Analyze data -Generate data	-Design Models	-Pattern Recog. -Abstraction

2D Simulation

Planting. Having carefully analyzed the graphs, compared the equations, and discussed how each factor may have played a role in germination, students are prompted to develop a simulation in Scratch with the focus of helping potential "future gardeners" decide the optimal conditions for germinating cucumber seeds. The simulation would allow the users to make choices regarding absence or presence of heat maps and grow lights as well as the day of the observation. This is followed by an image of a plug tray whose certain number of cells turn green (representing germination) for the selected day. For this, students create conditionals specifying the number of cells turning green based on the observed number of seeds (See Figure 5).

Figure 5. Scratch Simulation of Observed Findings in Scratch

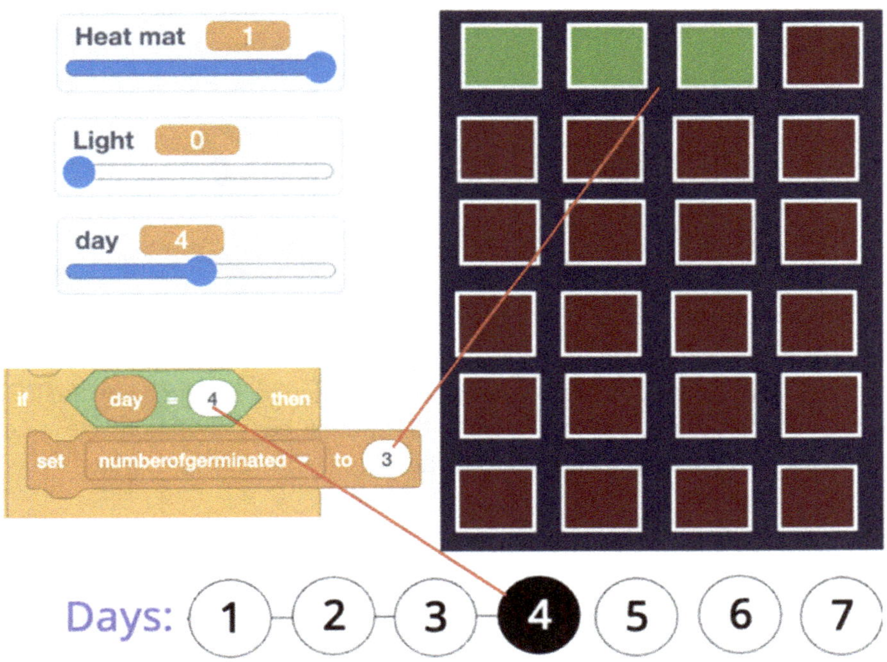

A more challenging level of this activity would build on the trendlines and the equations generated based on the earlier investigation results. The PST would guide students to code these equations in simulation that will match the user's choices of any given day, which will be used to determine and display the percentage of the tray that would need to be colored.

Pollination. A variation or a follow up activity on seed germination, related to food access, may include pollination. Worldwide, animal pollinators are needed for approximately 35% of the food crops to reproduce, which represents "one out of every three bites we eat" (U.S. Department of Agriculture, n.d.a), and play a vital role in the quantity and quality of crop yields impacting food security (Khalifa et al., 2021). After a brief introduction on bees as pollinators and their role in pollination, data from the U.S. Department of Agriculture (USDA) (n.d.b) can be presented to show varying numbers of bee populations over time with a prompting question- "*How may bee populations impact crop yields?*" Visualized datasets based on the findings of a study (Wood et al., n.d.), which would include the size of bee colonies in two farms and their respective crop yields are presented to help students discuss, predict, even visualize the crop yields changing over time in the state of Indiana (IN) as an example (see Figure 6).

Figure 6. Size of a Bee Colony in a Period of Time and Prompt for Crop Yields

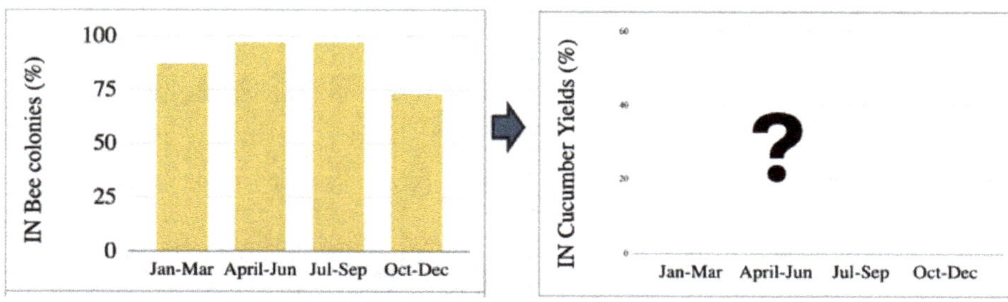

Students, then, are guided to run a simplified simulation developed by the PST, displaying cucumber yields in two farms with different bee population sizes (e.g., Farm A-dense and Farm B-sparse) (See Figure 7).

Figure 7. Scratch Simulation of Cucumber Crops in Two Farms with Different Size of Bee Colonies

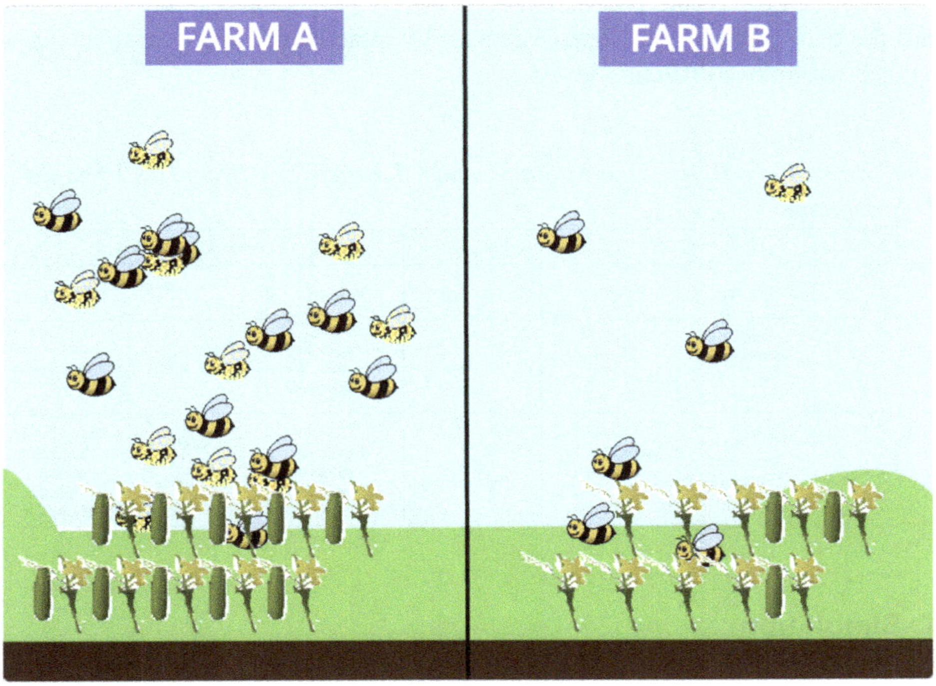

Each plant yields a cucumber when it is touched by a bee as long as the bee has acquired "pollens" initially from another plant's flower. Bees randomly move around in their designated farm until a certain time, after which the total yields in each area will be counted for comparison. Students are asked to run the simulation multiple times and note the total number of cucumbers each time. They discuss the relationship between the number of bees and the yields in each area, and compare it to the dataset presented earlier.

A more challenging level of this activity starts with the discussion of discrepancies between the results of the simulation and the observed outcomes of the presented study, and how the simulation can be modified to produce results similar to the actual outcomes. The PST introduces a few factors such as parasites, pesticides, or even the number of pollinator visitors needed per flower. A visual based on the data set from USDA (n.d.b) can also display the percentages of bee colonies impacted by various such stressors over time. Students can be guided to work in groups to focus on one factor of their choice and to take it into account in modifying the existing simulation. The activity takes a few days (or a week depending on the needs to facilitate their exploration of the factor and coding the project). In the end, students share their projects, carefully analyze the simulations, and develop a consolidated plan for strategies to help pollination and increase crop yields. Table 3 below outlines the two learning tasks, inquiry stages, CT practices & processes that can be engaged within two difficulty levels.

Table 3. Learning Tasks, Inquiry Stage, and CT Practices / Processes Engaged in 2D-Simulation

Dif. Level	Task		Inquiry	Computational Thinking		
	Planting	Pollination	5E Stages	Data Practice	Sim/Mod Practice	Process
Low	Simulation of germinated seeds for observed days	Simulation of crops in two areas with bee population	-Explain	-Analyze data -Visualize data -Generate data	-Assess models	-Pattern Recog.
High	Simulation of germinated seeds for <u>any given</u> day	Simulation of crops based on <u>a given factor impacting pollination</u>	-Explain <u>-Elaborate</u>	-Analyze data -Visualize data -<u>Generate data</u>	-Assess Models -<u>Design Models</u> <u>-Construct Models</u>	-Pattern Recog. <u>-Debug/T.shoot</u> <u>-Algorithm/ Auto.</u> <u>-Abstraction</u>

3D Simulation

Planting. Small scale farming is also critical to healthy food access (Blackwell, 2016). Yet, sustainability of food from such sources is challenging given the difficulty of farming. To make farming feasible, agricultural robots have been explored as they can automate various dull tasks such as picking, harvesting, weeding, or monitoring for farmers (Dao, 2020; Robotics Online Marketing Team, 2017). While experimenting with such robots may not be feasible due to their high cost, platforms such as Minecraft have been explored to model a variety of robotics tasks (Aluru et al., 2015). An example learning activity can focus on programming an autonomous agent in a Minecraft farm with the following question: "*A large number of cucumber seeds need be planted in a family-owned farm but it takes a lot of work for the family to prepare the soil and plant the seeds. Can we automate these tasks such that they are more efficiently completed for a specified planting area layout as well as for any given planting layout*? Having discussed the questions, students work in groups, tasked with automating the preparation of soil and planting in a block-layout. They use Code Builder to make the agent execute simple tasks such as tilling and placing seeds in each block in front of the agent, move it forward, turn left or right until each available block is taken care of. Each group displays their farm world and explains their algorithms (See Figure 8). They compare their algorithms and discuss why some may have resulted in faster task completions.

Figure 8. Minecraft Simulation of Tilling and Planting

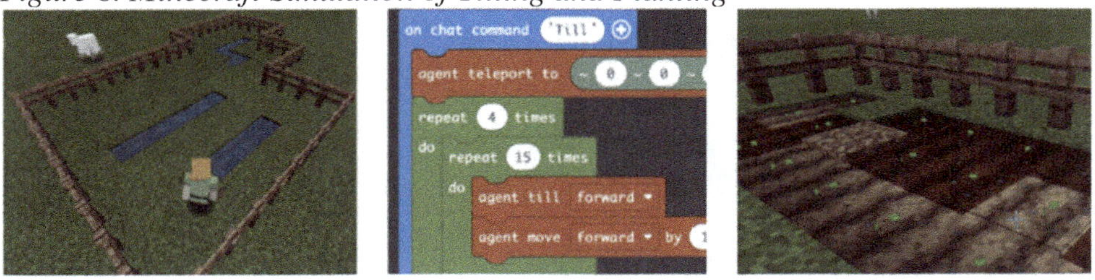

A more difficult activity building on the discussions prompts students to think about how to till the blocks and place the seeds for any given layout. How can we program the agent such that it would complete the same tasks without knowing the exact layout of a given field? The PST then shares with each group the link of Minecraft worlds that she previously created including a distinctly shaped planting area with borders made of fence blocks and a few rows of water. Students import the given worlds via the link and are tasked with generating a set of codes that can work for the given area. For this, students would first code a function that makes the agent move forward and plant a seed in each block in front (until a fence is reached), use a different code to make the agent turn left or right randomly until no fence is in front, and use the same function recursively.

Pollination. A variation activity in Minecraft Education may include pollination as well. Similar to the use of 2D Scratch, the PST can use USDA data on bee population over time and ask the following question to prompt the students – "*How may bee populations impact crop yields?*" Likewise, visualized datasets based on the findings of a study can be used to help students discuss, predict, even visualize the crop yields changing over time. This time, however, students can be guided to play with an existing Minecraft Education World that the PST develops earlier. With a given command, also developed earlier, they can see how a given area is tilled and planted while bees spawn and beehives are placed around. They are asked to navigate around the field, observe the bees, the pollen falling from them, and the crops growing in the next five minutes (see Figure 9).

Figure 9. Minecraft Simulation of Bee Pollinating Crops

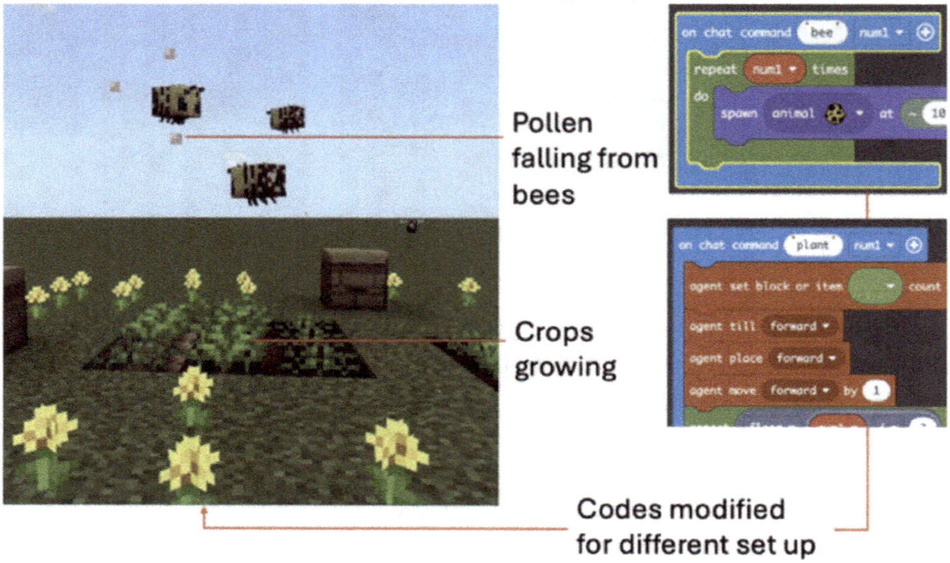

The next 15 minutes, students are guided to modify the coding such that it will provide a different set-up including the amount of bees spawn, the size of the tilled and planted area, the number of beehives. They discuss their observations and the impact of bees on crops.

A more challenging activity introduces additional factors impacting pollination such as the optimum number of hives for a given field size. While more bees may sound desirable, the excessive number of hives in a given area may lead to the starvation of the bees, negatively impacting pollination (Woodcock, 2012). Students are guided to test different algorithms that automate the number of bees spawn in relation to the size of the planted areaand observe which one may lead to a higher number of fully grown crops. In the end, they discuss the observed bee-crop relation with the earlier data set. Table 4 outlines the tasks, CT practices, and processes engaged within the 5E model.

Table 4. Learning Tasks, Inquiry Stage, and CT Practices / Processes Engaged in 3D-Simulation

Dif. Level	Task		Inquiry	Computational Thinking		
	Planting	Pollination	5E Stages	Data Practice	Sim/Mod Practice	Process
Low	Automation of planting & tilling in a predetermined virtual space	Modifying the automation of spawning a number of bees and placement of hives, and observe crops growth	-Explain	-Generate data	-Design Models -Construct Models	-Pattern Recog. -Debug/T.shoot -Algorithm/ Auto.
High	Automation of planting & tilling for any given virtual space	Automation in relation to the recommended bee population for the size of an area, and observe crops growth	-Explain -Elaborate	-Generate data -Analyze data	-Design Models -Construct Models -Assess Models	-Pattern Recog. -Debug/T.shoot -Algorithm/ Auto. -Abstraction

Robotics

Planting. Although the 3D simulations are useful to demonstrate the farming tasks, they may not be able to fully provide the concrete representations and the interactions of real physical objects. Robotics, which have been explored to promote computational thinking (Ioannou & Makridou, 2018), can provide more tangible experiences. Similar to the 3D simulation via Minecraft Education, the PST can help their students focus on the automation of farming tasks via affordable educational robotic tools such as Vincibot. In this activity, students, working in groups, would use MatataLab Coding to move VinciBot in a 4 X 6 square blocks-layout and make shaking actions to indicate tilling and planting in each "block" (*low difficulty*). A more challenging activity (*high difficulty*) focuses on avoiding objects in random locations of the same layout while continuing to till and plant in the same layout. Students also compare the efficiency of their algorithms regarding handling the obstacles placed (See Figure 10).

Figure 10. Robotic Simulation of Tilling and Planting while Avoiding a Random Object

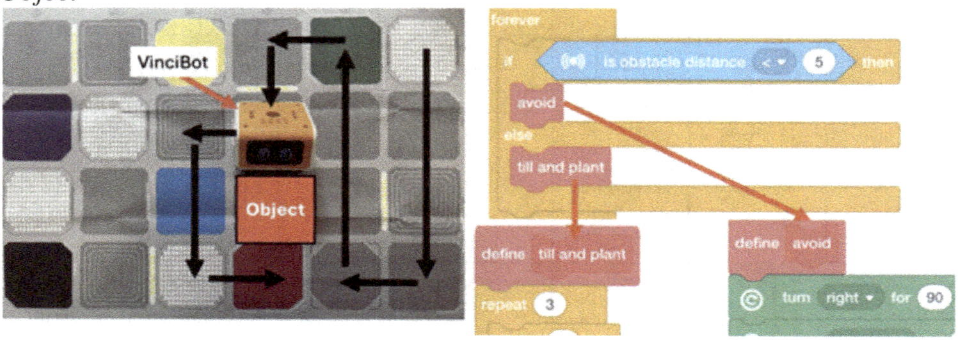

Pollination. A variation activity with the Vincibot may also focus on pollination. Like in the 3D simulation, the PST can introduce the importance of pollination regarding crop yield. An easier version of the activity (*low difficulty*) may first entail using simple art supplies to dress the Vincibot as a bee then using MatataLab Coding to make it move around to seek flowers (of crops) in the layout to simulate the pollination (e.g., "bee" collecting the pollens first time it touches a "flower" and continue to move around until finding another one to "transfer" the pollens to). A more challenging version of this activity (*high difficulty*) introduces and takes into account factors on pollination such as parasites (See Figure 11).

Figure 11. Robotic Simulation of Pollinating in Presence of Parasites

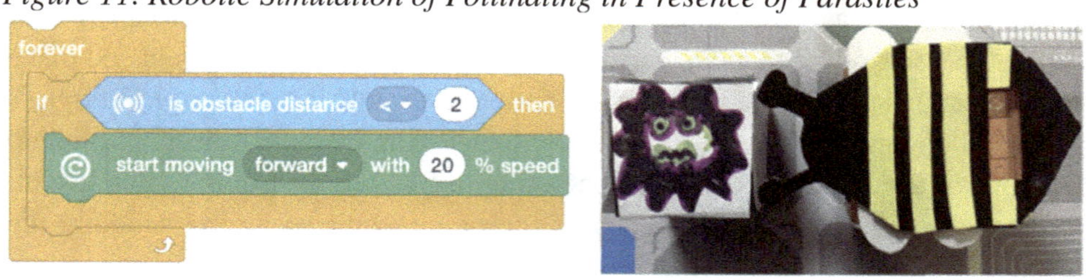

The students code not only to move Vincibot but also to variate its speed to simulate impaired foraging whenever it is "exposed" to a random block affected by a "parasite". They compare the efficiency of their algorithms regarding how the "bee" behaves and pollinates in relation to the "exposure". Table 5 below outlines the tasks, CT practices & processes that can be engaged within the 5E model.

Table 5. Learning Tasks, Inquiry Stage, and CT Practices / Processes Engaged in Robotics Simulation

Dif.	Task		Inquiry		Computational Thinking	
	Planting	Pollination	5E Stages	Data Practice	Sim/Mod Practice	Process
Low	Robot simulating planting & tilling in a physical space	Robot moving as bees pollinating "crops" located in predetermined physical space	-Explain	-Collect data -Analyze data	-Design Models -Construct Models	-Pattern Recog. -Debug/T.shoot -Algorithm/Auto.
High	Robot simulating planting & tilling in the same physical space and avoiding obstacles placed in random locations	Robot moving as bees pollinating "crops" located randomly and being slowed down when exposed to "pesticides" randomly	-Explain -Elaborate	-Collect data -Analyze data	-Design Models -Construct Models -Assess Models	-Pattern Recog. -Debug/T.shoot -Algorithm/Auto. -Abstraction

AI Extension

While the exemplified learning units in the previous section provide both a difficult and easy variation of the tasks, this section elaborates the use of the robotic system (MatataLab Coding and Vincibo) by presenting how machine learning, crucial to AI systems, can be promoted. Specifically, the section describes how the robotic system can be trained via its vision feature, focusing on identifying objects in its route and coding the robot to simulate various tasks.

After introducing the role of AIs in everyday lives (e.g., voice assistants such as Alexa or Siri), the PST can prompt the students about how AI systems "think" and "decide" like human beings or other living organisms. To relate this topic to the farming or pollination tasks discussed so far, questions such as "can a robot identify crops to harvest and weeds to avoid in a farm?" or "can we code a robot (dress as a bee) such that it can identify a flower to pollinate or weeds to avoid?" can be asked. Having discussed students' answers, the PST can highlight the need for training the robot to distinguish different objects (flowers versus weeds) and for informing robots' consequent decisions and actions accordingly.

The use of Vincibot and its training can then be demonstrated. This can start with the image modeling in the coding platform, which would require creating categories of images (e.g., weed versus flowers) and uploading the relevant image files from the computer or directly capturing from the vision kit attached on top of the robot (See Figure 12).

Figure 12. Adding Images Categorized to Prepare AI Training

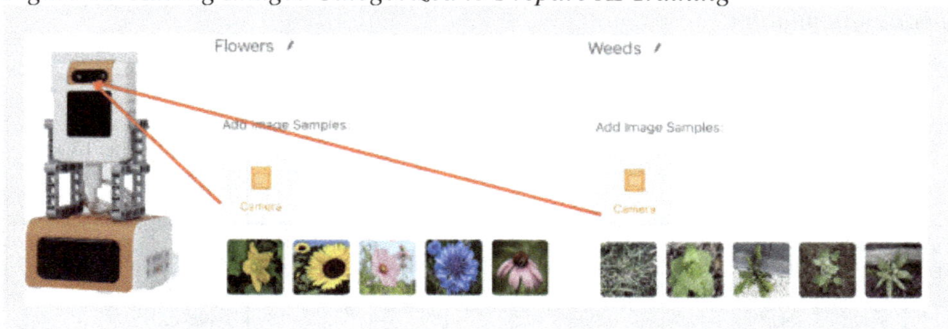

Next is the training of the model with various parameters. This produces an outcome regarding the accuracy of a prediction based on the uploaded images. Adding further images would likely improve the prediction accuracy, which the students could be prompted to try.

Once the trained model is deployed, the coding can be completed, which would make the "bee" avoid the weeds and pollinate the flowers when it detects an image via its vision kit. Students can be promoted to come up with the bees' behaviours of pollination or avoidance, and compare and justify their algorithms. Table 6 below outlines the tasks, CT practices & processes that can be engaged within the 5E model.

Table 6. Learning Tasks, Inquiry Stage, and CT Practices / Processes Engaged in Robotics Simulation

Dif. Level	**Task**	**Inquiry**		**Computational Thinking**	
	Pollination	5E Stages	Data Practice	Sim/Mod Practice	Process
High	Robot moving as a bee pollinating if the object detected is categorized as "flowers" and avoiding it if it is categorized as weeds	-Explain -Elaborate	-Create data -Collect data -Analyze data	-Design Models -Construct Models -Assess Models	-Pattern Recog. -Debug/T. shoot -Algorithm/ Auto. -Abstraction

ACTIVITIES IN A TEACHER EDUCATION COURSE

This section describes a suggested timeline of the previously mentioned learning units for a teacher education course (e.g., a method course) where PSTs can gradually develop their competence, increase their interest and recognize the value of CT in teaching. It is written based on a semester-long schedule with two sessions per week. The week numbers suggest that the activities start in the first week but these can be modified as needed. Further, depending on PSTs' current experiences with coding, the instructor may choose to cover the activities with low difficulty or high difficulty. Below is the schedule of the activities to be implemented (Figure 13) and their descriptions for the relevant weeks.

Figure 13. Suggested Timeline of Activities

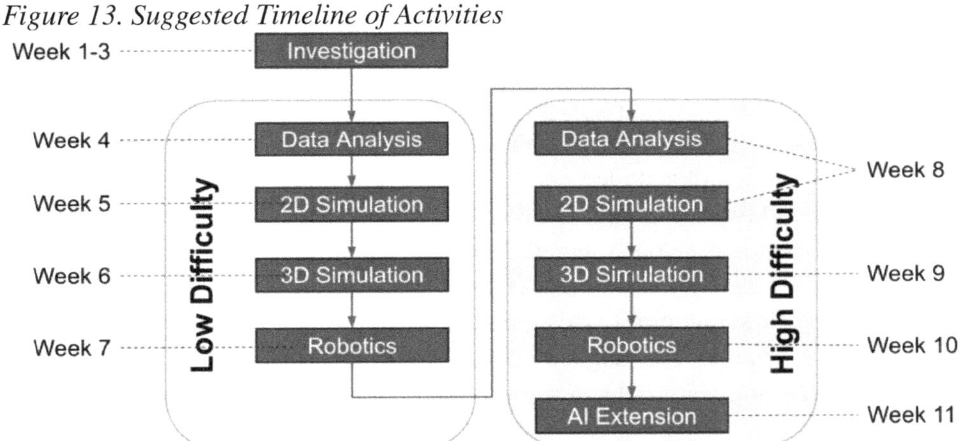

Week 1, 2, 3: Launch the Investigation

During the first session, the teacher education instructor introduces the inquiry-based learning approach focusing on the 5E model and provides Garden-based Learning (GBL) as its one specific form promoting data practices essential to students' CT regarding the issue of food access. Examples of GBL projects in public schools and relevant readings would have been shared with the PSTs prior to the session, and are reviewed and discussed in class. The remaining part of the session mainly focuses on the kind of data that K12 students can collect and analyze on the germination process (e.g., bar graphs regarding the number of seeds germinating). In the second session, the focus is to launch an investigation that PSTs can conduct. PSTs, split in four groups, are provided the equipment (e.g, trays, heat mats, lights, soil, and cucumber seeds seeds) work on setting up four conditions to examine how they impact the germination rates considering the levels of heat and light. They work in groups to plan what data they need to collect on daily bases for the next two weeks and how to analyze them in the end.

Week 4: Analyze the Result (Low Difficulty)

After two weeks, PSTs collect the data on the number of seeds that have by each day in their assigned condition. Either in the first or in the second session of the week, a guided discussion that prompts PSTs to compare the results per day focuses on identifying any patterns associated with each condition.

Week 5: 2D Simulation (Low Difficulty)

In the first session of this week, the instructor displays and runs a completed (Scratch) simulation that allows users to control multiple conditions discussed and to see their effects on the germination process. PSTs are given the link of the same simulation but without the codes, and be asked to develop their codes such that the simulation would function similar to the one the instructors displayed (prior to the session, PSTs would have been shared flashcards teaching basic coding in Scratch). PSTs are encouraged to share their codings and together discuss how to revise them for the desired outcomes. This guided practice is followed by the instructor's presentation explaining the original codings for comparison purposes. An online module fully demonstrating the development of the simulation can be shared with PSTs after the session. The session ends with PSTs being given an assignment to design their own simulations of any GBL activity of their choice before the second session of the week. Specifically, PSTs are to draw a sketch of the simulation on paper, develop a draft interface in Scratch, and a description of a learning activity that the simulation could be used for. They bring their assignments to the second session where they share their ideas with their peers, are guided by the instructor, and continue to develop their personal simulations.

Week 6, 7: 3D Simulation and Robotics (Low Difficulty)

Moving into the sustainability of food and automation of farming tasks, PSTs have similar practice opportunities with coding but this time by using 3D simulation (Minecraft Education) during week 6 and a robotics task during week 7 with low difficulty levels (both growth and pollination themes). Similar to week 5, the activities involve (a) guided practice opportunities to generate the displayed simulation and the robotic task in the first session, (b) an online module for the full demonstration of the simulation and robotic task, (c) an assignment for designing own personal simulations after the session, and (d) sharing and the full development of their personal simulation and the robotic task in the second session.

Week 8, 9, 10, 11: Analysis, 2D-3D Simulation, Robotics, and AI Extension (High Difficulty)

The activities in each of the next four weeks have the same structure – session 1 for guided practice, online module and assignment for designing own simulation after session 1, and session 2 for sharing and continuing to develop the projects. This time, however, the high difficulty levels of the growth and pollination themes are covered. The focus is on analysis of data and 2D simulation in Week 8, 3D simulation Week 9, robotics in Week 10 and AI extension in Week 11.

Assessing PST's CT Development

Building on the implementation activities described above, effective assessment can play a key role in evaluating both PSTs' learning progress and the impact of inquiry-based CT instruction. Assessment in this context can focus on two complementary areas: (1) PSTs' perceptions of CT and (2) their ability to design CT-integrated lessons. Together, these dimensions provide insight into not only what PSTs can do with CT, but also how they value and internalize it as future educators.

Regarding perceptions, various instruments can be employed, drawing on the expectancy-value theory. Table 7 presents the concepts and brief descriptions as well as example measurement items used in our previous studies all of which demonstrated high reliability (see Kale & Wang 2025 for reliability scores).

Table 7. Measurements Scale, Description

Broader Concepts	Specific Concepts measured	Brief description and a sample survey item
Expectancy of Success	Competence	Skills to use CT techniques in teaching: *"I feel comfortable teaching computational thinking"*
Subjective Task Values	Utility Value	Degree to which CT tasks are perceived as relevant for teaching or aspects of an individual's life: *"Using computational thinking is relevant to my future teaching"*
	Triggered Interest	Interest in CT triggered / sparked by initial perceptions or factors: *"I think computational thinking is very interesting"*
	Maintained Interest	A more focused and persistent psychological state of interest in CT due to learning. *"My experience in this class makes me want to use computational thinking in my future teaching"*
	Personal Interest	A well-developed individual interest in CT due to increased knowledge and perceived value of it: *"It is personally important to me that I teach computational thinking"*
Achievement Performance	Usage of CT	Use of CT techniques in daily life and teaching: *"I use computational thinking techniques in my teaching efforts"*

For the lesson design aspect, PSTs can be prompted to create a lesson of their choice that reflects the ideas and understandings gained from the sessions. The various components of CT, along with corresponding rubric criteria (see Table 8), can guide their designs. These criteria are based on the proposed classification of CT illustrated earlier in Figure 1.

Table 8. CT Components with Rubric Criteria

CT	Components	Criteria		
		Not acceptable	Acceptable	Exemplary
Data Practices	● Collecting data ● Creating data ● Manipulating data ● Analyzing data ● Visualizing data	No CT practices are present	Students engage in at least one CT practice	Students engage in at least one Data practice and one Modeling & Simulation practice
Simulation & Modeling Practices	● Using com. models to unders. concepts/ find/test solutions ● Assessing com. models ● Designing comp. models ● Construct. com. models			

continued on following page

Table 8. Continued

CT	Components		Criteria		
Processes	● Confrontation ● Decomposition ● Pattern recognition ● Abstraction ● Algorithm/Automation ● Test/Debug		No activities present to engage students in any of CT processes	Students decompose a given problem and identify patterns	Students develop algorithms for automation, generate a generic solution (abstraction), or debug in their coding
Concepts	Basics ● Sequences ● Loops ● Events ● Parallelism	Advanced ● Conditionals ● Operators ● Data	No activities present to engage students in any CT concepts	Students engage in at least one of the basic CT concepts	Students engage in at least one of the advanced CT concepts

A reflective element piece can also be included in the assessment. PSTs may be asked to respond to prompts focusing on CT components, such as:

1. What CT processes would students engage in during this lesson? At what points in the lesson would these processes occur?
2. What CT practices would students engage in? When in the lesson would these practices take place?
3. What CT concepts would students develop an understanding of through the activities?

Collectively, these assessments, spanning perceptions, performance, and reflection, offer a comprehensive understanding of PSTs' growth in both the motivation and application of CT.

CONCLUSION

This chapter has sought to address a critical gap in CT and teacher-education research: the limited attention to PSTs' motivational development and pedagogical readiness to teach CT. While prior studies have described CT's cognitive dimensions and disciplinary applications (Brennan & Resnick, 2012; Weintrop et al., 2016; Yadav et al., 2017), explicitly connections between CT instruction and a motivational theory as well as inquiry-based frameworks such as the 5E model that naturally elicit CT processes through data practices are yet to exist. By integrating these orientations, the chapter extends existing frameworks in three key ways.

First, it advances a motivation-centered conceptualization of CT in teacher education, emphasizing the interplay of competence, interest, and utility value in shaping

PST engagement. Second, it demonstrates how inquiry-based learning structures can translate CT principles into practice through 2D, 3D, robotics, and AI-enhanced activities. Third, it provides a scaffolded implementation model that connects theory to curriculum design, offering a practical pathway for teacher educators to embed CT in methods courses. Ultimately, the inquiry-based CT framework proposed here contributes to a more holistic understanding of CT in teacher preparation, which unites cognitive, pedagogical, and motivational dimensions. By situating CT within both the expectancy–value theoretical orientation and inquiry-based pedagogy, this chapter not only addresses a gap in current literature but also offers a replicable model for cultivating PSTs who are motivated, competent, and prepared to nurture computationally literate, future-ready learners.

REFERENCES

Adler, R. F., Hibdon, J., Kim, H., Mayle, S., Pines, B., & Srinivas, S. (2023). Assessing computational thinking across a STEM curriculum for pre-service teachers. *Education and Information Technologies*, *28*(7), 8051–8073. DOI: 10.1007/s10639-022-11508-4

Aghasaleh, R., Enderle, P., & Puvirajah, A. (2019). From Computational Thinking to Political Resistance. *Journal for Activist Science and Technology Education*, *10*(1), 29–44. DOI: 10.33137/jaste.v10i1.32915

Aghazadeh, S. (2020). *Inquiry-based Learning and its Impact on Teaching and Learning of the Humanities. (NIE Working Paper Series No. 19)*. National Institute of Education., https://repository.nie.edu.sg/server/api/core/bitstreams/47e655d5-20f5-4bb0-af80-a8a9c6212179/content

Aluru, K. C., Tellex, S., Oberlin, J. G., & MacGlashan, J. (2015). Minecraft as an experimental world for AI in robotics. *AAAI Fall Symposia,* Retrieved from https://h2r1.cs.brown.edu/wp-content/uploads/2015/09/aluru15.pdf

Angeli, C., & Valanides, N. (2020). Developing young children's computational thinking with educational robotics: An interaction effect between gender and scaffolding strategy. *Computers in Human Behavior*, *105*, 105954. DOI: 10.1016/j.chb.2019.03.018

Barr, D., Harrison, J., & Conery, L. (2011). Computational thinking: A digital age skill for everyone. *Learning and Leading with Technology*, *38*(6), 20–23.

Barr, V., & Stephenson, C. (2011). Bringing computational thinking to K-12: What is Involved and what is the role of the computer science education community? *ACM Inroads*, *2*(1), 48–54. DOI: 10.1145/1929887.1929905

Blackwell, A. (2016). Best practices for creating a sustainable and equitable food system in the United States. Center for American Progress. Retrieved from https://www.americanprogress.org/issues/poverty/reports/2016/05/12/137306/best-practices-for-creating-a-sustainable-and-equitable-food-system-in-the-united-states/

Blessinger, P., & Carfora, J. M. (2014). Innovative approaches in teaching and learning: An introduction to inquiry-based learning for the arts, humanities, and social sciences. In *Inquiry-based learning for the arts, humanities, and social sciences: A conceptual and practical resource for educators* (Vol. 2, pp. 3–25). Emerald Group Publishing Limited. DOI: 10.1108/S2055-364120140000002030

Bocconi, S., Chioccariello, A., Dettori, G., Ferrari, A., Engelhardt, K., Kampylis, P., & Punie, Y. (2016). Exploring the field of computational thinking as a 21st century skill. In *EDULEARN16 Proceedings* (pp. 4725-4733). IATED.

Braught, G., Miller, C. S., & Reed, D. (2004). Core empirical concepts and skills for computer science. *SIGCSE Bulletin, 36*(1), 245–249. DOI: 10.1145/1028174.971388

Brennan, K., & Resnick, M. (2012, April). New frameworks for studying and assessing the development of computational thinking. In *Proceedings of the 2012 annual meeting of the American educational research association,* Vancouver, Canada (Vol. 1, p. 25).

Breslyn, W., & McGinnis, J. R. (2019). Investigating preservice elementary science teachers' understanding of climate change from a computational thinking systems perspective.

Brophy, J. (2008). Developing students' appreciation for what is taught in school. *Educational Psychologist, 43*(3), 132–141. DOI: 10.1080/00461520701756511

Brophy, J. (2010). *Motivating students to learn* (3rd ed.). Routledge.

Bybee, R. (2015). *The BSCS 5E instructional model: Creating teachable moments.* NSTA Press.

Cetin, I., & Dubinsky, E. (2017). Reflective abstraction in computational thinking. *The Journal of Mathematical Behavior, 47*, 70–80. DOI: 10.1016/j.jmathb.2017.06.004

Cocieru, O. C., Lyle, M. C., & McDonald, M. A. (2021). An exploration of the dynamic nature of psychological ownership in a classroom-as-organization. *Journal of Experiential Education, 44*(3), 293–307. DOI: 10.1177/1053825920973704

Code.org, CSTA, ECEP Alliance. (2024). 2024 State of Computer Science Education. Retrieved from https://advocacy.code.org/stateofcs

Crook, S. (2009). Embedding Scratch in the Classroom. *International Journal of Learning and Media, 1*(4), 17–21. DOI: 10.1162/ijlm_a_00035

Dao, E. (2020). This professor wanted to make farming more sustainable, so he started a company to build a fleet of smart robot. *theRising*, May 2020, Retrieved from https://therising.co/2020/05/18/earthsense-robots-farming-more-sustainable/

Dohn, N. B., Kafai, Y., Mørch, A., & Ragni, M. (2022). Survey: Artificial intelligence, computational thinking and learning. *Kunstliche Intelligenz, 36*(1), 5–16. DOI: 10.1007/s13218-021-00751-5

Domingos, P. (2015). *The master algorithm: How the quest for the ultimate learning machine will remake our world*. Basic Books.

Dong, W., Li, Y., Sun, L., & Liu, Y. (2024). Developing pre-service teachers' computational thinking: A systematic literature review. *International Journal of Technology and Design Education, 34*(1), 191–227. DOI: 10.1007/s10798-023-09811-3 PMID: 36816094

Eccles, J. S., & Wigfield, A. (2002). Motivational beliefs, values, and goals. *Annual Review of Psychology, 53*(1), 109–132. DOI: 10.1146/annurev.psych.53.100901.135153 PMID: 11752481

Fang, X., Ng, D. T. K., Tam, W. T., & Yuen, M. (2025). Design mobile computational thinking-integrated mathematics lessons based on the 5E instructional model for primary students. *Educational Technology Research and Development*, *73*(4), 1–30. DOI: 10.1007/s11423-025-10513-x

Furness, W. W., & Gallaher, C. M. (2018). Food access, food security and community gardens in Rockford, IL. *Local Environment*, *23*(4), 414–430. DOI: 10.1080/13549839.2018.1426561

Gonzalez-Maldonado, D., Pugnali, A., Tsan, J., Eatinger, D., Franklin, D., & Weintrop, D. (2022, August). Investigating the use of planning sheets in young learners' open-ended scratch projects. In *Proceedings of the 2022 ACM Conference on International Computing Education Research-Volume 1* (pp. 247-263). DOI: 10.1145/3501385.3543972

Grover, S., Basu, S., & Schank, P. (2018, February). What we can learn about student learning from open-ended programming projects in middle school computer science. In *Proceedings of the 49th ACM technical symposium on computer science education* (pp. 999-1004). DOI: 10.1145/3159450.3159522

Grover, S., & Pea, R. (2013). Computational thinking in K–12: A Review of the state of the field. *Educational Researcher, 42*(1), 38–43. DOI: 10.3102/0013189X12463051

Hanuscin, D. L., & Lee, M. H. (2008). Using the learning cycle as a model for teaching the learning cycle to preservice elementary teachers. *Journal of Elementary Science Education, 20*(2), 51–66. DOI: 10.1007/BF03173670

Harel, I., & Papert, S. (1991). *Constructionism*. Ablex Publishing.

Hmelo-Silver, C. E., Duncan, R. G., & Chinn, C. A. (2007). Scaffolding and achievement in problembased and inquiry learning: A response to Kirschner, Sweller, and. *Educational Psychologist, 42*(2), 99–107. DOI: 10.1080/00461520701263368

Hsu, T. C., & Chen, M. S. (2024). Effects of students using different learning approaches for learning computational thinking and AI applications. *Education and Information Technologies*, *30*(6), 7549–7571. DOI: 10.1007/s10639-024-13116-w

Hsu, T. C., & Hsu, T. P. (2025). Teaching AI with games: The impact of generative AI drawing on computational thinking skills. *Education and Information Technologies*, *30*(15), 21499–21518. DOI: 10.1007/s10639-025-13624-3

Hulleman, C. S., Godes, O., Hendricks, B. L., & Harackiewicz, J. M. (2010). Enhancing interest and performance with a utility value intervention. *Journal of Educational Psychology*, *102*(4), 880–895. DOI: 10.1037/a0019506

Ioannou, A., & Makridou, E. (2018). Exploring the potentials of educational robotics in the development of computational thinking: A summary of current research and practical proposal for future work. *Education and Information Technologies*, *23*(6), 2531–2544. DOI: 10.1007/s10639-018-9729-z

Jaipal-Jamani, K., & Angeli, C. (2017). Effect of robotics on elementary preservice teachers' self-efficacy, science learning, and computational thinking. *Journal of Science Education and Technology*, *26*(2), 175–192. DOI: 10.1007/s10956-016-9663-z

Kafai, Y. B., & Proctor, C. (2021). A Revaluation of Computational Thinking in K–12 Education: Moving Toward Computational Literacies. *Educational Researcher*, *51*(2), 146-151. (Original work published 2022)DOI: 10.3102/0013189X211057904

Kafai, Y. B., Proctor, C., & Lui, D. (2019, July). From theory bias to theory dialogue: Embracing cognitive, situated, and critical framings of computational thinking in k-12 cs education. *In Proceedings of the 2019 ACM Conference on International Computing Education Research* (pp. 101-109). DOI: 10.1145/3291279.3339400

Kale, U., Akcaoglu, M., Cullen, T., Goh, D., Devine, L., Calvert, N., & Grise, K. (2018). Computational what? Relating computational thinking to teaching. *TechTrends*, *62*(6), 574–58. DOI: 10.1007/s11528-018-0290-9

Kale, U., & Wang, Y. (2025). Future science educators' usage, interest, competence, and utility value for computational thinking. *Journal of Science Teacher Education*, •••, 1–28. DOI: 10.1080/1046560X.2025.2535035

Kale, U., Wang, Y., Aldebyan, A., Mann, T., & O'Brian, N. (2024, April 14). *Future teachers' interest, competence, and perception of utility value regarding computational thinking in teaching science* [Conference session]. American Educational Research Association Annual Conference, Philadelphia, PA.

Kaya, E., Newley, A., Yesilyurt, E., & Deniz, H. (2020). Measuring computational thinking teaching efficacy beliefs of preservice elementary teachers. *Journal of College Science Teaching*, *49*(6), 55–64. DOI: 10.1080/0047231X.2020.12290665

Kazakoff, E. R., Sullivan, A., & Bers, M. U. (2013). The Effect of a Classroom-Based Intensive Robotics and Programming Workshop on Sequencing Ability in Early Childhood. *Early Childhood Education Journal*, *41*(4), 245–255. DOI: 10.1007/s10643-012-0554-5

Kazempour, M., Amirshokoohi, A., & Blamey, K. (2020). Putting theory to practice: Teaching the 5E learning cycle through immersive experiences for pre-service teachers. *European Journal of Science and Mathematics Education*, *8*(1), 67–75. DOI: 10.30935/scimath/9547

Khalifa, S. A. M., Elshafiey, E. H., Shetaia, A. A., El-Wahed, A. A. A., Algethami, A. F., Musharraf, S. G., AlAjmi, M. F., Zhao, C., Masry, S. H. D., Abdel-Daim, M. M., Halabi, M. F., Kai, G., Al Naggar, Y., Bishr, M., Diab, M. A. M., & El-Seedi, H. R. (2021). Overview of Bee Pollination and Its Economic Value for Crop Production. *Insects*, *12*(8), 688. DOI: 10.3390/insects12080688 PMID: 34442255

Kramer, J. (2007). Is abstraction the key to computing? *Communications of the ACM*, *50*(4), 36–42. DOI: 10.1145/1232743.1232745

Kwon, K., Brush, T. A., Kim, K., & Seo, M. (2024). Embodied Learning for Computational Thinking in a Mixed-Reality Context. *Journal of Educational Computing Research*, *62*(8), 1719–1740. DOI: 10.1177/07356331241291173

Kwon, K., Kim, K., Zhou, C., & Jeon, M. (2025). *Embodied Learning Experiences of Early Elementary Students in Computational Thinking Education*. Technology, Knowledge and Learning., DOI: 10.1007/s10758-025-09826-w

Lee, C. H., & Soep, E. (2016). None but ourselves can free our minds: Critical computational literacy as a pedagogy of resistance. *Equity & Excellence in Education*, *49*(4), 480–492. DOI: 10.1080/10665684.2016.1227157

Lee, H. S., Pallant, A., Pryputniewicz, S., Lord, T., Mulholland, M., & Liu, O. L. (2019). Automated text scoring and real-time adjustable feedback: Supporting revision of scientific arguments involving uncertainty. *Science Education*, *103*(3), 590–622. DOI: 10.1002/sce.21504

Mayer, R. E., & Wittrock, M. C. (2006). Problem solving. In Alexander, P. A., Winne, P. H., Alexander, P. A., & Winne, P. H. (Eds.), *Handbook of educational psychology* (pp. 287–303). Lawrence Erlbaum Associates Publishers.

McGinnis, J. R., Hestness, E., Mills, K., Ketelhut, D., Cabrera, L., & Jeong, H. (2020). Preservice science teachers' beliefs about computational thinking following a curricular module within an elementary science methods course. *Contemporary Issues in Technology & Teacher Education, 20*(1), 85–107.

National Center for Education Statistics. (2023). Teacher Openings in Elementary and Secondary Schools. *Condition of Education*. U.S. Department of Education, Institute of Education Sciences. Retrieved from https://nces.ed.gov/programs/coe/indicator/tls

Nouri, J., Zhang, L., Mannila, L., & Norén, E. (2020). Development of computational thinking, digital competence and 21st century skills when learning programming in K-9. *Education Inquiry, 11*(1), 1–17. DOI: 10.1080/20004508.2019.1627844

OECD. (2003). PISA 2003 assessment framework: Mathematics, reading, science and problem solving knowledge and skills. *OECD Publishing*. Retrieved from https://www.oecd.org/edu/school/programmeforinternationalstudentassessmentpisa/33694881.pdf

OECD. (2013). *OECD skills outlook 2013: First results from the survey of adult skills*. OECD Publishing., DOI: 10.1787/9789264204256-

OECD. (2015). OECD skills outlook 2015: Youth, skills and employability. *OECD Publishing*. Retrieved from https://www.oecd.org/edu/oecd-skills-outlook-2015-9789264234178-en.htm

Ozogul, G., Karlin, M., & Ottenbreit-Leftwich, A. (2018). Preservice teacher computer science preparation: A case study of an undergraduate computer education licensure program. *Journal of Technology and Teacher Education, 26*(3), 375–409.

Palop, B., Díaz, I., Rodriguez-Muniz, L. J., & Santaengracia, J. J. (2025). Redefining computational thinking: A holistic framework and its implications for K-12 education. *Education and Information Technologies, 30*(10), 1–26. DOI: 10.1007/s10639-024-13297-4

Pewkam, W., & Chamrat, S. (2022). Pre-Service Teacher Training Program of STEM-based activities in Computing Science to Develop Computational Thinking. *Informatics in Education, 21*(2), 311–329.

Popenici, S. A. D., & Kerr, S. (2017). Exploring the impact of artificial intelligence on teaching and learning in higher education. *Research and Practice in Technology Enhanced Learning, 12*(1), 22. DOI: 10.1186/s41039-017-0062-8 PMID: 30595727

Preston, L., Harvie, K., & Wallace, H. (2015). Inquiry-based learning in teacher education: A primary humanities example. *The Australian Journal of Teacher Education*, *40*(12), 73–85. DOI: 10.14221/ajte.2015v40n12.6

Rich, K. M., Yadav, A., & Schwarz, C. V. (2019). Computational thinking, mathematics, and science: Elementary teachers' perspectives on integration. *Journal of Technology and Teacher Education*, *27*(2), 165–205. DOI: 10.70725/303733vqleui

Robotics Online Marketing Team. (2017). Robotics in agriculture: Types and applications. *Association for Advancing Automation* (blog), December 12, 2017, Retrieved from https://www.automate.org/blogs/robotics-in-agriculture-types-and-applications

Suters, L. (2021). Elementary preservice teacher coursework design for developing science and mathematics computational thinking practices. *Contemporary Issues in Technology & Teacher Education*, *21*(2), 360–440.

Tagare, D. (2024). Factors That Predict K-12 Teachers' Ability to Apply Computational Thinking Skills. *ACM Transactions on Computing Education*, *24*(1), 1–26. DOI: 10.1145/3633205

Tissenbaum, M., Sheldon, J., & Abelson, H. (2019). From computational thinking to computational action. *Communications of the ACM*, *62*(3), 34–36. DOI: 10.1145/3265747

Tsarava, K., Moeller, K., Román-González, M., Golle, J., Leifheit, L., Butz, M. V., & Ninaus, M. (2022). A cognitive definition of computational thinking in primary education. *Computers & Education*, *179*, 104425. DOI: 10.1016/j.compedu.2021.104425

U.S. Department of Agriculture. (n.d.a). The importance of pollinators. https://www.usda.gov/about-usda/general-information/initiatives-and-highlighted-programs/peoples-garden/importance-pollinators

U.S. Department of Agriculture. (n.d.b). National Agricultural Statistics Service. https://quickstats.nass.usda.gov/#3F7820DC-AC84-3DC9-B409-FC613BFD0EE4

Vakil, S. (2014). A critical pedagogy approach for engaging urban youth in mobile app development in an after-school program. *Equity & Excellence in Education*, *47*(1), 31–45. DOI: 10.1080/10665684.2014.866869

Voogt, J., Fisser, P., Good, J., Mishra, P., & Yadav, A. (2015). Computational thinking in compulsory education: Towards an agenda for research and practice. *Education and Information Technologies*, *20*(4), 715–728. DOI: 10.1007/s10639-015-9412-6

Walkington, C., & Bernacki, M. L. (2019). Personalizing algebra to students' individual interests in an intelligent tutoring system: Moderators of impact. *International Journal of Artificial Intelligence in Education, 29*(1), 58–88. DOI: 10.1007/s40593-018-0168-1

Weintrop, D., Beheshti, E., Horn, M., Orton, K., Jona, K., Trouille, L., & Wilensky, U. (2016). Defining computational thinking for mathematics and science classrooms. *Journal of Science Education and Technology, 25*(1), 127–147. DOI: 10.1007/s10956-015-9581-5

Wigfield, A., & Eccles, J. S. (2000). Expectancy-value theory of achievement motivation. *Contemporary Educational Psychology, 25*(1), 68–81. DOI: 10.1006/ceps.1999.1015 PMID: 10620382

Wigfield, A., Eccles, J. S., Roeser, R. W., & Schiefele, U. (2008). Development of achievement motivation. In Damon, W., & Lerner, R. M. (Eds.), *Child and adolescent development: An advanced course* (pp. 406–434). John Wiley and Sons.

Wilson, B., DeBruin, J., Higgins, A., Gross, T., Gum, H., & Cannon, T. (2018). *Bringing our farms into focus: Specialty food crops, farm viability and market profitability in West Virginia.* Organization Name. Retrieved from http://foodjustice.wvu.edu/wp-content/uploads/2018/12/WV-Farm-viability_study_final.pdf

Wing, J. M. (2008). Computational thinking and thinking about computing. *Philosophical Transactions. Series A, Mathematical, Physical, and Engineering Sciences, 366*(1881), 3717–3725. DOI: 10.1098/rsta.2008.0118 PMID: 18672462

Wing, J. M. (2014). *Computational thinking benefits society. 40th anniversary blog of social issues in computing*, 2014, 26. http://socialissues.cs.toronto.edu/index.html%3Fp=279.html

Wood, T., Milbrath, M., & Szendrei, Z. (n.d.). *Maximizing honey bee pollination in pickling cucumbers.* Michigan State University Extension. https://pollinators.msu.edu/sites/_pollinators/assets/File/PollinationPicklingCucumbers.pdf

Woodcock, T. S. (2012). *Pollination in the agricultural landscape: best management practices for crop pollination. Canadian Pollination Initiative (NSERCCANPOLIN).* University of Guelph., https://seeds.ca/pollinator/bestpractices/images/Pollination%20in%20Agricultural%20Landscape_Woodcock_Final.pdf

Yadav, A., Stephenson, C., & Hong, H. (2017). Computational thinking for teacher education. *Communications of the ACM, 60*(4), 55–62. DOI: 10.1145/2994591

Yilmaz, R., & Yilmaz, F. G. K. (2023). The effect of generative artificial intelligence (AI)-based tool use on students' computational thinking skills, programming self-efficacy and motivation. *Computers and Education: Artificial Intelligence*, *4*, 100147. DOI: 10.1016/j.caeai.2023.100147

Yun, M., & Crippen, K. J. (2024). Computational Thinking Integration into Pre-Service Science Teacher Education: A Systematic Review. *Journal of Science Teacher Education*, •••, 1–30.

Zhang, L., & Nouri, J. (2019). A systematic review of learning computational thinking through Scratch in K-9. *Computers & Education*, *141*, 103607. DOI: 10.1016/j.compedu.2019.103607

Zhu, M., Liu, O. L., & Lee, H. S. (2020). The effect of automated feedback on revision behavior and learning gains in formative assessment of scientific argument writing. *Computers & Education*, *143*, 103668. DOI: 10.1016/j.compedu.2019.103668

Chapter 6
eduMathStatAI: Enhancing Mathematics and Statistics Education Through Coding and Digital Tools

İsmail Yenilmez
https://orcid.org/0000-0002-3357-3898
Eskişehir Technical University, Turkey

ABSTRACT

This chapter introduces eduMathStatAI, a developing R package designed to enhance mathematics and statistics education by integrating coding and digital tools into teaching. Currently, it provides structured lesson module examples and customized functions that enable teachers to incorporate computational thinking into their instruction. Focusing on sustainable, non-formal teacher training, the chapter highlights strategies that ensure accessibility for educators with varying programming experience. By emphasizing scalable, modular, and open-access resources, eduMathStatAI aims to foster equitable digital transformation and align with international recommendations for inclusive STEM education. The chapter offers a practical guide for gradually expanding the toolkit and integrating coding into curriculum-aligned instruction while supporting sustainable development.

INTRODUCTION

The integration of digital tools into mathematics and statistics education has become both a necessity and an opportunity in the 21st-century learning environment. Traditional instructional approaches often rely on abstract explanations and procedural repetition, which can alienate students from deeper conceptual understanding (Boal-

DOI: 10.4018/979-8-3373-2660-3.ch006

er, 2016). In statistics education, learners frequently struggle to connect theoretical knowledge to real-world data contexts (Yenilmez, 2016). Technology-supported instruction may offer a more concrete and engaging means of exploring abstract mathematical and statistical ideas (Garfield et al., 2008).

Recent evidence highlights that coding and computational thinking enrich Science, Technology, Engineering, and Mathematics (STEM) learning by enabling mathematical modeling, dynamic visualization, and interactive problem-solving experiences (Al Hamad et al., 2024; Ye et al., 2023). These approaches support enhanced problem-solving skills, conceptual understanding, and motivation among students.

Despite these benefits, educators encounter barriers such as limited programming proficiency, institutional constraints, and a lack of curriculum-aligned resources (Rovshenov and Sarsar, 2023). These challenges often lead to continued reliance on rote instruction and outdated pedagogical models. As such, accessible, scalable teaching solutions are critically needed.

In response, this chapter introduces eduMathStatAI, an open-source R package designed specifically for mathematics and statistics education. It offers custom R functions for modeling and visualization, interactive coding exercises, and structured lesson modules to help educators, regardless of their prior programming experience, confidently integrate coding and data analysis into their instruction.

Furthermore, the chapter proposes sustainable, non-formal teacher training strategies, particularly modular 40-minute lesson plans and open-access materials. These approaches support the integration of computational thinking into existing curricula without requiring fundamental changes to established pedagogical structures.

The chapter is structured around five core themes:

- The need for digital transformation in math and statistics education;
- The design and core functionality of the eduMathStatAI;
- Teacher training with R using the package;
- Creation of coding-based digital educational resources;
- Sustainability, scalability, and future implementation directions.

These themes aim to contribute to the evolving discourse on digital pedagogy and offer a practical roadmap for integrating coding into mathematics and statistics instruction.

BACKGROUND

To understand the motivation behind the development of the eduMathStatAI package and the objectives of this chapter, it is essential to first examine the broader context in which this work is situated. This section outlines the key challenges and opportunities driving the integration of coding and digital tools into mathematics and statistics education. Specifically, it addresses (1) the limitations of traditional instruction in fostering deep conceptual understanding; (2) the growing need for digital transformation in educational practice; and (3) the potential of coding and artificial intelligence (AI) to serve as powerful tools for modern pedagogy. Together, these elements form the foundation for the design and implementation of the eduMathStatAI presented in the following sections.

Challenges of Traditional Mathematics and Statistics Instruction

Instruction that emphasizes procedural fluency and rote memorization often fails to foster deep conceptual understanding or real-world application (Boaler, 2016). This emphasis contributes to disengagement and math anxiety while hindering learners' ability to transfer learned concepts beyond standardized problems (Yenilmez, 2016). In statistics education, complex concepts, such as variability, inference, and probability, are frequently taught abstractly, disconnected from authentic datasets, which restricts students' development of statistical reasoning (Garfield et al., 2008).

Importance of Digital Transformation in Education

Digital transformation involves much more than the mere deployment of devices; it requires redefining pedagogy, curriculum design, and learner engagement. Embracing technology-integrated methods supports the development of data literacy, computational thinking, and collaboration, essential competencies for the modern learner (Al Hamad et al., 2024).

Recent empirical studies highlight that the successful integration of digital and AI-based learning tools relies heavily on teachers' technological self-efficacy and pedagogical readiness. For instance, Sat and Kadirhan (2024) demonstrated that computer science teachers with stronger coding self-efficacy displayed higher levels of adaptive teaching competence and classroom innovation. Likewise, Mah and Groß (2024) found that faculty members' self-efficacy profiles significantly influenced how effectively they adopt and sustain AI tools in higher-education contexts. Complementing these results, Ng et al. (2023) emphasized that teachers' AI-related digital competencies and 21st-century skills are critical enablers in transforming emerging technologies into meaningful learning opportunities.

Collectively, these findings reinforce this chapter's focus on pairing open-source analytical tools with sustained, practice-oriented professional development to enhance educators' confidence and capacity for inclusive, technology-enhanced instruction.

Platforms like R and Python provide equitable access to scalable and interactive STEM learning environments (Bamigboye, 2024).

The digital transformation of mathematics and statistics education has evolved through several key stages. In the 1980s, the introduction of programming-based learning tools such as LOGO demonstrated how computers could help students visualize and explore mathematical structures interactively (Papert, 1980). During the 2000s, dynamic software like GeoGebra, Excel, and VUstat advanced visualization and modeling capabilities, promoting experimentation and enhancing students' engagement with statistical reasoning (Yenilmez and Yavuz, 2016; Zhang et al., 2023). By the 2010s, cloud-based learning platforms and open-source programming environments (e.g., R, Python) made computational thinking accessible to a wider audience (Grover and Pea, 2013; Çetinkaya-Rundel and Ellison, 2021). The 2020s have seen AI integrated into learning environments, enabling adaptive feedback, personalization, and intelligent tutoring (Zawacki-Richter et al., 2019). This chronological trajectory highlights how digital pedagogy has continuously evolved to make abstract mathematical reasoning more concrete, interactive, and inclusive.

Coding and AI as Tools for Modern Pedagogy

When thoughtfully implemented, coding and AI can transition instruction from passive consumption to active exploration. Engaging with programming fosters hypothesis testing, simulation, and visual modeling, deepening students' conceptual insights (Ye et al., 2023). AI tools have been shown to support personalization through adaptive feedback and pacing, which can improve engagement and outcomes (Xhako et al., 2025). For educators, these technologies support the creation of dynamic, real-world-aligned lesson content and facilitate more meaningful assessment practices.

MAIN FOCUS OF THE CHAPTER

This chapter emphasizes the urgent need for digital transformation in mathematics and statistics education, highlighting the evolving demands of 21st-century learning. It introduces eduMathStatAI, an innovative teaching and learning package designed to integrate AI and coding into the classroom, thereby enhancing both instructional delivery and student engagement. Central to the chapter is the professional development of educators, particularly in building their capacity to use coding tools effectively within the eduMathStatAI framework. The chapter also explores how this package supports the creation of dynamic, digital educational resources that foster interactive and personalized learning experiences. Finally, it addresses key considerations for ensuring the sustainability and scalability of such technological solutions, offering forward-looking insights into their role in shaping the future of math and statistics education.

The Need for Digital Transformation in Math and Statistics Education

Digital transformation, particularly through coding and computational thinking, offers a practical way to address the limitations of traditional math instruction. It supports active learning, real-time feedback, and higher student engagement, helping students conceptualize abstract mathematical ideas in more concrete and meaningful ways.

Challenges of traditional mathematics instruction

Traditional mathematics education often relies on abstract content delivery, emphasizing rote learning and procedural memorization over conceptual understanding. This method creates barriers for many students, particularly those with limited working memory capacity. Alloway and Passolunghi (2011) found a significant relationship between working memory, IQ, and math performance in children, showing that learners with reduced working memory capacity struggle more with mathematics tasks that require mental manipulation and storage of sequential steps.

A critical psychological factor affecting mathematics learning is math anxiety. Research by Ashcraft and Krause (2007) demonstrated that math anxiety interferes with working memory, impairing students' ability to solve problems. This is especially damaging in traditional classroom settings that emphasize speed and correctness over exploration. Similarly, Ramirez et al., (2013) showed that math anxiety emerges as early as elementary school and has lasting effects on performance. These issues are often exacerbated by teaching environments where students fear failure and are not encouraged to engage deeply with concepts.

Furthermore, traditional instruction tends to reflect fixed-mindset ideologies. Rattan et al. (2012) found that instructors who believed mathematical ability is fixed were more likely to offer comfort rather than encouragement when students struggled, inadvertently lowering student motivation and performance. This form of instruction limits students' resilience and growth in mathematics.

The passive nature of traditional instruction also reduces engagement. As Boaler (2016) emphasized, mathematical mindsets can be transformed when students are encouraged to explore problems, make mistakes, and engage visually and collaboratively. Boaler argues that all students are capable of high-level mathematical thinking if given the opportunity to learn through inquiry, exploration, and positive reinforcement.

Studies also show that pedagogical practices relying on teacher-led instruction do not consistently support deep learning. Hiebert and Grouws (2007) highlighted that effective learning requires classroom structures that foster conceptual understanding alongside procedural skills. Unfortunately, many traditional approaches do not sufficiently balance these two components.

In addition, systemic issues contribute to learning gaps. According to Darling-Hammond (2010), inequitable access to quality instruction and resources creates disparities in student outcomes, particularly in under-resourced schools. Mangarin and Caballes (2024) further observed that students face difficulties in mathematics when teaching lacks differentiation, feedback, and student-centered strategies, common traits in traditional math classrooms.

While these challenges are significant, they underscore the urgent need for transformation, one that prioritizes engagement, equity, and deep conceptual learning.

However, the adoption of digital pedagogy is not uniform across regions. In contexts such as developing and underdeveloped countries, educators often face barriers such as limited access to devices, lack of localized content, and insufficient training in computational methods. Studies (e.g., Mangarin and Caballes, 2024) indicate that while technologically advanced regions focus on depth and integration of coding, developing regions emphasize equitable access and teacher support. Addressing these disparities through open-source and language-accessible resources like eduMathStatAI is essential to ensure inclusive and sustainable digital transformation. Beyond regional disparities, international organizations such as UNESCO (2025) and the OECD (2023) have called for integrating computational thinking into global competency frameworks. Their recommendations emphasize equitable digital access, teacher professionalization, and open-source collaboration. By aligning with these principles, eduMathStatAI not only supports local capacity building but also contributes to international goals for inclusive and sustainable digital education.

The role of coding in making abstract concepts more tangible

Digital transformation and the rapid advancement of technology have introduced coding and computational thinking into education, creating powerful opportunities to improve how students engage with mathematics. Coding has increasingly been recognized not only as a technical skill but also as a cognitive tool that supports logical reasoning and creative problem-solving (Grover and Pea, 2013). Coding helps make abstract concepts more tangible by allowing students to model, simulate, and visualize mathematical ideas in dynamic ways. By translating mathematical relationships into executable code, learners can witness how changes in parameters affect outcomes; thereby transforming abstract formulas into observable phenomena.

Papert (1980) was among the first to propose that programming could serve as a mathematical learning tool. He argued that children could build knowledge more effectively by constructing and debugging code, which encourages active learning and problem-solving. This aligns with Wing's (2006) notion of computational thinking, which refers to a set of problem-solving processes that include abstraction, decomposition, pattern recognition, and algorithmic design (Wing, 2006; Grover and Pea, 2013). In educational contexts, computational thinking enables learners to approach mathematical problems systematically and to design step-by-step solutions much like computer scientists do.

These benefits are supported by recent research. Ye et al. (2023) conducted a systematic review on computational thinking-based mathematics instruction and found that integrating coding with math significantly enhances student achievement in both domains. Coding helps learners grasp complex, abstract mathematical ideas by engaging them in tasks that are interactive and iterative.

Incorporating coding into instruction also improves engagement and motivation, especially for students who may struggle with traditional symbolic representations. Bajarin (2016) emphasized that students must go beyond basic coding skills and learn how coding can be used as a tool to understand larger systems, such as mathematical models and statistical patterns. Bajarin (2016) stressed that integrating coding into core subjects equips students with essential skills for problem-solving in today's technology-driven world.

Freeman et al. (2014) found that active learning strategies, including coding tasks, improve learning outcomes and reduce failure rates in STEM fields. Their study confirmed that students learn better when they actively engage with material, collaborate, and receive real-time feedback, features commonly embedded in coding-based math instruction.

Ultimately, coding empowers students to explore math through experimentation and creation, rather than memorization. As digital tools become more accessible, the integration of coding into mathematics and statistics instruction offers a practical and effective path to make abstract ideas more concrete, engaging, and meaningful.

Introducing eduMathStatAI: A Teaching and Learning Package

Building on the preceding discussion of digital transformation and pedagogical challenges, eduMathStatAI is presented as a comprehensive, user-friendly digital resource designed to transform the teaching and learning of mathematics and statistics through the integration of coding and AI. At its core, the package provides a robust set of tools that empower educators to deliver more engaging, data-driven lessons and foster critical thinking among students. Central to the package are custom R functions tailored for mathematical modeling, data visualization, and interactive problem-solving. These functions simplify complex computations and allow users to explore mathematical concepts dynamically, making abstract ideas more concrete and accessible.

In addition, eduMathStatAI includes a collection of pre-built lesson modules that are ready for immediate use in the classroom. These modules align with curriculum standards and can be easily adapted to suit various educational contexts, making the package both versatile and practical for educators seeking to modernize their instructional approaches.

Several digital learning environments share the goal of integrating coding into mathematics education. Python-based frameworks such as *Jupyter Notebook*, *Google Colab*, and *Matplotlib* have demonstrated how coding can foster mathematical reasoning through visualization and experimentation. Similarly, R-based environments such as *LearnR* and *R Commander* offer statistical interactivity for classroom contexts. However, eduMathStatAI distinguishes itself through its ready-to-use lesson modules, curriculum alignment, and focus on non-formal teacher training. Unlike platforms designed primarily for professional programmers, eduMathStatAI emphasizes accessibility and pedagogical scaffolding, allowing teachers with limited programming experience to adopt coding as a teaching tool effectively.

For example, a high-school teacher might use the roll_dice_experiment() function to simulate probability outcomes during a classroom activity, while a university instructor could apply grade_correlation() to analyze relationships in real student datasets. These examples illustrate how eduMathStatAI bridges theoretical concepts and practical application through interactive, inquiry-based learning.

The eduMathStatAI package (version 0.1.0) is designed as a specialized educational package that supports teaching and learning in mathematical statistics and AI. The package provides a practical set of tools and functions that enable educators and students to explore core statistical concepts through hands-on coding activities (Yenilmez, 2025). Its core functionalities include support for descriptive statistics, Monte Carlo simulations, and simple regression analysis, all of which are essential topics in undergraduate-level statistics and introductory AI education.

Built in R and integrating widely used packages such as *MASS*, *dplyr*, *matrixcalc*, *stats*, *tidymodels*, and *utils*, eduMathStatAI ensures compatibility with modern data science workflows. The package introduces custom R functions designed specifically for educational use, allowing users to perform mathematical modeling, generate data visualizations, and engage in interactive problem-solving activities.

In addition to its computational tools, eduMathStatAI also offers a set of pre-built lesson modules, making it easy for educators to integrate the package into existing curricula. These modules are designed with ease of use and pedagogical alignment in mind, supporting classroom instruction, lab activities, and independent learning. With a focus on accessibility, reproducibility, and interactivity, eduMathStatAI represents a significant step forward in the digital transformation of mathematics and statistics education.

The eduMathStatAI offers a set of carefully designed R functions that support essential mathematical and statistical concepts through computational thinking, coding, and interactive visualizations. These functions allow students and teachers to move beyond static textbook examples and into dynamic, code-driven inquiry-based learning. The selected examples were developed to be accessible at the high school and pre-college levels, and each is intended to promote critical thinking, conceptual understanding, and engagement.

The functions cover a wide range of topics from descriptive statistics to regression analysis, probability experiments, and mathematical patterns such as the Fibonacci sequence. Each function includes both analytical components (e.g., mean, correlation, trend lines) and visual outputs (e.g., histograms, scatter plots, ratio graphs) to promote dual coding and deeper cognitive processing. Additionally, students are encouraged to modify inputs and test hypotheses, strengthening their programming and mathematical reasoning skills. The R scripts in Table 1 illustrate some of the functions of the package, summarized.

Table 1. Some of the centralized R scripts in the package

Function Name	Concept	R Topics Used
mean_median_mode.R	Central tendency comparison	Descriptive statistics, visualization
quadratic_explorer.R	Quadratic functions & root finding	Polynomials, graphing
simulate_dice.R	Probability distribution of dice	Sampling, simulation, histograms
height_distribution.R	Descriptive information	Mean, median, standard deviation
roll_dice_ experiment.R	Experimental probability with dice	Proportions, bar plot, randomness
grade_correlation.R	Relationship between two or more variables	Scatter plots, regression, correlation
liking_analysis.R	Analysis likert-scale feedback	Mode, frequency tables, Likert scales
reading_trend.R	Age and reading habits trends	Trend analysis, linear regression
attendance_vs_grade.R	Impact of absences on performance	Data frames, regression, interpretation
fibonacci_ratio.R	Golden Ratio via Fibonacci sequence	Sequences, ratios, visual convergence

Each function is open-source, editable, and compatible with standard R-based learning environments. They are modular by design and require no additional software outside of base R and common *tidyverse* packages, ensuring maximum classroom portability and technical accessibility.

Pre-built lesson module example for easy classroom integration:

To maximize usability in teaching contexts, each custom function is paired with a ready-to-use lesson module. These modules follow a consistent instructional structure:

1. Concept Introduction

A brief overview of the mathematical or statistical idea, often accompanied by real-world context or visual anchor.

2. Interactive Coding Task

Students run and modify the relevant R function. Input data is either pre-loaded or collected live in class. The code is written in plain, understandable syntax with explanatory comments.

3. Guided Interpretation

Students interpret outputs, answer prompts, and engage in group discussion or reflection. Visualizations (e.g., histograms, scatter plots, regression lines) support interpretation and concept reinforcement.

4. Extension and Exploration

Learners are encouraged to change parameters, compare results, or design a small experiment of their own using the same structure. Example: "What happens to the average when you add an outlier?"

Example: Lesson Flow Using grade_correlation.R

- Objective: Explore whether math and physics grades are correlated.
- Activity:
  - Students input data into the grade_correlation() function.
  - The function generates a scatter plot and fits a regression line.
  - The correlation coefficient is printed to guide interpretation.
- Discussion Questions:
  - What does a positive correlation mean in this context?
  - Could there be other factors influencing this relationship?

- o How would you expect the graph to change if the sample included more students?

Pedagogical Impact

These lessons are designed to promote:

- Data literacy and visual interpretation
- Mathematical modeling skills
- Hands-on coding fluency using R
- Deeper understanding of abstract concepts through simulation and exploration
- Student agency, allowing learners to ask questions and test hypotheses with real data

Open Access and Modularity

All functions and modules are freely available within the eduMathStatAI package under the MIT license. They can be adapted for:

- In-person or remote instruction
- Project-based learning
- Self-guided enrichment or flipped classrooms
- Teacher professional development in coding and digital pedagogy

Training Teachers in Coding with eduMathStatAI

One of the critical pillars of the eduMathStatAI project is the professional development of mathematics and statistics teachers in digital education and coding. Recognizing that many educators have little to no prior programming experience, this initiative prioritizes *non-formal*, *hands-on*, and *sustainable* approaches to teacher training. The emphasis is not on turning teachers into professional programmers but on empowering them to incorporate computational tools that deepen students' mathematical thinking and engagement.

The package includes interactive R-based exercises that are designed with accessibility and pedagogy in mind. By working with clear, well-documented functions such as fibonacci_ratio(), grade_correlation(), and roll_dice_experiment(), educators gradually build confidence in using code to teach mathematical ideas, explore patterns, and create visual explanations.

Hands-on approaches to learning R for educators

Rather than beginning with abstract programming syntax, the training modules start with meaningful mathematical problems and visual outputs. Teachers engage with fully functioning R scripts, make small edits (e.g., changing values, adjusting inputs), and immediately see how these changes impact the graph or output.

Each function acts as a scaffolded learning unit, with built-in explanations and prompts. Through short group workshops or individual practice, teachers gradually become more comfortable interpreting results, reading error messages, modifying code, and using the RStudio environment. This strategy bridges the gap between traditional math instruction and digital pedagogy.

Guidelines for practical implementation across educational levels:

To facilitate classroom adoption, eduMathStatAI provides adaptable lesson templates mapped to different educational levels:

- Primary (ages ~10–12): Simple, exploratory activities (e.g., simulate_dice.R, mean_median_mode.R) that visualize frequency and central tendency; teacher-facing scaffolds reduce code exposure and focus on interpretation.
- Secondary (ages ~13–17): Scaffolded investigations (e.g., fibonacci_ratio(), grade_correlation()) that combine code modification with conceptual prompts, suitable for 40-minute lessons.
- Higher education / tertiary: Extended projects and data-analysis tasks using simulations, regression, and reproducible workflows; students can adapt functions and contribute to package extensions.

Repository links direct users to "starter" and "advanced" lesson folders and hosted RStudio or Posit Cloud sessions so teachers can run demos without local installation.

Using to teach patterns Fibonacci, sequences, and convergence:

The fibonacci_ratio() function demonstrates how abstract mathematical sequences can be brought to life using simple code. Teachers guide students to explore how the ratio between Fibonacci terms converges to the Golden Ratio and to use a dynamic graph to visualize this limit.

```
# fibonacci_ratio.R
# Explore how Fibonacci ratios approach the golden ratio
```

```
fibonacci_ratio <- function(n = 20) {
  fib <- numeric(n)
  fib[1:2] <- 1
  for (i in 3:n) {
    fib[i] <- fib[i - 1] + fib[i - 2]
  }
  ratios <- fib[2:n] / fib[1:(n - 1)]

  plot(ratios, type = "b", col = "blue", pch = 19, ylim =
c(1.5, 1.7),
       main = "Fibonacci Ratios Approaching Golden Ratio",
       xlab = "Term Index", ylab = "Ratio")
  abline(h = 1.618, col = "red", lty = 2)
  text(n / 2, 1.62, "Golden Ratio ≈ 1.618", col = "red")

  return(invisible(ratios))
}
```

This example fosters deep discussions about limits and visual thinking. Teachers gain experience running loops, using vectors, and modifying code interactively.

Making data relationships tangible with correlation functions:

Teachers use the grade_correlation() function to analyze hypothetical or real classroom data. This supports learning about regression, scatter plots, and interpreting correlation coefficients visually and numerically.

```
# grade_correlation.R
# Plot and compute correlation between two subjects

grade_correlation <- function(math, physics) {
  if (length(math) != length(physics)) stop("Vectors must be
of same length.")

  plot(math, physics, col = "blue", pch = 19,
       xlab = "Math Grade", ylab = "Physics Grade",
       main = "Math vs Physics Correlation")
  abline(lm(physics ~ math), col = "red")

  corr <- cor(math, physics)
```

```
    cat("Correlation coefficient:", round(corr, 2), "\n")
    return(invisible(corr))
  }
```

Teachers recognize and teach how to create and analyze scatter plots, understand linear relationships, and interpret simple models within an accessible coding environment.

Using simulation to explain probability in practice:

The roll_dice_experiment() function helps teachers simulate and visualize the outcomes of rolling a six-sided die. This bridges theoretical probability with empirical results and supports concepts such as frequency, randomness, and distribution.

```
  # roll_dice_experiment.R
  # Simulate rolling a die multiple times and visualize the
results

  roll_dice_experiment <- function(n = 10) {
    set.seed(42)
    rolls <- sample(1:6, n, replace = TRUE)
    freq <- table(rolls)
    props <- prop.table(freq)

    barplot(freq, col = rainbow(6), main = paste("Die Rolls (n
=", n, ")"),
            xlab = "Face", ylab = "Frequency")

    print(round(props, 3))
    return(invisible(list(frequency = freq, proportion =
props)))
  }
```

This function supports exploratory learning, encouraging teachers to test the Law of Large Numbers, understand variability, and use visual representations to communicate probabilistic concepts effectively.

Interactive Coding Exercises Tailored for Teachers

Each function is part of a training module that includes:

- Guided walkthroughs of the code structure and logic
- Editable scripts with scaffolded comments
- Reflection questions encouraging pedagogical connections (e.g., "How would you use this in class?")
- Debugging practice, giving teachers experience reading and fixing common coding issues

For example:

- *What happens if I change the sample size from 10 to 1000 in roll_dice_experiment()?*
- *Can we use students' actual math and physics scores in grade_correlation() to explore relationships?*

Non-Formal and Sustainable Strategies

Training is designed to be:

- Low-cost and open-access: All materials are open-source, licensed under MIT, and runnable in free environments like RStudio.
- Modular: Teachers can engage with one concept at a time (e.g., just correlation or sequences), without needing a full course.
- Peer-facilitated: Modules can be shared among colleagues or used in teacher communities of practice.
- Reinforcing: Teachers strengthen their skills through repetition across different contexts (e.g., all plots, all simulations use the same base syntax).

As shown in Table 2, each function supports specific teacher professional development goals such as visualizing sequences, exploring correlations, and conducting simulations.

Table 2. Summary of Pedagogical Advantages

Function	Pedagogical Focus / Instructional Objectives
fibonacci_ratio()	Facilitating conceptual visualization of mathematical limits, recursive patterns, and sequence convergence
grade_correlation()	Supporting data interpretation through scatter plot analysis, linear regression modeling, and relational reasoning
roll_dice_experiment()	Promoting statistical reasoning via simulation-based inquiry, understanding randomness, and comparing empirical and theoretical distributions

Building Digital Educational Resources with eduMathStatAI

The integration of coding and digital tools into mathematics and statistics education offers students a deeper understanding of core concepts while also developing computational thinking and problem-solving skills. The eduMathStatAI is designed to support educators in building innovative, engaging lesson plans that use coding as a pedagogical tool. This section outlines how to design effective 40-minute coding-integrated lesson plans, the benefits of open-access teaching materials for computational thinking, and practical strategies for incorporating coding-based problem-solving into existing curricula.

Designing 40-Minute Coding-Integrated Lesson Plans

A structured 40-minute lesson plan allows students to experience coding in a way that connects mathematical theory with computational practice. The key elements of a successful coding lesson are clarity, engagement, and exploration. The lesson should start with clear learning objectives and guide students through an interactive activity that incorporates coding to explore the underlying mathematical concept. Below is a template for designing a 40-minute coding-integrated lesson plan:

1. Introduction (5 minutes)
   - Goal: Introduce the topic and provide the context for why coding is relevant.
   - Example: Start by discussing the concept of central tendency (mean, median, and mode) and explain how coding can help us calculate these values dynamically for large datasets.
2. Concept Introduction and Setup (10 minutes)
   - Goal: Provide students with basic code snippets and explain the key concepts.
   - Example: Introduce the mean_median_mode.R function. Guide students through the process of computing the mean, median, and mode for a set of test scores using R.
3. Interactive Coding Activity (15 minutes)
   - Goal: Students run the code, explore different inputs, and observe how the outputs change.
   - Example: Let students modify the dataset (e.g., changing the values of the test scores) and observe how the mean and median change. Encourage them to reflect on the differences between these statistical measures.
4. Reflection and Discussion (5 minutes)

- Goal: Discuss the results and tie them back to real-world examples.
- Example: Begin by showing two small datasets that represent real-life classroom scenarios; for instance, students' exam scores.

Dataset A: 60, 65, 70, 72, 68, 95

Dataset B: 60, 65, 70, 72, 68, 70

Ask students:

What is the mean and median of each dataset?

How does the score of 95 in Dataset A affect the mean compared to the median?

Why might the median be a better measure of central tendency when there are extreme scores (outliers)?

Then, connect to a real-world teaching context:

"Imagine you are a teacher analyzing your class's test results. How might using the median instead of the mean give you a fairer sense of student performance?"

Encourage students to discuss in small groups and share examples from their own experiences.

This approach makes the activity more accessible to teachers and teacher candidates, illustrating how statistical reasoning can directly inform classroom assessment practices.

5. Wrap-Up and Homework/Extension (5 minutes)
   - Goal: Summarize the key takeaways and give students a task to reinforce learning.
   - Example: Ask students to extend the code by adding additional statistical calculations (e.g., standard deviation) or experiment with larger datasets.

Open-Access Teaching Materials for Computational Thinking in Math

Open-access teaching materials serve as a practical and sustainable means of supporting computational thinking in mathematics education. By providing freely available and adaptable content, educators can integrate coding-based activities without dependence on commercial software or costly textbooks.

The eduMathStatAI adopts this principle by offering an initial set of open-source R scripts and structured lesson examples that demonstrate how coding can be used to explore mathematical and statistical concepts. Instead of presenting a complete instructional system, the package provides a foundation upon which teachers can build, modify, and contextualize resources for their own classroom needs.

Each included function, such as fibonacci_ratio(), grade_correlation(), and roll_dice_experiment(), is accompanied by basic documentation and sample classroom tasks. These examples illustrate how changes in parameters influence outcomes, helping students connect abstract formulas to visual or empirical representations.

To enhance accessibility, the toolkit is designed to run on widely available platforms such as RStudio or Posit Cloud, allowing teachers and students to experiment without extensive technical setup. Supporting files (e.g., simple documentation, README notes) are provided to facilitate implementation and adaptation.

While still in its early stage of development, eduMathStatAI aims to contribute to the growing body of open-access educational tools that encourage hands-on, data-driven learning in mathematics and statistics. Future iterations will focus on expanding lesson materials and refining user guidance based on classroom feedback and educator collaboration.

Strategies for Integrating Coding-Based Problem-Solving into Existing Curricula

Integrating coding-based problem-solving into existing curricula requires careful alignment with traditional learning objectives. It is essential to design coding activities that complement traditional math instruction, rather than disrupt or replace it.

Below are some strategies for integration:

1. Mapping Code to Existing Curriculum Topics: A first step involves mapping coding functions to existing curriculum areas where computational exploration can enrich conceptual understanding. For instance, the grade_correlation() function can support lessons on correlation and regression by enabling students to visualize data relationships and explore linear trends dynamically. Similarly, the mean_median_mode.R function can be applied in units on descriptive statistics to compute measures of central tendency and discuss the sensitivity of these measures to extreme values.
2. Problem-Solving Approach: Framing coding as a medium for mathematical problem solving promotes inquiry-oriented learning. Through simulation and modeling, students can test hypotheses, analyze variability, and interpret outcomes. For example, the roll_dice_experiment()function provides an accessible means to investigate randomness and probability by comparing empirical and theoretical distributions.
3. Collaboration and Pair Programming: Collaborative coding environments encourage dialogue around computational logic and mathematical reasoning. Pair programming or small-group collaboration allows students to co-construct understanding while debugging and optimizing code. For example, in a lesson

on linear regression, use grade_correlation() to have students analyze real-world data in groups. Have them collaborate to explore how different factors might influence the results.
4. Project-Based Learning (PBL): PBL provides a broader framework for integrating coding into mathematics education. Through authentic, open-ended projects, learners can connect abstract mathematical models to real-world contexts. For instance, a population growth modeling activity using recursive functions and simulations can help students explore exponential patterns and parameter effects.

The integration of coding within mathematics and statistics education enhances students' problem-solving, critical thinking, and data literacy skills (Al Hamad et al., 2024; Boaler, 2016). The U.S. National Research Council (2010) highlights the importance of computational thinking as a core competency for the 21st century. Complementary findings emphasize that coding-based learning environments foster interactivity and engagement, which are especially effective for developing understanding of abstract mathematical concepts (Freeman et al., 2014; Al Hamad et al., 2024).

Sustainability, Scalability, and Future Directions

Ensuring Long-Term Impact Through Open-Source Development

The sustainability of eduMathStatAI is supported as an open-source project. By leveraging R's open-source ecosystem, the package allows for continuous improvement, community contributions, and long-term accessibility. Unlike proprietary educational software, open-source resources such as eduMathStatAI may reduce institutional dependence on proprietary platforms, thereby making digital transformation more financially viable, especially in under-resourced educational settings.

Maintaining the package through transparent documentation, version control (e.g., via GitHub), and community-driven development can ensure that the package evolves with pedagogical needs and technological advances. Contributors, including teachers, researchers, and developers, may adapt and expand functions to fit local curricula or unique classroom contexts, contributing to a growing repository of digital education assets that could support diverse learning environments.

Furthermore, sustainability is reinforced by alignment with reproducible research practices. Lessons and analyses created using eduMathStatAI can be shared, reused, and validated, facilitating both academic integrity and collaborative learning.

Expanding the Package with Additional Educational Resources

To enhance scalability and responsiveness to educational demand, the next stages of development for eduMathStatAI may include the expansion of both content and functionality:

- Curriculum-specific extensions: Modules targeting specific national and international math and statistics standards (e.g., Common Core, IB Math, IGCSE Statistics) could increase classroom relevance.
- Multilingual support: Translating lessons and documentation into major world languages may allow broader adoption in non-English speaking regions, promoting global educational equity.
- AI-enhanced features: Future iterations aim to explore intelligent tutoring features using R's AI capabilities, such as auto-hint generation, mistake diagnosis, and adaptive learning feedback, potentially personalizing student learning pathways.
- Gamification and interactive dashboards: Adding R Shiny-based applications and game-like elements will increase student engagement through visual interactivity and rewards-based feedback.

These developments will ensure that eduMathStatAI continues to meet the needs of diverse learners and educators in an evolving educational landscape.

Recommendations for Integrating Coding into National Curricula

To enhance the broader impact of tools such as eduMathStatAI, supportive measures at the policy level may be beneficial. Integrating coding and computational thinking into national mathematics and statistics curricula could be considered not merely as optional enrichment, but as components that contribute to developing digital literacy.

Possible considerations include:

Incorporating coding into teacher training frameworks: National guidelines might encourage pre-service and in-service teacher programs to include foundational programming and data literacy skills.

Supporting open-source educational initiatives: Governments and institutions could prioritize funding and endorsement of open-source educational technologies, which may foster equity and innovation.

Developing flexible curricular models: Curriculum guidelines can allow modular integration of coding into math and statistics topics, providing opportunities for gradual and adaptable implementation.

Enhancing infrastructure and technical support: Equipping schools with adequate devices, reliable internet access, and ongoing technical assistance to facilitate effective use of digital learning resources.

Creating incentive mechanisms for adoption of digital pedagogy: Recognizing and encouraging schools and educators who implement technology-enhanced instruction may help stimulate innovation and reflective practice.

Such measures could help position coding and computational thinking as integral aspects of mathematics education in the 21st century, rather than peripheral skills.

SOLUTIONS AND RECOMMENDATIONS

To address the multifaceted challenges confronting mathematics and statistics education, particularly those linked to traditional pedagogy, inequitable access to digital tools, and insufficient teacher preparedness, several targeted strategies are suggested. These solutions aim to support sustainable digital transformation, encourage computational thinking, and facilitate effective integration of tools such as eduMathStatAI into diverse educational settings.

Professional Development Through Modular, Practice-Based Training

One of the most pressing barriers to the integration of coding in education is the limited programming proficiency among in-service educators. To address this, teacher training can benefit from adopting modular, non-formal formats that prioritize accessibility and practical application over theoretical instruction. Short, iterative workshops, built around 40-minute lessons using the eduMathStatAI, allow teachers to gradually develop coding fluency without disrupting their instructional responsibilities. These sessions could be scaffolded to support progression from novice to more confident users, incorporating both pedagogical and technical components.

Curriculum Alignment and Pedagogical Integration

To ensure relevance and uptake, coding tools should be aligned as closely as possible with national and regional curriculum standards. Lesson modules and R functions in eduMathStatAI can be mapped to learning objectives, such as central tendency, probability, or linear modeling. This alignment allows educators to integrate computational approaches into existing units of instruction without requiring extensive curriculum redesign. Furthermore, adopting interdisciplinary perspectives, linking mathematics with subjects such as physics, economics, or environmental science, may help contextualize learning and increase student engagement.

Scalable Infrastructure and Technical Accessibility

Technical limitations remain a barrier, particularly in under-resourced contexts. eduMathStatAI has been designed with a lightweight structure that is compatible with standard R installations and modest computing requirements. Schools and institutions might consider investing in basic infrastructure, such as shared computer labs or mobile learning devices, while leveraging cloud-based solutions and open-access platforms to reduce cost burdens. Partnerships with local universities or NGOs could help bridge infrastructure gaps through shared services or community outreach programs.

Policy Support for Open-Source and Computational Pedagogy

Sustained implementation of coding-based instruction would benefit from policy-level endorsement. Curriculum authorities could consider embedding computational thinking as a core competency across STEM disciplines and offering recognition for teacher training programs that involve tools like eduMathStatAI. Policies might also recommend open-source educational technologies, ensuring that cost-effective, adaptable, and locally relevant solutions are recommended over proprietary alternatives.

Fostering a Growth-Oriented, Inclusive Learning Culture

Addressing math anxiety and fixed mindsets may require a pedagogical shift toward inclusive and exploratory learning environments. Coding activities can contribute to this by encouraging iteration, experimentation, and productive failure. Teachers might be supported in creating psychologically safe spaces where mistakes are framed as learning opportunities. Lesson materials could incorporate Universal Design for Learning (UDL) principles to ensure accessibility for learners with diverse needs, including language learners and students with disabilities.

Ongoing Evaluation and Collaborative Development

The long-term success of tools like eduMathStatAI likely depends on continuous feedback and iterative development. Establishing communities of practice among educators using the package can facilitate knowledge sharing, co-creation of resources, and real-time troubleshooting. Regular evaluations, including surveys, classroom observations, and performance analytics, should inform future updates to both the package and its associated pedagogical materials.

FUTURE RESEARCH DIRECTIONS

The impact of coding-based learning on student engagement, cognitive load, and learning outcomes represents a crucial area for further investigation. Future research might conduct comparative analyses between traditional teaching methods and coding-enhanced instruction. By applying experimental designs, one group could be taught using eduMathStatAI and coding-integrated lesson plans, while another group receives conventional instruction. This may allow for insights into how coding-based education influences various learning outcomes.

Future research should investigate how coding-based learning influences student engagement, cognitive load, and measurable learning outcomes. Engagement levels might be measured through tracking systems. These insights would help understand how coding influences student motivation and performance in STEM education.

Moreover, qualitative case studies could provide an in-depth analysis of the successful implementation of eduMathStatAI in diverse educational settings. Case studies focusing on real classroom environments can provide a more nuanced understanding of how coding tools like eduMathStatAI are adopted by educators, the challenges they face, and the strategies they employ to integrate technology effectively.

Future studies may also explore longitudinal research to assess the long-term retention of coding-based learning. By investigating how students retain and transfer problem-solving skills and conceptual understanding over time, researchers can determine the sustainability and efficacy of coding-enhanced education for long-term academic success. Furthermore, future research could examine how different student demographics, such as varying levels of prior coding experience or learning abilities, respond to coding-enhanced instruction, thereby providing insights into the scalability and inclusivity of tools like eduMathStatAI in diverse educational contexts.

CONCLUSION

The eduMathStatAI package provides educators with a systematically designed, pedagogically aligned digital toolkit that facilitates the integration of coding into mathematics and statistics instruction. The package promotes accessibility and sustainability by aligning with open-source principles and utilizing widely adopted R-based technologies. In doing so, it addresses critical gaps in computational literacy and supports development of essential 21st-century competencies among both teachers and learners.

Far from being a mere technological supplement, eduMathStatAI may contribute to evolving practices in mathematics and statistics pedagogy. Its design aims to support interactive, learner-centered experiences. Constructivist learning principles are reflected through inquiry-based exploration, dynamic visualization, and iterative problem-solving via hands-on coding activities.

The long-term impact and scalability of the package are supported by ongoing open-source development, planned expansion of modular educational content, and alignment with evolving educational frameworks. These elements collectively ensure that eduMathStatAI remains adaptable to diverse instructional contexts while supporting systemic digital transformation in STEM education.

As collaboration among educators, decision-makers, and developers continues, the integration of coding and computational thinking into mainstream curricula may gradually extend beyond experimental or extracurricular domains. It has potential to become a supportive pedagogical approach that encourages critical thinking, equitable access to digital skills, and readiness for data-driven environments.

Future iterations would benefit from empirical evaluation, longitudinal tracking, and international collaboration. By combining evidence-based assessment with ongoing open-source development, the project may evolve into a valuable resource for integrating computational thinking across mathematics and statistics curricula.

ACKNOWLEDGMENT

This chapter is based on the ongoing work from the Erasmus+ project proposal titled *Digital Skills for Teacher Training: Sustainable and Non-Formal Methods in Maths and Stats with Coding and AI.* While the project was still under review at the time this chapter was prepared, the author was informed of its acceptance during the revision stage. The chapter was written by Dr. İsmail Yenilmez during the project evaluation phase and submitted for consideration as part of the project's preparatory outputs.

The eduMathStatAI package and all materials associated with it are the original work of Dr. Yenilmez and were developed independently, without external funding. The classroom implementation examples and pilot workshops are planned future activities within the accepted Erasmus+ project and will be carried out in schools in Spain, Italy, and Türkiye. Based on the findings of these upcoming studies, subsequent versions of the package and training materials will be refined. The perspectives and recommendations presented here reflect preliminary development work and proposed directions for integrating coding and AI into mathematics and statistics education.

Declaration of Generative AI and AI-Assisted Technologies in the Writing Process:

During the preparation of this manuscript, the author used ChatGPT to assist in improving the readability and clarity of the text. After using this tool, the authors thoroughly reviewed and edited the content as needed and takes full responsibility for the final version. The AI-assisted technology was used only to enhance the manuscript's clarity and presentation, in accordance with ethical guidelines.

REFERENCES

Al Hamad, N. M., Adewusi, O. E., Unachukwu, C. C., Osawaru, B., & Onyebuchi, N. C. (2024). A review on the innovative approaches to STEM education. *International Journal of Science and Research Archive, 11*(1), 244–252. DOI: 10.30574/ijsra.2024.11.1.0026

Alloway, T. P., & Passolunghi, M. C. (2011). The relationship between working memory, IQ, and mathematical skills in children. *Learning and Individual Differences, 21*(1), 133–137. DOI: 10.1016/j.lindif.2010.09.013

Ashcraft, M. H., & Krause, J. A. (2007). Working memory, math performance, and math anxiety. *Psychonomic Bulletin & Review, 14*(2), 243–248. DOI: 10.3758/BF03194059 PMID: 17694908

Bajarin, T. (2016, March 16). *Why schools should teach more than basic coding*. TIME. https://time.com/4261554/why-schools-should-teach-more-than-basic-coding/

Bamigboye, K. (2024). Supporting STEM success: Digital curriculum innovations to foster student retention. [IJSRM]. *International Journal of Scientific Research and Management, 11*(4), 982–1000. DOI: 10.18535/ijsrm/v11i04.ec3

Boaler, J. (2016). *Mathematical mindsets: Unleashing students' potential through creative math, inspiring messages, and innovative teaching*. Jossey-Bass.

Çetinkaya-Rundel, M., & Ellison, V. (2021). A fresh look at introductory data science. *Journal of Statistics and Data Science Education : An Official Journal of the of the American Statistical Association, 29*(sup1, S1), S16–S26. DOI: 10.1080/10691898.2020.1804497

Darling-Hammond, L. (2010). *The flat world and education: How America's commitment to equity will determine our future*. Teachers College Press.

Freeman, S., Eddy, S. L., McDonough, M., Smith, M. K., Okoroafor, N., Jordt, H., & Wenderoth, M. P. (2014). Active learning increases student performance in science, engineering, and mathematics. *Proceedings of the National Academy of Sciences of the United States of America, 111*(23), 8410–8415. DOI: 10.1073/pnas.1319030111 PMID: 24821756

Garfield, J. B., Ben-Zvi, D., Chance, B., Medina, E., Roseth, C., & Zieffler, A. (2008). *Developing students' statistical reasoning: Connecting research and teaching practice*. Springer., DOI: 10.1007/978-1-4020-8383-9

Grover, S., & Pea, R. (2013). Computational thinking in K–12: A review of the state of the field. *Educational Researcher, 42*(1), 38–43. DOI: 10.3102/0013189X12463051

Hiebert, J., & Grouws, D. A. (2007). The effects of classroom mathematics teaching on students' learning. In Lester, F. K. (Ed.), *Second handbook of research on mathematics teaching and learning* (pp. 371–404). Information Age Publishing / National Council of Teachers of Mathematics. DOI: 10.1108/978-1-28141-200-320251013

Mah, D.-K., & Groß, N. (2024). Artificial intelligence in higher education: Exploring faculty use, self-efficacy, distinct profiles, and professional development needs. *International Journal of Educational Technology in Higher Education, 21*(58), 58. Advance online publication. DOI: 10.1186/s41239-024-00490-1

Mangarin, R. A., & Caballes, D. O. (2024). Difficulties in learning mathematics: A systematic review. *International Journal of Innovation and Scientific Research, 11*(9), 401–405. DOI: 10.51244/IJRSI.2024.1109037

National Research Council. (2010). *Report of a workshop on the scope and nature of computational thinking*. The National Academies Press., DOI: 10.17226/12840

Ng, D. T. K., Leung, J. K. L., Su, J., Ng, R. C. W., & Chu, S. K. W. (2023). Teachers' AI digital competencies and twenty-first century skills in the post-pandemic world. *Educational Technology Research and Development*, *71*(1), 137–161. DOI: 10.1007/s11423-023-10203-6 PMID: 36844361

OECD. (2023). *OECD digital education outlook 2023: Towards an effective digital education ecosystem*. OECD Publishing., DOI: 10.1787/c74f03de-

Papert, S. (1980). *Mindstorms: Children, computers, and powerful ideas*. Basic Books.

Ramirez, G., Gunderson, E. A., Levine, S. C., & Beilock, S. L. (2013). Math anxiety, working memory, and math achievement in early elementary school. *Journal of Cognition and Development*, *14*(2), 187–202. DOI: 10.1080/15248372.2012.664593

Rattan, A., Good, C., & Dweck, C. S. (2012). "It's ok—not everyone can be good at math": Instructors with an entity theory comfort (and demotivate) students. *Journal of Experimental Social Psychology*, *48*(3), 731–737. DOI: 10.1016/j.jesp.2011.12.012

Rovshenov, A., & Sarsar, F. (2023). Research trends in programming education: A systematic review of articles published between 2012–2020. *Journal of Educational Technology & Online Learning*, *6*(1), 48–81. DOI: 10.31681/jetol.1201010

Sat, M., & Kadirhan, Z. (2024). Unveiling competence in the classroom: A multidimensional assessment of computer science teachers' self-efficacy in coding education. *Education and Information Technologies*, *29*, 1–29. DOI: 10.1007/s10639-024-12503-7

UNESCO Institute for Statistics. (2025). *National education statistical capacity assessment: Global analysis based on a maturity model* (Report No. UIS/2025/ED/SD/1). UNESCO. https://unesdoc.unesco.org/ark:/48223/pf0000394897

Wing, J. M. (2006). Computational thinking. *Communications of the ACM*, *49*(3), 33–35. DOI: 10.1145/1118178.1118215

Xhako, D., Hoxhaj, S., Hyka, N., & Spahiu, E. (2025). Integrating AI applications into university STEM study programs using Python. *International Journal of Innovative Research and Scientific Studies*, *8*(1), 2374–2384. DOI: 10.53894/ijirss.v8i1.4995

Ye, H., Liang, B., Ng, O.-L., & Chai, C. S. (2023). Integration of computational thinking in K-12 mathematics education: A systematic review on CT-based mathematics instruction and student learning. *International Journal of STEM Education*, *10*(1), 3. DOI: 10.1186/s40594-023-00396-w

Yenilmez, İ. (2016). *İstatistiksel kavramların teknoloji ile öğretiminin matematik didaktiği perspektifinden incelenmesi [Evaluation of teaching statistical concepts using technology from the perspective of the didactics of mathematics]* (Unpublished master's thesis). Marmara University, İstanbul, Türkiye.

Yenilmez, İ. (2025). eduMathStatAI: An R package for math and statistics education (Version 1.0). GitHub. https://github.com/IsmailYenilmez/eduMathStatAI

Yenilmez, İ., & Yavuz, İ. (2016). Using technology in statistical education at high school level: VUstat software and a case of Eskişehir Tepebaşı. In *Proceedings of the 7th International Congress on New Trends in Education* (pp. 55). Antalya, Türkiye.

Zawacki-Richter, O., Marín, V. I., Bond, M., & Gouverneur, F. (2019). Systematic review of research on artificial intelligence applications in higher education – where are the educators? *International Journal of Educational Technology in Higher Education, 16*(1), 39. DOI: 10.1186/s41239-019-0171-0

Zhang, Y., Wang, P., Jia, W., Zhang, A., & Chen, G. (2023). Dynamic visualization by GeoGebra for mathematics learning: A meta-analysis of 20 years of research. *Journal of Research on Technology in Education*. Advance online publication. DOI: 10.1080/15391523.2023.2250886

ADDITIONAL READING

Yenilmez, İ. (2025). eduMathStatAI: An R package for math and statistics education (Version 1.0). GitHub. https://github.com/IsmailYenilmez/eduMathStatAI

KEY TERMS AND DEFINITIONS

Computational Thinking: A problem-solving process that includes logical reasoning and the design of algorithms.

Digital Pedagogy: The use of digital tools and methods to support teaching and learning.

eduMathStatAI: An open-source R package developed to integrate coding into math and statistics education.

Interactive Coding Exercises: Hands-on coding tasks designed to support conceptual learning in a subject area.

Math Modeling: Using mathematical representations to simulate real-world situations.

Non-formal Training: Educational activities that occur outside the formal school curriculum.

Open Educational Resources (OER): Freely accessible, openly licensed teaching and learning materials.

APPENDIX 1

Visualizing Key Concepts in Mathematics and Statistics with eduMathStatAI

This appendix presents a series of educational visualizations created using the eduMathStatAI package. These examples illustrate how computational and visual tools can enhance conceptual understanding and engagement in mathematics and statistics education. The figures demonstrate the pedagogical value of interactive, R-based visualizations in supporting visual reasoning, data interpretation, and the exploration of mathematical relationships.

Figure 1 presents a composite visualization generated using the eduMathStatAI package. The figure includes four pedagogically aligned outputs that demonstrate key mathematical and statistical concepts through interactive R-based visualizations. These plots exemplify how computational tools can support visual thinking, data analysis, and conceptual understanding in mathematics and statistics education.

Figure 1. Composite output from the eduMathStatAI package, illustrating diverse educational visualizations

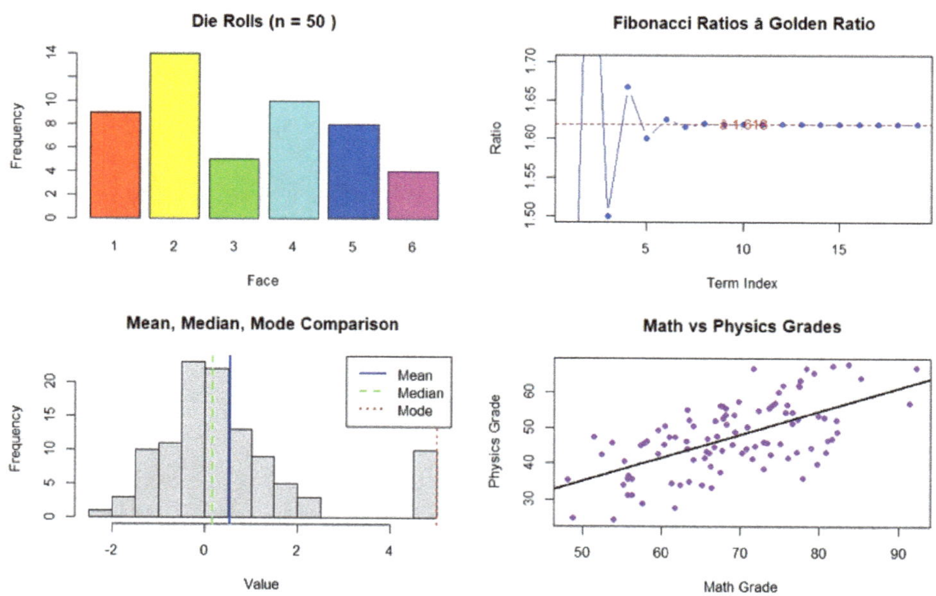

(a) Experimental probability distribution from roll_dice_experiment.R,
(b) Convergence of Fibonacci ratios from fibonacci_ratio.R,
(c) Comparison of mean, median, and mode from mean_median_mode.R, and
(d) Correlation between math and physics scores from grade_correlation.R.

Figure 2 represents the progressive visualizations of die roll distributions using the roll_dice_experiment.R function from the eduMathStatAI. As the sample size increases from (a) $n = 50$ to (d) $n = 5000$, the empirical frequencies gradually converge towards the theoretical uniform distribution, demonstrating how increasing data size leads to a more accurate approximation of expected outcomes. The red dashed lines across each subplot indicate the expected frequency for each die face (n / 6), highlighting the underlying principle of the *Law of Large Numbers*. This visual progression allows students to observe the diminishing variability in the empirical distribution as the number of rolls increases, thus reinforcing the conceptual link between probability theory and real-world data.

Figure 2. Progressive visualization of die roll distributions at increasing sample sizes

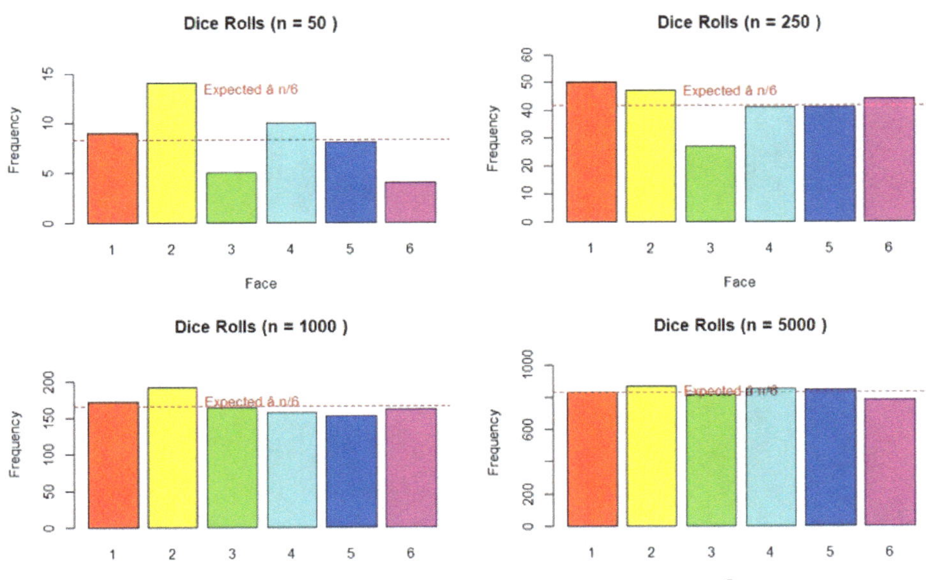

The visualizations presented in this appendix exemplify the pedagogical potential of eduMathStatAI in fostering data-driven reasoning and conceptual understanding. By integrating computational tools and visual representations into mathematics and statistics education, teachers and students can explore patterns, relationships, and theoretical principles in a more interactive and meaningful way.

Chapter 7
Educational Neuroscience of Programming:
Cognitive and Neural Perspectives

Özgür Örün
https://orcid.org/0000-0001-7131-7265
Izmir Institute of Technology, Turkey

ABSTRACT

The integration of programming and coding into education and research has gained prominence. These skills are viewed as both core technical competencies and tools for enhancing cognitive development. This chapter reviews research from neuroscience, education, and cognitive psychology to examine the cognitive and neural processes involved in programming. The chapter examines how programming fosters critical skills like problem-solving, creative thinking, and critical analysis, alongside its demands on analytical intelligence and metacognitive abilities. It delves into the neural mechanisms involved, highlighting the activation of various brain regions responsible for working memory, language processing, and executive control. The chapter highlights neuroplastic changes in gray matter volume and neural efficiency, showcasing how the brain adapts to programming learning across ages. It also explores the cognitive effects of coding education, emphasizing its integration into curricula and its impact on cognitive development through an interdisciplinary research approach.

INTRODUCTION

Programming is a broad and complex skill that involves efficiently addressing and solving problems using computational principles and methods (Badiee et al.,

DOI: 10.4018/979-8-3373-2660-3.ch007

2023; Arfé et al., 2020). It combines essential elements of mathematical reasoning, recursive thinking, and language processing, which makes error tracing in these tasks particularly challenging (Castelhano et al., 2019; Medeiros et al., 2019). The fundamental skills required for programming include understanding the problem, breaking it down into smaller parts, generating algorithms (often represented through flowcharts or pseudocode), and implementing solutions using a programming language (Doukakis, 2019).

Programming requires analytical skills to develop solutions to problems, translate abstract constructs into precise execution commands, and evaluate the outcomes (Çiftçi & Bildiren, 2020). These processes foster some of the essential 21st-century skills, such as creative thinking, questioning, problem-solving, and critical thinking (Çiftçi & Bildiren, 2020). Besides, coding, a subset of programming, is primarily the practical skill of writing computer code and creating software. It is generally considered a less theoretical endeavor than computational thinking itself (Tsarava et al., 2019). Coding involves the direct application of problem-solving strategies, including planning and design, which are fundamental for achieving successful coding outcomes (Çiftçi & Bildiren, 2020). Specifically, coding requires the organization of tasks through step-by-step logic, analysis of inputs and outputs, and formulation of clear problem-solving steps (Çiftçi & Bildiren, 2020). Additionally, coding enhances metacognitive skills by allowing students to articulate their thoughts, monitor their results, and clarify their thinking processes through trial and error (Çiftçi & Bildiren, 2020).

The view of programming education in schools has undergone a common transformation in recent years, with a broad consensus on the necessity of incorporating computational thinking (CT) and active exposure to digital technologies into school curricula (Arfé et al., 2020; Nardelli & Ventre, 2015; Shute et al., 2017). This shift reflects the understanding that coding ability is now an essential skill for students entering the technology-driven global labour market (Çiftçi & Bildiren, 2020; Bers et al., 2014; Burke, 2012; Grover & Pea, 2013; Yen et al., 2012). As a result, the number of studies focusing on CT and its pedagogical integration through coding has been increasing consistently (Arfé et al., 2020; Roman-Gonzalez & Vazquez-Cano, 2017; Shute et al., 2017; Tuomi et al., 2018).

The educational aspects of programming are combined with its capacity to develop various cognitive skills, including creativity, reasoning, and mathematical abilities (Scherer et al., 2019). Learning activities are increasingly designed to include computational thinking dimensions before students start programming, especially for solving authentic problems (Psycharis & Kallia, 2017). This emphasis is evident in various practices in different countries. For example, in Italy, the Code.org platform provided by the 'Programma il futuro' initiative was used to introduce coding to children, allowing them to create sequences of commands by moving blocks (Arfé et al.,

2020). This platform provides immediate visual and written feedback and gradually increases task difficulty, forcing children to maintain a problem-solving approach by switching between computational functions such as sequencing, debugging, and loops (Arfé et al., 2020). Similarly, a study from Türkiye reported that Code.org based coding courses implemented for 4- to 5-year-old preschool children resulted in an increase in nonverbal cognitive abilities (Çiftçi & Bildiren, 2020). Another study from Iran investigated the effectiveness of brain-compatible courseware on computer programming learning achievement and retention of vocational school students and showed improvements compared to traditional methods (Badiee et al., 2023). At the university level, a 15-week course on 'Processing' language for novices in Japan led to structural neuroplastic changes in students' brains (Hongo et al., 2023). Furthermore, 'Brain-Based Programming', an introductory programming concept based on neurodidactic principles tested in Austria, led to significantly better exam performance for students in experimental groups (Sabitzer & Pasterk, 2014). This global trend highlights the growing acceptance of programming as a vital component of contemporary education, promoting cognitive growth beyond mere technical competence (Scherer et al., 2019).

The cognitive and neural processes involved in programming intersect with various domains, including language processing, mathematics, and logic. Programming comprehension activates regions like Brodmann Areas (BA) 6, 21, 40, 44, and 47, which are responsible for working memory, semantic and syntactic processing, and executive control (Peitek et al., 2018; Siegmund et al., 2017). Moreover, code comprehension and debugging tasks engage deductive reasoning and divided attention, highlighting programming's demands on higher-order cognition (Castelhano et al., 2019; Hongo et al., 2023).

Notably, programming has been shown to facilitate both near and far cognitive transfer. Learners benefit not only in coding-related tasks but also in broader domains such as mathematical reasoning, spatial cognition, and metacognitive strategies (Scherer et al., 2019). This convergence of evidence underscores the dual role of programming as both a technical and cognitive discipline. It opens up interdisciplinary pathways for investigating the neural underpinnings of learning and informs curriculum design grounded in educational neuroscience.

By examining programming through a neurocognitive lens, this chapter aims to synthesize findings across neuroscience, education, and cognitive psychology. The following sections will explore neural mechanisms, structural and functional brain adaptations, cognitive outcomes, and implications for instructional design and future research.

NEURAL MECHANISMS UNDERLYING PROGRAMMING AND CODING

The fields of programming and coding are complex cognitive tasks that significantly alter human interaction with technology and demand a broad spectrum of cognitive skills (Castelhano et al., 2019).Programming is characterised as a systematic solution development activity that requires the transformation of abstract conceptual designs into precise, executable commands, followed by a rigorous analytical evaluation of the outputs produced by these commands (Çiftçi & Bildiren, 2020; Arfé et al., 2020). This complex process goes beyond mere technical execution and requires breaking down complex problems into manageable units, abstracting key features, iteratively refining potential solutions, and generalising basic principles (Arfé et al., 2020). It requires innate creative thinking, critical analysis and an enquiring approach; these skills are considered critical for navigating the contemporary environment (Çiftçi & Bildiren, 2020). Coding, on the other hand, is often understood as a specific subset of programming and refers to the act of translating these broader programming designs into concrete, machine-readable instructions using a specific programming language (Scherer et al., 2019). It serves as the primary means by which computational thinking is introduced and nurtured in educational contexts (Arfé et al., 2020).

The act of programming engages a distributed network of brain regions responsible for a wide array of cognitive functions. It requires real-time integration of symbolic processing, syntactic reasoning, visuospatial working memory, and performance monitoring. Far from being localized in any one region, the cognitive operations intrinsic to programming are mapped across the cerebral cortex, drawing on both domain-general and domain-specific systems. Functional magnetic resonance imaging (fMRI) studies have played a crucial role in identifying these activations and elucidating how they vary by task and experience level. fMRI is a technique that indirectly measures brain activity by detecting changes in the "blood oxygen level-dependent" (BOLD) signal. This method is based on the principle that more oxygenated blood is sent to the region to meet the increased energy demand of active neurons. The fact that oxygenated and deoxygenated blood have different magnetic properties allows fMRI to detect this hemodynamic response and thus map brain activity (Logothetis, 2008).

Figure 1. fMRI Device (Resource: https://www.braindynamics.ca/fmri)

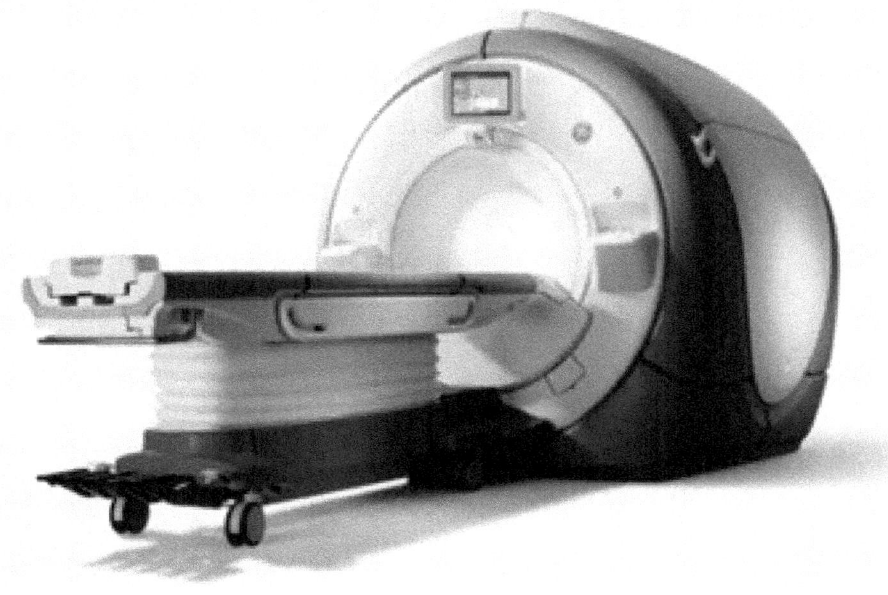

Cognitive Processes and Brain Region Activations

As mentioned before, cognitive processes associated with programming are multifaceted and often overlap with general intellectual abilities. Programming requires problem-solving strategies such as identifying problems, decomposing them, creating algorithms and implementing solutions (Doukakis, 2019). It involves logical thinking and formal logical inference in depth; neural resources for code comprehension share common ground with these functions (Liu et al., 2020). In this context, language processing is an important aspect as understanding computer languages involves cognitive skills similar to learning a second natural language (Hishikawa et al., 2023). Specific brain regions, including Brodmann areas (BA) 21, 44 and 47, form a critical 'language network' for building syntactic structures and extracting semantic information from code (Peitek et al., 2018; Siegmund et al., 2017).

Figure 2. A diagram showing the division of Brodmann Areas in left and right hemispheres (Rahman, 2014; p. 37)

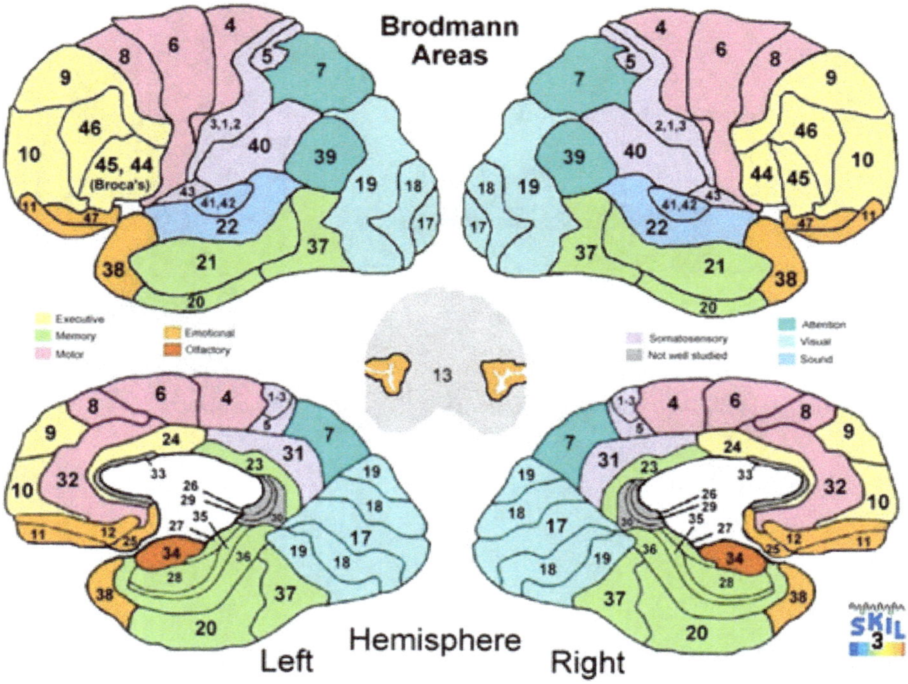

Note: Brodmann areas are regions of the cerebral cortex defined by their cellular structure and organization. This map was originally created based on anatomical differences, but it remains an important reference in neuroscience. These areas are closely linked to specific brain functions.

Working memory plays a critical role in keeping track of variables and values in the 'phonological loop', especially during comprehension (Siegmund et al., 2014; Siegmund et al., 2017). Programmers also show divided attention, distributing their focus on various cognitive activities, such as understanding expressions and processing data simultaneously (Siegmund et al., 2014). The increasing complexity of the source code is associated with a higher need for concentration (Peitek et al., 2018).

Furthermore, programming tasks for beginners involve deductive reasoning; the right middle frontal gyrus is involved in executing and monitoring the cognitive processes necessary to translate rules into reasoning conclusions (Hongo et al., 2023). Bug tracking and bug detection are also fundamental cognitive tasks and are particularly challenging due to the integration of language, logic and mathematical skills (Castelhano et al., 2019). Expert programmers use specific knowledge structures and eye movement patterns during code review (Hishikawa et al., 2023; Uwano et al., 2006; Busjahn et al., 2015).

Brain Regions and Networks

The neural mechanisms underlying programming and coding are spread across a variety of specialized and domain-specific brain regions and networks (Castelhano et al., 2019).

Multiple Demand (MD) System: Programme comprehension is a fundamental component of both activities, consistently activating the Multiple Demand (MD) system, which encompasses domain-specific executive regions located in the forehead and parietal lobes and anterior cingulate cortex (ACC) regions (Ivanova et al., 2020; Shashidhara et al., 2019). This widespread activation highlights a significant dependence on general executive brain functions for code processing (Ivanova et al., 2020). This network is characterised by its domain-specific cognitive core, which shows activation across a broad range of cognitive demands, including those related to mathematics and logic (Ivanova et al., 2020; Duncan, 2010, 2013; Fedorenko et al., 2013). It has been noted that no particular region in the MD system is functionally specialised for code comprehension, reinforcing its role as a flexible, domain-specific rather than programming-specific system (Ivanova et al., 2020; Liu et al., 2020; Weber et al., 2021).

Brodmann Areas (BAs): Specific Brodmann Areas (BAs) are involved in the cognitive processes underlying programming and coding (See Figure 2):

- BA 6 and 40: consistently associated with working memory, attention, problem solving and divided attention capacity, which are critical for the mental manipulation of numerical and linguistic values during programme comprehension (Peitek et al., 2018; Siegmund et al., 2014; Endres et al., 2021). BA 6 and 40 are particularly linked to problem-solving activities, including the phonological loop, which processes verbal and numerical information, and strategic thinking to solve problems embedded in the programme (Siegmund et al., 2014; Peitek et al., 2018).
- BA 21, 44 and 47: Relate to language processing, covering both syntactic and semantic aspects of artificial and natural languages, thus enabling programmers to create syntactic structures and extract meaning from programme tokens (Peitek et al., 2018; Castelhano et al., 2019; Ivanova et al., 2020; Liu et al., 2020). BA 21 is vital for processing semantic information at the word level and enables inference from individual programme markers (Siegmund et al., 2017; Peitek et al., 2018). This region is also a classic natural language processing area, suggesting commonalities in how the brain processes linguistic input, whether natural or artificial (Siegmund et al., 2017). BA 44 is primarily involved in forming syntactic structures (Siegmund et al., 2014; Peitek et al., 2018). This highlights the brain's involvement in parsing the

grammatical rules and hierarchical organisation of programming languages. BA 47 functions as a semantic executive system responsible for organising and controlling the retrieval, selection and evaluation of semantic information (Peitek et al., 2018). This suggests an active role in integrating the meanings of various code elements to form a coherent understanding.

- BA 39: It functions as a cross-modal integration centre that integrates multisensory information necessary for understanding events, manipulating mental representations, solving known problems, and directing attention to relevant information (Peitek et al., 2018; Siegmund et al., 2017). This area emphasises the multimodal integration required for holistic code comprehension.
- Insula (BA 13): The insula, particularly BA 13, plays a prominent role in heuristic expert error detection in computer code (Castelhano et al., 2019). Its activity levels are significantly correlated with the sensitivity of error detection and initial, often subconscious, suspicion towards errors (Castelhano et al., 2019). The insula, as a component of the salience network, is modulated by levels of task difficulty and uncertainty, indicating its role in assessing and responding to challenging or uncertain situations encountered during debugging (Lamichhane et al., 2016; Castelhano et al., 2019). Top-down modulations from the anterior cingulate cortex (BA 32) and anterolateral frontal regions (BA 10) have been observed to causally influence decision processes within the insula, which correlates with activity in mathematical processing regions of the early parietal cortex (Castelhano et al., 2019).

Prefrontal Cortex (PFC): The PFC is broadly implicated in higher-order cognitive functions required for programming (Wallis, 2007; Castelhano et al., 2019). In particular, specific Brodmann Areas within the PFC, such as BA 9, 10 and 46, are associated with causal reasoning and the fusion of information from various mnemonic sources, which enables integrating various pieces of information to form a coherent understanding and design (Castelhano et al., 2019; Baddeley, 2000; Baddeley, 1992). The frontal pole, a subregion of the PFC, is linked to goal-orientated persistence and metacognitive control (Collins & Koechlin, 2012; Hosoda et al., 2020; Strange et al., 2001; Sakai & Passingham, 2002; Daw et al., 2006; Okuda et al, 2007; Badre & Nee, 2018), and increases in grey matter volume (GMV) positively correlated with programming learning performance in novices (Hongo et al., 2023). The right medial frontal gyrus is also part of the PFC and is prominently associated with deductive reasoning and with executing and monitoring cognitive processing, including transformation and modification of rules during learning and application of programming knowledge (Hongo et al., 2023).

The neural processes underlying programming involve the reuse of brain regions that have evolved for other functions, similar to the reuse of brain areas for reading and writing (Castelhano et al., 2019). According to Floyd et al. (2017), although neural representations of programming languages often differ from natural languages, greater expertise may lead to a more similar pattern of neural activation between code and prose.

Relationship with Memory and Cognitive Load

The relationship between memory and programming is multifaceted because cognitive processes require constant interaction with various forms of memory, especially during frequent interruptions or complex problem-solving tasks (Parnin, 2010). Programmers often face difficulties in retaining relevant task knowledge due to frequent interruptions and the need to change tasks (Parnin, 2010). This highlights the critical role of understanding how programmers actively manage their task memory to inform the development of more effective cognitive theories and programming tools (Parnin, 2010).

Working memory is defined as the cognitive system that holds and manipulates information for short periods of time during cognitive tasks (Baddeley, 2001). Research has consistently shown that strong working memory is essential for programming skills and that programming training can potentially improve it (Robins et al., 2003; Çiftçi & Bildiren, 2020; Scherer et al., 2019). During programme comprehension, certain brain regions associated with working memory are activated. For example, Brodmann Areas 6 and 40 are linked to the phonological loop, which is responsible for holding verbal and numerical material while processing code step by step (Siegmund et al., 2014; Peitek et al., 2018). This requires divided attention as programmers mentally track values and relationships within the code. The anterior frontal cortex is also well recognised as a critical area for working memory function (Fuster, 2001; D'Esposito et al., 1998).

Cognitive load, the cognitive load experienced during the coding or programming process, significantly affects an individual's working memory capacity. Program comprehension inherently imposes a high cognitive load, especially when it is based on understanding code expression by expression (a bottom-up approach) without relying on domain-specific knowledge or recognizable patterns (Siegmund et al., 2017; Peitek et al., 2018). This load directly affects working memory as programmers need to memorise and manipulate the values of variables while processing source code (Siegmund et al., 2014). Brain regions associated with working memory, particularly the phonological loop for verbal and numerical material, are continuously activated during program comprehension tasks (Siegmund et al., 2014; Peitek et al., 2018). As source code complexity increases, the demand for concentration also increases, which can further strain working memory (Peitek et al., 2018). Research suggests that the size of the vocabulary in a code snippet is particularly taxing on programmers' working memory (Peitek et al., 2021). If the number of variables or the overall complexity exceeds a programmer's working memory capacity, program comprehension can be impaired (Siegmund et al., 2014). Some research suggests that mental effort can reach saturation at very high levels of complexity (Medeiros et al., 2019), while others show that poor source code dictionary and readability can significantly increase a developer's cognitive load (Fakhoury et al., 2018; Weber et al., 2021). Cognitive demands are also modulated by level of expertise; experienced programmers use cognitive resources more efficiently, potentially reducing the load on working memory when interacting with familiar programming languages (Weber et al., 2021; Crk et al., 2015; Peitek et al., 2018).

Neuroimaging Methods and Contributions

Neuroimaging studies have advanced our understanding of the cognitive processes underlying programming, providing unprecedented insights into how the human brain processes computer code (Siegmund et al., 2014; Medeiros et al., 2019; Weber et al., 2021). These studies, mainly using techniques such as fMRI, Electroencephalography (EEG) and functional Near Infrared Spectroscopy (fNIRS), provide objective and direct measures of brain activity during programming tasks (Endres et al., 2021; Floyd et al., 2017; Doukakis, 2019; Krueger et al., 2020; Medeiros et al., 2019; Peitek et al., 2021). These studies contribute to our understanding in several critical ways:

Specific brain regions and networks are precisely identified: They precisely identify specific brain regions and networks that are activated during programming activities (Siegmund et al., 2014). For example, sustained activation of the Multiple Demand (MD) system and parts of the language network have highlighted their integral role in code comprehension and other programming tasks (Ivanova et al., 2020; Siegmund et al., 2014). The unique involvement of the insula in heuristic error detection is another example of such sensitivity (Castelhano et al., 2019).

Linking brain activation patterns to cognitive processes: Neuroimaging enables researchers to directly relate observed brain activation patterns to underlying cognitive processes (Siegmund et al., 2014). For example, activations in specific Brodmann Areas (See Figure 2; BA 6, 21, 40, 44, 47) during code comprehension have been linked to functions such as working memory, attention, linguistic processing (syntax and semantics), and problem solving (Siegmund et al., 2014; 2017; Peitek et al., 2018). This helps to analyse the complex cognitive load involved in programming.

Empirical validation of cognitive theories: These studies provide empirical confirmation or falsification of existing cognitive theories of programme comprehension (Siegmund et al., 2017).

The relationship between programming and other cognitive domains: Neuroimaging research has shed light on the relationship between programming and other cognitive domains, revealing both shared neural resources and distinct processing pathways (Liu et al., 2020; Weber et al., 2021).

Evidence of neuroplastic changes: These studies provide evidence of neuroplastic changes induced by programming learning (Hongo et al., 2023).

Pedagogical insights: Neuroimaging findings provide pedagogical insights into how programming training can be optimised (Badiee et al., 2023; Doukakis, 2019).

Predicting future performance: Preliminary research suggests that brain activation patterns in beginners can predict future programming performance (Endres et al., 2021).

NEUROPLASTICITY AND LONG-TERM EFFECTS

Limited research using advanced neuroimaging techniques such as fMRI and EEG continues to shed light on the complex neural mechanisms underlying programming activities (Castelhano et al., 2019).

Effects of Coding Activities on Neuroplasticity, Structural and Functional Changes, and the Meaning of Research

Coding activities lead to observable neuroplastic changes in the brain, encompassing both structural and functional changes (Hongo et al., 2023; Siegmund et al., 2014; Peitek et al., 2018). Structurally, learning programming has been associated with significant increases in grey matter volume (GMV) in several brain regions, including the left and right frontal poles, right medial frontal gyrus, left cuneus, bilateral pallidum, left lateral cerebellum (especially posterior lobule and tuber), and medial cerebellum (uvula and tonsil) (Hongo et al., 2023). These structural changes demonstrate the brain's capacity to reorganise itself in response to novel learning experiences (Hongo et al., 2023; Zatorre et al., 2012).

Research on these neuroplastic effects is meaningful as it provides important insights to advance educational practices (Doukakis, 2019). Understanding the neurological underpinnings of coding can inform the design of more effective learning curricula and help identify optimal learning pathways for future developers (Doukakis, 2019). It also has the potential to answer fundamental questions such as how to predict an individual's programming ability, the effects of new programming languages and tools on comprehension, and how best to train programmers for greater efficiency and effectiveness (Siegmund et al., 2014).

The Effect of Coding on Grey Matter Volume (GMV) and Brain Region Connectivity

Coding visibly affects GMV, which generally indicates neuroplastic changes in the brain. A longitudinal study of university students learning the programming language "Processing" over a 15-week course found significant changes in GMV in eight specific brain regions: bilateral frontal poles, right medial frontal gyrus, left cuneus, bilateral pallidum, left lateral cerebellum (posterior lobule and tuber), and medial cerebellum (uvula and tonsil) (Hongo et al., 2023). Furthermore, the degree of GMV change in the right frontal pole was positively correlated with the final product score of the programming course, suggesting a link to goal achievement-related functions (Hongo et al., 2023). Similarly, GMV changes in the right medial frontal gyrus and bilateral pallidum were positively correlated with test scores, implying their role in deductive reasoning and reward functions, respectively (Hongo et al., 2023). These findings highlight that multiple brain regions are activated and structurally altered during programming learning through different functions (Hongo et al., 2023).

In terms of brain region connectivity, sources emphasise changes in activation and volume, but also refer to changes in functional connectivity (Castelhano et al., 2019). For example, in expert error detection, anterior regions of the cingulate (BA32) and middle frontal gyrus (BA10) are reported to causally modulate the insula. The insula, in turn, functionally influences parietal regions (BA 40) and higher-order sensory processing regions (BA 18) (Castelhano et al., 2019). The concept of 'dynamic restructuring of human brain networks during learning' is also being introduced in the context of cognitive training (Taya et al., 2015; Bassett et al., 2011), suggesting that learning, including programming, can lead to changes in the way different brain regions interact and communicate.

Structural and Functional Changes Resulting from Regular Programming Participation

Regular participation in programming can lead to both structural and functional changes in the brain that are indicative of neural adaptation and efficiency. Structurally, increases in grey matter volume identified in studies involving programming courses, even in as little as 15 weeks, suggest that consistent programming practice contributes to the development and maintenance of brain tissue in key cognitive areas (Hongo et al., 2023).

Functionally, regular engagement improved the cognitive processes used during programming (Siegmund et al., 2017; Peitek et al., 2018). Novice programmers exhibit different patterns of brain activity when distinguishing coding from natural language processing or mental rotation (Endres et al., 2021). As programmers gain experience, they exhibit a phenomenon known as "neural efficiency", where they show lower activation in specific brain areas for the same task (Siegmund et al., 2017; Peitek et al., 2018). This reduced activity means that less neural effort is required to perform familiar tasks, which is in line with general theories of expertise (Siegmund et al., 2017). For example, experts may use different neural strategies for code comprehension compared to novices, potentially relying more on semantic cues and less on a tedious, bottom-up approach, leading to reduced brain activation (Siegmund et al., 2017). This efficiency is particularly striking in Brodmann areas 21 and 44, which are critical for language and syntactic processing, and BA 40 for semantic integration (Siegmund et al., 2017).

Development of Skills such as Problem Solving Speed, Cognitive Flexibility and Mental Adaptability through Coding Practice

Coding practice promotes the development of critical cognitive skills, including problem solving speed, cognitive flexibility and mental adaptability. Programming is inherently a problem-solving activity and requires skills that are also vital for other cognitive domains such as parsing, abstraction, iteration, and generalisation (Scherer et al., 2019). Successful coding requires the ability to develop solutions to problems, transform plans into precise commands, and analytically evaluate the results of these commands (Çiftçi & Bildiren, 2020). This process encourages structured thinking, as evidenced by the need to organize work logically step by step and formulate solutions (Çiftçi & Bildiren, 2020).

The meta-analysis by Scherer et al. (2019) provides strong evidence for the transferability of computer programming learning to various cognitive skills. They found an overall moderate transfer effect, strong "near transfer" to related programming tasks, and moderate "far transfer" to dissimilar cognitive challenges (Scherer et al., 2019). Positive transfer was observed for creative thinking, mathematical skills and metacognition, followed by spatial skills and reasoning (Scherer et al., 2019). This suggests that the iterative nature of coding, which involves continuous testing and debugging, reinforces metacognitive skills and encourages a trial-and-error approach, which is critical for cognitive flexibility (Çiftçi & Bildiren, 2020). The coding process also encourages students to express their thoughts clearly, monitor results, and improve their thinking processes (Çiftçi & Bildiren, 2020).

Neuroplastic Responses of Different Age Groups to Programming

Neuroplastic responses to learning programming vary between different age groups, reflecting their developmental stages and educational contexts.

Children: Even at preschool age (4-5 years), coding interventions have shown positive effects. One study observed an increase in non-verbal cognitive abilities in preschool children who participated in a computer programming course (Çiftçi & Bildiren, 2020). This suggests that early exposure to coding promotes cognitive development, although this particular study found no statistically significant difference in problem-solving skills for this age group (Çiftçi & Bildiren, 2020). The push for the inclusion of computational thinking and digital technologies in school curricula is widely recognised (Arfé et al., 2020). Programming activities can significantly improve children's planning and prevention skills (Arfé et al., 2020). A meta-analysis examining the transfer effects of programming has generally included primary and secondary school students, suggesting that many interventions target these age ranges (Scherer et al., 2019).

Adolescents and Young Adults: Most neuroimaging studies on programming, especially fMRI studies, have focused on advanced undergraduates and professionals (Endres et al.) Studies in university students (e.g., first-semester computer science students or those with no prior programming experience) reveal structural neuroplastic changes in grey matter volume after a dedicated programming course (Hongo et al., 2023). For example, 20 software development experts with formal master's and/or PhD degrees and more than 3 years of C language programming experience were recruited for the fMRI error detection study (Castelhano et al., 2019). Research on young programmers has also examined brain activity differences between visual and textual programming languages (Doukakis, 2019).

Elder: Research in 33 countries on the role of education in cognitive decline and brain ageing also provides a framework for understanding brain changes across the lifespan, including old age (Fjell et al., 2025). This suggests the potential for programming to contribute to cognitive health in older adults, although empirical research is needed and direct evidence is lacking.

Comparison of Neuroplastic Effects of Programming with Other Higher-Level Cognitive Activities

The neuroplastic effects of programming are effectively comparable to those of other higher-order cognitive activities such as music, mathematics and second language learning, revealing both shared and distinct neural underpinnings.

Programming is fundamentally similar to mathematical problem solving, as both require basic cognitive skills such as parsing, abstraction, iteration and generalisation (Scherer et al., 2019). Code learning has been shown to improve mathematical calculation skills (Çiftçi & Bildiren, 2020). Neuroimaging studies investigate whether the neural signature of code comprehension is more closely aligned with other culturally derived symbol systems, such as logic and mathematics, or with natural language (Liu et al., 2020; Weber et al., 2021). Although some studies have found that expert error detection does not activate classical maths processing regions (e.g., intraparietal sulcus), this may be because the nature of error detection primarily involves simple syntactic analysis (Castelhano et al., 2019). Conversely, other research highlights that programming may activate areas in the parietal and frontal lobes that are also involved in mathematical processing (Castelhano et al., 2019).

An important aspect of programme comprehension involves language processing (Siegmund et al., 2014). In particular, several Brodmann Areas 21, 44 and 47 are critical for both natural and artificial language processing and are consistently activated during programme comprehension tasks (Siegmund et al., 2014; Peitek et al., 2018; Siegmund et al., 2017). This similarity suggests a shared neural substrate for the processing of structured information. However, recent studies distinguish the neural processing of code and natural language. Although language regions are often activated during code comprehension, some research suggests that code comprehension relies primarily on domain-specific executive brain regions and is not functionally specialised for code within the language system (Ivanova et al., 2020). Furthermore, brain activity during writing code and reading prose has been shown to activate different brain regions, although there is some overlap in traditional language domains such as BA 44 and 45 (Krueger et al., 2020). This means that while programming makes use of some general linguistic capacities, it also utilises unique neural pathways. However, this distinction tends to diminish with increasing expertise (Floyd et al., 2017; Weber et al., 2021).

The effect of music training on cognitive transfer has been the subject of a meta-analysis (Sala & Gobet, 2017a, cited in Scherer et al., 2019). Although one study has investigated the effect of music on brain activity during programming, its results are inconclusive (Ikramov et al., 2019; Weber et al., 2021). However, music training, especially for professional pianists, has been associated with cortical activations in primary and secondary motor areas during complex two-handed movements (Jäncke et al., 2000). This highlights that complex skills, whether programming or music, can lead to specific neural adaptations related to the motor and cognitive demands of the task (Peitek et al., 2018).

After learning a second foreign language, structural neuroplastic changes were observed in Brodmann area 44 in the right frontal lobe, such as increases in grey matter volume and strengthened connections in associated areas (Hosoda et al., 2013). This finding is particularly striking as BA 44 is also activated during programme comprehension (Siegmund et al., 2014; Peitek et al., 2018), suggesting a common neural substrate for the acquisition of complex symbolic systems (whether a spoken language or a programming language).

In conclusion, the neuroplastic effects of programming overlap considerably with mathematical and linguistic processing, exploiting domain-specific executive functions. While sharing some neural resources, it also appears to promote unique adaptations and efficiencies, positioning it as a distinct but interconnected high-level cognitive activity with significant potential for brain development.

COGNITIVE IMPACT OF LEARNING TO CODE

Programming and coding learning are significantly intertwined with the development and enhancement of various cognitive abilities, which makes their study critical for understanding human cognition and improving educational methodologies. The growing emphasis on the inclusion of computational thinking (CT) and digital technologies in school curricula emphasises the necessity to investigate the cognitive effects of these new learning activities (Arfé et al., 2020).

Broad Spectrum of Cognitive Skills

It has been stated that programming and coding are related to a broad spectrum of cognitive skills that are considered as basic 21st-century skills such as creative thinking, questioning, problem solving, and critical thinking (Çiftçi & Bildiren, 2020). In addition, the process includes logical reasoning, mathematical skills, metacognition, planning, design and spatial abilities (Psycharis & Kallia, 2017; Scherer et al., 2019; Çiftçi & Bildiren, 2020; Hishikawa et al., 2023). The basic understanding of computer language, code and algorithm identification required for successful programming overlaps with the skills used in traditional spoken and written languages, suggesting a partial overlap in neural structures and processes for language learning (Hishikawa et al., 2023).

Research shows that programming interventions lead to a moderate overall transfer effect on cognitive skills, with strong proximal transfer effects to programming skills and moderate distal transfer effects to other cognitive domains such as creative thinking, mathematical skills, metacognition, spatial skills and general reasoning (Scherer et al., 2019). This effect extends to neuroplastic changes in the brain, with observed changes in grey matter volume in brain regions related to goal achievement, deduction and reward functions (Hongo et al., 2023). The overall effects highlight that learning programming is not just about acquiring a technical skill, but can profoundly affect a student's cognitive architecture (Siegmund et al., 2014; Peitek et al., 2018; Hongo et al., 2023). These effects are worth investigating as, despite the increasing integration of coding into education, little attention has been paid to its cognitive benefits (Arfé et al., 2020) and understanding these neural correlates is critical for education, training and the design of programming tools and languages (Siegmund et al., 2014).

Variation with Age and Experience Level

The effects of programming activities on cognitive development can vary significantly with age and experience level (Çiftçi & Bildiren, 2020; Hishikawa et al., 2023; Hongo et al., 2023). For preschool children, coding courses showed an increase in non-verbal cognitive abilities, but their effects on problem-solving skills were not statistically significant, which may be due to differences in educational programme goals for different age groups (Çiftçi & Bildiren, 2020). In older age groups, in university students with no previous programming experience, a 15-week course in "Processing" language led to noticeable improvements in programming skills, significantly increasing programming task accuracy (Hishikawa et al., 2023; Hongo et al., 2023).

In terms of experience level, comparative studies between novices and experts reveal different neural activation patterns. Novice programmers tend to show greater activation in brain areas linked to spatial ability and task difficulty compared to experts (Endres et al., 2021). Conversely, the right middle frontal gyrus and inferior frontal gyrus show more activity in programming experts than in novices (Hongo et al., 2023). As expertise increases, the neural distinction between programming languages and natural languages becomes less differentiated, suggesting that skilled programmers process code more similarly to natural language (Floyd et al., 2017; Weber et al., 2021). This phenomenon, known as neural efficiency, is also observed where lower brain activation indicates more efficient cognitive processing; experts show higher power in the Beta range on EEG measures, indicating more efficient use of brain resources (Siegmund et al., 2017; Weber et al., 2021; Lee et al., 2016). Cognitive demands have also been observed to depend on the level of expertise (Weber et al., 2021; Crk et al., 2015).

Strengthening Cognitive Skills such as Problem Solving, Logical Reasoning and Computational Thinking

Cognitive skills such as problem solving, logical reasoning and computational thinking are significantly strengthened through programming and coding. Problem solving is naturally supported as coding tasks require the development of solutions, the transformation of plans into precise commands, and the analytical evaluation of results (Çiftçi & Bildiren, 2020). This involves applying strategies such as planning, systematic organisation and situation analysis to formulate problem solutions (Çiftçi & Bildiren, 2020). Programming interventions show positive transfer effects to tasks requiring problem solving, creative thinking, mathematical skills and metacognition (Scherer et al., 2019).

Computational thinking (CT) is explicitly promoted in educational curricula through active exposure to digital technologies and coding (Arfé et al., 2020). CT is characterised as a conceptual framework for solving problems effectively and efficiently, algorithmically and with reusable solutions (Tsarava et al., 2019). It also encompasses a creative capacity for self-expression through digital tools (Tsarava et al., 2019).

Logical reasoning is naturally applied through programming, which requires analytical thinking and algorithmic procedures (Psycharis & Kallia, 2017). The cognitive processes involved in programming, interpreting and modifying rules and then applying this knowledge to derive responses, are aligned with the functions of the medial frontal gyrus, a brain region associated with deductive reasoning (Hongo et al., 2023). Furthermore, neuroimaging studies show that computer code comprehension shares neural resources with formal logical inference within the fronto-parietal network (Liu et al., 2020). This suggests that the brain processes logical structures within code with similar mechanisms used for abstract logical inference.

Mathematical skills are also reinforced, as coding practices can help students express their thoughts clearly and concisely and help them organise and evaluate their work throughout the problem-solving process (Çiftçi & Bildiren, 2020). Finally, metacognitive skills come into play through the iterative process of trial and error in coding, where students test their codes, monitor the results and improve their thinking processes (Çiftçi & Bildiren, 2020).

Relationship with Executive Functions

Programming and coding activities exhibit a close relationship with executive functions, including cognitive flexibility, response inhibition and attentional control, and lead to positive changes in these areas. Programming skills are understood to rely on traditional intellectual abilities such as executive functions (Hishikawa et al., 2023), and there is direct evidence that coding training can positively affect planning and inhibition skills (Arfé et al., 2020).

In particular, experimental groups exposed to coding interventions showed significant improvements in both NEPSY-II inhibition time and total inhibition errors and STROOP inhibition time and total inhibition errors from pretest to posttest, and most of these improvements were maintained or even increased at follow-up (Arfé et al., 2020). In terms of planning, significant improvements were observed in the experimental group in "Encoding Time planning," "Encoding Accuracy," "Elithorn Accuracy," and "Tower of London Accuracy" (Arfé et al., 2020).

Attention is a crucial component of programming because program comprehension activates brain regions involved in attention (Siegmund et al., 2014; Peitek et al., 2018). Programming tasks often require divided attention, such as visually discriminating multiple features simultaneously (Siegmund et al., 2014). The challenging nature of coding, especially the textual dimension of a code, has been shown to divert programmers' attention (Peitek et al., 2021). Although not explicitly labelled as 'cognitive flexibility', the requirement to translate plans into precise commands, evaluate results (Çiftçi & Bildiren, 2020), and engage in iterative trial and error processes (Çiftçi & Bildiren, 2020) implicitly involves a high degree of cognitive flexibility. Furthermore, after programming learning, structural neuroplastic changes have been observed in brain regions associated with enhanced executive functions and decision-making, such as the right frontal pole and right medial frontal gyrus, which correlate with functions such as persistence and deductive reasoning related to goal achievement (Hongo et al., 2023).

Benefits in Daily Life and Academic Achievement

The cognitive benefits of programming and coding can be observed in both daily life and academic achievement through various mechanisms. In terms of academic achievement, studies have shown that brain-compatible courseware significantly improves students' learning achievement and retention in computer programming courses (Badiee et al., 2023). Furthermore, pedagogical approaches such as "Brain-Based Programming" have been shown to increase learning outcomes and success rates in introductory programming courses, with some evidence even suggesting a particular benefit for female students (Sabitzer & Pasterk, 2014). Neuroimaging studies reveal that neural activation patterns can predict future programming performance and that changes in grey matter volume in specific brain regions (right frontal pole, right medial frontal gyrus and bilateral pallidum) are positively correlated with final project and test scores in programming (Endres et al., 2021; Hongo et al., 2023).

Beyond programming-specific metrics, programming education improves performance on tasks requiring general problem solving and logical reasoning (Psycharis

& Kallia, 2017; Scherer et al., 2019) and shows positive transfer to mathematical skills (Scherer et al., 2019; Çiftçi & Bildiren, 2020). Advanced metacognitive skills such as strategic trial and error and self-monitoring of thought processes developed through coding can also be transferred to other academic learning contexts (Çiftçi & Bildiren, 2020).

In everyday life, benefits arise through remote transfer effects, where skills acquired in programming are directly transferred to situations outside the coding domain. This includes moderate improvements in creative thinking, spatial skills and general reasoning abilities (Scherer et al., 2019). The systematic and logical problem-solving approach developed in programming provides a generalisable framework for addressing real-life challenges (Çiftçi & Bildiren, 2020; Psycharis & Kallia, 2017). Computational thinking, a broader cognitive concept, goes beyond computer-specific applications and promotes analytical thinking, organised problem solving and efficient evaluation in everyday reasoning (Tsarava et al., 2019; Çiftçi & Bildiren, 2020). The brain's capacity to 'reuse' existing neural circuits for new, complex functions such as programming, as it adapts for reading, suggests a profound cognitive adaptability that could benefit a variety of complex tasks in everyday life (Castelhano et al., 2019).

CODING EDUCATION AND COGNITIVE DEVELOPMENT

The integration of coding education into curricula has garnered significant attention due to its potential to foster a broad array of cognitive skills and influence brain activity. Research employing various neuroimaging techniques and educational studies has begun to delineate the specific mental processes engaged and enhanced by learning computer programming, as well as the ways in which these educational approaches can be effectively implemented and evaluated (Arfé et al., 2020; Badiee et al., 2023; Çiftçi & Bildiren, 2020; Doukakis, 2019; Endres et al., 2021; Hongo et al., 2023; Ivanova et al., 2020; Peitek et al., 2021; Psycharis & Kallia, 2017; Sabitzer & Pasterk, 2014; Scherer et al., 2019; Siegmund et al., 2014; Siegmund et al., 2017; Tsarava et al., 2019; Wang et al., 2023; Weber et al., 2021).

Coding education contributes to the development of several mental skills that are crucial for cognitive development. These include planning and inhibition skills, as demonstrated by improvements observed in children participating in coding activities compared to control groups (Arfé et al., 2020). Beyond these, computer programming supports creative thinking, questioning, problem-solving, and critical thinking, which are considered fundamental 21st-century abilities (Çiftçi & Bildiren, 2020; Psycharis & Kallia, 2017). Solving problems through coding specifically requires the development of solutions, the ability to transform plans into precise executable commands, and the analytical skills needed to evaluate command results (Çiftçi & Bildiren, 2020). The learning process embedded in coding also encourages students to articulate their thoughts, monitor outcomes, and clarify their thinking processes, thereby engaging metacognitive skills and reinforcing a trial-and-error approach (Çiftçi & Bildiren, 2020). Furthermore, coding practices can assist students in analyzing their thoughts clearly and concisely, and in organizing and evaluating their work throughout the problem-solving process, reinforcing various mathematical skills (Çiftçi & Bildiren, 2020). A meta-analysis confirmed that learning computer programming leads to positive transfer effects on creative thinking, mathematical skills, metacognition, spatial skills, and reasoning (Scherer et al., 2019). Structural neuroplastic changes in the brain regions associated with persistent attempts to accomplish tasks (goal achievement-related function), deduction, and reward functions have been observed in programming beginners, with these changes correlating positively with learning performance, indicating the involvement of multiple brain regions in programming learning through distinct functions (Hongo et al., 2023).

Regarding cognitive differences between block-based and text-based programming languages in educational environments, a field study explored potential differences in brain activity during programming with a visual programming language versus a textual one among novice programmers (Doukakis, 2019). Surprisingly, the type of programming language did not significantly affect the students' brain activity (Doukakis, 2019). However, six out of eight students needed more time to successfully develop programs with the first programming language they used, regardless of whether it was visual or textual, suggesting a learning curve effect that transcends the specific language type (Doukakis, 2019). This study found no reduction or increase in brain activity or development time for most students as they spent more time on tasks (Doukakis, 2019). In contrast, a meta-analysis on transfer effects of programming education noted that most studies used visual rather than text-based programming tools in their interventions, suggesting a potential preference or perceived suitability for younger learners (Scherer et al., 2019). Another study investigating a blended computational thinking course that incorporated both unplugged activities and plugged-in interventions using Scratch (a block-based environment) and Scratch for Arduino, and a robot simulation environment, did not explicitly detail cognitive differences between the programming language types but showed the effectiveness of the combined approach (Tsarava et al., 2019).

Text-based coding environments are often perceived to require more mental effort due to factors related to code complexity and the cognitive processes involved in their comprehension. Functional magnetic resonance imaging (fMRI) studies have been instrumental in investigating the neural correlates of program comprehension, contrasting it with tasks like locating syntax errors or reading natural language (Peitek et al., 2021; Siegmund et al., 2014; Siegmund et al., 2017; Weber et al.,

2021). Program comprehension itself is a complex cognitive process that places a high cognitive load on programmers (Siegmund et al., 2017; Yousoof et al., 2007). Research indicates that a code's textual size drives programmers' attention, and vocabulary size burdens programmers' working memory, contributing to the perceived difficulty (Peitek et al., 2021). When source code is obfuscated, such as through word scrambling, it becomes more difficult to understand, forcing programmers to rely more on bottom-up comprehension, which is inherently tedious and associated with high cognitive load, and can make immediate understanding challenging (Siegmund et al., 2017). This increased mental effort is reflected in neural efficiency, where lower brain activation indicates a more efficient and easier cognitive process (Siegmund et al., 2017). For instance, bottom-up comprehension, particularly with obfuscated code, leads to stronger activation in brain areas related to natural and artificial language processing (BAs 21, 44) and integration of semantic information (BA 40), compared to comprehension aided by semantic cues (Siegmund et al., 2017; Siegmund et al., 2014). This suggests that when clear semantic cues (like meaningful variable names or formatting) are absent, programmers exert more effort to extract meaning from the basic syntactic and lexical information (Siegmund et al., 2017). The relationship between mental effort and learning outcomes is complex; while high cognitive load can hinder learning, engaging in challenging tasks can also promote deeper processing and the development of more efficient neural pathways over time (Taya et al., 2015).

Beyond coding, computational thinking (CT) promotes development in various cognitive areas through its inherent problem-solving strategies and analytical demands. CT is understood as a set of problem-solving strategies, such as planning and design, which are fundamental to computer science education and central to successful coding outcomes (Çiftçi & Bildiren, 2020). It involves thinking like a computer scientist, which encompasses concepts like decomposition, pattern recognition, abstraction, and algorithms (Tsarava et al., 2019). CT is recognized as supporting high-level abilities for everyone, including creative thinking, questioning, problem solving, and critical thinking (Çiftçi & Bildiren, 2020; Psycharis & Kallia, 2017). A meta-analysis demonstrated that learning computer programming, which is often a vehicle for CT, yields positive transfer effects on reasoning, creative thinking, metacognition, and mathematical and spatial skills (Scherer et al., 2019). Although direct evidence on CT's impact beyond coding in sources is limited, the strong correlation between programming and these cognitive skills implies that CT fosters these broader abilities, making it an early predictor of academic success (Tsarava et al., 2019).

The effects of coding education vary across different age groups. For preschool children (4-5 years old), coding courses have shown an increase in non-verbal cognitive abilities, although no statistically significant difference in problem-solving skills was observed in one study, possibly due to curriculum differences for various age groups (Çiftçi & Bildiren, 2020). The curriculum for 4-year-olds focuses on creativity and problem-solving, while for 5-year-olds, it emphasizes preparation for primary school (Çiftçi & Bildiren, 2020). A meta-analysis also included studies on kindergarten children, finding a transfer effect of 0.41 (Scherer et al., 2019). For primary and secondary school students, the meta-analysis found positive transfer effects on cognitive skills, with a strong effect for near transfer (e.g., programming skills) and a moderate effect for far transfer (e.g., reasoning, mathematical skills, creative thinking, spatial skills, metacognition) (Scherer et al., 2019). For high school students, computer programming education has been shown to improve reasoning skills (Psycharis & Kallia, 2017). Among university students (novices), learning computer programming (a 15-week course) induced significant structural neuroplastic changes in eight brain regions associated with goal achievement, deduction, and reward functions, with these changes correlating positively with learning outcomes (Hongo et al., 2023). Studies on advanced undergraduates and professionals, often using fMRI, reveal that expert programmers exhibit neural efficiency, meaning lower brain activation for the same task, indicating more efficient cognitive processing (Siegmund et al., 2017; Endres et al., 2021). Novice coding, in contrast, generally shows more activation in areas associated with spatial ability and task difficulty (Endres et al., 2021). These findings suggest that coding education promotes a range of cognitive developments, from basic non-verbal abilities in young children to more efficient neural processing in experienced learners.

Programming-based teaching approaches can be effectively integrated into general education curricula by drawing on insights from neuroeducation and cognitive science. There is a general consensus on the need to introduce computational thinking and active exposure to digital technologies in school curricula (Arfé et al., 2020). One approach involves utilizing brain-compatible courseware, which has been shown to significantly improve students' learning achievement and retention in computer programming compared to conventional methods (Badiee et al., 2023). This highlights the importance of instructional materials designed to align with how the brain learns. Another effective strategy is through neurodidactical principles, as implemented in "Brain-based Programming" concepts, which structure lessons as open learning units allowing students to follow their own learning rhythm and choose tasks, topics, and collaboration styles based on individual knowledge, needs, and interests (Sabitzer & Pasterk, 2014). This approach also suggests dividing students into groups such as professionals (peer-tutors), amateurs, and real beginners, offering diverse activities to match individual preconditions and competencies (Sabitzer & Pasterk, 2014). Furthermore, the use of blended learning models incorporating both "unplugged" (offline, conceptual activities like board games) and "plugged-in" (computer-based coding environments and robot simulations) interventions can effectively foster computational thinking (Tsarava et al., 2019). Such integrated approaches ensure that students are actively engaged, and that learning activities prior to coding focus on problem-solving strategies like planning and design (Çiftçi & Bildiren, 2020; Psycharis & Kallia, 2017).

IMPLICATIONS FOR EDUCATION AND FUTURE RESEARCH

Neuroscientific findings can significantly inform the integration of programming and coding into school curricula, enabling innovative approaches within the scope of instructional design (Sabitzer & Pasterk, 2014; Arfé et al., 2020).

Instructional Design and Curriculum Implementation

Research suggests that brain-compatible courseware can significantly improve students' learning achievement and retention in computer programming compared to non-brain-compatible courseware and conventional methods, inferring its greater effectiveness (Badiee et al., 2023). This indicates a direct application of neuroscientific principles to the design of instructional materials.

Furthermore, the field of neurodidactics explicitly aims to leverage understandings of the learning brain to propose effective teaching and learning strategies, integrating insights from neuroscience with educational science, progressive pedagogy, didactics, and psychology (Sabitzer & Pasterk, 2014). An empirical study demonstrated a significant positive impact of a concept rooted in Caine's principles of "brain-based learning" in science classes, suggesting the potential of such principles for programming education (Sabitzer & Pasterk, 2014). This holistic approach allows for a diverse educational methodology for program development and helps in identifying optimal learning pathways (Doukakis, 2019).

In terms of curriculum design, incorporating computational thinking skills can be achieved through blended courses that combine unplugged activities (such as life-size board games to introduce CT concepts) with plugged-in interventions (like applying CT concepts in Scratch, transferring them to Scratch for Arduino, and simulating robots in Open Roberta Lab) (Tsarava et al., 2019). Such a restructured curriculum, emphasizing critical thinking skills, has been shown to foster positive attitudes towards computer science and enhance mathematical calculation abilities (Çiftçi & Bildiren, 2020). Moreover, brain enhancement systems, informed by neurotechnology and an understanding of brain cognitive functions, hold the promise of improving cognitive performance and accelerating the learning process. These systems could benefit from real-time monitoring of cognitive workloads using electroencephalography (EEG) biomarkers to flexibly adjust the difficulty levels of training tasks, thereby preventing cognitive overload and mental fatigue that can hinder learning gains (Taya et al., 2015). This demonstrates a direct link between neuroscientific monitoring and dynamic instructional adjustment.

Studies have already explored the cognitive impacts of coding on preschool children (4-5 years old), demonstrating an increase in their non-verbal cognitive abilities (Çiftçi & Bildiren, 2020). However, differences in preschool education programs, which might focus on creativity and problem-solving for 4-year-olds versus reading and writing preparation for 5-year-olds, could influence the observed outcomes in problem-solving skills (Çiftçi & Bildiren, 2020). This highlights the need for age-appropriate curriculum design that aligns with developmental goals, such as using motion blocks or control flow concepts like message passing, repeat loops, timing, endless loops, looks, and triggering commands for young children (Strawhacker & Bers, 2019).

Interdisciplinary Approaches and Research Collaborations

To comprehensively understand the cognitive impacts of programming and coding education, interdisciplinary research models that integrate insights from diverse fields are essential. Historically, little attention has been paid to the neural and cognitive impacts of incorporating computational thinking (CT) and coding into schools. This gap necessitates a multidisciplinary approach to assess impact and inform curriculum planning (Arfé et al., 2020; Doukakis, 2019). Research on cognitive processes during programming already encompasses general cognitive theories such as problem solving, knowledge acquisition and construction, and solution design (Doukakis, 2019).

An interdisciplinary model for understanding the cognitive effects of programming and coding, educational neuroscience draws heavily from neuroscience, educational science, and psychology, including their theories, concepts, and methods. According to Sabitzer and Pasterk (2014), neurodidactics, a term primarily used in German-speaking countries that refers to educational concepts such as educational neuroscience, neuropedagogy, brain-based learning, or mind, brain, and education science, can assist students in understanding difficult and complex subjects. This approach aims to provide a comprehensive view of the learning brain to inform effective teaching strategies (Sabitzer & Pasterk, 2014). A key application involves brain enhancement systems that leverage neurophysiological signals, such as EEG biomarkers, for real-time monitoring of cognitive workloads. This allows for dynamic adjustment of task difficulty during cognitive training interventions, preventing overload and maximizing learning gains (Taya et al., 2015). Such systems can accelerate learning performance, which is particularly beneficial for struggling students (Taya et al., 2015). Empirical studies on program comprehension have already benefited from interdisciplinary teams comprising psychologists, neurobiologists, linguists, computer scientists, and software engineers to interpret complex neuroimaging data and discuss the relevance of various cognitive processes to programming (Siegmund et al., 2014). Such collaborative interpretation is crucial because individual brain regions are often associated with multiple cognitive processes (Siegmund et al., 2014).

Future research requires models that explicitly compare coding with other cognitive domains. For instance, studies are needed to investigate whether the neural signature of code comprehension is akin to other culturally derived symbol systems, such as logic and mathematics, or if it more closely resembles natural language processing (Liu et al., 2020). This involves designing tasks that differentiate between code comprehension, fake code, mathematical problems, logical inference, and natural language comprehension (Liu et al., 2020). Similarly, research should explore how brain activity during coding relates to tasks involving prose reading or spatial visualization (mental rotation), as findings suggest distinct neural patterns but also some overlap (Endres et al., 2021). The question of whether code comprehension primarily relies on domain-general executive brain regions or more specialized language systems also points to a model integrating cognitive science and neuroimaging expertise (Ivanova et al., 2020).

The study of structural neuroplastic changes associated with programming learning is another area requiring interdisciplinary effort, combining neuroimaging techniques with educational assessments (Hongo et al., 2023). The use of triangulation techniques, long-term studies, and continuous learner tracking are crucial methodological components in these interdisciplinary models to provide robust findings (Doukakis, 2019). Finally, the emerging field of computational neuroscience, which involves studying convergent representations of computer programs in human and artificial neural networks, signifies another frontier for interdisciplinary collaboration to deepen the understanding of programming's cognitive impact (Srikant et al., 2022).

Collaborations between instructional technologies, neuroscience, and learning and educational sciences are driving new areas of research and application to better understand the role of coding in cognitive training. A key emerging area is the development and implementation of "brain-compatible courseware," which has demonstrated superior effectiveness in improving learning success and retention in programming (Badiee et al., 2023). This highlights the direct application of neuroscientific insights to educational software design. Furthermore, the synergy between these disciplines allows for in-depth investigations into program comprehension at the neurological level. Research using fMRI has sought to validate long-standing theories of program comprehension, such as "pointers," "plans," and "semantic chunking," and to explore the concept of "neural efficiency," which indicates a more efficient cognitive process (Siegmund et al., 2017). This area of research may lead to new applications in optimizing learning efficiency and designing programming languages and tools that are more neurally compatible and easier to understand (Siegmund et al., 2014). These studies also pave the way for predicting programming aptitude or expertise based on neural activity patterns (Siegmund et al., 2014).

The observed cognitive benefits from coding, including improved nonverbal cognitive abilities in preschool children (Çiftçi & Bildiren, 2020) and the relationships between coding aptitude, computational thinking, creative thinking, and working memory in young children (Wang et al., 2023), highlight the importance of this interdisciplinary work for early childhood education. New application areas include designing age-appropriate coding curricula and tools that target these specific cognitive developments.

In terms of research methods, collaboration has fostered the use of neurophysiological data (fMRI, EEG, fNIRS, heart rate, skin conductance, eye tracking) to predict various mental states (e.g., cognitive load, emotional state, perceived progress, uninterruptibility, stress) and task performance during software development activities (Weber et al., 2021). This has given rise to the concept of neuroadaptive systems, which can support users in real time by automatically adjusting to their cognitive and emotional states, thus improving human-computer interaction (Weber et al., 2021). The growing trend of multimodal data collection, combining various neurophysiological methods with behavioral data such as eye tracking, allows for more detailed analyses and a holistic understanding of cognitive processes in real-world programming scenarios (Weber et al., 2021). This ongoing integration also paves the way for a new generation of neuroscientists who will need to be proficient in coding, signaling a deepening interdependence between these fields (Juavinett, 2022).

Research Methods and Measurement Approaches

Future research aiming to uncover the effects of programming and coding on cognitive development can utilize a variety of methodological approaches, methods, techniques, and tools. As is well known, robust research designs are crucial. Experimental or quasi-experimental designs, particularly pretest-posttest control group designs, are critical for establishing causal relationships between coding interventions and cognitive outcomes (Arfé et al., 2020; Çiftçi & Bildiren, 2020; Scherer et al., 2019). To account for developmental changes, cross-sectional and longitudinal studies are essential to assess effects at different ages and over extended periods of time (Arfé et al., 2020). Given the potential instability of executive functions over time, researchers should employ strategies such as using multiple tasks for the same executive function measure to increase reliability (Arfé et al., 2020).

Advances in neuroimaging offer powerful tools. fMRI can be used to identify brain regions activated during code comprehension and error detection, and to compare neural signatures of programming with natural language, logic, or mathematical processing (Castelhano et al., 2019; Endres et al., 2021; Ivanova et al., 2020; Liu et al., 2020; Siegmund et al., 2014; Weber et al., 2021). EEG, with its high temporal resolution and portability, is valuable for assessing cognitive workload and distinguishing brain activation patterns across different programming languages or task difficulties (Doukakis, 2019; Medeiros et al., 2019; Weber et al., 2021). fNIRS offers a balance of spatial and temporal resolution to measure neural activity during mental workload and cognitive load (Endres et al., 2021; Weber et al., 2021). These brain activity measurements are often complemented by behavioral data such as task performance, response time, and accuracy (Weber et al., 2021).

To capture the dynamic nature of cognitive processes, eye-tracking measurements, including fixations, saccades, pupil dilation, and blink rates, can provide detailed insights into visual attention and cognitive load during code comprehension (Weber et al., 2021). Furthermore, multimodal data collection, combining various neurophysiological methods with behavioral data, is increasingly important to provide a more holistic understanding of cognitive states, as one modality can compensate for the limitations of another (Weber et al., 2021). Longitudinal analysis of gray matter volume (GMV) using MRI can reveal structural neuroplastic changes associated with programming learning and relate these changes to learning outcomes (Hongo et al., 2023). For large-scale studies, General Additive Mixed Models (GAMM), Linear Mixed Models, and Principal Component Analysis (PCA) are advanced statistical tools for analyzing the relationships between training, brain structure, and cognitive function over time (Fjell et al., 2025). Triangulation techniques and long-term student monitoring are also critical for a comprehensive understanding (Doukakis, 2019).

In this context, it is recommended to use various standardized and validated instruments, which have been included in similar studies accessible in the literature, albeit in limited numbers:

Executive Function (EF) tasks: These include measures of planning (e.g., Encoding Time planning, Elithorn Time planning, Tower of London) and response inhibition (e.g., NEPSY-II Inhibition, STROOP Inhibition) (Arfé et al., 2020).

Cognitive abilities: Tests such as the Colored Progressive Matrices Test for non-verbal cognitive abilities and the Problem Solving Skills Scale (PSSS) for young children can be used (Çiftçi & Bildiren, 2020).

Computational Thinking (CT) assessments: Focusing on flow-of-control concepts, Mühling et al. (2015), the Variable Assessment for various CT concepts (Weintrop & Wilensky, 2015), tablet-based cognitive assessments (Ambrosio et al., 2015), or the Code Development (CODE) Test for preschoolers (Tsarava et al., 2019).

General cognitive skills: Standardized tests for creative thinking (e.g., Torrance Test of Creative Thinking), reasoning (e.g., Cornell's Critical Thinking Test), and spatial skills (2D/3D object understanding tests) (Scherer et al., 2019). Measures of working memory span (WRS), calculation (CALC), multiplication (MUL), and computational problem solving (COM) may also be relevant (Tsarava et al., 2019). Neuroimaging data interpretation: Tools such as the Talairach daimon are used to attribute active voxel clusters to specific Brodmann areas (Siegmund et al., 2017).

Behavioral performance tests: Researcher-administered programming tests for achievement and retention (Badiee et al., 2023) and specific code snippets designed to elicit bottom-up or semantic cue comprehension, with syntax error tasks as controls (Siegmund et al., 2014; Siegmund et al., 2017).

Self-report measures and questionnaires: Assess programming experience and Java knowledge (Siegmund et al., 2014), but these should be critically evaluated for potential biases (Weber et al., 2021).

Code metrics: Software complexity measures (e.g., McCabe, Halstead) to characterize stimuli (Siegmund et al., 2014; Peitek et al., 2018).

To measure the long-term cognitive effects of coding training, a comprehensive evaluation framework combining longitudinal studies with various evaluation methodologies can be developed. Such a framework might include:

1. *Longitudinal Study Design:* Conduct studies that follow participants over extended periods of time with multiple measurement points to capture long-term changes beyond just pretest and posttest (Arfé et al., 2020; Doukakis, 2019; Fjell et al., 2025; Hongo et al., 2023).
2. *Variety of Cognitive Assessments:* Use a battery of validated tests to measure a wide range of cognitive skills identified as benefiting from coding (planning, inhibition, creative thinking, problem solving, critical thinking, mathematical skills, metacognition, reasoning, and spatial skills) (Arfé et al., 2020; Çiftçi & Bildiren, 2020; Scherer et al., 2019; Wang et al., 2023). This should include both standardized and non-standardized tests when appropriate (Scherer et al., 2019).
3. *Neuroimaging Techniques:* Integrating neuroimaging methods such as fMRI, EEG, and fNIRS to observe structural and functional brain changes over time. Longitudinal analysis of gray matter volume (GMV) can reveal neuroplastic changes that correlate with learning outcomes (Hongo et al., 2023), while fMRI can identify specific brain region activation patterns associated with different cognitive processes during encoding tasks (Siegmund et al., 2014; Siegmund et al., 2017). Measuring neural efficiency can indicate the development of more efficient cognitive processing with expertise (Siegmund et al., 2017).
4. *Predicting Future Performance:* Incorporating deep learning and/or AI-assisted analyses to determine whether early neural activation patterns or cognitive performance metrics can predict long-term programming performance or transfer effects to other academic domains (Endres et al., 2021).

5. *Control Group Methodologies*: Using untreated control groups to isolate the specific effects of coding training from other learning experiences (Scherer et al., 2019).
6. *Considering Moderating Variables:* Collecting and analyzing data on potential moderating variables such as participant age, prior experience, learning environment (e.g., extracurricular vs. regular lessons), and specific programming tools or languages used (Scherer et al., 2019).
7. *Qualitative Data and Behavioral Metrics:* Supplementing neuroimaging and standardized testing with behavioral measures (e.g., task completion time, accuracy) and qualitative data (e.g., self-reports, interviews) to provide a holistic understanding of cognitive processes and learning experiences (Siegmund et al., 2014; Siegmund et al., 2017).

It is hoped that integrating the various methodological approaches, frameworks, methods, techniques, and tools mentioned in this section will contribute to future research producing a more nuanced and comprehensive understanding of how programming and coding education profoundly affects cognitive development.

CONCLUSION

The research-based findings reviewed in this section demonstrate that coding, encompassing the broader category of programming, is not merely a technical skill but also a cognitively demanding process that engages multiple brain regions. Programming can have effects on problem solving, memory, executive functions, and neuroplasticity. Furthermore, its educational applications have the potential to be a useful tool for cognitive development. The findings examined from a limited number of studies suggest the need for further research on the cognitive mechanisms underlying programming and the development of neuroscience-inspired teaching methodologies. Future research is recommended to explore how coding can be used for cognitive development and develop pedagogical strategies to enhance its potential benefits.The integration of computer programming and coding into educational curricula represents a significant transformation, driven by the recognition of their role as essential technical competencies and powerful catalysts for broader cognitive development. This field, broadly termed the educational neuroscience of programming, underscores the profound implications of programming for enhancing diverse cognitive functions.

Learning to program is understood as a high-level, complex skill that requires problem-solving based on computational principles, integrating mathematical, recursive thinking, and language processing. Coding, as a subset, focuses on the practical skill of writing computer code and building programs. These activities cultivate crucial 21st-century abilities, including creative thinking, questioning, problem-solving, and critical thinking, and significantly bolster skills such as logical reasoning, mathematical proficiency, metacognition, planning, design, and spatial abilities. Notably, programming has been empirically shown to induce moderate overall transfer effects to other cognitive skills, including strong "near transfer" to related programming tasks and moderate "far transfer" to dissimilar cognitive challenges, extending benefits to creative thinking, mathematical skills, and metacognition.

The neuroscientific underpinnings reveal that programming is a cognitively demanding process that engages multiple brain regions. Functional neuroimaging techniques (fMRI, EEG, fNIRS) have shown consistent activation in areas related to working memory (Brodmann Areas 6, 40), language processing (BAs 21, 44, 47), attention, and problem-solving. The Multiple Demand (MD) system, a domain-general executive network, is consistently recruited, indicating a broad engagement of higher-order cognitive functions. The insula, specifically BA 13, plays a distinct role in intuitive expert bug detection. Importantly, programming learning induces significant structural neuroplastic changes, observed as increases in gray matter volume (GMV) in regions like the frontal poles, medial frontal gyrus, and pallidum, with these changes correlating positively with learning performance and test scores. This demonstrates that learning to program physically alters brain structures, akin to the brain's reutilization of regions for new complex activities like reading.

Differences in brain activation patterns are observed with experience; expert programmers exhibit neural efficiency, meaning lower brain activation for the same task, indicating more efficient processing. For experts, the neural representation between programming code and natural language becomes less differentiated, suggesting that code is processed more like a native language. Cognitive demands, including working memory load, are significantly impacted by code complexity and vocabulary size, with understanding obfuscated code imposing a particularly high cognitive load.

The findings have crucial implications for education and future research. Understanding the neurological underpinnings can inform the design of more effective learning curricula and help in identifying optimal learning pathways. Concepts like brain-compatible courseware and neurodidactical principles have already shown promise in improving learning achievement and retention in programming. Age-appropriate curricula are vital, as even preschool children show increases in non-verbal cognitive abilities from coding interventions.

To advance this understanding, interdisciplinary research models are essential, integrating insights from neuroscience, educational science, psychology, and computer science. Future research needs to employ robust methodologies, including longitudinal study designs, diverse cognitive assessments, and advanced neuroimaging techniques (fMRI, EEG, fNIRS, eye-tracking) to measure both structural and functional brain changes over time. These comprehensive approaches will enable the development of pedagogical strategies to further enhance how coding can be used for cognitive development and to fully realize its potential benefits.

REFERENCES

Arfé, B., Vardanega, T., & Ronconi, L. (2020). The effects of coding on children's planning and inhibition skills. *Computers & Education, 148*, 103807. DOI: 10.1016/j.compedu.2020.103807

Baddeley, A. (1992). Working Memory. *Science, 255*(5044), 556–559. Advance online publication. DOI: 10.1126/science.1736359 PMID: 1736359

Baddeley. (2000). The episodic buffer: A new component of working memory? *Trends in Cognitive Sciences, 4*(11), 417–423. http:// www.ncbi.nlm.nih.gov/pubmed/11058819

Badiee, E., Nili, M. R., & Abedini, Y. (2023). Brain-compatible courseware impact on learning computer programming. *International Journal of Technology Enhanced Learning, 15*(1), 1–13. DOI: 10.1504/IJTEL.2023.127933

Badre, D., & Nee, D. E. (2018). Frontal cortex and the hierarchical control of behavior. *Trends in Cognitive Sciences, 22*(2), 170–188. DOI: 10.1016/j.tics.2017.11.005 PMID: 29229206

Bassett, D. S., Wymbs, N. F., Porter, M. A., Mucha, P. J., Carlson, J. M., & Grafton, S. T. (2011). Dynamic reconfiguration of human brain networks during learning. *Proceedings of the National Academy of Sciences of the United States of America, 108*(18), 7641–7646. DOI: 10.1073/pnas.1018985108 PMID: 21502525

Bers, M. U., Flannery, L., Kazakoff, E. R., & Sullivan, A. (2014). Computational thinking and tinkering: Exploration of an early childhood robotics curriculum. *Computers & Education, 72*, 145–157. DOI: 10.1016/j.compedu.2013.10.020

Burke, W. Q. (2012). *Coding & composition: Youth storytelling with Scratch programming* (Unpublished doctoral dissertation). Available from ProQuest Dissertations & Theses Global, 1–144. University of Pennsylvania. (1021379799).

Busjahn, T., Bednarik, R., Begel, A., Crosby, M., Paterson, J. H., Schulte, C., . . . Tamm, S. (2015, May). Eye movements in code reading: Relaxing the linear order. In *2015, IEEE 23rd International Conference on Program Comprehension* (pp. 255-265). IEEE.

Castelhano, J., Duarte, I. C., Ferreira, C., Duraes, J., Madeira, H., & Castelo-Branco, M. (2019). The role of the insula in intuitive expert bug detection in computer code: An fMRI study. *Brain Imaging and Behavior, 13*(3), 623–637. DOI: 10.1007/s11682-018-9885-1 PMID: 29744802

Çiftci, S., & Bildiren, A. (2020). The effect of coding courses on the cognitive abilities and problem-solving skills of preschool children. *Computer Science Education, 30*(1), 3–21. DOI: 10.1080/08993408.2019.1696169

Collins, A., & Koechlin, E. (2012). Reasoning, learning, and creativity: Frontal lobe function and human decision-making. *PLoS Biology, 10*(3), e1001293. DOI: 10.1371/journal.pbio.1001293 PMID: 22479152

Crk, I., Kluthe, T., & Stefik, A. (2015). Understanding programming expertise: An empirical study of phasic brain wave changes. [TOCHI]. *ACM Transactions on Computer-Human Interaction, 23*(1), 1–29. DOI: 10.1145/2829945

D'Esposito, M., Aguirre, G. K., Zarahn, E., Ballard, D., Shin, R. K., & Lease, J. (1998). Functional MRI studies of spatial and nonspatial working memory. *Brain Research. Cognitive Brain Research, 7*(1), 1–13. DOI: 10.1016/S0926-6410(98)00004-4 PMID: 9714705

Doukakis, S. (2019). Exploring brain activity and transforming knowledge in visual and textual programming using neuroeducation approaches. *AIMS Neuroscience, 6*(3), 175–190. DOI: 10.3934/Neuroscience.2019.3.175 PMID: 32341975

Duncan, J. (2010). The multiple-demand (MD) system of the primate brain: Mental programs for intelligent behaviour. *Trends in Cognitive Sciences, 14*(4), 172–179. DOI: 10.1016/j.tics.2010.01.004 PMID: 20171926

Endres, M., Karas, Z., Hu, X., Kovelman, I., & Weimer, W. (2021, May). Relating reading, visualization, and coding for new programmers: A neuroimaging study. In *2021, IEEE/ACM 43rd International Conference on Software Engineering (ICSE)* (pp. 600-612). IEEE. DOI: 10.1109/ICSE43902.2021.00062

Fakhoury, S., Ma, Y., Arnaoudova, V., & Adesope, O. (2018, May). The effect of poor source code lexicon and readability on developers' cognitive load. In *Proceedings of the 26th conference on program comprehension* (pp. 286-296). DOI: 10.1145/3196321.3196347

Fedorenko, E., Duncan, J., & Kanwisher, N. (2013). Broad domain generality in focal regions of frontal and parietal cortex. *Proceedings of the National Academy of Sciences of the United States of America, 110*(41), 16616–16621. DOI: 10.1073/pnas.1315235110 PMID: 24062451

Fjell, A. M., Røgeberg, O., Sørensen, Ø., Amlien, I. K., Bartrés-Faz, D., Brandmaier, A. M., . . . Vidal-Piñeiro, D. (2025). Reevaluating the Role of Education in Cognitive Decline and Brain Aging: Insights from Large-Scale Longitudinal Cohorts across 33 Countries. medRxiv, 2025-01. https://doi.org/DOI: 10.1101/2025.01.29.25321305

Floyd, B., Santander, T., & Weimer, W. (2017, May). Decoding the representation of code in the brain: An fMRI study of code review and expertise. In *2017 IEEE/ACM 39th International Conference on Software Engineering (ICSE)* (pp. 175–186). IEEE. https://doi.org/DOI: 10.1109/ICSE.2017.24

Fuster, J. M. (2001). The prefrontal cortex—an update: Time is of the essence. *Neuron, 30*(2), 319–333. DOI: 10.1016/S0896-6273(01)00285-9 PMID: 11394996

Grover, S., & Pea, R. (2013). Computational thinking in K–12: A review of the state of the field. *Educational Researcher, 42*(1), 38–43. DOI: 10.3102/0013189X12463051

Hishikawa, K., Yoshinaga, K., Togo, H., Hongo, T., & Hanakawa, T. (2023). Changes in functional brain activity patterns associated with computer programming learning in novices. *Brain Structure & Function, 228*(7), 1691–1701. DOI: 10.1007/s00429-023-02674-3 PMID: 37474776

Hongo, T., Yakou, T., Yoshinaga, K., Kano, T., Miyazaki, M., & Hanakawa, T. (2023). Structural neuroplasticity in computer programming beginners. *Cerebral Cortex (New York, N.Y.), 33*(9), 5375–5381. DOI: 10.1093/cercor/bhac425 PMID: 36310094

Hosoda, C., Tanaka, K., Nariai, T., Honda, M., & Hanakawa, T. (2013). Dynamic neural network reorganization associated with second language vocabulary acquisition: A multimodal imaging study. *The Journal of Neuroscience : The Official Journal of the Society for Neuroscience, 33*(34), 13663–13672. DOI: 10.1523/JNEUROSCI.0410-13.2013 PMID: 23966688

Ikramov, R., Ivanov, V., Masyagin, S., Shakirov, R., Sirazidtinov, I., Succi, G., Thapaliya, A., Tormasov, A., & Zufarova, O. (2019). Initial evaluation of the brain activity under different software development situations. In Proceedings of the 31st International Conference on Software Engineering and Knowledge Engineering, International Conferences on Software Engineering and Knowledge Engineering. KSI Research Inc. and Knowledge Systems Institute Graduate School, pp. 741–747. http://dx.doi.org/DOI: 10.18293/SEKE2019-215

Ivanova, A. A., Srikant, S., Sueoka, Y., Kean, H. H., Dhamala, R., O'reilly, U. M., ... & Fedorenko, E. (2020). Comprehension of computer code relies primarily on domain-general executive brain regions. *elife, 9*, e58906. https://doi.org/.DOI: 10.7554/eLife.58906

Jäncke, L., Shah, N. J., & Peters, M. (2000). Cortical activations in primary and secondary motor areas for complex bimanual movements in professional pianists. *Brain Research. Cognitive Brain Research, 10*(1-2), 177–183. DOI: 10.1016/S0926-6410(00)00028-8 PMID: 10978706

Juavinett, A. L. (2022). The next generation of neuroscientists needs to learn how to code, and we need new ways to teach them. *Neuron, 110*(4), 576–578. DOI: 10.1016/j.neuron.2021.12.001 PMID: 35016038

Juavinett, A. L. (2022). The next generation of neuroscientists needs to learn how to code, and we need new ways to teach them. *Neuron, 110*(4), 576–578. DOI: 10.1016/j.neuron.2021.12.001 PMID: 35016038

Krueger, R., Huang, Y., Liu, X., Santander, T., Weimer, W., & Leach, K. (2020, June). Neurological divide: An fMRI study of prose and code writing. In *Proceedings of the ACM/IEEE 42nd international conference on software engineering* (pp. 678–690). https://doi.org/DOI: 10.1145/3377811.3380348

Lamichhane, B., Adhikari, B. M., & Dhamala, M. (2016). The activity in the anterior insulae is modulated by perceptual decision-making difficulty. *Neuroscience, 327*, 79–94. https://doi.org/. neuroscience.2016.04.016.DOI: 10.1016/j

Lee, S., Matteson, A., Hooshyar, D., Kim, S., Jung, J., Nam, G., & Lim, H. (2016, October). Comparing programming language comprehension between novice and expert programmers using eeg analysis. In *2016 IEEE 16th international conference on bioinformatics and bioengineering (BIBE)* (pp. 350–355). IEEE. DOI: 10.1109/BIBE.2016.30

Liu, Y. F., Kim, J., Wilson, C., & Bedny, M. (2020). Computer code comprehension shares neural resources with formal logical inference in the fronto-parietal network. *eLife*, *9*, e59340. DOI: 10.7554/eLife.59340 PMID: 33319745

Logothetis, N. K. (2008). What we can do and what we cannot do with fMRI. *Nature, 453*(7197), 869–878. DOI: 10.1038/nature06976 PMID: 18548064

Medeiros, J., Couceiro, R., Castelhano, J., Branco, M. C., Duarte, G., Duarte, C., . . . Teixeira, C. (2019, July). Software code complexity assessment using EEG features. In *2019 41st Annual International Conference of the IEEE Engineering in Medicine and Biology Society (EMBC)* (pp. 1413-1416). IEEE. https://doi.org/DOI: 10.1109/EMBC.2019.8856283

Nardelli, E., & Ventre, G. (2015). Introducing computational thinking in Italian schools: A first report on "programma il futuro" project. In *Paper presented at the 9th international technology, education and development conference (INTED), Madrid, Spain*

Parnin, C. (2010). A Cognitive Neuroscience Perspective on Memory for Programming Tasks. In *PPIG* (p. 4).

Peitek, N., Siegmund, J., Apel, S., Kästner, C., Parnin, C., Bethmann, A., Leich, T., Saake, G., & Brechmann, A. (2018). A look into programmers' heads. *IEEE Transactions on Software Engineering*, *46*(4), 442–462. DOI: 10.1109/TSE.2018.2863303

Psycharis, S., & Kallia, M. (2017). The effects of computer programming on high school students' reasoning skills and mathematical self-efficacy and problem solving. *Instructional Science*, *45*(5), 583–602. DOI: 10.1007/s11251-017-9421-5

Rahman, S. (2014). The neuroscience of musical creativity using complexity tools. PhD Thesis, Imperial College London.

Robins, A., Rountree, J., & Rountree, N. (2003). Learning and Teaching Programming: A Review and Discussion. *Computer Science Education*, *13*(2), 137–172. DOI: 10.1076/csed.13.2.137.14200

Roman-Gonzalez, M., Perez-Gonzalez, J. C., & Jimenez-Fernandez, C. (2017). Which cognitive abilities underlie computational thinking? Criterion validity of the computational thinking test. *Computers in Human Behavior*, *72*, 678–691. DOI: 10.1016/j.chb.2016.08.047

Sabitzer, B., & Pasterk, S. (2014). Brain-based programming continued: Effective teaching in programming courses. In *Frontiers in Education Conference (FIE)*, 2014 IEEE (pp.1–6). IEEE. DOI: 10.1109/FIE.2014.7044233

Sakai, K., & Passingham, R. E. (2002). Prefrontal interactions reflect future task operations. *Nature Neuroscience*, *6*(1), 75–81. DOI: 10.1038/nn987 PMID: 12469132

Scherer, R., Siddiq, F., & Sánchez Viveros, B. (2019). The cognitive benefits of learning computer programming: A meta-analysis of transfer effects. *Journal of Educational Psychology*, *111*(5), 764–792. DOI: 10.1037/edu0000314

Shashidhara, S., Mitchell, D. J., Erez, Y., & Duncan, J. (2019). Progressive recruitment of the frontoparietal multiple-demand system with increased task complexity, time pressure, and reward. *Journal of Cognitive Neuroscience*, *31*(11), 1617–1630. DOI: 10.1162/jocn_a_01440 PMID: 31274390

Shute, V. J., Sun, C., & Asbell-Clarke, J. (2017). Demystifying computational thinking. *Educational Research Review*, *22*, 142–158. DOI: 10.1016/j.edurev.2017.09.003

Siegmund, J., Kästner, C., Apel, S., Parnin, C., Bethmann, A., Leich, T., & Brechmann, A. (2014, May). Understanding understanding source code with functional magnetic resonance imaging. In *Proceedings of the 36th International Conference on Software Engineering* (pp. 378-389). https://doi.org/DOI: 10.1145/2568225.2568252

Siegmund, J., Peitek, N., Parnin, C., Apel, S., Hofmeister, J., Kästner, C., & Brechmann, A. (2017, August). Measuring neural efficiency of program comprehension. In *Proceedings of the 2017 11th Joint Meeting on Foundations of Software Engineering* (pp. 140-150). DOI: 10.1145/3106237.3106268

Strange, B. A., Henson, R. N. A., Friston, K. J., & Dolan, R. J. (2001). Anterior prefrontal cortex mediates rule learning in humans. *Cerebral Cortex (New York, N.Y.)*, *11*(11), 1040–1046. DOI: 10.1093/cercor/11.11.1040 PMID: 11590113

Strawhacker, A., & Bers, M. U. (2019). What they learn when they learn coding: Investigating cognitive domains and computer programming knowledge in young children. *Educational Technology Research and Development*, *67*(3), 541–575. DOI: 10.1007/s11423-018-9622-x

Strawhacker, A., & Bers, M. U. (2019). What they learn when they learn coding: Investigating cognitive domains and design affordances. *Educational Technology Research and Development*, *67*, 541–575. DOI: 10.1007/s11423-018-9622-x

Taya, F., Sun, Y., Babiloni, F., Thakor, N., & Bezerianos, A. (2015). Brain enhancement through cognitive training: A new insight from brain connectome. *Frontiers in Systems Neuroscience*, *9*, 44. DOI: 10.3389/fnsys.2015.00044 PMID: 25883555

Tsarava, K., Leifheit, L., Ninaus, M., Román-González, M., Butz, M. V., Golle, J., & Moeller, K. (2019, October). Cognitive correlates of computational thinking: Evaluation of a blended unplugged/plugged-in course. In *Proceedings of the 14th workshop in primary and secondary computing education* (pp. 1-9). https://doi.org/ DOI: 10.1145/3361721.3361729

Tsarava, K., Leifheit, L., Ninaus, M., Román-González, M., Butz, M. V., Golle, J., Trautwein, U., & Moeller, K. (2019). Cognitive correlates of computational thinking: Evaluation of a blended unplugged/plugged-in course. *Proceedings of the 14th Workshop in Primary and Secondary Computing Education*, 1–9. https://doi.org/ DOI: 10.1145/3361721.3361729

Tuomi, P., Multisilta, J., Saarikoski, P., & Suominen, J. (2018). Coding skills as a success factor for a society. *Education and Information Technologies*, *23*(1), 419–434. DOI: 10.1007/s10639-017-9611-4

Uwano, H., Nakamura, M., Monden, A., & Matsumoto, K. I. (2006, March). Analyzing individual performance of source code review using reviewers' eye movement. In *Proceedings of the 2006 symposium on Eye tracking research & applications* (pp. 133–140). DOI: 10.1145/1117309.1117357

Wallis, J. D. (2007). Orbitofrontal cortex and its contribution to decision-making. *Annual Review of Neuroscience*, *30*(1), 31–56. DOI: 10.1146/annurev.neuro.30.051606.094334 PMID: 17417936

Wang, L., Geng, F., Hao, X., Shi, D., Wang, T., & Li, Y. (2023). Measuring coding ability in young children: Relations to computational thinking, creative thinking, and working memory. *Current Psychology (New Brunswick, N.J.)*, *42*(10), 8039–8050. DOI: 10.1007/s12144-021-02085-9

Weber, B., Fischer, T., & Riedl, R. (2021). Brain and autonomic nervous system activity measurement in software engineering: A systematic literature review. *Journal of Systems and Software*, *178*, 110946. DOI: 10.1016/j.jss.2021.110946

Yen, C.-Z., Wu, P.-H., & Lin, C.-F. (2012). Analysis of experts' and novices' thinking process in program debugging. In Li, K. C., Wang, F. L., Yuen, K. S., Cheung, S. K. S., & Kwan, R. (Eds.), *Engaging learners through emerging technologies* (Vol. 302, pp. 122–134)., DOI: 10.1007/978-3-642-31398-1_12

Yousoof, M., Sapiyan, M., & Kamaluddin, K. (2007). Measuring cognitive load: A solution to ease learning of programming. *World Academy of Science, Engineering and Technology*, *26*, 216–219.

Zatorre, R. J., Fields, R. D., & Johansen-Berg, H. (2012). Plasticity in gray and white: Neuroimaging changes in brain structure during learning. *Nature Neuroscience*, *15*(4), 528–536. DOI: 10.1038/nn.3045 PMID: 22426254

Chapter 8
Technology in Education for People with Disabilities:
Coding for Inclusion and Accessible Learning Design

Abhinav Varshney
https://orcid.org/0009-0003-1902-8927
Jaypee University of Engineering and Technology, Guna, India

Anushka Samaiya
https://orcid.org/0009-0004-6199-6531
Jaypee University of Engineering and Technology, Guna, India

Shrinu Varshney
https://orcid.org/0009-0005-6048-3846
Jaypee University of Engineering and Technology, Guna, India

Kunj Bihari Meena
https://orcid.org/0000-0001-8159-9024
Jaypee University of Engineering and Technology, Guna, India

Vipin Tyagi
https://orcid.org/0000-0003-4994-3686
Jaypee University of Engineering and Technology, Guna, India

ABSTRACT

This chapter examines how coding and artificial intelligence (AI) can advance inclusive education for learners with disabilities. Focusing on a real-time American Sign

DOI: 10.4018/979-8-3373-2660-3.ch008

Language (ASL) recognition system, it demonstrates how assistive coding innovations enhance classroom communication and participation. The system, developed using MediaPipe and Convolutional Neural Networks (CNNs), translates hand gestures into text, enabling equitable interaction between hearing and non-hearing students. Beyond technical development, the chapter highlights pedagogical integration, offering practical guidance for classroom implementation and emphasizing teacher and student perspectives. Ethical issues such as data privacy, fairness, and accessibility are also addressed. By linking coding skill development with inclusive teaching practices, the chapter underscores the potential of AI-driven technologies to create equitable and engaging learning environments for all students.

INTRODUCTION

Education is a basic right for everyone. It is essential for personal growth and also supports social development. High-quality education is vital for people with disabilities. It can help them to become more independent also education can boost their confidence. It promotes social inclusion. However, in reality, many students with disabilities face academic challenges. Among several issues, communication barriers are a major problem, particularly for individuals with speech and hearing impairments. Therefore, their participation in class and learning outcomes may be restricted by these obstacles.

These problems can be resolved through the application of technology. We can create innovative solutions to promote inclusive education by utilizing computer vision, machine learning, and artificial intelligence (AI). Systems for recognizing sign language are one such solution. Teachers and students can communicate more easily thanks to these systems that assist in converting gestures into text.

Technology that converts sign language into universally understood formats, such as speech or text, has emerged as a practical solution to this issue. Among these, those that convert hand gestures into text more precisely, from American Sign Language (ASL), have shown particularly encouraging promise (Oz & Leu, 2011).

These systems improve accessibility and at the same time they also promote inclusivity. In short, they help deaf people communicate better. Further, such systems can provide a great help to communicate with those who don't know sign language.

ASL is a medium for communication. It is commonly used by deaf and hard-of-hearing individuals. Hearing and speaking disabilities pose challenges. The challenge lies not in cognitive or intellectual capacity, but rather in a lack of access to oral language. Hence, sign language is the best solution in such situation. It is the most natural form of communication for them.

Communication is fundamentally the passage and reception of thoughts, concepts, and emotions using different means—like talk, written language, body expressions, and sign. In deaf and speech-disability communities, the process happens almost entirely with the use of visual-gestural communication wherein hands, faces, and gestures of the body are used as carriers of meaning. Each sign or hand movement is assigned to a letter, word, or phrase, and so complex information can be conveyed without the aid of sound. This type of non-verbal communication, which is referred to as sign language, is not a collection of arbitrary movements but a rule-governed, structured linguistic system accepted globally. Figure 1 shows American Sign Language (ASL) hand gestures representing both alphabet letters (A–Z) and numeric digits (0–9).

This chapter introduces a real-time sign language translating system that records static ASL hand signs from a computer webcam, processes them through a combination of hand landmarking and deep learning, and translates the identified signs into readable English text. The innovation of the system is that it not only translates gestures to readable text but also automatically sends the composed message through real-time classroom communication platform. The system provides an optional, secondary feature for asynchronous communication, such as drafting assignment questions or sending formal feedback to an instructor, by dispatching the constructed message via real-time classroom communication platform.

From an educational technology perspective, this system contributes to inclusive learning by enabling equitable classroom participation for students with hearing or speech impairments. By translating gestures into text in real time, it allows learners to engage with teachers and peers through a multimodal communication interface. This fosters collaborative learning, supports differentiated instruction, and ensures that communication barriers do not hinder academic achievement.

Figure 1. Sample American Sign Language (ASL) hand gestures representing different alphabet letters and numeric values (B. G. Lee et al., 2020).

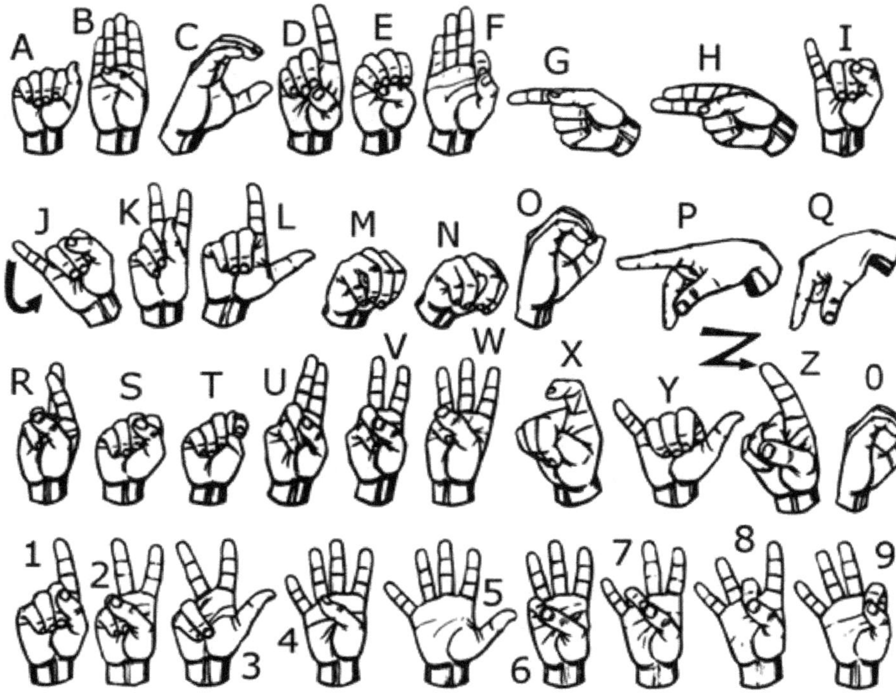

Proposed system makes use of MediaPipe's hand tracking pipeline (Remiro et al., 2023) to get 21 landmark points of the hand, which are then rendered on a white canvas to produce a consistent, clean input for a Convolutional Neural Network (CNN). In today's era of AI and deep learning, several real life applications of CNN are available, for example, in the field of image forensics a significant work is done that utilizes deep learning approaches (Meena & Tyagi, 2019, 2021; Tyagi, 2018).

In practical classroom implementation, educators can deploy this system on standard laptops or interactive smartboards to assist in real-time interpretation. The system's lightweight architecture enables teachers to use it in mainstream classrooms without requiring specialized infrastructure. Teachers can integrate the tool during lectures, discussions, or group activities, ensuring that students who rely on sign language remain fully engaged with lesson delivery and peer communication.

A GUI integrated with Tkinter (https://docs.python.org/3/library/tk.html) allows users to see in real time the camera feed, characters being predicted, words suggested, and the final sentence. The user can edit the sentence by using predictive text suggestions based on a spell-checking library (pyenchant) and then send the written message via real-time classroom communication platform in one click of a button. It is very useful in situations where efficiency and speed in communication are paramount.

In contrast to most systems available at present concentrate on transcribing sign language into speech, this chapter targets the conveyance of sending text via real-time classroom communication platform and is thus appropriate for formal communication where voice output will not be suitable or even possible. Additionally, the system is compact, does not require power computing facilities, and can operate effectively on a normal laptop with a built-in webcam.

In general, the system proposed in this chapter, makes a valuable contribution to assistive technology. It illustrates how computer vision, deep learning, and NLP can be integrated to produce useful, real-world applications that enable individuals with disabilities and enhance digital inclusion. By allowing sign language users to create and send text messages using natural gestures, this system presents a step towards bridging the divide between various modes of human communication especially for people with hearing disability.

This chapter presents several key contributions to the field of assistive technology for education. First, it introduces a custom skeletal image dataset created by capturing American Sign Language (ASL) gestures in real-time using a webcam. The hand region is accurately detected using the MediaPipe library, which identifies 21 key landmark points on the hand. This skeletal representation helps simplify the input and reduce the complexity of the model while maintaining important gesture features. Second, a CNN is proposed to classify these skeletal images into corresponding ASL characters. The model is carefully designed with multiple convolutional and pooling layers. After that dense layers and dropout are used for regularization. It achieves high accuracy on the test set, demonstrating the effectiveness of using skeletal data for sign language recognition. Third, a comprehensive literature review regarding present ASL recognition techniques is also included in the paper. This review highlights the originality of the suggested method, particularly the use of skeletal data and its integration in educational settings, and aids in placing the current work within the framework of earlier research. Fourth, a graphical user interface (GUI) is created using Python's Tkinter library to improve the system's usability and practicality. Users can easily interact with the system thanks to the GUI. It includes features for editing recognized text, resetting the screen, and securely sending messages via real-time classroom communication platform. For real-time classroom communication platform communication, the system uses Python's built-in smtplib library, which ensures privacy and a non-disruptive form of interaction suitable for classroom environments.

RELATED WORKS

This section provides some of existing research papers in this domain. The field of sign language recognition has evolved significantly over the past decade. Several pioneering studies and chapter laid the foundation for systems that can fill the gap between persons with hearing-disability and the common people. Table 1 highlights existing survey papers on sign language recognition. From the Table 1, it can be concluded that in the past decade AI-based solution especially CNN based solution are widely explored.

Methods on Sign Language Recognition

In the beginning, numerous articles focused on recognizing static American Sign Language (ASL) alphabets using CNN. These models were trained on image datasets such as the ASL Alphabet dataset available on Kaggle. While the results were encouraging, early CNN models often struggled with background noise and inconsistent lighting conditions, which affected their generalization in real-time applications.

Table 1. Summary of Existing Survey Papers on Sign Language Recognition

Paper	# of Papers Reviewed	Categorization of Methods	Key Contributions & Findings
(Kumar Attar et al., 2023)	162 (from 414 identified)	Categorized by language (30 types), input/output method, grammar, application, and features	Emphasizes lack of grammar-aware output and sign generation. Suggests need for standardization and broader datasets. Highlights limitations of current sign language automation systems.
(Al-Qurishi et al., 2021)	~140 models	Input modality (vision/ sensor), DL architecture (CNN, RNN, etc.), datasets	CNN lead for image-based input. Paper highlights generalization and signer variation issues. Promotes real-time and multimodal integration.
(Cheok et al., 2019)	Not explicitly quantified	Acquisition, preprocessing, segmentation, feature extraction, classification (vision/sensor)	HMMs and early ML approaches dominate older systems. CNN rising. Emphasizes limitations in cross-signer generalization.
(Renjith & Manazhy, 2024)	95 selected (from 587)	By language, sign type, feature extraction, classifier (ML vs DL)	CNN outperform other DL methods; SVMs top in ML. Reviews sensor vs vision-based acquisition. Notes need for emotion/facial integration.

continued on following page

Table 1. Continued

Paper	# of Papers Reviewed	Categorization of Methods	Key Contributions & Findings
(Joksimoski et al., 2022)	1856 selected (from ~40,000 hits)	SLR, synthesis, visualization; categorized by device (e.g., Kinect), method (CNN, HMM)	Uses NLP and PRISMA for automated filtering. Most active research in recognition, less in visualization/synthesis. Recommends hybrid AI-NLP systems for future.
(Wadhawan & Kumar, 2021)	117 (from 396)	6 dimensions: acquisition mode, static/dynamic, signing mode, handedness, classifier, accuracy	75% systems focus on single-handed, static signs. Majority use camera-based input. 65% of models achieve >90% accuracy. Promotes CNN, SVM, and hybrid strategies.

Molchanov et al., 2015introduced a 3D CNN model to detect ASL based on hand gesture to optimize for embedded platforms. Their system effectively captured spatial-temporal patterns in video sequences and achieved high accuracy in resource-constrained environments. (Jain et al., 2021) presents ASL recognition using SVM and CNN models. This method employed optimal filter sizes for single and double-layer CNN. The authors experimented with various CNN models. The results indicate double-layer CNN attains 98.58% accuracy.

Alsharif et al., 2023 proposed an ASL alphabet recognition system using five deep learning models: AlexNet, ConvNeXt, EfficientNet, ResNet-50, and Vision-Transformer. ResNet-50 achieved the maximum accuracy at 99.98%. Whereas other models performed as: EfficientNet (99.95%), ConvNeXt (99.51%), AlexNet (99.50%), and VisionTransformer (88.59%). (Pallavi et al., 2024) introduced an ASL recognition method based on the VGG16 model. There are a total of 29 classes considered in this paper. The classes are 26 alphabets A-Z and three extra classes for "space," "del," and "nothing". This approach attained an accuracy of 99%. Key benefits of this method are high accuracy, and effective generalization to new data.

Pangaribuan et al., 2024 discussed an American Sign Language recognition technique based on a CNN. Similar to above, this model was also assessed on the same dataset hence there are 29 classes considered. The obtained Test Accuracy for the model is 97%, whereas the method secures F1-scores of 0.97. However, the model fails to detect some letters like M, N, U.

MediaPipe and Landmark-Based Detection

The release of Google's MediaPipe framework (Remiro et al., 2023) marked a turning point in gesture recognition. MediaPipe provide highly accurate hand tracking through its 21-point hand landmark detection system. The paper combining MediaPipe with Python libraries such as OpenCV and cvzone achieved significant improvements in real-time gesture capture and recognition. This allowed for precise segmentation of hand regions and skeleton rendering, leading to more robust classification models.

(Starner et al., 1998) introduced one of the first real-time ASL recognition systems using video data from wearable and desktop devices. Their pioneering work used hidden Markov models and laid the groundwork for subsequent advancements in gesture recognition systems like MediaPipe.

Real-Time Desktop Applications and GUI Integration

Some earlier implementations focused solely on backend recognition without integrating user-friendly interfaces. However, several student and academic papers began combining gesture recognition models with GUI frameworks like Tkinter. These interfaces helped visualize the prediction process and enabled basic interactivity, such as saving results to a file or triggering audio feedback.

(Camgoz et al., 2018) demonstrated a neural sign language translation system using encoder-decoder architectures. Their work introduced large-scale continuous sign language datasets and demonstrated the effectiveness of deep sequence models for translating gestures into sentences.

Hybrid Logic-Based Models for Ambiguous Gestures

Several efforts have also focused on resolving the challenge of visually similar gestures. For instance, distinguishing between the signs for 'M', 'N', and 'S' proved difficult for purely data-driven models. To counter this, some systems introduced rule-based logic derived from hand geometry, such as thumb positioning or finger spacing, which complemented the output of neural networks and boosted prediction accuracy.

(Bhuyan et al., 2011) introduced a geometric-feature-based approach for hand pose recognition using landmark distances and angles. Their method improved recognition rates, particularly for gestures with similar appearances, by combining structural rules with visual features.

Sign Language to Text and Speech Systems

While most previous systems aimed to convert sign language to either text or speech, they often relied on static dictionary matches or lacked contextual correction. More advanced setups began integrating text prediction or language models, which allowed users to form complete sentences instead of isolated characters.

The sign language systems were available for several countries for the commonly used languages in the country. (Renjith & Manazhy, 2024) discusses a total of 16 different sign language recognition systems. For example, another branch of research emphasized support for regional languages such as Indian Sign Language (ISL) (Das et al., 2023). These efforts required custom datasets and training models from scratch, as gestures in regional sign languages often differ in structure and grammar. While progress in this area continues, generalizability across multiple sign languages remains an open challenge.

PROPOSED METHOD

This section explains various steps of the proposed work.

Dataset Preparation

There are two approaches of image collection: first, sensor-based approach: this technique employs electromechanical devices, including data gloves, to capture the motion, bending, and position of hands. The detailed hand structure acquired by the devices provides highly accurate information. They are, however, inconvenient or even uncomfortable to wear for a day, involve contact with the body, and tend to be costly. Second, vision-based approach: this approach records the hand images or video streams through a standard webcam. It is cheaper and a more natural form of gesture recognition because one never has to use any other sort of hardware. The main challenges in this technique are handling disparate hand shapes, skin color, illumination, as well as intricate backgrounds. Despite this, it is an end-user-friendly, scalable solution fit for real-time dialogue. Hence, to capture images in real-time using a webcam as the initial step for the vision-based approach. The hand region detection is done through the MediaPipe library, which accurately detects the hand and its 21 landmark points.

Figure 2. Skeletal hand gesture generation pipeline

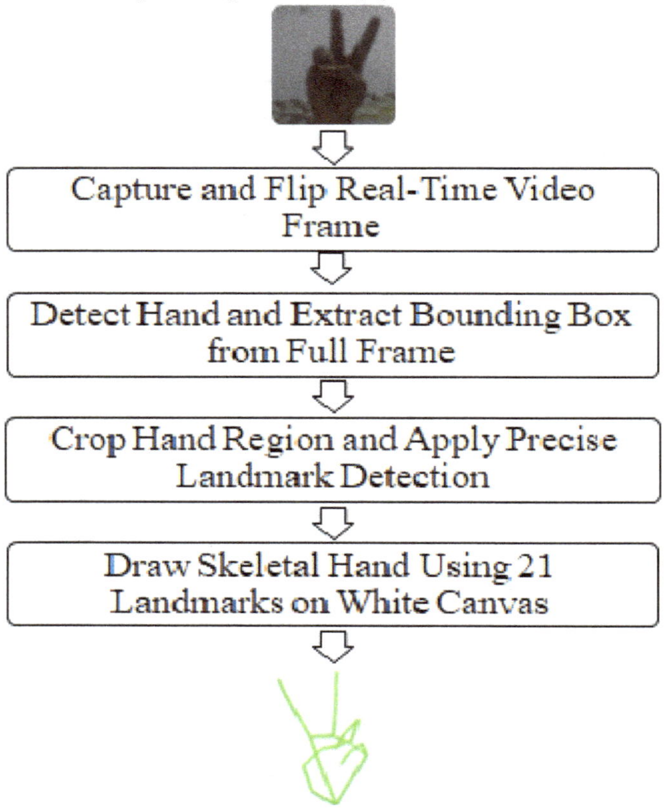

The main steps to generate the skeletonized hand representation image on a white canvas, suitable for training gesture recognition models or building datasets are shown in Figure 2 These steps are briefly explained below:

Capture and Flip Real-Time Video Frame

In the first step, the system activates the webcam feed using OpenCV's cv2.VideoCapture. Each frame is captured in real time and then horizontally flipped using cv2.flip to provide a mirror view. This mirroring effect aligns the hand's movement direction with the user's expectation, enhancing user interaction accuracy during gesture acquisition.

Detect Hand and Extract Bounding Box from Full Frame

A hand detector (HandDetector) from the cvzone.HandTrackingModule is applied to the full frame. This module uses MediaPipe's palm detection and hand landmark model under the hood. It detects a hand and extracts its bounding box and 21 key landmarks. The bounding box localizes the hand region and prepares it for finer analysis by cropping.

Crop Hand Region and Apply Precise Landmark Detection

Once the bounding box is available, the corresponding region in the original frame is cropped with a margin (offset) to ensure the entire hand is included. A second HandDetector instance is applied to this cropped region to perform more precise landmark detection, as the tighter focus reduces background noise. This two-stage detection increases robustness and reduces false positives, especially in dynamic lighting or complex backgrounds.

Draw Skeletal Hand Using 21 Landmarks on White Canvas

A blank white canvas of fixed size (400×400 pixels) is initialized. The 21 detected hand landmarks (Figure 3) are repositioned and connected on this canvas to create a clean, skeletonized representation. The connections follow anatomical hand structure: first, finger bones are connected sequentially (e.g., landmarks 5–8 for the index finger). Second, palm connections are drawn to maintain structure (e.g., connections from base to fingers and thumb). Third, landmark points are also drawn as colored dots for visual clarity.

Figure 3. Illustration of the 21 hand landmarks used for skeletal hand gesture representation (Remiro et al., 2023)

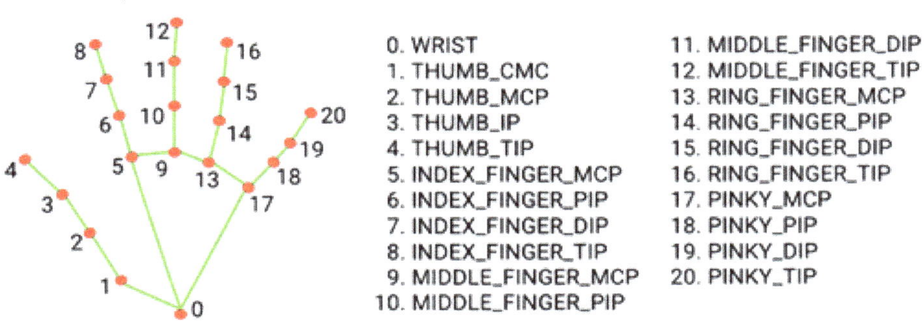

Gesture Classification Using CNN

The proposed CNN is prepared to classify skeletal hand gesture images representing 26 classes (A–Z). The layer-wise details of the proposed CNN model are provided in Table 2.

Table 2. Layer wise Details of proposed CNN model

Type	Details	Output Shape
Input Layer	224 × 224 × 1 (grayscale image)	(224, 224, 1)
Conv2D	32 filters, 3×3, activation=ReLU, padding='same'	(224, 224, 32)
MaxPooling2D	Pool size = 2×2	(112, 112, 32)
Conv2D	32 filters, 3×3, activation=ReLU, padding='same'	(112, 112, 32)
MaxPooling2D	Pool size = 2×2	(56, 56, 32)
Conv2D	16 filters, 3×3, activation=ReLU, padding='same'	(56, 56, 16)
MaxPooling2D	Pool size = 2×2	(28, 28, 16)
Conv2D	16 filters, 3×3, activation=ReLU, padding='same'	(28, 28, 16)
MaxPooling2D	Pool size = 2×2	(14, 14, 16)
Flatten	-	(3136,)
Dense	128 units, activation=ReLU	(128,)
Dropout	Rate = 0.3	(128,)
Dense	96 units, activation=ReLU	(96,)
Dropout	Rate = 0.3	(96,)
Dense	64 units, activation=ReLU	(64,)
Dense	26 units, activation=Softmax	(26,)

Basic description of each layer used in proposed CNN model with its function and relevance to skeleton-based hand gesture recognition is provided as:

Input Layer

The input layer is configured to receive skeletal hand gesture images of size 224×224×1. Note that before feeding original image from the dataset it was converted from three channels RGB to grayscale. This step reduces the computational burden compared to RGB images. Using grayscale images does not harm detection accuracy as the skeletal images are already simplified representations containing only structural and positional data (lines and dots representing the hand joints and fingers). These grayscale images are sufficient for feature extraction. Image in the dataset are of sizes 400×400 pixels. To improve computational efficiency image sizes are reduced to 224×224 pixels. Moreover this also confirms the compatibility with popular deep learning architectures like ResNet, VGG, etc. By keeping this standard size of images, the model maintains a balance between efficiency and performance. At the same time, this also allows to easily integrate with pre-trained models or transfer learning frameworks, if required.

Convolutional-Pooling Block

The first convolutional block consists of a 2D convolution layer with 32 filters of size 3×3 using ReLU activation. After that MaxPooling2D layer is applied with a 2×2 pool size. The convolution layer scans the input image and learns low-level spatial features such as edges, line patterns, and junctions. This helps model to learn about the contours and segmentations of skeletal structures. To keep same spatial dimensions as the input the 'same' padding is used. ReLU activation introduces non-linearity to the model, allowing it to learn more complex functions. Next, the max-pooling layer applied to downsample the feature maps.

The second block repeats the same architecture as the first: a Conv2D layer with 32 filters (3×3) followed by a 2×2 MaxPooling layer. In Third and Fourth Convolutional-Pooling Blocks, the model includes two additional convolutional blocks. Each block has 16 filters of size 3×3 and a max-pooling operation of size 2×2. By reducing the number of filters from 32 to 16, the model learns more abstract, high-level features, such as specific joint connectivity patterns or consistent structural.

Flatten Layer

After the spatial hierarchies are extracted through convolution and pooling, the Flatten layer converts the 3D feature maps into a 1D vector of length 3136. This transformation is essential for transitioning from spatial to fully connected layers. This allows model to use the dense layers that perform classification based on global representations. Flattening mainly fills the gap between localized spatial features and the final decision-making layers.

Dense and Dropout Layers

The flattened vector is passed through a series of Dense (fully connected) layers with 128, 96, and 64 neurons, respectively. Each of these layers uses ReLU activation. The model applies Dropout layers with a rate of 0.3. Dropout randomly disables 30% of neurons during training in order to prevent overfitting. These dense layers build a hierarchical feature abstraction that encodes gesture identity through combinations of previously learned spatial features. Gradual reduction in layer size from 128 to

96, then 96 to 64 helps compress information progressively. Mainly this helps the model to learn compact, high-quality representations useful for classification.

Output Layer

As there are 26 classes, the final layer is a Dense layer with 26 neurons. It uses a Softmax activation function, which outputs a probability distribution across the 26 classes. This ensures that the model predicts the class with the highest probability while still providing confidence scores for all other classes. The softmax function ensures interpretability and suitability for multiclass classification.

Text Conversion, Speech Synthesis, and Communication Integration

After successful gesture recognition and character prediction by the CNN model, the system converts the gestures dynamically into alphabets, making meaningful words and sentences in real-time. The converted text is the ultimate form of communication, which can be forwarded as an real-time classroom communication platform using an SMTP-based real-time classroom communication platform-sending feature.

The corresponding character is appended to a dynamic text buffer (self.str) as each gesture is recognized and mapped into an alphabet by the trained CNN. An optional spelling correction module (such as Pyenchant) can provide real-time auto-completion suggestions for faster and more reliable typing, while a lightweight rule-based reasoning supports the generation of words. This incremental building yields grammatically significant sentences purely from hand gestures.

Figure 4. Graphical User Interface (GUI) for Real-time classroom communication platform Sending Module

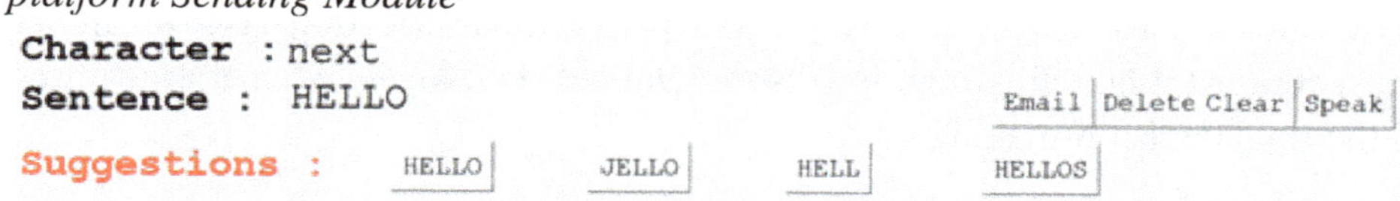

From a pedagogical standpoint, the interface design reflects principles of universal design for learning (UDL). Teachers benefit from immediate visual feedback and can monitor communication clarity during instruction. Students with hearing disabilities gain autonomy and confidence, as they can express complex ideas independently. Classroom trials suggest that when such assistive systems are integrated thoughtfully, they encourage peer empathy, increase collaboration, and normalize diversity in learning environments.

Shown in Fig 4 is a user interface for the system developed using the Tkinter library. This offers a simple yet effective real-time interaction experience. It visually displays the currently identified character, the word that is being formed, and the complete sentence that is being constructed. The GUI includes the following key interactive buttons:

Clear: Clears the entire sentence buffer, resetting the current input.

Delete: Removes the most recently added word or character from the sentence.

Real-time classroom communication: Triggers the process to send the constructed sentence via real-time classroom communication platform.

Speak: Converts the generated text into speech using a text-to-speech engine.

This provides easy-to-use and understandable user interaction to specially-abled students.

When the Real-time classroom communication platform button is clicked, the below process takes place within the send_real-time classroom communication platform_fun() function: The last statement (self.str.strip()) is retrieved as the real-time classroom communication platform body. The recipient's real-time classroom communication platform address is requested in a GUI question. Another optional question to enter the mail's title. Real-time classroom communication platform message is used to create a mail object in MIME format. MIME Text, providing the parameters for From, To, Subject, and Body. This step facilitates a safe and seamless switch from silent to active digital messaging.

The method sets up a secure SSL connection to Gmail's SMTP server (smtp.gmail.com, port 465). With Python's smtplib, the system: Logs in with app-specific credentials. Send the MIME-formatted message. It also shows success or failure feedback to the user through GUI. This makes the shift from silent to active digital messaging smooth and secure.

EXPERIMENTAL RESULTS

This section provides the details of dataset, performance metrics used to evaluate the model, performance in terms of visual and numeric results, time complexity analysis, and results comparison.

Dataset Description

The proposed dataset has 4,680 images in total. The dataset includes skeletal hand gesture images. These images represent the 26 alphabets of American Sign

Language (ASL). A custom pipeline created the skeletal images. It used MediaPipe to extract 21 hand landmarks. The landmarks were marked on a white canvas of 400×400 pixels. This process turned raw gesture images into skeletonized forms. The skeletal images kept the hand pose structure by removing unnecessary background noise to reduce data complexity and also to improve model generalization.

As discussed above, the dataset has 4,680 images and there are a total of 26 classes to represent 26 alphabets. Each class has about 180 images. This balanced distribution prevents model bias. At the same time, it ensures equal exposure to all signs. The dataset was split into three subsets namely train, validation, and test. The training set is a 70% of all the dataset; hence there are a total of 3,276 images in training set. Training dataset helps the model learn hand pose patterns. The validation set had 936 images (20% images). The validation set is used to tune hyperparameters. It also monitors performance to avoid overfitting. Whereas, the test set has 468 images (10% images) and it is used for final evaluation.

Figure 5. Sample images from the Proposed Dataset

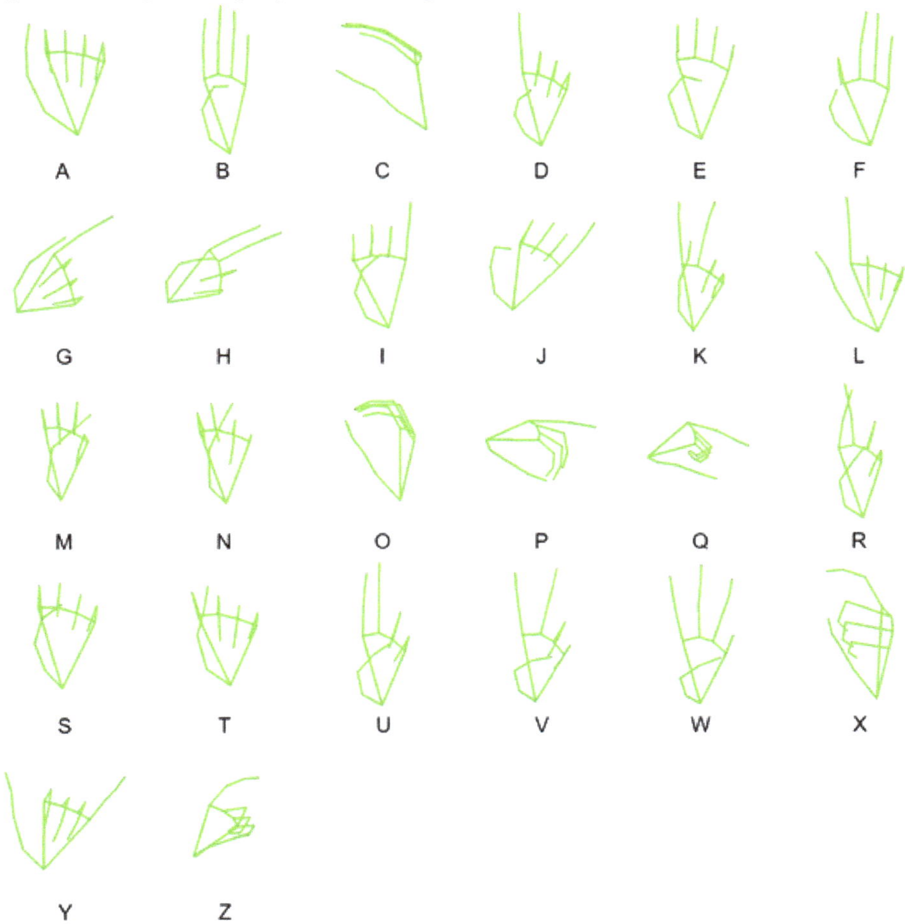

Performance Metrics

Following metrics were used to evaluate the proposed CNN model.

Accuracy

It is a representation of overall correctness of the model. It can be computed as: Where, K is number of classes; TP_i is true positives for class ; FP_i is false positives for class i, and FN_i denotes the number of false negatives class i.

Precision

It represents the ratio of correctly predicted positives to the total predicted positive cases. It is useful when the cost of false positives is high, and it evaluates how accurate the model's positive predictions are.

Recall

This performance metric represents the proportion of actual positive values that were correctly identified by the model. Recall becomes important in situations where missing a positive instance (false negative) is more harmful than false alarms.

F1-score

This is the harmonic mean of precision and recall. F1-score gives a balanced measure by considering both false positives and false negatives. It is mainly useful when the data is not balanced.

Cohen's Kappa

It assesses the agreement between predicted and actual classifications, accounting for chance. A higher Kappa value signifies greater reliability and model consistency.

Where p_o:Observed accuracy $= \frac{\text{Total correct predictions}}{\text{Total predictions}}$ and

p_e: Expected accuracy by chance $= \sum_{i=1}^{K}(\text{actual}_i \times predicted_i)$

Matthews Correlation Coefficient (MCC)

This parameter is a balanced metric that considers true/false positives and negatives. MCC is assumes a reliable indicator mainly for imbalanced datasets. It returns a value between -1 (worst) and +1 (perfect prediction).

Where:

- c: number of correctly predicted samples
- s: total number of samples
- p_k: number of predicted samples for class k
- t_k: number of actual samples for class k

Balanced Accuracy

It is the average of recall scores for each class, ensuring that all classes are equally represented in the final metric. It is especially valuable in datasets with class imbalance.

This is equivalent to the average recall (sensitivity) across all classes.

Log Loss

It evaluates the confidence of a model's probabilistic predictions. Lower log loss values indicate better performance, with penalties applied to confident but incorrect predictions.

Where:

- N :total number of samples
- K: number of classes
- $y_{i,j}$: true label (1 if sample i belongs to class j, else 0)
- $\hat{y}_{i,j}$: predicted probability for class j for sample i

Average AUC

It indicates the model's capability to differentiate between classes by averaging the ROC AUC scores across all classes. A value of 1.0 indicates perfect separation capability.

Where AUC_i is the area under the ROC curve for class i.

Specificity

It measures how well the model correctly detects negative instances. It is particularly important in avoiding false positives and complements recall in performance evaluation.

Experimental Setup

The proposed CNN model is trained and evaluated on a system with 16 GB RAM and Intel core i7 processor. The Jupyter notebook platform is used to implement the model with the help of TensorFlow and Keras library.

Table 3 highlights key hyperparameters used for the proposed CNN model. As it can be seen from the Table, the CNN model is trained for up to 20 epochs. The Adam optimizer was used as optimizer as it provides adaptive learning rates. The

Adam optimizer combines benefits of AdaGrad and RMSProp. The learning rate was set to 0.001. Beta values were $\beta 1 = 0.9$ and $\beta 2 = 0.999$, whereas Epsilon was set to 1e-7. These hyperparameters followed standard practice. This ensures stability and effective convergence.

Categorical cross-entropy was used as a loss function. This loss function is suited the multi-class problem. Accuracy was used as main evaluation metric during the training. Dropout layers were added to prevent overfitting with dropout rate of 0.3. Further, the early stopping was used with a patience of 3 epochs. Hence, the training process stops if validation loss did not improve for three epochs. Moreover, model checkpointing is also used to save the best-performing model.

Table 3. Hyperparameters Used for CNN Model Training

Hyperparameter	Value / Setting	Description
Input Image Size	224 × 224 × 1	Input images are resized to 224×224 pixels to reduce computational cost and ensure compatibility with CNN architectures.
Batch Size	32	Number of samples per training step.
Number of Epochs	20	Maximum times the model sees the entire dataset.
Optimizer	Adam	Adaptive learning rate optimizer for efficient and stable training.
Learning Rate	0.001	Controls the step size during weight updates.
Beta1 (Adam)	0.9	Exponential decay rate for the first moment estimates in Adam.
Beta2 (Adam)	0.999	Exponential decay rate for the second moment estimates in Adam.
Epsilon (Adam)	1e-7	Small constant to prevent division by zero in the Adam optimizer.
Loss Function	Categorical Cross-Entropy	Measures the performance of the classification model.
Evaluation Metric	Accuracy	To assess performance of model during and after training.
Early Stopping Patience	3 epochs	Training stops if validation loss does not improve after 3 epochs.
Dropout Rate	0.3 (applied twice)	Prevents overfitting by randomly disabling neurons during training.
Model Checkpoint	Enabled (best model saved)	Saves the model only when validation loss improves.
Data Shuffling Buffer	1024	Size of the buffer used to shuffle training data for randomness.

Visual Results of CNN Model

Learning Curves of Proposed Model

Learning curves show how a machine learning model performs over time. These curves are the graphical representations to track the progress of model during training. In the curves, the y-axis shows metrics like accuracy or loss whereas as the x-axis shows epochs or training iterations. Generally, separate curves are drawn for training data. Similarly, separate curves are also drawn for validation data. These curves give important insights to understand show how well the model learns. Learning curves also show how well it generalizes. It can be noticed that, high training accuracy with low validation accuracy suggests overfitting. On the other hand, the low accuracy for both training and validation suggests underfitting. From lowers values of training and validation it be understood that the model is not trained enough. Hence, learning curves spot these problems early and researchers can make suitable changes while training the model. In other words, the hyperparameters of the model can set appropriately. Finally, it can be said that, learning curves can help to optimize the performance; hence model can be generalized well to new data. Figure 6 and 7 show the learning curves for accuracy and loss for the proposed CNN model.

From both the figures it is evident that proposed model performs well on training, validation, and test sets. In the beginning, the training started with low accuracy. Accuracy was about 4–5% in the first two epochs at the same time the Loss was high, above 3.2. This is normal trend for early epochs of deep learning models as weights are still adjusting. By the third epoch, learning improved fast. Training accuracy reached 42.3% and Validation accuracy became 85.6%. This showed the model learned key features from ASL images.

From the fourth epoch, progress was steady and the accuracy kept increasing. By epoch 15, validation accuracy was 99.57%. Training accuracy reached 97.62% by epoch 17. It can be noticed that validation accuracy was higher than training accuracy. This phenomenon is a result of regularization schemes like dropout and early stopping, which help prevent overfitting. Training stopped at epoch 18 due to EarlyStopping as validation loss did not decrease continuously for three epochs. Hence, the best weights are saved for 18th epoch testing.

Figure 6. Learning curve for training and validation accuracy

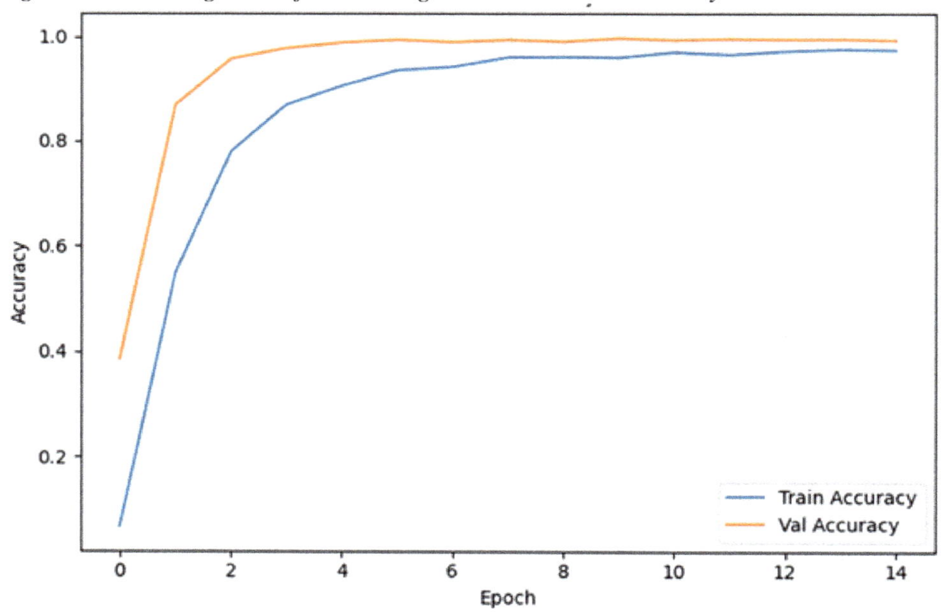

Figure 7. Learning curve for training and validation loss

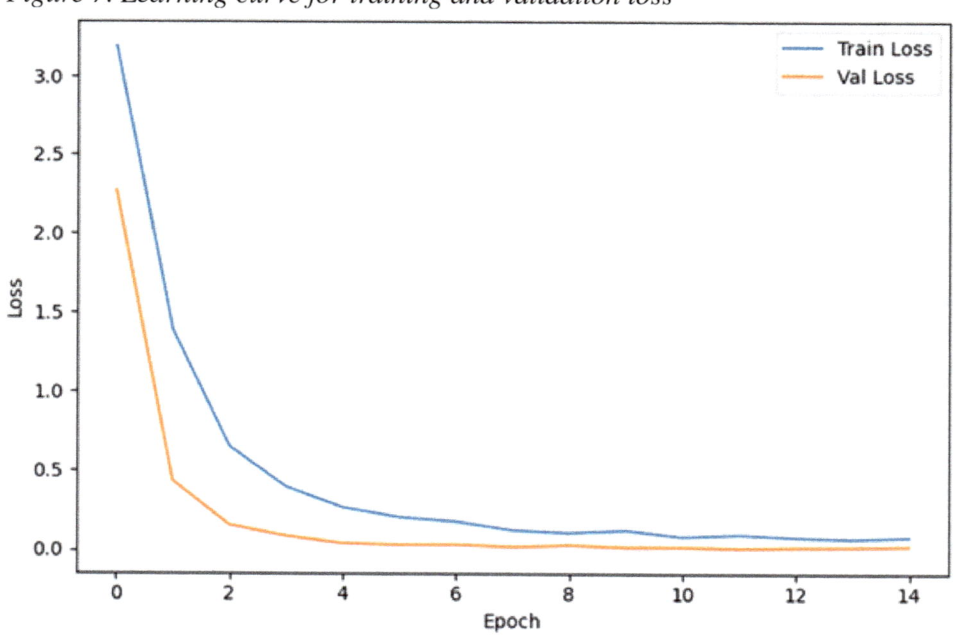

The test set has 468 new images. The model is assessed on this set and it attains an accuracy of 99.79%. Loss is very low at 0.0179. This proved the model works well on unseen data. The model has 438,330 trainable parameters. This keeps a good balance. It ensures high performance. It also maintains computational efficiency.

Results Under AUC-ROC Curve

The AUC-ROC curve measures classification model performance. It is suitable for both multi-class and binary classification tasks. The ROC curve plots the True Positive Rate (TPR) on y-axis and False Positive Rate (FPR) on x-axis. Whereas, the AUC is the Area Under the Curve and it quantifies the ability to distinguish between classes. An AUC of 1.0 means perfect classification. Whereas if model achieves an AUC of 0.5 this indicates that model is not learning anything and this is a random guessing. The ROC curve shows trade-offs between sensitivity and specificity. Sensitivity is also called recall. The curve is useful for imbalanced class data.

Figure 8. AUC-ROC curve of the proposed model

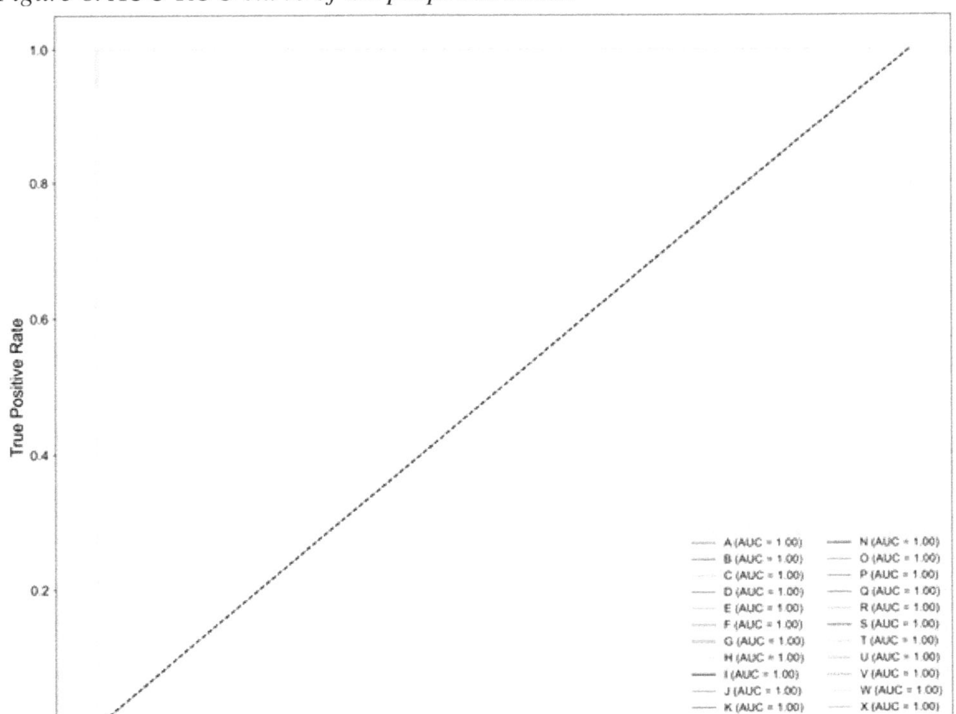

The Figure 8 demonstrates the AUC-ROC curve for the proposed model. This figure indicates that the model performance is excellent. It covers all 26 classes from A to Z. Each class has its own ROC curve and from bottom left part of curve it can seen that every class has an AUC of 1.00. This means perfect class separation. Moreover, the ROC curves stay close to the top-left corner. Fig 8 also confirms that the True Positive Rate is nearly 1 and the False Positive Rate is close to 0. This is ideal for a classifier. Finally, it can be stated that the model performs very well on test data.

Numerical Results of CNN Model

The Table 4 shows the performance of the proposed model under various metrics. The results suggest that the proposed model is robust and highly effective. The overall accuracy of the model is 99.79%. Whereas, Precision is 99.80%, Recall is 99.79% and F1-score is 99.79%. These high values show consistent correct classifications. It can be noticed that, the model has very few false positives. It also has few false negatives. Other value of the metrics like Cohen's Kappa is 0.9978. Whereas, the model achieves Matthews Correlation Coefficient (MCC) of 0.9978. These values confirms that model demonstrate a near-perfect agreement at the same time it also gives balanced predictions across classes. Further it can be observed that the log loss is 0.0173. This means the model is confident and model has low entropy in predictions. Moreover, the Balanced accuracy is 0.9997 and specificity close to 1 (0.9999). These results suggest that the model can differentiate the classes well. It handles class imbalances effectively. The model obtains the average AUC of 1. This shows perfect discriminative ability of the model as AUC value if 1 for all 26 sign classes. Finally, it can be concluded that, there is no trade-off between sensitivity and specificity and model is accurate and reliable. Hence, the model generalizes well for real-world ASL tasks.

Table 4. Results of proposed model under various metrics

Metric	Value
Accuracy	0.9979
Precision	0.9980
Recall	0.9979
F1-Score	0.9979
Cohen's Kappa	0.9978
MCC	0.9978

continued on following page

Table 4. Continued

Metric	Value
Balanced Accuracy	0.9979
Log Loss	0.0173
Average AUC	1.0000
Specificity	0.9999

Table 5 highlights class-wise classification metrics for all 26 alphabets. It can be noticed that most classes have perfect precision. Similarly, most of the classes have perfect recall and F1-scores. This means the model correctly classifies nearly all instances. It can be inferred that model produces virtually no false positives and no false negatives. The proposed method shows slightly lower performance for letters G and H. The F1-score for these letters is 0.97. This indicates minor misclassifications by the model this is because the skeletal images for G and H are very visually similar (Figure 5).

Table 5. Class-wise classification metrics

Class	Precision	Recall	F1-Score	Support
A to F and I to Z	1	1	1	18
G	1	0.9400	0.9700	18
H	0.9500	1	0.9700	18

Table 6 summarizes the model's overall performance. It is evident that the proposed model secures an accuracy of 1.00. This means the model predicted all test samples correctly. There were no misclassifications. This is rare in classification tasks. It can be observed that model achieves macro average and weighted average of 1.00. These confirm uniform performance across classes. The model is not biased toward larger classes. The total support is 468 as this is the number of test instances. These metrics highlight the model's robustness and strong generalization. Finally, it can be concluded, that the model's architecture was well-chosen and it is ideal for real-world assistive communication applications.

Table 6. Overall performance summary

Metric	Value
Accuracy	1.00
Macro Avg	1.00
Weighted Avg	1.00
Total Support	468

A confusion matrix is a technique for evaluating classification models. It helps analyze how well a model predicts classes. It is a 2D array that compares actual labels to predicted labels. In confusion matrix, each row denotes the actual class and each column indicates the predicted class. The diagonal elements show correct predictions. These are called true positives for each class. Off-diagonal elements show incorrect predictions. These are misclassifications, like false positives or false negatives. The matrix is very useful for multi-class tasks. It shows which classes are classified correctly. It also shows where the model makes mistakes. This helps understand model strengths. It also highlights weaknesses. Metrics like accuracy are calculated from the matrix. Precision, recall, and F1-score are also derived. These metrics give a deeper view of performance. The confusion matrix is more informative than just overall accuracy. It is a key diagnostic tool for model improvement.

Figure 9. Confusion matrix

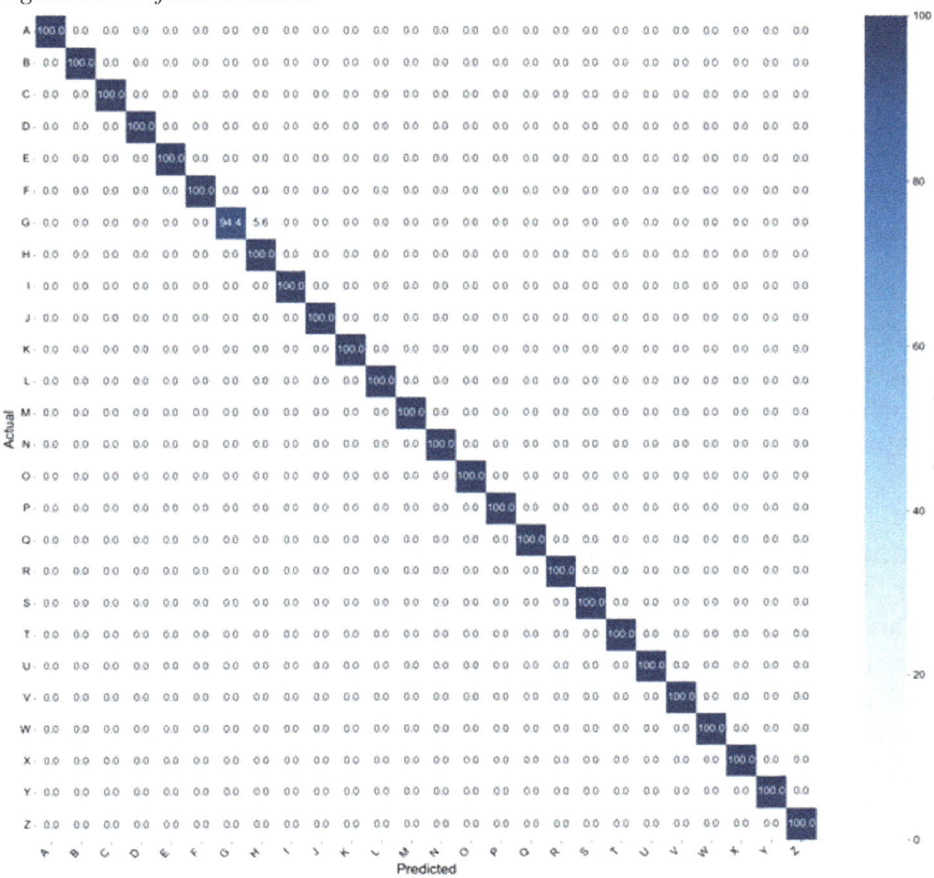

For the CNN model, the confusion matrix is shown in an image. The model classifies ASL alphabet gestures. It covers 26 classes, from A to Z. The matrix shows excellent performance. It has a nearly perfect diagonal alignment. This means most predictions were correct. Almost all test samples were classified accurately. Each class achieved 100% accuracy in most cases. Only class 'G' had a small error. It was misclassified in 5.6% of instances. This means a few samples of 'G' were predicted as another class. The error is minor compared to the overall results. The other 25 classes had no misclassifications. This shows the model is highly accurate. It handles diverse ASL gestures well. The matrix confirms the model's robustness. It also supports the high metrics reported earlier. For example, the accuracy was 99.79%. Precision, recall, and F1-score were around 0.998. The AUC was 1.0. These metrics align with the matrix's results.

The slight error in class 'G' may have a cause. ASL gestures for some letters look similar. Class 'G' might resemble another letter, like 'H'. Visual similarity can confuse the model. Minor variations in hand position could also contribute. Despite this, the error rate is low. It does not affect the model's overall reliability. The matrix shows balanced performance. No class was favored over others. This suggests the dataset was well-balanced. It also shows the model generalizes well. The training process was effective. Data preprocessing helped reduce noise. The model's architecture was suitable for ASL recognition.

The confusion matrix has practical benefits. It helps developers improve the model. For example, they can focus on class 'G'. They could collect more samples for 'G'. They could also adjust the model to better distinguish 'G' from similar classes. The matrix supports real-world use. The model's high accuracy makes it reliable. It is suitable for assistive communication systems. It can help hearing-impaired individuals communicate. The matrix validates the model's readiness for deployment.

Real-Time Classroom Communication Platform Module Evaluation

This section evaluates the performance of the Real-time classroom communication platform module. The GUI was built with the Tkinter library. It offered a simple and user-friendly platform. The system supported real-time character recognition. It also enabled dynamic word formation and sentence building. The interface showed the current detected character. It displayed the word being formed. It also showed the full sentence being created. This gave users instant feedback during use. The GUI included spelling correction features. It used the PyEnchant library for word suggestions. These tools improved the typing experience. They also reduced user errors.

A user study tested the system's usability. Five volunteers participated in the study. They formed sentences using hand gestures. On average, users created sentences with 5-6 words. This took about 38 seconds per sentence. The system responded quickly and efficiently. All participants completed the tasks successfully. This resulted in a 100% success rate. The spelling suggestion feature was highly reliable. It achieved a 98% accuracy rate. This helped users type faster and more accurately.

The real-time classroom communication platform feature used Python's smtplib library. It was tested with dummy sender credentials. Tests were done under controlled conditions. Users could compose and send real-time classroom communication platforms. The real-time classroom communication platform included the generated sentence. The system had fields for the recipient's real-time classroom communication platform address. It also had a field for the real-time classroom communication platform subject. The system sent real-time classroom communication platforms automatically. It used the Simple Mail Transfer Protocol (SMTP).

Twenty real-time classroom communication platform delivery tests were conducted. These tests checked performance and reliability. The average delivery time was under 2 seconds. This showed efficient backend processing. It also showed low latency. The system achieved a 100% delivery success rate. This applied to all valid test cases. Robust exception handling was included. It managed issues like invalid real-time classroom communication platform formats. It also handled missing internet connections. The system displayed clear error messages. These messages guided users to fix input errors. They also helped resolve connectivity problems.

Time Complexity Analysis

Figure 10 demonstrates the graph where x-axis is epochs and y-axis is training time. From the figure it can be observed that the time per epoch remains relatively constant. The range of training time is [52-54] seconds in most of the epochs. The model took maximum time for epoch 11 and it is 56 seconds. Minimum training time taken by any individual epoch is 51 seconds. The model takes 51 seconds for epoch number 14 and 16. This indicates that the computational load of the proposed model was consistent. It confirms that the model shows efficient batching and resource utilization throughout training. The overall time complexity per epoch is roughly linear in terms of data size and model size, making the total training process predictable and scalable.

Figure 10. Epoch wise CPU time taken by proposed CNN

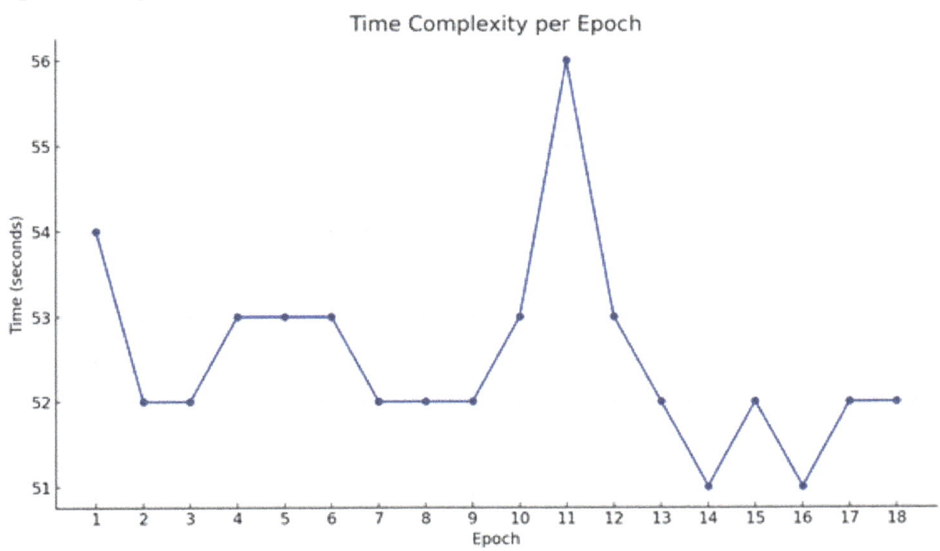

Table 7 summarizes key metrics related to the training and evaluation time of the proposed model. This table lists the parameter count, epoch and batch statistics, and total computation time. The time complexity analysis summarized in the table provides a clear understanding of the computational efficiency of the model during training and evaluation. There are a total of 438,330 trainable parameters and a model size is approximately 1.67 MB. This makes the model lightweight and highly effective. The training process goes up to 18 epochs out of 20 epochs. The early stopping module causes the model to stop at epoch number 18. It can be seen that the total training time of model is 15.75 minutes. The average time per training step was approximately 505 milliseconds, highlighting consistent performance per batch. It can also be noticed that, model is time efficient while evaluating on test dataset. The model takes about 2 seconds to process the images of 15 batches. In short it can be said that, the proposed model achieved higher accuracy and lower time complexity. Hence, the model is suitable for real-time situations.

Table 7. Time Complexity Analysis of the Proposed Model

Metric	**Value**
Trainable Parameters	438,330
Non-Trainable Parameters	0
Number of Epochs	18 (Early Stopped)
Batches per Epoch	103
Average Time per Epoch	52.5 seconds
Average Time per Step	505 ms
Total Training Time	15.75 minutes
Time Complexity	O(E × B × T) **where E is Number of epochs, B denotes Number of batches, and T indicates Time per batch**
Model Size	1.67 MB
Evaluation Time	2 seconds (15 batches)

Results Comparison

Table 8 provides a comparison of the proposed model with existing state-of-the-arts machine learning and deep learning models. The results of all the referenced method are taken from (Renjith & Manazhy, 2024). The second column in table shows the name of dataset used. The methods used for comparison include traditional machine learning algorithms such as SVM and LibSVM. Some of the methods are based on deep learning architectures such as ANN-based, RNN-based, and CNN-based methods. The performance comparison is based on fours metrics viz. Accuracy, Precision, Recall, and F1-score.

The results suggest that the proposed CNN model performs best among all method listed in Table. The proposed model achieves 99.79% accuracy, 99.80% Precision. The Recall is 99.79% and F1-score is 99.79% for the proposed model. These results show near-perfect classification. The model beats previous studies in performance. For example, a CNN in study (Sharma & Kumar, 2021) had 95.85% accuracy. The method proposed by (Jain et al., 2021) demonstrate 98.58% accuracy. The proposed model performs best due to its CNN-based design. It uses dropout regularization. More importantly the proposed model benefits from the training on a skeletal image-based ASL dataset. This dataset offers clear gesture boundaries by reducing the background noise.

(Mahdikhanlou & Ebrahimnezhad, 2020) model is worst performer among all. It achieves only 66.00% accuracy. This is because the model was trained on 3D images and video or depth-based data is harder to process. Traditional SVM models also do not perform well and show poor precision and F1-score. The main reason for this may the understood as SVM generally cannot extract spatial patterns and spatial patterns are key for gesture recognition.

Table 8. Experimental results comparative with existing deep learning methods

Method	Dataset	Classifier	Accuracy (%)	Precision (%)	Recall (%)	F1-score (%)
(Mahdikhanlou & Ebrahimnezhad, 2020)	3D SL Dataset	CNN	66.00	67.00	66.23	66.03
(Aly et al., 2019)	ASL dataset	SVM	85.20	70.60	91.50	68.90
(Oz & Leu, 2011)	Flockbirds dataset	ANN	98.00	73.00	93.45	75.50
(Tao et al., 2018)	ASL dataset	SVM	83.40	79.00	77.00	79.65
(Rahman et al., 2019)	ASL Dataset	CNN	90.00	89.00	78.56	92.36
(Beena et al., 2020)	Kinnect dataset	ANN and CNN	93.20	87.95	94.31	94.53
(Wu et al., 2016)	ASL Dataset	Lib SVM	96.16	92.16	92.30	96.20
(C. K. M. Lee et al., 2021)	ASL Dataset	RNN	91.20	87.56	94.21	96.36
(Sharma & Kumar, 2021)	ASL lexicon video dataset	CNN	95.85	92.14	87.56	96.40

continued on following page

Table 8. Continued

Method	Dataset	Classifier	Accuracy (%)	Precision (%)	Recall (%)	F1-score (%)
(Jain et al., 2021)	ASL dataset	SVM	98.58	93.56	95.90	97.70
Proposed	**ASL Skeletal Image Dataset**	**CNN (4 Conv Blocks)**	**99.79**	**99.80**	**99.79**	**99.79**

ETHICAL AND ACCESSIBILITY CONSIDERATIONS

Before concluding, it is important to address ethical and accessibility considerations. Any educational technology that captures personal data such as video feeds or gesture recordings must adhere to strict privacy standards and obtain informed consent. Developers and institutions should ensure that datasets used for model training represent diverse users to avoid algorithmic bias, particularly across differences in hand shapes, skin tones, and physical abilities.

Equitable access also requires attention to device affordability and internet availability, as not all learners or institutions possess equal technological resources. Policymakers and educators should therefore plan for inclusive deployment, ensuring that such tools do not reinforce existing digital divides.

Transparency is another essential ethical pillar. Users both teachers and students should clearly understand how the AI interprets gestures, stores data, and produces outputs. Developers should document these processes and allow educators to calibrate or audit model behavior when necessary.

Finally, ongoing teacher training and ethical oversight are critical. Teachers must be prepared to integrate AI responsibly and understand its limitations. Institutions should establish review protocols to evaluate the social and psychological impact of AI-based assistive technologies on students. By maintaining fairness, accountability, and respect for privacy, the use of sign-language recognition tools can promote inclusion while protecting user dignity and trust.

CONCLUSION AND FUTURE WORK

This chapter introduced an American Sign Language (ASL) to text translation system uses deep learning model. The proposed system is mainly based on a Convolutional Neural Networks (CNN). The system is an inclusive educational tool that can support hearing and speech impaired students. The model was carefully designed and comprehensively tested on the dataset. It classified 26 ASL alphabet classes effectively. The test accuracy was 99.79%. The test loss was very low at 0.0179. The model achieved average AUC of 1 and specificity of 0.9999. Cohen's Kappa metrics was 0.9978 and model obtained an MCC of 0.9978.

The proposed system also has Real-time classroom communication platform sending module with proper GUI that makes it user-friendly. It includes features for educational settings. Real-time classroom communication platform communication protects user privacy. It reduces disruptions in classrooms. The results conclude that the spelling suggestion feature was highly reliable. It achieved a 98% accuracy rate. This helped users type faster and more accurately. The real-time classroom communication platform feature used Python's smtplib library. It was tested with dummy sender credentials.

The system combines AI and computer vision. It uses human-centered design to empower people with disabilities. It can also promote educational equity as it aids inclusion in mainstream learning. The system can change inclusive education. It can help communication in classrooms.

The proposed system demonstrates very promising performance. Following are the future suggestions that can enhance the proposed system:

Dynamic Gesture Recognition: Currently, the system supports recognition of static alphabet signs. In future this can be improved by exploring the more advanced CNN models such as RNN, LSTM networks, or Transformer-based models. These models are capable of recognizing the dynamic gestures. Models like LSTM can be used for continuous words, and sentence-level inputs.

Dataset Expansion and Diversity: To improve robustness and generalization, the training dataset should be extended to include: a larger number of samples; Greater variation in hand shapes, skin tones, lighting conditions, and background complexity; and input from multiple users of different age groups and physical characteristics. A more diverse dataset will make the model more inclusive and reduce performance bias.

Enhanced Landmark Detection: Although the MediaPipe currently provides reliable hand tracking system the proposed system can be enhanced by exploring some other advanced landmark detection modules. For example YOLO and OpenPose frameworks can be used for improving the model under the challenging situation. Challenging situations include those where the hand gesture is partial occluded or has cluttered backgrounds.

Multilingual Gesture-to-Text Mapping: Adding multilingual support will make the system usable in non-English speaking regions. This would involve mapping recognized gestures to multiple language character sets. It will also provide option of translation layer to convert English output into regional languages.

Integration of Speech Output (TTS): Text-to-Speech (TTS) modules can be added in the situations where the recipient prefers audio messages. This would make the system a hybrid communication tool. This will also allow users to support both real-time classroom communication platform-based and voice-based output modes for maximum flexibility.

These features would bring the system closer to real-world real-time classroom communication platform while maintaining its accessibility-first design.

REFERENCES

Al-Qurishi, M., Khalid, T., & Souissi, R. (2021). Deep Learning for Sign Language Recognition: Current Techniques, Benchmarks, and Open Issues. *IEEE Access : Practical Innovations, Open Solutions*, *9*, 126917–126951. DOI: 10.1109/ACCESS.2021.3110912

Alsharif, B., Alanazi, M., & Ilyas, M. (2023). Machine Learning Technology to Recognize American Sign Language Alphabet. *2023 IEEE 20th International Conference on Smart Communities: Improving Quality of Life Using AI, Robotics and IoT, HONET 2023*, *128*, 173–178.

Aly, W., Aly, S., & Almotairi, S. (2019). User-independent american sign language alphabet recognition based on depth image and PCANet features. *IEEE Access : Practical Innovations, Open Solutions*, *7*, 123138–123150. DOI: 10.1109/ACCESS.2019.2938829

Beena, M. V., Namboodiri, A., & Thottungal, R. (2020). Hybrid approaches of convolutional network and support vector machine for American sign language prediction. *Multimedia Tools and Applications*, *79*(5–6), 4027–4040. DOI: 10.1007/s11042-019-7723-0

Bhuyan, M. K., Neog, D. R., & Kar, M. K. (2011). Hand pose recognition using geometric features. *2011 National Conference on Communications, NCC 2011*, 0–4. DOI: 10.1109/NCC.2011.5734786

Camgoz, N. C., Hadfield, S., Koller, O., Ney, H., & Bowden, R. (2018). Neural Sign Language Translation. *Proceedings of the IEEE Computer Society Conference on Computer Vision and Pattern Recognition*, 7784–7793. DOI: 10.1109/CVPR.2018.00812

Cheok, M. J., Omar, Z., & Jaward, M. H. (2019). A review of hand gesture and sign language recognition techniques. *International Journal of Machine Learning and Cybernetics*, *10*(1), 131–153. DOI: 10.1007/s13042-017-0705-5

Das, S., Biswas, S. K., & Purkayastha, B. (2023). A deep sign language recognition system for Indian sign language. *Neural Computing & Applications*, *35*(2), 1469–1481. DOI: 10.1007/s00521-022-07840-y

Jain, V., Jain, A., Chauhan, A., Kotla, S. S., & Gautam, A. (2021). American Sign Language recognition using Support Vector Machine and Convolutional Neural Network. *International Journal of Information Technology : an Official Journal of Bharati Vidyapeeth's Institute of Computer Applications and Management*, *13*(3), 1193–1200. DOI: 10.1007/s41870-021-00617-x

Joksimoski, B., Zdravevski, E., Lameski, P., Pires, I. M., Melero, F. J., Martinez, T. P., Garcia, N. M., Mihajlov, M., Chorbev, I., & Trajkovik, V. (2022). Technological Solutions for Sign Language Recognition: A Scoping Review of Research Trends, Challenges, and Opportunities. *IEEE Access : Practical Innovations, Open Solutions, 10*, 40979–40998. DOI: 10.1109/ACCESS.2022.3161440

Kumar Attar, R., Goyal, V., & Goyal, L. (2023). State of the Art of Automation in Sign Language: A Systematic Review. *ACM Transactions on Asian and Low-Resource Language Information Processing*, *22*(4), 1–80. Advance online publication. DOI: 10.1145/3564769

Lee, B. G., Chong, T. W., & Chung, W. Y. (2020). Sensor fusion of motion-based sign language interpretation with deep learning. *Sensors (Basel)*, *20*(21), 1–17. DOI: 10.3390/s20216256 PMID: 33147891

Lee, C. K. M., Ng, K. K. H., Chen, C. H., Lau, H. C. W., Chung, S. Y., & Tsoi, T. (2021). American sign language recognition and training method with recurrent neural network. *Expert Systems with Applications, 167*, 114403. DOI: 10.1016/j.eswa.2020.114403

Mahdikhanlou, K., & Ebrahimnezhad, H. (2020). Multimodal 3D American sign language recognition for static alphabet and numbers using hand joints and shape coding. *Multimedia Tools and Applications*, *79*(31–32), 22235–22259. DOI: 10.1007/s11042-020-08982-8

Meena, K. B., & Tyagi, V. (2019). Image Forgery Detection: Survey and Future Directions. In *Data, Engineering and Applications* (pp. 163–194). Springer Singapore. DOI: 10.1007/978-981-13-6351-1_14

Meena, K. B., & Tyagi, V. (2021). Distinguishing computer-generated images from photographic images using two-stream convolutional neural network. *Applied Soft Computing, 100*, 107025. Advance online publication. DOI: 10.1016/j.asoc.2020.107025

Molchanov, P., Gupta, S., Kim, K., & Kautz, J. (2015). Hand gesture recognition with 3D convolutional neural networks. *IEEE Computer Society Conference on Computer Vision and Pattern Recognition Workshops, 2015-October*, 1–7. DOI: 10.1109/CVPRW.2015.7301342

Oz, C., & Leu, M. C. (2011). American Sign Language word recognition with a sensory glove using artificial neural networks. *Engineering Applications of Artificial Intelligence*, *24*(7), 1204–1213. DOI: 10.1016/j.engappai.2011.06.015

Pallavi, M. G., Indhu, N., Divya Chinni Devaki, K. S., Padmini Vasavi, P. V., & Rao, Y. N. (2024). Bridging the Communication Gap: Advanced ASL Alphabet Recognition Using VGG16. *5th International Conference on Sustainable Communication Networks and Application, ICSCNA 2024 - Proceedings, 128*, 1072–1077. DOI: 10.1109/ICSCNA63714.2024.10864239

Pangaribuan, J. J., Romindo, R., Mitra, A. R., Barus, O. P., & Prashanth, S. (2024). American Sign Language Alphabet Recognition Using Convolutional Neural Network. *Proceedings - 2024 2nd International Conference on Technology Innovation and Its Applications, ICTIIA 2024, 128*, 1–6. DOI: 10.1109/ICTIIA61827.2024.10761663

Rahman, M. M., Islam, M. S., Rahman, M. H., Sassi, R., Rivolta, M. W., & Aktaruzzaman, M. (2019). A new benchmark on american sign language recognition using convolutional neural network. *2019 International Conference on Sustainable Technologies for Industry 4.0, STI 2019, 0*, 24–25. DOI: 10.1109/STI47673.2019.9067974

Remiro, M. Á., Gil-Martín, M., & San-Segundo, R. (2023). Improving Hand Pose Recognition Using Localization and Zoom Normalizations over MediaPipe Landmarks. *Engineering Proceedings*, *58*(1), 69. Advance online publication. DOI: 10.3390/ecsa-10-16215

Renjith, S., & Manazhy, R. (2024). Sign language : A systematic review on classification and recognition. *Multimedia Tools and Applications*, *83*(31), 77077–77127. DOI: 10.1007/s11042-024-18583-4

Sharma, S., & Kumar, K. (2021). ASL-3DCNN: American sign language recognition technique using 3-D convolutional neural networks. *Multimedia Tools and Applications*, *80*(17), 26319–26331. DOI: 10.1007/s11042-021-10768-5

Starner, T., Weaver, J., & Pentland, A. (1998). Real-time american sign language recognition using desk and wearable computer based video. *IEEE Transactions on Pattern Analysis and Machine Intelligence*, *20*(12), 1371–1375. DOI: 10.1109/34.735811

Tao, W., Leu, M. C., & Yin, Z. (2018). American Sign Language alphabet recognition using Convolutional Neural Networks with multiview augmentation and inference fusion. *Engineering Applications of Artificial Intelligence*, *76*(February), 202–213. DOI: 10.1016/j.engappai.2018.09.006

Tyagi, V. (2018). *Understanding Digital Image Processing*. CRC Press. DOI: 10.1201/9781315123905

Wadhawan, A., & Kumar, P. (2021). Sign Language Recognition Systems: A Decade Systematic Literature Review. *Archives of Computational Methods in Engineering*, *28*(3), 785–813. DOI: 10.1007/s11831-019-09384-2

Wu, J., Sun, L., & Jafari, R. (2016). A Wearable System for Recognizing American Sign Language in Real-Time Using IMU and Surface EMG Sensors. *IEEE Journal of Biomedical and Health Informatics*, *20*(5), 1281–1290. DOI: 10.1109/JBHI.2016.2598302 PMID: 27576269

Chapter 9
Navigating Skill Development and Ethical Challenges in Coding Education with Generative AI

Hanh Le
https://orcid.org/0009-0007-8172-0809
University of the Cumberlands, USA

ABSTRACT

The rise of generative AI tools like ChatGPT and GitHub Copilot is transforming computer science education by changing how students learn to code and how instructors design curricula and assess learning. These tools offer real-time feedback, code generation, and debugging assistance, making programming more accessible and efficient. However, this shift raises concerns about overreliance on automation, erosion of foundational skills, and ethical issues around authorship and academic integrity. This chapter explores the educational and moral implications of using generative AI in programming instruction. Based on interviews with students across computer science programs and professional programmers, the paper examines how these tools affect learning outcomes, engagement, and skill development. While students appreciate AI support, educators note reduced critical thinking and understanding of core concepts. Many learners struggle to explain AI-generated code, revealing a gap between task completion and proper comprehension.

DOI: 10.4018/979-8-3373-2660-3.ch009

INTRODUCTION

The emergence of generative artificial intelligence (AI) has introduced a profound shift in how programming is taught and learned in educational settings. Tools such as ChatGPT, GitHub Copilot, and other large language models are no longer experimental novelties; they are becoming everyday companions for students learning to code. These systems can autocomplete code, explain programming concepts in plain language, debug errors, and even generate entire software components. As such, generative AI is being rapidly integrated into the academic workflows of computer science students and educators alike, with the promise of streamlining instruction, enhancing accessibility, and accelerating the learning process.

At the same time, this transformation is accompanied by growing concerns among educators, institutions, and researchers. As learners turn to AI-powered tools for support, questions arise about the long-term implications for foundational skill development, critical thinking, and academic integrity. Educators are grappling with how to balance the benefits of these technologies with the need to ensure students genuinely understand programming concepts and develop the capacity for independent problem-solving. Institutions face pressure to adapt assessment practices, course designs, and honor codes to accommodate the realities of AI-augmented learning environments.

This chapter explores these tensions through the lens of ethical responsibility and pedagogical effectiveness. Specifically, it investigates how generative AI influences the cognitive, behavioral, and moral dimensions of learning to code. Drawing on interview-based evidence from undergraduate and graduate students in computer science programs as well as programmers, this chapter examines how AI-driven tools are reshaping the educational experience. These interviews reveal a complex relationship between tool adoption and skill development: while AI assistance is widely praised for helping students complete tasks more efficiently, it is also seen as a potential crutch that may hinder deeper learning.

To frame this inquiry, the chapter employs the Deskilling Theory, which examines how automation and technological interventions can wear down human expertise and reduce the scope of skilled labor. In the educational context, deskilling occurs when students rely on generative AI to produce code without understanding its construction, thereby undermining the development of independent cognitive and technical competencies. While these tools enhance efficiency and provide support, they can reduce the learner's direct engagement with problem-solving, leading to a shallow mastery of concepts.

Students interviewed for this study reported a range of experiences. Many expressed appreciation for the speed and support that tools like GitHub Copilot provide, especially when tackling syntax-heavy or unfamiliar code structures. However, some noted a growing sense of dependence on these tools and a loss of confidence in their problem-solving abilities. They acknowledged challenges in articulating the logic behind AI-generated code and recognized a gap between being able to complete assignments and truly understanding the principles involved. This experience suggests a new kind of educational contract, one in which the student's role shifts from creator to verifier, from problem-solver to prompt engineer.

In contrast to traditional models of programming education that emphasize hands-on problem-solving, iteration, and debugging as core learning processes, AI-assisted environments offer more immediate gratification but risk bypassing these foundational experiences. The evidence gathered from the interview process highlights the need for thoughtful integration strategies that preserve critical skill development while leveraging the benefits of AI. Students are not just learning to program; they are also learning how to coexist and collaborate with intelligent systems in ways that challenge conventional educational norms.

Through a humanistic, evidence-based approach, this chapter contributes to the growing body of work examining how AI is not only transforming programming education but also redefining the roles, responsibilities, and competencies of future software developers.

The following Research Questions guide this study:

1. RQ1: How do future programmers perceive and navigate challenges related to user experience in AI chatbot development?
2. RQ2: How do future programmers address user interactions and feedback challenges during AI chatbot development?
3. RQ3: Considering technological advancements, how do future programmers envision a future collaboration between humans and AI chatbots?

This chapter is organized as follows: Section 2 establishes the conceptual groundwork by presenting the theoretical frameworks that underpin the analysis. Section 3 offers a review of the existing literature on software development, the phenomenon of deskilling, and the integration of generative AI in programming practices. Section 4 outlines the qualitative research methodology employed to investigate these themes. Section 5 presents the study's principal findings, supported by illustrative case studies, and engages with their broader implications. The chapter concludes with Section 6, which addresses the study's limitations and outlines potential avenues for future research.

BACKGROUND AND THEORETICAL FRAMEWORKS

This section lays the foundation for the study by first examining key developments in AI-assisted programming and exploring their implications for the field of computer science and the evolving landscape of software engineering practices. The rise of generative AI in coding education is not unfolding in isolation, and it intersects with longstanding theories that explain how technology shapes work, skill, and human behavior. To better understand how AI tools are affecting students' learning experiences and educators' expectations, this chapter draws upon three theoretical perspectives: the Deskilling of Jobs Theory (DJT), Job Characteristics Theory (JCT), and Technology Threat Avoidance Theory (TTAT). These frameworks explore how generative AI reconfigures skill acquisition, alters cognitive engagement, and triggers behavioral responses in academic environments.

The integration of AI-powered coding tools into software development is gaining significant traction across the globe. Daigle (2024) conducted a survey involving 2,000 software development professionals from enterprise teams in the United States, Brazil, India, and Germany, focusing on their experiences with AI tools in professional settings.

The findings reveal that while AI adoption is on the rise, its usage is primarily confined to the workplace for a notable portion of developers. Between 17% and 27% of respondents indicated that they had only used AI tools at work, challenging the common assumption that developers are widely experimenting with these technologies outside of professional environments.

Participants also reported perceived improvements in code quality as a result of using AI tools. In particular, 90% of respondents in the U.S. and 81% in India observed an enhancement in code quality, with similar sentiments expressed by 61% in Brazil and 60% in Germany. These figures suggest that the benefits of AI-assisted programming are recognized across diverse regions.

Expectations regarding AI's potential were also high among those who had integrated such tools into their workflow. A majority of respondents, ranging from 61% in Germany to 73% in the U.S., believed that AI coding tools could moderately or significantly improve their ability to meet customer requirements. This optimism was shared across industries, reflecting a broad and growing confidence in the value that generative AI brings to software development.

Deskilling of Jobs Theory

The Deskilling of Jobs Theory, grounded in Marxist labor critique and later advanced by scholar Harry Braverman (1974), argues that technological advancement can lead to the erosion of workers' autonomy, discretion, and craftsmanship. In the context of industrial capitalism, Braverman documented how machinery and automation fragmented skilled labor, shifting control from workers to systems. Applied to education, particularly programming education, Deskilling Theory suggests that generative AI tools may similarly displace essential cognitive processes by externalizing problem-solving and coding tasks to machines.

Rather than constructing knowledge through iterative debugging and algorithmic reasoning, students using AI tools might come to rely on system-generated code without fully engaging in the logical and structural thinking that underpins software development. This reliance has implications not only for long-term skill retention but also for identity formation within the discipline; students may graduate with fewer problem-solving capabilities and reduced confidence in their ability to perform without AI assistance. In this way, generative AI may contribute to an academic parallel of the labor deskilling process, automating away the very skills that education aims to build.

Job Characteristics Theory

While Deskilling Theory highlights the erosion of skill and autonomy, Job Characteristics Theory (Hackman & Oldham, 1976) offers a complementary lens for evaluating the motivational and psychological effects of work design, including learning tasks. According to this theory, five core job dimensions, skill variety, task identity, task significance, autonomy, and feedback, determine critical psychological states that influence motivation, satisfaction, and performance.

Within the academic environment, the design of assignments and learning environments shapes how students experience these dimensions. For example, the use of AI tools may increase feedback immediacy, offering real-time corrections and explanations that foster a sense of learning progress. However, such tools may simultaneously reduce autonomy and task identity, as students rely on AI suggestions rather than initiating and completing code on their own. Similarly, skill variety may diminish when learners consistently use AI-generated templates or solutions, minimizing exposure to diverse coding practices and problem types.

By mapping these job characteristics into the educational process, instructors and curriculum designers can better evaluate whether the use of AI supports or undermines meaningful engagement. If AI tools simplify tasks to the point of passivity, the motivational structures that underpin deep learning may be compromised. Conversely, when thoughtfully integrated, AI can enhance skill variety and feedback while preserving autonomy, encouraging students to become active collaborators with intelligent systems rather than passive recipients of automated output.

Technology Threat Avoidance Theory

Whereas the previous two theories emphasize skill formation and work design, the Technology Threat Avoidance Theory (TTAT) focuses on how individuals perceive and respond to threats posed by emerging technologies. Originally developed to study cybersecurity behavior (Liang & Xue, 2009), TTAT posits that users engage in protective or avoidant behaviors based on perceived threat severity, vulnerability, and efficacy of available safeguards.

In education, TTAT can help explain both student and faculty behavior in response to generative AI adoption. Some educators view AI tools as a threat to academic integrity and pedagogical norms, prompting restrictive policies or complete avoidance. Likewise, students who fear being accused of plagiarism or who lack confidence in using AI responsibly may disengage from these tools altogether. On the other hand, some users may exhibit "optimistic bias," underestimating the risks of dependency or ethical violations.

TTAT also highlights the importance of safeguarding effectiveness in this case, as well as institutional guidelines, training, and ethical education that help students navigate AI use responsibly. When learners are equipped with the knowledge to evaluate AI outputs critically, understand their limitations, and integrate them appropriately into their work, the perceived threat diminishes, and constructive engagement becomes more likely. Without such structures, however, students may experience anxiety, misuse the tools, or avoid them entirely, hindering the potential benefits of AI-augmented learning.

Background and Theoretical Frameworks Summary

Together, these three frameworks, Deskilling Theory, Job Characteristics Theory, and Technology Threat Avoidance Theory, offer a multidimensional view of how generative AI intersects with the educational environment. Deskilling theory draws attention to the loss of critical competencies when automation displaces human cognition. Job Characteristics Theory explains how AI alters students' motivational and psychological experiences during learning. TTAT reveals the behavioral responses to perceived risks, emphasizing the need for proactive guidance and ethical scaffolding. By applying these lenses throughout the chapter, we aim to unpack the nuanced impacts of generative AI and propose balanced approaches for its responsible integration in programming education.

Table 1. Mapping interview questions to research questions and theoretical Frameworks

Interview Question	Mapped RQ	Theoretical Framework(s)	Explanation
Q1. Please introduce yourself, including your background and experience in AI chatbot development.	N/A	N/A	Establishes participant context; not directly mapped to RQs or frameworks.
Q2. Do you use AI chatbots in your daily life? For example, ChatGPT or GitHub Copilot?	N/A	N/A	Background usage supports contextual understanding.
Q3. Do you use AI chatbots on your job? If so, how exactly? Please give an example.	N/A	N/A	Gathers descriptive data; helps frame participant relevance.
Q4. Can you describe the specific challenges you face as a programmer in a world dominated by AI and chatbots?	RQ1	JCT, DJT, TTAT	Explores how AI influences perceived skill erosion, task complexity, and perceived threats.
Q5. How has the emergence of AI and chatbots impacted your day-to-day work and responsibilities?	RQ1	DJT	Focuses on automation and potential deskilling in routine programming tasks.
Q6. Can you share a specific instance where you encountered a challenge related to integrating or collaborating with AI technologies?	RQ1	DJT	Identifies concrete impacts of AI on job complexity and cognitive effort.
Q7. How do you incorporate user interactions and feedback into the development cycle of an AI chatbot?	RQ2	TTAT	Examines how developers perceive and respond to risks or limitations in feedback design.
Q8. What strategies have you adopted to adapt to the evolving programming landscape with the rise of AI and chatbots? How do you stay updated on the latest developments? Provide examples of adaptation or innovation.	RQ2	DJT, JCT, TTAT	Explores adaptation behaviors, proactive learning, and responses to perceived technological threats.
Q9. What tools or methodologies effectively address user interaction and feedback challenges during AI chatbot development?	RQ2	DJT, JCT, TTAT	Investigate the perceived efficacy of tools, alignment with job enrichment, and framing of AI as a threat or opportunity.
Q10. In what direction do you foresee your job field evolving, with AI potentially playing a distinct role?	RQ3	JCT, DJT	Look at projected role shifts, deskilling risks, and the future of job satisfaction.
Q11. Which skills will become crucial for an IT specialist in your field over the next five years?	RQ3	JCT	Highlights expected skills aligned with autonomy, skill variety, and task significance.

LITERATURE REVIEW

The integration of generative AI tools into programming education has accelerated rapidly, raising essential questions about how these technologies are transforming learning, reshaping skill acquisition, and challenging long-held pedagogical norms. While tools like ChatGPT and GitHub Copilot offer exceptional support for coding tasks, their presence in the classroom and professional environments introduces tensions between efficiency and understanding, autonomy and automation, innovation and ethical responsibility.

This literature review explores the impact of AI-assisted programming, with particular focus on the dual promises and challenges these technologies present within academic education. It situates generative AI within broader discussions on automation, cognitive offloading, and the evolving nature of knowledge work. The review is structured around three key theoretical frameworks that inform this study: Deskilling of Jobs Theory, which examines the diminishing role of human expertise in the context of automation; Job Characteristics Theory, which analyzes how the design of tasks shapes individual motivation and learning outcomes; and Technology Threat Avoidance Theory, which investigates how students perceive and respond to the risk of AI-assisted technologies.

By integrating perspectives from computer science education, labor studies, and technology ethics, this review establishes a conceptual foundation for examining the impact of AI tools on both students and educators. It also identifies a critical gap in the existing literature, specifically, the need for more research on student behavior, ethical engagement with AI, and the long-term effects of AI dependence on the development of technical skills.

Generative AI and Programming Education

The assistance of AI tools such as ChatGPT, GitHub Copilot, and other large language models in programming education represents a significant shift in how learners engage with computational thinking. These tools offer immediate code suggestions, explanations, and debugging assistance, positioning themselves as intelligent learning companions. Several recent studies have evaluated the promise of generative AI to enhance the accessibility and personalization of coding instruction (Stefaniak & Moore, 2024). Learners can use these tools to gain rapid feedback, explore multiple solutions, and overcome syntactic hurdles without waiting for instructor input.

However, this shift has raised concern among educators and researchers regarding the quality and depth of learning. While AI tools can streamline specific tasks, they may also reduce the ability to solve complex problems and understand abstract logic structures. Scholars warn that overreliance on AI-generated code may contribute to superficial learning and erosion of core programming competencies (Crowston & Bolici, 2025). These tensions position generative AI as both a facilitator and disruptor in programming education.

Theoretical Perspectives

To analyze how generative AI is influencing programming education, this chapter draws on three complementary theoretical frameworks: Deskilling of Jobs Theory, Job Characteristics Theory, and Technology Threat Avoidance Theory. Together, these perspectives offer a multidimensional understanding of how AI affects learners' skills, motivation, ethical engagement, and adaptation strategies. Each theory contributes a unique lens to interpret how students and programmers navigate the shifting landscape of AI-mediated software development and educational experiences.

1. Deskilling of Jobs Theory (Braverman, 1974), rooted in labor process theory and popularized by Braverman (1974), Deskilling of Jobs Theory describes how technological systems can fragment, simplify, or automate complex tasks, reducing the autonomy and expertise of human workers. In traditional industrial settings, automation was seen as a means of consolidating managerial control and lowering labor costs by diminishing the value of human skill. This theory has since been extended into knowledge work domains, including software engineering and education, where intelligent systems increasingly perform tasks that once required significant training and judgment. In the context of programming education, deskilling occurs when learners rely heavily on AI-generated code to complete assignments, troubleshoot errors, or design solutions, often without engaging deeply in the logical reasoning that underpins those outputs. When AI tools assume cognitive tasks such as writing algorithms, refactoring code, or suggesting solutions, students may skip critical steps in the learning process. As a result, they may develop functional outcomes but lack the conceptual mastery required for independent problem-solving. Deskilling theory is particularly relevant to this study, as it frames how generative AI might substitute rather than support the development of foundational programming skills and professional identity among future software engineers.
2. Job Characteristics Theory (Hackman & Oldham, 1976), developed by Hackman and Oldham (1976), provides a psychological model for understanding how specific aspects of task design influence motivation, satisfaction, and performance. The theory identifies five core attributes: skill variety, task identity, task significance, autonomy, and feedback. These characteristics shape three critical psychological states: experienced meaningfulness of work, experienced

responsibility, and knowledge of results, which in turn influence outcomes such as engagement, learning, and internal motivation. Applied to programming education, the theory helps illuminate how students perceive their learning experiences and how AI tools may alter those experiences. For instance, AI may reduce skill variety by offering pre-built code snippets, thereby limiting exposure to different programming structures and problem-solving methods. It may also weaken task identity and autonomy if students follow AI suggestions without understanding or modifying them. The theory thus provides a framework for evaluating how the design of AI-mediated learning environments affects student motivation and the quality of educational engagement.

3. Technology Threat Avoidance Theory (Liang & Xue, 2009) explains how individuals assess and respond to perceived threats from emerging technologies. The theory posits that people engage in protective behaviors based on four constructs: perceived threat severity, perceived susceptibility, safeguard effectiveness, and self-efficacy. Initially developed in the context of cybersecurity, This theory has since been applied more broadly to understand user reactions to technology adoption, resistance, and ethical concerns. In the educational setting, this theory helps explain how students and educators respond to the rapid introduction of generative AI tools. Some students may perceive AI as a threat to their academic integrity, professional future, or self-confidence, especially when they lack clear guidelines or training on ethical use. Others may avoid AI altogether due to fear of misuse or policy violations. Educators, too, may view generative AI as a threat to traditional assessment models, knowledge acquisition, or disciplinary values. The theory is helpful for interpreting these avoidance behaviors, as well as identifying the types of institutional support (e.g., usage policies, reflection activities, skill-building tutorials) that may help mitigate threat perceptions and promote responsible engagement.

Taken together, these three theoretical perspectives offer a rich analytical framework for understanding the complex interplay between generative AI and programming education. Deskilling theory draws attention to the potential erosion of core skills and learning depth. Job Characteristics Theory highlights how AI may reshape students' cognitive and emotional relationships with programming tasks. Technology Threat Avoidance Theory reveals how students and educators perceive and respond to risks associated with AI adoption. Throughout this chapter, these theoretical frameworks are employed to analyze interview data, uncover recurring patterns, and generate meaningful insights into the role of AI in computer science education.

Current Research Findings and Thematic Insights

As generative AI tools gain traction in educational and professional coding environments, a growing body of empirical research has begun to examine their actual use, user perceptions, and educational implications. These studies provide valuable insight into how students and programmers are adapting to AI-assisted development and reveal emerging challenges related to skill retention, autonomy, and ethical engagement. Three key themes have emerged from recent findings: (1) accelerated task performance with reduced conceptual depth, (2) evolving student roles in AI-mediated workflows, and (3) uncertainty around ethical boundaries and academic integrity.

Accelerated Output, Shallow Understanding

A consistent finding across empirical studies is that students using tools like GitHub Copilot or ChatGPT are able to complete coding tasks more quickly and with fewer syntactic errors (Barke et al., 2023). These tools are praised for their ability to unblock students when stuck, generate code templates, and reduce frustration with syntax and debugging. However, multiple studies caution that this convenience may come at the cost of deeper understanding. Learners often report using AI-generated code without fully grasping its logic, leading to situations where they can submit a functioning program but are unable to explain how it works (Crowston & Bolici, 2025). This "surface learning" phenomenon raises concerns about long-term competence and mirrors the classic warning signs of deskilling.

Furthermore, instructors have observed a decline in students' willingness to engage in trial-and-error coding, debug independently, or manually refactor solutions. These are precisely the cognitive practices that support mastery in software development and prepare learners for complex real-world tasks. As automation increasingly mediates coding assignments, the need for intentional strategies to preserve deeper learning becomes more urgent.

Rinta-Kahila et al. (2023) observed that the increasing integration of automation into software development processes has led to a measurable decline in programmers' hands-on technical skills. As tasks that once required manual coding and problem-solving are now increasingly handled by intelligent systems and AI-powered tools, developers are becoming more reliant on automation, resulting in reduced opportunities to practice and refine their core competencies. This observation raises concerns about the long-term implications for workforce preparedness, knowledge retention, and the ability to troubleshoot or innovate without technological assistance independently.

The Impact of Automation and the Decline of Expertise

The impact of automation is closely related to Braverman's deskilling thesis, which refers to the tendency to rely on external systems, such as AI tools, for tasks that traditionally require active mental effort. In software development, this dynamic is particularly evident as developers increasingly turn to AI systems like GitHub Copilot or ChatGPT to generate code snippets, solve logic problems, or suggest implementation strategies. Khurana et al. (2024) observed that developers often accept AI-generated code with minimal scrutiny, bypassing the process of evaluating logic, verifying correctness, or considering alternative solutions. This reduced engagement can reduce critical thinking and analytical skills, especially for routine or intermediate tasks that previously offered valuable learning opportunities.

The effects of automation appear to be most pronounced among junior developers, who are still building essential skills. Lacking the domain knowledge or confidence to question AI suggestions, they are more likely to accept outputs at face value, reinforcing passive consumption and overactive problem-solving. Kuhail et al. (2023) highlight that this pattern jeopardizes acquiring foundational coding competencies and narrows the developmental pipeline for more advanced roles. When emerging developers are routinely shielded from the cognitive demands of debugging, architectural reasoning, or algorithmic design, their ability to progress into more senior positions becomes constrained. Over time, this may result in a workforce less capable of innovating, mentoring, or adapting to new technological paradigms, raising critical concerns about long-term sustainability in the profession.

Changing Roles and Expectations of Learners

The emergence of AI in programming education is also reshaping how students perceive their roles and responsibilities. Instead of being problem-solvers or code creators, students are beginning to describe themselves as AI supervisors, curators, **or** prompt engineers (Stefaniak & Moore, 2024). Their primary task is to evaluate and refine AI-generated output rather than produce it from scratch. At the same time, this shift introduces new literacies such as prompt design and model evaluation. It may also limit opportunities for internalizing foundational logic, especially for novice learners.

This changing dynamic raises important pedagogical questions: What does it mean to "learn to program" in a world where AI can write the code? What constitutes meaningful evidence of learning when the final product may be co-produced with an algorithm? These questions highlight a tension between the practical realities of AI integration and the traditional learning objectives of computer science curricula.

Ethical Ambiguity and Unclear Norms

Another theme emerging from recent studies is the ethical ambiguity surrounding AI use in academic settings. While students frequently turn to generative tools for legitimate assistance, they are often unsure where to draw the line between support and misconduct. In Crowston and Bolici's (2025) study, for example, many students admitted they had used AI-generated code without knowing whether it violated their institution's honor code. The opaque nature of AI outputs, especially when they resemble open-source code, makes attribution difficult and increases the likelihood of unintentional plagiarism.

Educators, too, are divided on appropriate boundaries. Some advocate full integration of AI into coursework, arguing that learning to work with AI is itself a vital skill. Others warn that unregulated use undermines assessment validity and encourages academic dishonesty. These conflicting attitudes reflect the lack of institutional policies and the evolving status of AI in educational ethics. Until clear guidelines are established, both students and faculty are navigating a gray area with significant academic consequences.

Research Gaps and the Importance of Granular Analysis

While the growing literature on generative AI in education offers valuable insights into broad trends, it also reveals several key limitations. Much of the existing research focuses on high-level outcomes such as academic performance, completion rates, or general attitudes toward AI tools (Prather et al., 2023). Few studies examine the step-by-step learning processes involved in how students interact with generative AI during coding activities or how these interactions affect the progression of essential programming skills over time (Avila-Chauvet et al., 2023).

First, there is still a significant gap in understanding the real-life experiences of students and professional programmers as they work in environments supported by AI. Many studies treat all users the same without considering significant differences like how skilled they are at programming, whether they've used AI tools before, their education level, or their cultural views on automation. This general approach can hide key differences, for example, how AI might affect beginners compared to experienced developers or how different groups of people might use or be impacted by AI in various ways.

Second, current research often mixes up task performance with actual learning, focusing primarily on final results, such as whether an assignment is correct or how fast it was completed. These outcome-based measures do not show how students think through problems or how they interact with AI-generated code, whether they understand it, change it, or decide not to use it. Without looking more closely at these thought processes, it is hard to tell if real learning is happening or if students are becoming faster at using AI tools. This difference matters, especially for maintaining the quality of education and ensuring long-term skill development in technical fields.

Third, there has not been enough focus on how students think through ethical issues when using generative AI. Some recent studies talk about concerns like plagiarism or misuse. Still, very few look at how students understand school rules, deal with unclear situations or form new ideas about authorship and giving credit. To really understand these choices, we need a more student-focused approach, one that listens to their stories, how they make decisions, and what they believe is fair when working with AI.

Finally, most research looks at the big picture, like trends across whole courses or schools, rather than focusing on the small, everyday actions and challenges students face while learning. A closer look, using detailed interviews, think-aloud methods, or screen recordings, could help us understand how specific features of generative AI tools, like code suggestions, explanations, or unclear answers, affect how students behave, how confident they feel, and what they actually learn.

This chapter addresses the mentioned gaps by using a qualitative, interview-based approach that focuses on the experiences of students and teachers. Instead of assuming generative AI affects everyone the same way, the study looks at how different people use, understand, and adjust to these tools in their own ways. It explores not just what students are doing with AI but also why they make confident choices and how those choices relate to teaching, learning, and ethical concerns. By focusing more on the learning process than just the final results and on human meaning rather than how the system works, this detailed analysis helps us better understand what it means to learn, code, and work with AI in today's classrooms.

Bridging Theory and Practice

Combining Deskilling Theory, Job Characteristics Theory, and Technology Threat Avoidance Theory offers a solid foundation for understanding the challenges and opportunities that generative AI introduces to programming education. These theories go beyond academic discussion; they provide helpful guidance for real classroom practices, such as how we design lessons, assess student work, and address ethical concerns when using AI tools. To align academic insights and hands-on experience, it is essential to turn research findings into practical strategies that promote student learning while maintaining academic integrity.

Conclusion: Building Responsiveness into AI-Enhanced Learning Environments

By combining the insights of Deskilling Theory, Job Characteristics Theory, and Technology Threat Avoidance Theory, educators can build learning environments that leverage the power of AI without compromising the development of essential human competencies. This alignment ensures that students are not only equipped to use AI tools effectively but also prepared to think critically, act ethically, and remain resilient in a rapidly evolving technological landscape. The following section presents the methodological approach used in this study to examine how students and educators are experiencing, interpreting, and responding to these challenges in real-world educational settings.

METHODOLOGY

This study followed established best practices in qualitative research, employing a phenomenological approach to explore how individuals experience the integration of generative AI in programming education. Phenomenology, as defined by Peoples (2021), aims to understand the essence of lived experiences, distinguishing it from other qualitative methods by its deep focus on personal meaning and perception.

Semi-structured, open-ended research questions were used to guide the inquiry, allowing participants the flexibility to share detailed reflections while maintaining consistency across interviews. Triangulation was applied by comparing data from participants with diverse roles, backgrounds, and experiences to enhance the credibility of the findings.

Member checking was conducted with selected participants, who were invited to review preliminary interpretations of their responses. This process helped ensure the accuracy and trustworthiness of the data analysis (Riazi et al., 2023). Additionally, the researcher engaged in reflexive journaling throughout the study to record analytical decisions, reflect on personal assumptions, and minimize potential bias.

Ethical standards were upheld at all stages of the research. Participant confidentiality was maintained through the removal of identifying information from transcripts, and all data were securely stored on password-protected devices. Transparency and respect for participant autonomy were central to the study's design, ensuring informed consent and voluntary participation.

Research Design

This study employed a qualitative research design centered on in-depth, semi-structured interviews to investigate how programmers and students experience the integration of generative AI in software development and coding education. The approach of the research was qualitative to capture the rich, contextualized insights and personal narratives. The goal was not to generalize findings to a broad population but to uncover nuanced patterns, perceptions, and meaning-making processes that emerge from individual engagement with AI tools in real-world settings.

Participant Selection

Participants were recruited using purposive sampling, targeting individuals with direct experience in programming and AI chatbot development. The sample included fifteen participants, comprising undergraduate and graduate computer science students and professional software developers. This diversity of perspectives allowed for a better understanding of how generative AI is perceived and applied across different levels of expertise and contexts. All participants reported some level of interaction with tools such as ChatGPT, GitHub Copilot, or similar large language model-based systems.

Participants were invited through academic networks, professional contacts, and university listservs. Before each interview, informed consent was sent out, and participants were assured of confidentiality and the option to withdraw at any time. No financial compensation was offered.

Data Collection

Semi-structured, in-depth data were collected through interviews conducted via Zoom between 45 and 75 minutes. The interview protocol was designed to elicit reflections on several core topics, including experiences with AI-assisted coding, perceptions of skill development and task ownership, ethical considerations, strategies for adapting to AI in the workplace or classroom, and visions for future human-AI collaboration.

Interviews followed a flexible structure, allowing participants to expand on issues that were most salient to them. This format enabled the researcher to probe deeper into emergent themes while maintaining consistency across interviews. All sessions were recorded with participant consent and subsequently transcribed verbatim for analysis.

Analytical Approach

Data analysis followed a thematic coding approach, combining both inductive and deductive strategies. Transcripts were first reviewed holistically to identify recurring concepts, language patterns, and points of emphasis. Initial codes were generated based on both participant responses and the theoretical frameworks guiding this study, namely, Deskilling Theory, Job Characteristics Theory, and Technology Threat Avoidance Theory.

Subsequent rounds of coding involved grouping similar responses, identifying contradictions or tensions, and mapping findings to the three research questions:

- RQ1: How do programmers perceive and navigate challenges related to user experience in AI chatbot development?
- RQ2: How do programmers address user interactions and feedback challenges during AI chatbot development?
- RQ3: Considering technological advancements, how do programmers envision a future collaboration between humans and AI chatbots?

Coding and organization of thematic categories were conducted using qualitative data analysis software (MaxQDA), which facilitated data visualization and ensured consistency in identifying themes across interviews.

Trustworthiness

This study followed several best practices in qualitative research. Triangulation was employed by comparing data across participants with varied roles and experiences. Member checking was conducted with select participants who reviewed preliminary interpretations of their responses to confirm accuracy. In addition, reflexive journaling was used by the researcher to document analytical decisions and reduce potential bias in the interpretation of data.

The study also upheld ethical research principles, including confidentiality, transparency, and respect for participant autonomy. All data were stored on password-protected devices, and identifiers were removed from transcripts during analysis.

FINDINGS

The interview data provided detailed and thoughtful insights into how students, teachers, and professionals use generative AI tools in software development and chatbot programming. This section shares the findings based on the three main research questions. Each part is centered around a key theme that reflects common patterns in what participants said. The discussion also connects these findings to the study's theories to help explain what they mean for learning, building skills, and working in real-world settings.

RQ1: How do programmers perceive and navigate challenges related to user experience in AI chatbot development?

Theme 1: From Creator to Curator of UX Design

Programmers increasingly rely on generative AI to generate conversational flows and UX interactions, shifting their role from constructing user journeys to selecting and modifying AI-generated suggestions.

One participant reflected on how AI has changed his development workflow, noting a shift in his role. "It feels like I'm editing more than building," he said. Instead of starting from scratch, he often begins with AI-generated code and then spends time refining, correcting, or tailoring it to fit the project's needs. While this approach speeds up specific tasks, it also leaves him questioning the depth of his creative involvement. "I'm still coding," he explained, "but it's more about steering and revising than actually constructing something from the ground up."

Theme 2: Diminished Conceptual Engagement and Skill Confidence

Participants reported difficulty articulating the logic behind AI-generated outputs, revealing a gap between successful task completion and deep understanding, a core concern of Deskilling Theory.

One participant admitted to accepting AI-generated code without fully understanding it, driven by the pressure of tight deadlines. "Honestly, I didn't have time to dig into what the code was doing," he shared. "I just needed to get it done and move on." For him, the immediate need to deliver results often outweighed the opportunity for deeper learning or verification. His experience reflects a common challenge, balancing efficiency with comprehension in fast-paced development environments where time constraints can lead to a reliance on AI without critical evaluation.

Theme 3: Tension Between Speed and Design Ownership

While AI improved efficiency, it reduced programmers' sense of task ownership and autonomy in user experience design, echoing Job Characteristics Theory's concern about loss of task identity.

One participant expressed appreciation for how AI tools streamlined his development process, especially under tight deadlines. "It's so much faster to get things done now," he explained. "Before, I'd spend hours manually writing out repetitive code or debugging small issues. Now, the AI takes care of that in seconds." He emphasized that what used to be time-consuming and labor-intensive tasks have become more efficient, freeing him up to focus on higher-level decisions. "I don't have to do the manual work anymore," he said. "It helps me deliver on time and stay productive, especially when juggling multiple priorities." For him, AI wasn't just a convenience; it was a practical solution to the demands of modern development.

RQ2: How do programmers address user interactions and feedback challenges during AI chatbot development?

Theme 1: Partial Automation with Human Oversight

Participants described using AI for everyday interactions while reserving complex or sensitive user feedback tasks for human intervention, a strategy to maintain quality and ethical control.

One participant embraced a hybrid approach to software development, combining human oversight with AI-driven automation. He made it clear that trusting the AI wasn't a primary concern for him. "I don't really worry about whether I fully trust it," he said. "If it works and saves time, I'm fine with that." For him, the priority was efficiency and output rather than deep scrutiny of every AI-generated line of code.

He accepted automation as a natural evolution of development work, viewing AI as a collaborator that could handle routine or repetitive tasks. "I still review the important stuff, but I don't waste energy second-guessing every suggestion," he explained. "There's no point fighting it; automation is here, and it's helping me move faster." This pragmatic mindset reflects a growing trend among developers who are more focused on results than on maintaining complete control over every detail of the coding process. By blending AI assistance with selective human judgment, he found a balance that met both his technical and time-related demands.

Theme 2: Unstable Feedback Loops and Iterative Limitations

AI systems lacked contextual learning over time, which limited their ability to adapt meaningfully to evolving user feedback. Programmers had to intervene manually, disrupting natural UX improvement cycles.

One participant highlighted the challenges of working with AI by pointing to what he described as "unstable feedback loops" and limitations in iterative refinement. "Sometimes, the more you try to fix or clarify a prompt, the worse the output gets," he said. He explained that instead of improving with each iteration, the AI would occasionally drift further from the intended result, creating a cycle of corrections that felt unproductive. "It doesn't always learn from previous steps the way a human would," he noted. "I end up re-explaining things that should have been obvious from the context." This inconsistency made it difficult to rely on AI for complex or layered tasks that required subtle adjustments or continuity. His experience underscores a critical limitation: while AI can accelerate development, its lack of memory across iterations and its sensitivity to prompt phrasing can introduce frustrating inefficiencies, especially in workflows that depend on stable, cumulative feedback.

Theme 3: Adaptive Strategies and Skillful Workarounds

Some programmers developed conscious workarounds, custom fallbacks, layered guardrails, or model tuning to manage unpredictability. These practices reinforced their sense of skill and responsibility (autonomy and task significance in JCT).

One participant described developing a technique to learn alongside AI assistance. "I needed to understand what the code output was, so I repeated the process without looking at the code," he explained. This proactive approach not only boosted his confidence in handling AI-generated results but also fostered a greater sense of ownership over the system's evolving quality.

RQ3: Considering technological advancements, how do programmers envision a future collaboration between humans and AI chatbots?

Theme 1: Ambivalence Toward Role Redefinition

Participants expressed both enthusiasm for AI-augmented roles such as AI strategies and concern about losing technical relevance, mirroring TTAT's mix of opportunity and threat perception.

One participant voiced both excitement and apprehension about the increasing role of AI. "I'm amazed by what it can do," she remarked, "but I am also concerned about how dependent we might become on it." Her comments reflect a standard tension of admiration for AI's potential, mixed with concern about its long-term effects.

Theme 2: Emergence of Hybrid Competencies

There was a widespread belief that future programmers would need a blend of coding, prompt engineering, ethical reasoning, and domain-specific insight, expanding the definition of programming literacy.

One participant saw the rise of AI as a call to expand his skill set. "It's no longer just about knowing a programming language and having debugging skills," he explained. "You need to understand prompt engineering, ethics, and how models behave." To prepare, he enrolled in online courses on AI alignment and conversational UX, viewing them as critical skills for the future. "The best developers in five years," he predicted, "will be the ones who can read the prompt."

Theme 3: Reframing Human-AI Collaboration as a Shared Cognitive Task

Rather than replacing human work, many envisioned AI as a thinking partner that augments human creativity and critical reasoning, suggesting a shift toward co-agency, not subordination.

One participant described his approach to chatbot development as a collaborative partnership with AI rather than simply a tool-based interaction. "It's like having a co-developer who's fast and tireless, but you still have to guide it with clarity and intent," he said. For him, building effective AI-driven systems meant more than just writing code; it required an understanding of prompt engineering, user experience, and ethical design.

"It's not just about syntax and debugging anymore," he explained. "You have to think about how the AI interprets your instructions, how users will interact with it, and what unintended consequences might arise." To keep pace with this evolving landscape, he took online courses in AI alignment and conversational UX design, viewing these as essential skills for modern developers. "The best developers in five years," he added, "will be the ones who know how to speak the language of prompts and think critically about the AI's role in their code." His experience highlights a growing mindset among developers: embracing AI not just as a productivity tool but as an intelligent partner in shaping the future of software.

Summary of Findings

This study explored how students and professional developers engage with generative AI tools in programming and chatbot development contexts. Drawing from qualitative interviews grounded in Deskilling Theory, job characteristics theory, and technology threat avoidance theory, the findings reveal a complex, evolving relationship between human programmers and AI systems. Each research question uncovered three distinct themes, further illustrated by real-world case studies that highlight how individuals adapt, struggle, and reimagine their roles in the age of AI.

RQ1: How do future programmers perceive and navigate challenges related to user experience in AI chatbot development?

Programmers reported a notable transformation in their approach to user experience (UX) design in AI chatbot development, primarily driven by their adoption of generative AI tools. A recurring pattern among participants was the shift from traditional roles as active creators of chatbot UX to curators of AI-generated content. Many described using tools like GitHub Copilot or ChatGPT to draft conversation flows or suggest interaction responses and then simply selecting or refining the most relevant options. While this increased efficiency, several participants felt that their creative control had diminished, and they no longer had full authorship over the final design.

A decline in conceptual engagement with UX logic accompanied this transition. Although participants successfully implemented functional chatbot flows, some admitted they could not explain the underlying decision logic or predict how the system would behave in nuanced cases. The ease of copying or modifying AI-generated code often replaces the deeper learning that comes from building interactions manually. For some, this reliance on automation raised doubts about their competence, with one participant questioning whether they were truly learning or simply becoming dependent on AI suggestions.

The tension between efficiency and ownership emerged as a central concern. While participants appreciated the speed at which they could produce and test chatbot designs using AI tools, many acknowledged a reduction in reflective thinking and purposeful design. Their roles had become more reactive, focused on evaluating or correcting AI output rather than proactively designing user experiences from the ground up. As a result, they experienced a loss of autonomy and task identity, key elements of intrinsic motivation according to Job Characteristics Theory.

RQ2: How do future programmers address user interactions and feedback challenges during AI chatbot development?

When it came to integrating user interactions and feedback into AI chatbot systems, programmers described a complex balancing act between leveraging automation and ensuring ethical, accurate, and contextually appropriate responses. Most participants developed hybrid approaches to user interaction management, allowing AI to handle routine tasks while reserving high-risk or ambiguous situations for human oversight. For instance, some implemented escalation mechanisms that redirected sensitive queries to human agents. This selective automation strategy allowed developers to maintain a level of quality control and ethical responsibility for the system's behavior.

Despite these efforts, participants expressed frustration with the limitations of current AI models in adapting to feedback. Several developers noted that while users provided corrections or flagged errors, these interactions did not result in persistent learning unless the developers manually retrained or re-prompted the system. As a result, chatbot responses often repeat the same mistakes, making the iterative refinement process feel disconnected and inefficient. This lack of integration disrupted the expected agile feedback loop and challenged participants' expectations for continuous improvement in user-centered design.

To manage these shortcomings, many programmers created skillful workarounds and adaptation strategies. Some designed layered fallback logic, others fine-tuned prompts based on error logs, and a few established monitoring systems to track user dissatisfaction. These practices allowed them to regain a sense of autonomy and agency over the chatbot's learning process. Rather than abandoning AI entirely, these developers embraced a more proactive and reflective role, demonstrating that, while AI might reduce manual work, the need for human skill and oversight remains indispensable in dynamic, user-facing systems.

RQ3: Considering technological advancements, how do future programmers envision a future collaboration between humans and AI chatbots?

Most participants recognized the value of AI as a tool that enhances productivity, facilitates ideation, and automates repetitive coding tasks. On the other hand, some expressed concern that the increasing capability of generative AI might reduce the role of human developers to that of overseers or validators, individuals who approve AI-generated solutions rather than design them. This ambiguity reflected a broader anxiety about the future relevance of human creativity and expertise in the face of accelerating automation.

In response to these shifts, participants articulated the need for new, hybrid skill sets that go beyond traditional coding abilities. Many emphasized that future programmers must be fluent not only in programming languages but also in prompt engineering, ethical reasoning, data stewardship, and cross-disciplinary communication. Several described actively upskilling themselves in these areas, anticipating that success in a future AI-mediated development environment will depend on the ability to think critically, frame meaningful problems, and guide AI systems responsibly.

Interestingly, a few participants articulated an aspirational vision of AI as a cognitive collaborator rather than a tool. They likened the development process to pair programming with a non-human partner, one that can brainstorm, generate, and iterate alongside them. This vision repositions human developers not as passive consumers of automation but as active participants in a co-creative process. In this emerging paradigm, human-AI collaboration becomes a symbiotic relationship, where AI amplifies human capability, and humans bring contextual intelligence, ethics, and intentionality to work. This reframing offers a promising path forward for sustaining meaningful, empowered engagement in a future shaped by intelligent systems.

DISCUSSION AND IMPLICATION

The findings of this study highlight the complex and evolving relationship between programmers and generative AI systems, particularly in educational and early-career development contexts. Across all three research questions, participants described a notable shift in how they engage with programming tasks, user experience design, and feedback processes. A duality characterized these shifts: while AI tools increased efficiency and accessibility, they also introduced new forms of dependency, cognitive disengagement, and ethical uncertainty. The discussion below examines how these findings intersect with the guiding theoretical frameworks and explores their broader implications for pedagogy and practice.

Deskilling Theory helps explain the decline in foundational programming skills observed in this study. Many participants relied on AI-generated code without understanding its underlying logic, reflecting a reduction in conceptual engagement and aligning with traditional patterns of automation-driven deskilling. However, several participants also demonstrated agency by manually correcting code, refining strategies, and critically evaluating AI outputs, indicating opportunities for reskilling when appropriate scaffolding and guidance are provided.

Job Characteristics Theory illustrates how AI use reshapes motivational factors in learning and development. Core job attributes such as autonomy, skill variety, task identity, and feedback were all affected. Although generative tools improved the immediacy of feedback, they often diminished autonomy and skill variety, mainly when learners used AI to shortcut problem-solving. These shifts risk lowering engagement and intrinsic motivation, as students may come to see themselves as passive curators of AI-generated content rather than active problem-solvers.

Technology Threat Avoidance Theory further clarifies participants' emotional and behavioral responses to AI. Some viewed AI as a threat, expressing anxiety about job displacement or ethical concerns, while others approached it with confidence, seeing it as a means for augmentation rather than replacement. These differing responses highlight the importance of perceived control, self-efficacy, and institutional support in shaping how individuals engage with AI tools.

Several strategies are recommended to address these challenges. Structured AI onboarding should provide students with clear training on AI capabilities, limitations, and critical usage. Mentorship programs can connect learners with experienced practitioners who model reflective and iterative engagement with AI. Hybrid workflows that alternate between manual and AI-assisted coding can help preserve foundational skills. Finally, career-aware design of learning activities should align AI use with students' experience levels and professional goals. Together, these strategies promote AI as an augmentative rather than a substitutive force in learning and development.

The findings of this study have several important implications for educators developing curricula that integrate AI tools into programming education.

First, promoting reflective use of AI is essential. Educators should encourage students to explain, critique, and revise AI-generated code to maintain conceptual engagement and prevent cognitive offloading. Assignments such as code walk-throughs, justification memos, or annotated reviews can help learners think critically about the reasoning behind AI outputs rather than accepting them at face value.

Second, rebalancing learning objectives is necessary to move beyond simple task completion. Course goals should emphasize metacognitive skills such as prompt engineering, ethical reasoning, and human–AI collaboration. These abilities align with current industry needs and prepare students to navigate increasingly hybrid work environments responsibly.

Third, preserving autonomy and challenge can help sustain motivation and engagement. To counter the passivity that automation may encourage, instructors should design activities that maintain elements of autonomy, skill variety, and complexity. Open-ended projects, real-world problem-solving, and team-based challenges foster deeper learning and a stronger sense of ownership.

Finally, establishing clear ethical guidelines is crucial. Participants in this study often expressed uncertainty about the boundaries of acceptable AI use. Institutions should provide transparent policies, model responsible practices, and integrate discussions of academic integrity into technical coursework. Requiring students to disclose their AI usage and reflect on their decision-making processes can promote ethical awareness and accountability.

The integration of generative AI into programming education is neither inherently detrimental nor wholly beneficial. As this study shows, its impact depends mainly on how learners and educators respond to its presence. Generative AI can enable creativity, productivity, and accessibility, but only if its use is framed within a pedagogical structure that prioritizes deep learning, ethical reasoning, and adaptive expertise. By grounding AI integration in theory and practice, we can ensure that today's learners become not just proficient coders but thoughtful, responsible collaborators in the age of intelligent automation.

LIMITATIONS

While this study provides important insights into how generative AI tools are reshaping programming education and chatbot development, several limitations must be acknowledged.

First, the study is based on a relatively small sample of twelve participants drawn from academic and professional settings. Although qualitative methods are well-suited to exploring complex experiences in depth, the findings are not statistically generalizable. The sample's diversity in terms of roles (students, educators, developers) adds richness to the data but also introduces variability that may limit the specificity of conclusions across particular subgroups.

Second, data were collected through self-reported interviews, which rely on participants' perceptions, memories, and reflections. While these narratives offer valuable subjective insight, they may not capture behaviors as accurately as observational or experimental methods. Some participants may have overstated or understated their engagement with AI tools due to social desirability, uncertainty, or lack of formal awareness regarding tool usage.

Third, the study focused primarily on experiences with a subset of generative AI tools, namely, ChatGPT and GitHub Copilot. As the field of AI-assisted development evolves rapidly, new tools, features, and integrations are emerging that may produce different impacts on learning, workflow, and ethical considerations. Consequently, the insights presented here reflect a snapshot of a particular moment in technological development and user adaptation.

Lastly, this research was framed by three theoretical lenses: Deskilling Theory, Job Characteristics Theory, and Technology Threat Avoidance Theory, which, while robust, do not exhaust the range of possible explanatory frameworks. Other perspectives, such as critical algorithm studies, could provide additional nuance and alternative interpretations.

CONCLUSION

This chapter explored how generative AI tools like ChatGPT and GitHub Copilot are changing the way students and future programmers learn and grow, especially in areas like AI chatbot design and programming education. Based on interviews with students, developers, and educators, the study looked at how AI affects user experience design, the way feedback is used, and how programmers see their roles. The findings showed that while AI can make coding faster, provide helpful support, and offer easy access to resources, it also brings challenges, such as the risk of losing hands-on skills, feeling less ownership over tasks, and facing unclear ethical situations.

Guided by Deskilling Theory, Job Characteristics Theory, and Technology Threat Avoidance Theory, this chapter highlighted how generative AI reconfigures key elements of the educational process, from how learners engage with problem-solving to how they define their roles in collaborative systems. The study found that students are transitioning from creators to curators, often relying on AI-generated outputs without fully understanding the underlying logic. Meanwhile, developers and educators are responding to these shifts with a mix of optimism and concern, seeking ways to preserve human agency, critical thinking, and ethical awareness in the face of increasingly capable automation.

The findings underscore the need for educational frameworks that go beyond technical proficiency to cultivate metacognitive, ethical, and adaptive skills. When thoughtfully integrated, AI can serve as a catalyst for innovation, not only in how students learn to code but also in how they learn to think, reason, and collaborate in hybrid human-machine systems. However, without intentional guidance, AI use risks reducing learners to passive consumers of algorithmic output, undermining the very goals of education.

REFERENCES

Avila-Chauvet, L., Mejía, D., & Acosta Quiroz, C. (2023). CHATGPT as a support tool for online behavioral task programming. *SSRN.* Retrieved from https://ssrn.com/abstract=4329020

Barke, S., James, M., & Polikarpova, N. (2023). Grounded copilot: How programmers interact with code-generating models. *Proceedings of the ACM on Programming Languages, 7*(OOPSLA1), 85-111. DOI: 10.1145/3586030

Braverman, H. (1974). *Labor and monopoly capital.* Monthly Review Press. DOI: 10.14452/MR-026-03-1974-07_1

Crowston, K., & Bolici, F. (2025). Deskilling and upskilling with AI Systems. *nformation Research an International Electronic Journal, 30*(iConf), 1009-1023. DOI: 10.47989/ir30iConf47143

Daigle, K. (2024). *Survey: The AI wave continues to grow on software development teams.* Retrieved from https://github.blog/author/kdaigle/

Hackman, J. R., & Oldham, G. R. (1976). Motivation through the design of work: Test of a theory. *Organizational Behavior and Human Performance, 16*(2), 250–279. DOI: 10.1016/0030-5073(76)90016-7

Khurana, A., Subramonyam, H., & Chilana, P. K. (2024). Why and when llm-based assistants can go wrong: Investigating the effectiveness of prompt-based interactions for software help-seeking. *arXiv.org.* Retrieved from /arxiv.2402.08030DOI: 10.1145/3640543.3645200

Kuhail, M. A., Mathew, S. S., Khalil, A., Khalil, A., & Shah, S. J. (2023). "Will I be replaced?" Assessing ChatGPT's effect on software development and programmer perceptions of AI tools. *arXiv.org.* Retrieved from DOI: 10.2139/ssrn.4571482

Liang, H., & Xue, Y. (2009). Avoidance of information technology threats: A theoretical perspective. *Management Information Systems Quarterly, 33*(1), 71–90. DOI: 10.2307/20650279

Peoples, K. (2021). *How to write a phenomenological dissertation: A step-by-step guide* (Vol. 56). SAGE.

Prather, J., Reeves, B. N., Denny, P., Becker, B. A., Leinonen, J., Luxton-Reilly, A., Powell, G., Finnie-Ansley, J., & Santos, E. A. (2023). "It's weird that it knows what I want": Usability and interactions with Copilot for novice programmers. *ACM Transactions on Computer-Human Interaction, 31*(1), 1–31. DOI: 10.1145/3617367

Riazi, M., Rezvani, R., & Ghanbar, H. (2023). Trustworthiness in L2 writing research: A review and analysis of qualitative articles in the Journal of Second Language Writing. *Research Methods in Applied Linguistics*, *2*(3), 100065. Advance online publication. DOI: 10.1016/j.rmal.2023.100065

Rinta-Kahila, T., Penttinen, E., Salovaara, A., Soliman, W., & Ruissalo, J. (2023). The vicious circles of skill erosion: A case study of cognitive automation. *Journal of the Association for Information Systems*, *24*(5), 1378–1412. DOI: 10.17705/1jais.00829

Stefaniak, J., & Moore, S. (2024). The Use of Generative AI to Support Inclusivity and Design Deliberation for Online Instruction. *Online Learning : the Official Journal of the Online Learning Consortium*, *28*(3), 181–205. DOI: 10.24059/olj.v28i3.4458

KEY TERMS AND DEFINITIONS

Academic Integrity: The commitment to honesty, fairness, and responsibility in academic work, including proper citation, avoiding plagiarism, and using AI tools ethically.

AI-Assisted Learning: A learning approach that incorporates artificial intelligence tools to enhance instruction, personalize content, provide feedback, and support student engagement and performance.

ChatGPT in Education: The use of ChatGPT, a conversational AI tool, to support teaching and learning through activities such as tutoring, content generation, feedback, coding help, and language assistance.

Continuous Learning: The ongoing development of skills and knowledge necessary to keep pace with technological advancements, especially in fast-evolving fields like software development.

Deskilling: The process by which the skills required to perform a job diminish, often due to automation or the introduction of technology that simplifies tasks.

Ethical Challenges: Dilemmas that arise when technology or decisions conflict with moral principles. In Generative AI, these include issues like privacy, bias, misinformation, and misuse.

Generative AI: Artificial intelligence that creates new content, such as text, images, or code, by learning patterns from existing data.

Responsible AI Use: The ethical and transparent application of artificial intelligence that ensures fairness, accountability, privacy, and alignment with societal values while minimizing potential harm.

Skill Development: The process of acquiring, enhancing, or refining abilities and competencies needed to perform tasks effectively in academic, professional, or personal contexts.

Skill Gaps: Rapid technological change often exacerbates the difference between the skills required for a job and the actual skills workers possess.

Software Engineering Education: The study and practice of teaching software development principles, tools, and methods to prepare individuals for designing, building, and maintaining software systems.

Compilation of References

Acar, İ. G., & Övez, F. D. (2022). The effect of block-based game development activities on the geometry achievement, computational thinking skills and opinions of seventh-grade students. *Journal of Educational Technology and Online Learning*, *5*(4), 1106–1121. DOI: 10.31681/jetol.1151170

Adıgüzel, S., Eryılmaz, S., Gencer, T., & Göksu, H. (2023). Coding activities in IT courses through the lenses of IT teachers. *Journal of Educational Technology and Online Learning*, *6*(2), 384–402. DOI: 10.31681/jetol.1219963

Adler, R. F., Hibdon, J., Kim, H., Mayle, S., Pines, B., & Srinivas, S. (2023). Assessing computational thinking across a STEM curriculum for pre-service teachers. *Education and Information Technologies*, *28*(7), 8051–8073. DOI: 10.1007/s10639-022-11508-4

Aghasaleh, R., Enderle, P., & Puvirajah, A. (2019). From Computational Thinking to Political Resistance. *Journal for Activist Science and Technology Education*, *10*(1), 29–44. DOI: 10.33137/jaste.v10i1.32915

Aghazadeh, S. (2020). *Inquiry-based Learning and its Impact on Teaching and Learning of the Humanities. (NIE Working Paper Series No. 19)*. National Institute of Education., https://repository.nie.edu.sg/server/api/core/bitstreams/47e655d5-20f5-4bb0-af80-a8a9c6212179/content

Aksu, F. N., & Durak, G. (2019). Robotics in Education: Examining Information Technology Teachers' Views. *Journal of Education and e-learning Research*, *6*(4), 162–168. DOI: 10.20448/journal.509.2019.64.162.168

Al Hamad, N. M., Adewusi, O. E., Unachukwu, C. C., Osawaru, B., & Onyebuchi, N. C. (2024). A review on the innovative approaches to STEM education. *International Journal of Science and Research Archive*, *11*(1), 244–252. DOI: 10.30574/ijsra.2024.11.1.0026

Alloway, T. P., & Passolunghi, M. C. (2011). The relationship between working memory, IQ, and mathematical skills in children. *Learning and Individual Differences, 21*(1), 133–137. DOI: 10.1016/j.lindif.2010.09.013

Allsop, Y. (2019). Assessing computational thinking process using a multiple evaluation approach. *International Journal of Child-Computer Interaction, 19*, 30–55. DOI: 10.1016/j.ijcci.2018.10.004

Almadhun, S., Swese, R. F., Ali, A., Nasef, A. A., Alasoud, A., & Rmis, A. (2024). Programming education in focus: Investigating and analyzing the present state in libyan primary and secondary schools. *Humanitarian and Natural Sciences Journal, 5*(1). Advance online publication. DOI: 10.53796/hnsj51/39

Almadhun, S., Toycan, M., & Adalıer, A. (2019). Vb2algo: An educational reverse engineering tool to enhance high school students' learning capacities in programming. *Revista de Cercetare si Interventie Sociala, 67*, 67–87. DOI: 10.33788/rcis.67.5

Al-Qurishi, M., Khalid, T., & Souissi, R. (2021). Deep Learning for Sign Language Recognition: Current Techniques, Benchmarks, and Open Issues. *IEEE Access : Practical Innovations, Open Solutions, 9*, 126917–126951. DOI: 10.1109/ACCESS.2021.3110912

Alsharif, B., Alanazi, M., & Ilyas, M. (2023). Machine Learning Technology to Recognize American Sign Language Alphabet. *2023 IEEE 20th International Conference on Smart Communities: Improving Quality of Life Using AI, Robotics and IoT, HONET 2023, 128*, 173–178.

Altadmri, A., & Brown, N. C. C. (2015). 37 million lines of code: Identifying common student mistakes in novice programs. *Proceedings of the 46th ACM Technical Symposium on Computer Science Education*, 278–283. https://doi.org/DOI: 10.1145/2676723.2677258

Al-Tahat, K. S. (2019). The impact of a 3d visual programming tool on students' performance and attitude in computer programming. *Journal of Cases on Information Technology, 21*(1), 52–64. DOI: 10.4018/JCIT.2019010104

Aluru, K. C., Tellex, S., Oberlin, J. G., & MacGlashan, J. (2015). Minecraft as an experimental world for AI in robotics. *AAAI Fall Symposia,* Retrieved from https://h2r1.cs.brown.edu/wp-content/uploads/2015/09/aluru15.pdf

Aly, W., Aly, S., & Almotairi, S. (2019). User-independent american sign language alphabet recognition based on depth image and PCANet features. *IEEE Access : Practical Innovations, Open Solutions, 7*, 123138–123150. DOI: 10.1109/ACCESS.2019.2938829

Amandha, S., Dani, R., Hierdawati, T., Armandito, A., & Rahmat, B. (2024). Workshop pengenalan web dan css dasar pada mahasiswa universitas muhammadiyah jambi. *KREATIF: Jurnal Pengabdian Masyarakat Nusantara*, *4*(1), 65–71. DOI: 10.55606/kreatif.v4i1.2842

Ameen, S. Y., & Mohammed, D. Y. (2022). Developing cross-platform library using flutter. *European Journal of Engineering and Technology Research*, *7*(2), 18–21. DOI: 10.24018/ejeng.2022.7.2.2740

Andonov, F. (2019). Comparative analysis of python with other programming languages. *Yearbook Telecommunications*, *6*, 1–15. DOI: 10.33919/YTelecomm.19.6.1

Angeli, C., & Valanides, N. (2020). Developing young children's computational thinking with educational robotics: An interaction effect between gender and scaffolding strategy. *Computers in Human Behavior*, *105*, 105954. DOI: 10.1016/j.chb.2019.03.018

Apple Education. (2020). *Everyone Can Code Curriculum*. Apple Inc.

Arendes, K., Kerkhoff, S. N., & Adhikari, B. (2024). Engaging students to learn coding in the ai era with emphasis on the process. *Edukasiana: Jurnal Inovasi Pendidikan*, *3*(2), 257–268. DOI: 10.56916/ejip.v3i2.728

Arfe, B., Vardanega, T., Montuori, C., & Lavanga, M. (2019). Coding in primary grades boosts children's executive functions. *Frontiers in Psychology*, *10*, 2713. Advance online publication. DOI: 10.3389/fpsyg.2019.02713

Arfé, B., Vardanega, T., & Ronconi, L. (2020). The effects of coding on children's planning and inhibition skills. *Computers & Education*, *148*, 103807. DOI: 10.1016/j.compedu.2020.103807

Ari, F., Arslan-Ari, I., & Vasconcelos, L. (2022). Early childhood preservice teachers' perceptions of computer science, gender stereotypes, and coding in early childhood education. *TechTrends*, *66*(3), 539–546. DOI: 10.1007/s11528-022-00725-w

Ashcraft, M. H., & Krause, J. A. (2007). Working memory, math performance, and math anxiety. *Psychonomic Bulletin & Review*, *14*(2), 243–248. DOI: 10.3758/BF03194059 PMID: 17694908

Avila-Chauvet, L., Mejía, D., & Acosta Quiroz, C. (2023). CHATGPT as a support tool for online behavioral task programming. *SSRN*. Retrieved from https://ssrn.com/abstract=4329020

Avramovic, S., Avramovic, I., & Wojtusiak, J. (2024). Exploring the impact of github copilot on health informatics education. *Applied Clinical Informatics*, *15*(05), 1121–1129. DOI: 10.1055/a-2414-7790

Bachiller, P., Barbecho, I., Calderita, L. V., Bustos, P., & Manso, L. J. (2020). Learnblock: A robot-agnostic educational programming tool. *IEEE Access : Practical Innovations, Open Solutions*, *8*, 30012–30026. DOI: 10.1109/ACCESS.2020.2972410

Baddeley. (2000). The episodic buffer: A new component of working memory? *Trends in Cognitive Sciences, 4*(11), 417–423. http:// www.ncbi.nlm.nih.gov/pubmed/11058819

Baddeley, A. (1992). Working memory. *Science*, *255*(5044), 556–559. DOI: 10.1126/science.1736359

Baddeley, A. D. (1986). *Working memory*. Oxford University Press.

Badiee, E., Nili, M. R., & Abedini, Y. (2023). Brain-compatible courseware impact on learning computer programming. *International Journal of Technology Enhanced Learning*, *15*(1), 1–13. DOI: 10.1504/IJTEL.2023.127933

Badre, D., & Nee, D. E. (2018). Frontal cortex and the hierarchical control of behavior. *Trends in Cognitive Sciences*, *22*(2), 170–188. DOI: 10.1016/j.tics.2017.11.005 PMID: 29229206

Bajarin, T. (2016, March 16). *Why schools should teach more than basic coding*. TIME. https://time.com/4261554/why-schools-should-teach-more-than-basic-coding/

Bamigboye, K. (2024). Supporting STEM success: Digital curriculum innovations to foster student retention. [IJSRM]. *International Journal of Scientific Research and Management*, *11*(4), 982–1000. DOI: 10.18535/ijsrm/v11i04.ec3

Barke, S., James, M., & Polikarpova, N. (2023). Grounded copilot: How programmers interact with code-generating models. *Proceedings of the ACM on Programming Languages, 7*(OOPSLA1), 85-111. DOI: 10.1145/3586030

Barr, D., Harrison, J., & Conery, L. (2011). Computational thinking: A digital age skill for everyone. *Learning and Leading with Technology*, *38*(6), 20–23.

Barr, V., & Stephenson, C. (2011). Bringing computational thinking to K-12: What is Involved and what is the role of the computer science education community? *ACM Inroads*, *2*(1), 48–54. DOI: 10.1145/1929887.1929905

Bassett, D. S., Wymbs, N. F., Porter, M. A., Mucha, P. J., Carlson, J. M., & Grafton, S. T. (2011). Dynamic reconfiguration of human brain networks during learning. *Proceedings of the National Academy of Sciences of the United States of America*, *108*(18), 7641–7646. DOI: 10.1073/pnas.1018985108 PMID: 21502525

Batiha, Q. A., Ashaari, N. S., Aini, N., & Mohd, N. (2022). Adoption of visual programming environments in programming learning. *International Journal on Advanced Science, Engineering and Information Technology*, *12*(5), 1921–1930. DOI: 10.18517/ijaseit.12.5.15500

BBC. (2021). *MicroPython and BBC micro:bit – Getting Started Guide.* https://microbit.org

Beddows, P. A., & Mallon, E. K. (2018). Cave pearl data logger: A flexible arduino-based logging platform for long-term monitoring in harsh environments. *Sensors (Basel)*, *18*(2), 530. DOI: 10.3390/s18020530

Beege, M., Schneider, S., Nebel, S., Zimm, J., Windisch, S., & Rey, G. D. (2021). Learning programming from erroneous worked-examples. Which type of error is beneficial for learning? *Learning and Instruction*, *75*, 101497. Advance online publication. DOI: 10.1016/j.learninstruc.2021.101497

Beena, M. V., Namboodiri, A., & Thottungal, R. (2020). Hybrid approaches of convolutional network and support vector machine for American sign language prediction. *Multimedia Tools and Applications*, *79*(5–6), 4027–4040. DOI: 10.1007/s11042-019-7723-0

Bers, M. U., Flannery, L., Kazakoff, E. R., & Sullivan, A. (2014). Computational thinking and tinkering: Exploration of an early childhood robotics curriculum. *Computers & Education*, *72*, 145–157. DOI: 10.1016/j.compedu.2013.10.020

Bhuyan, M. K., Neog, D. R., & Kar, M. K. (2011). Hand pose recognition using geometric features. *2011 National Conference on Communications, NCC 2011*, 0–4. DOI: 10.1109/NCC.2011.5734786

Bieg, T., Schmoigl-Tonis, M., Sturm, N., Nativel, C., & Sackl, A. (2022). Enabling cross-domain robot programming by end-users: the robxtask platform. 2022 *IEEE Symposium on Visual Languages and Human-Centric Computing* (VL/HCC). https://doi.org/DOI: 10.1109/VL/HCC53370.2022.9833136

Blackwell, A. (2016). Best practices for creating a sustainable and equitable food system in the United States. Center for American Progress. Retrieved from https://www.americanprogress.org/issues/poverty/reports/2016/05/12/137306/best-practices-for-creating-a-sustainable-and-equitable-food-system-in-the-united-states/

Blessinger, P., & Carfora, J. M. (2014). Innovative approaches in teaching and learning: An introduction to inquiry-based learning for the arts, humanities, and social sciences. In *Inquiry-based learning for the arts, humanities, and social sciences: A conceptual and practical resource for educators* (Vol. 2, pp. 3–25). Emerald Group Publishing Limited. DOI: 10.1108/S2055-364120140000002030

Boaler, J. (2016). *Mathematical mindsets: Unleashing students' potential through creative math, inspiring messages, and innovative teaching*. Jossey-Bass.

Bocconi, S., Chioccariello, A., Dettori, G., Ferrari, A., Engelhardt, K., Kampylis, P., & Punie, Y. (2016). Exploring the field of computational thinking as a 21st century skill. In *EDULEARN16 Proceedings* (pp. 4725-4733). IATED.

Bocconi, S., Chioccariello, A., Kampylis, P., Dagienė, V., Wastiau, P., Engelhardt, K., Earp, J., Horvath, M. A., Jasutė, E., Malagoli, C., Masiulionytė-Dagienė, V., & Stupurienė, G. (2022). *Reviewing computational thinking in compulsory education.* Publications Office of the European Union., DOI: 10.2760/126955

Brady, C. (2021). Patches as an expressive medium for exploratory multi-agent modelling. *British Journal of Educational Technology*, *52*(3), 1024–1042. DOI: 10.1111/bjet.13087

Braught, G., Miller, C. S., & Reed, D. (2004). Core empirical concepts and skills for computer science. *SIGCSE Bulletin*, *36*(1), 245–249. DOI: 10.1145/1028174.971388

Braverman, H. (1974). *Labor and monopoly capital.* Monthly Review Press. DOI: 10.14452/MR-026-03-1974-07_1

Brennan, K., & Resnick, M. (2012). New frameworks for studying and assessing the development of computational thinking. Paper presented at the annual meeting of the American Educational Research Association, Vancouver, BC, Canada. https://scratched.gse.harvard.edu/ct/files/AERA2012.pdf

Brennan, K., & Resnick, M. (2012, April). New frameworks for studying and assessing the development of computational thinking. In *Proceedings of the 2012 annual meeting of the American educational research association,* Vancouver, Canada (Vol. 1, p. 25).

Breslyn, W., & McGinnis, J. R. (2019). Investigating preservice elementary science teachers' understanding of climate change from a computational thinking systems perspective.

Brookings Institution. (2021). *Building skills for life: How to expand and improve computer science education around the world.* Center for Universal Education at Brookings. https://www.brookings.edu/articles/building-skills-for-life/

Brophy, J. (2008). Developing students' appreciation for what is taught in school. *Educational Psychologist*, *43*(3), 132–141. DOI: 10.1080/00461520701756511

Brophy, J. (2010). *Motivating students to learn* (3rd ed.). Routledge.

Burke, W. Q. (2012). *Coding & composition: Youth storytelling with Scratch programming* (Unpublished doctoral dissertation). Available from ProQuest Dissertations & Theses Global, 1–144. University of Pennsylvania. (1021379799).

Busjahn, T., Bednarik, R., Begel, A., Crosby, M., Paterson, J. H., Schulte, C., . . . Tamm, S. (2015, May). Eye movements in code reading: Relaxing the linear order. In *2015, IEEE 23rd International Conference on Program Comprehension* (pp. 255-265). IEEE.

Bybee, R. (2015). *The BSCS 5E instructional model: Creating teachable moments.* NSTA Press.

Cakir, R., Korkmaz, Ö., İdil, Ö., & Uğur Erdoğmuş, F. (2021). The effect of robotic coding education on preschoolers' problem solving and creative thinking skills. *Thinking Skills and Creativity*, *40*, 100812. Advance online publication. DOI: 10.1016/j.tsc.2021.100812

Çam, E., & Kıyıcı, M. (2022). The impact of robotics assisted programming education on academic success, problem solving skills and motivation. *Journal of Educational Technology and Online Learning*, *5*(1), 47–65. DOI: 10.31681/jetol.1028825

Camgoz, N. C., Hadfield, S., Koller, O., Ney, H., & Bowden, R. (2018). Neural Sign Language Translation. *Proceedings of the IEEE Computer Society Conference on Computer Vision and Pattern Recognition*, 7784–7793. DOI: 10.1109/CVPR.2018.00812

Castelhano, J., Duarte, I. C., Ferreira, C., Duraes, J., Madeira, H., & Castelo-Branco, M. (2019). The role of the insula in intuitive expert bug detection in computer code: An fMRI study. *Brain Imaging and Behavior*, *13*(3), 623–637. DOI: 10.1007/s11682-018-9885-1 PMID: 29744802

Cetin, I., & Dubinsky, E. (2017). Reflective abstraction in computational thinking. *The Journal of Mathematical Behavior*, *47*, 70–80. DOI: 10.1016/j.jmathb.2017.06.004

Çetinkaya-Rundel, M., & Ellison, V. (2021). A fresh look at introductory data science. *Journal of Statistics and Data Science Education : An Official Journal of the of the American Statistical Association*, *29*(sup1, S1), S16–S26. DOI: 10.1080/10691898.2020.1804497

Chandler, P., & Sweller, J. (1991). Cognitive load theory and the format of instruction. *Cognition and Instruction*, *8*(4), 293–332. DOI: 10.1207/s1532690xci0804_2

Chandler, P., & Sweller, J. (1992). The Split-Attention Effect as a Factor in the Design of Instruction. *The British Journal of Educational Psychology*, *62*(2), 233–246. DOI: 10.1111/j.2044-8279.1992.tb01017.x

Chen, C., Jong, M. S., & Tsai, C. (2022). A comparison of in-service teachers' conceptions of barriers to mobile technology-integrated instruction and technology-integrated instruction. *Australasian Journal of Educational Technology*, •••, 35–50. DOI: 10.14742/ajet.7299

Chen, O., Kalyuga, S., & Sweller, J. (2015). The worked example effect, the generation effect, and element interactivity. *Journal of Educational Psychology*, *107*(3), 689–704. DOI: 10.1037/edu0000018

Cheok, M. J., Omar, Z., & Jaward, M. H. (2019). A review of hand gesture and sign language recognition techniques. *International Journal of Machine Learning and Cybernetics*, *10*(1), 131–153. DOI: 10.1007/s13042-017-0705-5

Choleva, V., Stagakis, S., Choleva, E., & Patrikakis, C. Z. (2022). Integrating the 4cs into creating games by visual programming and project based learning. *European Conference on Games Based Learning, 16*(1), 147-154. https://doi.org/DOI: 10.34190/ecgbl.16.1.694

Çiftçi, S., & Bildiren, A. (2020). The effect of coding courses on the cognitive abilities and problem-solving skills of preschool children. *Computer Science Education*, *30*(1), 3–21. DOI: 10.1080/08993408.2019.1696169

Çoban, D., & Yıldız, D. G. (2025). An evaluation of the 10th grade robotic coding curriculum (2020) within a participant oriented curriculum evaluation approach. *Journal of Educational Technology and Online Learning*, *8*(2), 226–250. DOI: 10.31681/jetol.1568614

Cocieru, O. C., Lyle, M. C., & McDonald, M. A. (2021). An exploration of the dynamic nature of psychological ownership in a classroom-as-organization. *Journal of Experiential Education*, *44*(3), 293–307. DOI: 10.1177/1053825920973704

Code.org, CSTA, ECEP Alliance. (2024). 2024 State of Computer Science Education. Retrieved from https://advocacy.code.org/stateofcs

Code.org. (2023). *State of computer science education: Illuminating disparities*. https://advocacy.code.org/stateofcs

College Board. (2020). *AP computer science principles course and exam description.* https://apcentral.collegeboard.org/courses/ap-computer-science-principles

College Board. (2021). *AP program participation and performance data 2021.* https://research.collegeboard.org/programs/ap/data

Collins, A., & Koechlin, E. (2012). Reasoning, learning, and creativity: Frontal lobe function and human decision-making. *PLoS Biology, 10*(3), e1001293. DOI: 10.1371/journal.pbio.1001293 PMID: 22479152

Computer Science Teachers Association. (2021). *CSTA K-12 computer science standards* (Revised 2017). https://www.csteachers.org/page/standards

Computer Weekly. (2020, November 12). More than 1,300 teachers are trained by the National Centre for Computing Education. https://www.computerweekly.com/news/252492701/

Cooper, G., Tindall-Ford, S., Chandler, P., & Sweller, J. (2001). Learning by imagining. *Journal of Experimental Psychology. Applied, 7*(1), 68–82. DOI: 10.1037/1076-898X.7.1.68

Cooper, S., Dann, W., & Pausch, R. (2017). *Learning to Program with Alice* (3rd ed.). Pearson.

Corradini, I., Lodi, M., & Nardelli, E. (2018). An investigation of Italian primary school teachers' view on coding and programming. In Pozdniakov, S., & Dagienė, V. (Eds.), *Informatics in schools: Fundamentals of computer science and software engineering* (pp. 18–30). Springer., DOI: 10.1007/978-3-030-02750-6_18

Cowan, N. (1988). Evolving conceptions of memory storage, selective attention, and their mutual constraints within the human information-processing system. *Psychological Bulletin, 104*(2), 163–191. DOI: 10.1037/0033-2909.104.2.163

Cowan, N. (2001). The magical number 4 in short-term memory: A reconsideration of mental storage capacity. *Behavioral and Brain Sciences, 24*(1), 87–114. DOI: 10.1017/S0140525X01003922

Crk, I., Kluthe, T., & Stefik, A. (2015). Understanding programming expertise: An empirical study of phasic brain wave changes. [TOCHI]. *ACM Transactions on Computer-Human Interaction, 23*(1), 1–29. DOI: 10.1145/2829945

Crook, S. (2009). Embedding Scratch in the Classroom. *International Journal of Learning and Media, 1*(4), 17–21. DOI: 10.1162/ijlm_a_00035

Crowston, K., & Bolici, F. (2025). Deskilling and upskilling with AI Systems. *nformation Research an International Electronic Journal, 30*(iConf), 1009-1023. DOI: 10.47989/ir30iConf47143

D'Esposito, M., Aguirre, G. K., Zarahn, E., Ballard, D., Shin, R. K., & Lease, J. (1998). Functional MRI studies of spatial and nonspatial working memory. *Brain Research. Cognitive Brain Research, 7*(1), 1–13. DOI: 10.1016/S0926-6410(98)00004-4 PMID: 9714705

Daigle, K. (2024). *Survey: The AI wave continues to grow on software development teams*. Retrieved from https://github.blog/author/kdaigle/

Dao, E. (2020). This professor wanted to make farming more sustainable, so he started a company to build a fleet of smart robot. *theRising*, May 2020, Retrieved from https://therising.co/2020/05/18/earthsense-robots-farming-more-sustainable/

Darling-Hammond, L. (2010). *The flat world and education: How America's commitment to equity will determine our future*. Teachers College Press.

Das, S., Biswas, S. K., & Purkayastha, B. (2023). A deep sign language recognition system for Indian sign language. *Neural Computing & Applications, 35*(2), 1469–1481. DOI: 10.1007/s00521-022-07840-y

Delle-Vergini, S., Eacersall, D., Dann, C., Ally, M., & Chakraborty, S. (2023). Teaching project management to primary school children: A scoping review. *Australian Educational Researcher, 51*(4), 1035–1062. DOI: 10.1007/s13384-023-00627-7

Demir, B. E. (2021). *Okulöncesi eğitimde kodlama, robotik ve bilişimsel düşünme: magne-board'un gelişimi*. European Journal of Science and Technology., DOI: 10.31590/ejosat.842483

Deniz, T., & Korucu, A. T. (2023). The effect of coding education designed with different visual *programs on academic success and attitudes and self-efficiencies of secondary school students. Journal of Teacher Education and Lifelong Learning, 5*(1), 307–323. DOI: 10.51535/tell.1279547

Denning, P. J. (2017). Remaining trouble spots with computational thinking. *Communications of the ACM, 60*(6), 33–39. DOI: 10.1145/2998438

Denning, P. J., & Tedre, M. (2019). *Computational thinking*. MIT Press. DOI: 10.7551/mitpress/11740.001.0001

Department for Education. (2014). *National curriculum in England: Computing programmes of study*. UK Government. https://www.gov.uk/government/publications/national-curriculum-in-england-computing-programmes-of-study

Dohn, N. B., Kafai, Y., Mørch, A., & Ragni, M. (2022). Survey: Artificial intelligence, computational thinking and learning. *Kunstliche Intelligenz, 36*(1), 5–16. DOI: 10.1007/s13218-021-00751-5

Domingos, P. (2015). *The master algorithm: How the quest for the ultimate learning machine will remake our world.* Basic Books.

Dong, W., Li, Y., Sun, L., & Liu, Y. (2024). Developing pre-service teachers' computational thinking: A systematic literature review. *International Journal of Technology and Design Education, 34*(1), 191–227. DOI: 10.1007/s10798-023-09811-3 PMID: 36816094

Dönmez, O. (2022). A Cognitive Load Perspective to Instructional Design for Online Learning. In Durak, G., & Çankaya, S. (Eds.), *Handbook of Research on Managing and Designing Online Courses in Synchronous and Asynchronous Environments* (pp. 380–403). IGI Global Scientific Publishing., DOI: 10.4018/978-1-7998-8701-0.ch019

Dönmez, O., Akbulut, Y., Telli, E., Kaptan, M., Özdemir, İ. H., & Erdem, M. (2022). In search of a measure to address different sources of cognitive load in computer-based learning environments. *Education and Information Technologies, 27*(7), 10013–10034. DOI: 10.1007/s10639-022-11035-2

Doukakis, S. (2019). Exploring brain activity and transforming knowledge in visual and textual programming using neuroeducation approaches. *AIMS Neuroscience, 6*(3), 175–190. DOI: 10.3934/Neuroscience.2019.3.175 PMID: 32341975

Duncan, J. (2010). The multiple-demand (MD) system of the primate brain: Mental programs for intelligent behaviour. *Trends in Cognitive Sciences, 14*(4), 172–179. DOI: 10.1016/j.tics.2010.01.004 PMID: 20171926

Durak, G. (2014). The Effects of a Distance Education Programming Language Course on Student Performance/Uzaktan Eğitimle Verilen Programlama Dilleri Dersinin Öğrenen Başarısı Üzerine Etkisi. *Eğitimde Kuram ve Uygulama, 10*(1), 202–219.

Duran, R., Zavgorodniaia, A., & Sorva, J. (2022). Cognitive load theory in computing education research: A Review. *ACM Transactions on Computing Education, 22*(4), 1–27. DOI: 10.1145/3483843

Eccles, J. S., & Wigfield, A. (2002). Motivational beliefs, values, and goals. *Annual Review of Psychology, 53*(1), 109–132. DOI: 10.1146/annurev.psych.53.100901.135153 PMID: 11752481

Endres, M., Karas, Z., Hu, X., Kovelman, I., & Weimer, W. (2021, May). Relating reading, visualization, and coding for new programmers: A neuroimaging study. In *2021, IEEE/ACM 43rd International Conference on Software Engineering (ICSE)* (pp. 600-612). IEEE. DOI: 10.1109/ICSE43902.2021.00062

Ericson, B., Pearce, J. L., Rodger, S. H., Csizmadia, A., Garcia, R., Gutiérrez, F. J., & Bernuy, A. Z. (2023). Conducting multi-institutional studies of parsons problems. *Proceedings of the 2023 Conference on Innovation and Technology in Computer Science Education* v. 2. https://doi.org/DOI: 10.1145/3587103.3594211

Fakhoury, S., Ma, Y., Arnaoudova, V., & Adesope, O. (2018, May). The effect of poor source code lexicon and readability on developers' cognitive load. In *Proceedings of the 26th conference on program comprehension* (pp. 286-296). DOI: 10.1145/3196321.3196347

Fakhri, M. M., Fardan, M., Leo, M. A., Wulandari, W., & Hawari, M. D. (2023). Peningkatan kompetensi front end web programming: pelatihan bahasa pemrograman html dan css bagi mahasiswa. *Jurnal Sipakatau: Inovasi Pengabdian Masyarakat*, 35-45. https://doi.org/DOI: 10.61220/jsipakatau.v1i1.235

Fan, G., Liu, D., Zhang, R., & Pan, L. (2025). The impact of AI-assisted pair programming on student motivation, programming anxiety, collaborative learning, and programming performance: A comparative study with traditional pair programming and individual approaches. *International Journal of STEM Education*, *12*(16), 16. Advance online publication. DOI: 10.1186/s40594-025-00537-3

Fang, X., Ng, D. T. K., Tam, W. T., & Yuen, M. (2025). Design mobile computational thinking-integrated mathematics lessons based on the 5E instructional model for primary students. *Educational Technology Research and Development*, *73*(4), 1–30. DOI: 10.1007/s11423-025-10513-x

Farah, J. C., Spaenlehauer, B., Rodríguez-Triana, M. J., Ingram, S., & Gillet, D. (2022). Toward code review notebooks. *2022 International Conference on Advanced Learning Technologies (ICALT)*, 209-211. https://doi.org/DOI: 10.1109/ICALT55010.2022.00068

Fedorenko, E., Duncan, J., & Kanwisher, N. (2013). Broad domain generality in focal regions of frontal and parietal cortex. *Proceedings of the National Academy of Sciences of the United States of America*, *110*(41), 16616–16621. DOI: 10.1073/pnas.1315235110 PMID: 24062451

Felleisen, M., Findler, R. B., Flatt, M., & Krishnamurthi, S. (2018). *How to Design Programs: An Introduction to Programming and Computing* (2nd ed.). MIT Press.

Ferrari, S., & Pelizzari, F. (2023). *Coding and creativity: reflections and design proposals. Pedagogy*. Learning, and Creativity., DOI: 10.5772/intechopen.109971

Fjell, A. M., Røgeberg, O., Sørensen, Ø., Amlien, I. K., Bartrés-Faz, D., Brandmaier, A. M., . . . Vidal-Piñeiro, D. (2025). Reevaluating the Role of Education in Cognitive Decline and Brain Aging: Insights from Large-Scale Longitudinal Cohorts across 33 Countries. medRxiv, 2025-01. https://doi.org/DOI: 10.1101/2025.01.29.25321305

Floyd, B., Santander, T., & Weimer, W. (2017, May). Decoding the representation of code in the brain: An fMRI study of code review and expertise. In *2017 IEEE/ACM 39th International Conference on Software Engineering (ICSE)* (pp. 175–186). IEEE. https://doi.org/DOI: 10.1109/ICSE.2017.24

Flynn, D., Hughes, J., & Robb, J. (2023). Improving Mathematics Learning Through Computational Participation. *Journal of Educational Informatics*, *4*(1). Advance online publication. DOI: 10.51357/jei.v4i1.214

Ford, M., & Parnell, J. (2016). Teaching Ruby in the secondary school curriculum. *Journal of Computers in Education*, *4*(1), 15–29. DOI: 10.1007/s40692-015-0043-5

Foughali, M. (2023). Some thoughts on teaching introductory programming and the first language dilemma (discussion paper)., 1-8. https://doi.org/DOI: 10.1145/3631802.3631812

Fraser, G., Heuer, U., Körber, N., Obermüller, F., & Wasmeier, E. (2021). Litterbox: a linter for scratch programs.. https://doi.org/DOI: 10.1109/ICSE-SEET52601.2021.00028

Freeman, S., Eddy, S. L., McDonough, M., Smith, M. K., Okoroafor, N., Jordt, H., & Wenderoth, M. P. (2014). Active learning increases student performance in science, engineering, and mathematics. *Proceedings of the National Academy of Sciences of the United States of America*, *111*(23), 8410–8415. DOI: 10.1073/pnas.1319030111 PMID: 24821756

Furness, W. W., & Gallaher, C. M. (2018). Food access, food security and community gardens in Rockford, IL. *Local Environment*, *23*(4), 414–430. DOI: 10.1080/13549839.2018.1426561

Fuster, J. M. (2001). The prefrontal cortex—an update: Time is of the essence. *Neuron*, *30*(2), 319–333. DOI: 10.1016/S0896-6273(01)00285-9 PMID: 11394996

Gao, M., & Contreras, A. (2023). *A structured note-taking program to aid in data retention and promote organization using mobile devices as a medium*. Signal Image Processing and Multimedia., DOI: 10.5121/csit.2023.130923

Gao, X., Yang, Y., Du, Y., & Sun, D. (2025). Effect of mind mapping-based scaffolding on elementary students' computational thinking in block-based programming. *Journal of Educational Computing Research*, *63*(1), 236–271. DOI: 10.1177/07356331241303067

Garcia, F. W. S., Oliveira, S. R. B., & Carvalho, E. C. (2022). A second experimental study the application of a teaching plan for the algorithms subject in an undergraduate course in computing using active methodologies. *Informatics in Education*, *22*(2), 233–255. DOI: 10.15388/infedu.2023.12

Garfield, J. B., Ben-Zvi, D., Chance, B., Medina, E., Roseth, C., & Zieffler, A. (2008). *Developing students' statistical reasoning: Connecting research and teaching practice*. Springer., DOI: 10.1007/978-1-4020-8383-9

Gerritsen, J. (2019, November 27). New NZ digital curriculum set for 2020, are schools ready? *RNZ News*. https://www.rnz.co.nz/news/national/404558/new-nz-digital-curriculum-set-for-2020-are-schools-ready

Girardin, M., & Courtney, E. (2023, December 5). *Coding vs. programming: What's the difference?* Forage. https://www.theforage.com/blog/skills/coding-vs-programming

Glas, M., Vielberth, M., Reittinger, T., Böhm, F., & Pernul, G. (2023). Improving cybersecurity skill development through visual programming. *Information and Computer Security*, *31*(3), 316–330. DOI: 10.1108/ICS-11-2022-0170

Gonzalez-Maldonado, D., Pugnali, A., Tsan, J., Eatinger, D., Franklin, D., & Weintrop, D. (2022, August). Investigating the use of planning sheets in young learners' open-ended scratch projects. In *Proceedings of the 2022 ACM Conference on International Computing Education Research-Volume 1* (pp. 247-263). DOI: 10.1145/3501385.3543972

Goode, J., Chapman, G., & Margolis, J. (2014). Beyond curriculum: The Exploring Computer Science program. *ACM Inroads*, *3*(2), 47–53. DOI: 10.1145/2189835.2189851

Google & Gallup. (2016). *Trends in the state of computer science in U.S. K-12 schools*. https://services.google.com/fh/files/misc/trends-in-the-state-of-computer-science-report.pdf

Google. (2021). *Flutter & Dart Documentation*. https://flutter.dev

Grover, S., Basu, S., & Schank, P. (2018, February). What we can learn about student learning from open-ended programming projects in middle school computer science. In *Proceedings of the 49th ACM technical symposium on computer science education* (pp. 999-1004). DOI: 10.1145/3159450.3159522

Grover, S., Basu, S., & Schank, P. (2021). Scaling computational thinking through Tynker: A case study of a widely used platform. *Computers & Education, 164*, 104121. DOI: 10.1016/j.compedu.2021.104121

Grover, S., & Pea, R. (2013). Computational thinking in K–12: A review of the state of the field. *Educational Researcher, 42*(1), 38–43. DOI: 10.3102/0013189X12463051

Grover, S., & Pea, R. (2018). Computational thinking: A competency whose time has come. In Sentance, S., Barendsen, E., & Schulte, C. (Eds.), *Computer science education: Perspectives on teaching and learning in school* (pp. 19–38). Bloomsbury Academic. DOI: 10.5040/9781350057142.ch-003

Güleryüz, H. (2023). Attitudes of secondary school students towards robotics and coding in stem education with tinkercad. *Bayburt Eğitim Fakültesi Dergisi, 18*(38), 471–485. DOI: 10.35675/befdergi.1270169

Guo, P. J., Watson, C., & Li, X. (2020). Python usage in introductory computer science courses. *ACM Inroads, 11*(1), 28–33. DOI: 10.1145/3375880

Guzdial, M. (2015). *Learner-centered design of computing education: Research on computing for everyone*. Morgan & Claypool Publishers., DOI: 10.2200/S00684ED-1V01Y201511HCI033

Hackman, J. R., & Oldham, G. R. (1976). Motivation through the design of work: Test of a theory. *Organizational Behavior and Human Performance, 16*(2), 250–279. DOI: 10.1016/0030-5073(76)90016-7

Hanuscin, D. L., & Lee, M. H. (2008). Using the learning cycle as a model for teaching the learning cycle to preservice elementary teachers. *Journal of Elementary Science Education, 20*(2), 51–66. DOI: 10.1007/BF03173670

Harel, I., & Papert, S. (1991). *Constructionism*. Ablex Publishing.

Hassan, A. M. (2022). The design and implementation of a libyan salary mobile application using flutter. *Al-Mukhtar Journal of Sciences, 37*(3), 251–260. DOI: 10.54172/mjsc.v37i3.802

Hatami, Z., & Wolcott, P. (2020). Understanding students' identification and use of patterns while writing sql queries. *Proceedings of the 21st Annual Conference on Information Technology Education*, 20-25. https://doi.org/DOI: 10.1145/3368308.3415367

Hiebert, J., & Grouws, D. A. (2007). The effects of classroom mathematics teaching on students' learning. In Lester, F. K. (Ed.), *Second handbook of research on mathematics teaching and learning* (pp. 371–404). Information Age Publishing / National Council of Teachers of Mathematics. DOI: 10.1108/978-1-28141-200-320251013

Hishikawa, K., Yoshinaga, K., Togo, H., Hongo, T., & Hanakawa, T. (2023). Changes in functional brain activity patterns associated with computer programming learning in novices. *Brain Structure & Function, 228*(7), 1691–1701. DOI: 10.1007/s00429-023-02674-3 PMID: 37474776

Hmelo-Silver, C. E., Duncan, R. G., & Chinn, C. A. (2007). Scaffolding and achievement in problembased and inquiry learning: A response to Kirschner, Sweller, and. *Educational Psychologist, 42*(2), 99–107. DOI: 10.1080/00461520701263368

Hongo, T., Yakou, T., Yoshinaga, K., Kano, T., Miyazaki, M., & Hanakawa, T. (2023). Structural neuroplasticity in computer programming beginners. *Cerebral Cortex (New York, N.Y.), 33*(9), 5375–5381. DOI: 10.1093/cercor/bhac425 PMID: 36310094

Hosoda, C., Tanaka, K., Nariai, T., Honda, M., & Hanakawa, T. (2013). Dynamic neural network reorganization associated with second language vocabulary acquisition: A multimodal imaging study. *The Journal of Neuroscience : The Official Journal of the Society for Neuroscience, 33*(34), 13663–13672. DOI: 10.1523/JNEUROSCI.0410-13.2013 PMID: 23966688

Hsu, T. C., & Chen, M. S. (2024). Effects of students using different learning approaches for learning computational thinking and AI applications. *Education and Information Technologies, 30*(6), 7549–7571. DOI: 10.1007/s10639-024-13116-w

Hsu, T. C., & Hsu, T. P. (2025). Teaching AI with games: The impact of generative AI drawing on computational thinking skills. *Education and Information Technologies, 30*(15), 21499–21518. DOI: 10.1007/s10639-025-13624-3

Huang, A. Y. Q., Lin, C.-Y., Su, S.-Y., & Yang, S. J. H. (2025). The impact of GenAI-enabled coding hints on students' programming performance and cognitive load in an SRL-based Python course. *British Journal of Educational Technology, 00*(5), 1–31. DOI: 10.1111/bjet.13589

Huang, C., Hung, H., Jaw, F., & Young, Y. (2022). Comparison of the wii balance board system and foam posturography system in assessing postural balance. *Ear and Hearing, 43*(6), 1800–1806. DOI: 10.1097/AUD.0000000000001242

Hudin, S. S. (2023). A systematic review of the challenges in teaching programming for primary schools' students. *Online Journal for TVET Practitioners, 8*(1). Advance online publication. DOI: 10.30880/ojtp.2023.08.01.008

Hu, L. (2024). Programming and 21st century skill development in K-12 schools: A multidimensional meta-analysis. *Journal of Computer Assisted Learning, 40*(2), 610–636. DOI: 10.1111/jcal.12904

Hulleman, C. S., Godes, O., Hendricks, B. L., & Harackiewicz, J. M. (2010). Enhancing interest and performance with a utility value intervention. *Journal of Educational Psychology, 102*(4), 880–895. DOI: 10.1037/a0019506

Ikramov, R., Ivanov, V., Masyagin, S., Shakirov, R., Sirazidtinov, I., Succi, G., Thapaliya, A., Tormasov, A., & Zufarova, O. (2019). Initial evaluation of the brain activity under different software development situations. In Proceedings of the 31st International Conference on Software Engineering and Knowledge Engineering, International Conferences on Software Engineering and Knowledge Engineering. KSI Research Inc. and Knowledge Systems Institute Graduate School, pp. 741–747. http://dx.doi.org/DOI: 10.18293/SEKE2019-215

indeed. (2025, March 28). *Understanding the difference between coding vs. programming*. indeed. https://ca.indeed.com/career-advice/career-development/coding-vs-programming

Indriasari, T. D., Luxton-Reilly, A., & Denny, P. (2020). A review of peer code review in higher education. *ACM Transactions on Computing Education, 20*(3), 1–25. DOI: 10.1145/3403935

Ioannou, A., & Makridou, E. (2018). Exploring the potentials of educational robotics in the development of computational thinking: A summary of current research and practical proposal for future work. *Education and Information Technologies, 23*(6), 2531–2544. DOI: 10.1007/s10639-018-9729-z

Israel, M., Pearson, J. N., Tapia, T., Wherfel, Q. M., & Reese, G. (2015). Supporting all learners in school-wide computational thinking: A cross-case qualitative analysis. *Teaching Exceptional Children, 47*(6), 308–316. DOI: 10.1177/0040059915579868

Ivanova, A. A., Srikant, S., Sueoka, Y., Kean, H. H., Dhamala, R., O'reilly, U. M., ... & Fedorenko, E. (2020). Comprehension of computer code relies primarily on domain-general executive brain regions. *elife, 9*, e58906. https://doi.org/.DOI: 10.7554/eLife.58906

Jain, V., Jain, A., Chauhan, A., Kotla, S. S., & Gautam, A. (2021). American Sign Language recognition using Support Vector Machine and Convolutional Neural Network. *International Journal of Information Technology : an Official Journal of Bharati Vidyapeeth's Institute of Computer Applications and Management, 13*(3), 1193–1200. DOI: 10.1007/s41870-021-00617-x

Jaipal-Jamani, K., & Angeli, C. (2017). Effect of robotics on elementary preservice teachers' self-efficacy, science learning, and computational thinking. *Journal of Science Education and Technology, 26*(2), 175–192. DOI: 10.1007/s10956-016-9663-z

Jäncke, L., Shah, N. J., & Peters, M. (2000). Cortical activations in primary and secondary motor areas for complex bimanual movements in professional pianists. *Brain Research. Cognitive Brain Research, 10*(1-2), 177–183. DOI: 10.1016/S0926-6410(00)00028-8 PMID: 10978706

Joksimoski, B., Zdravevski, E., Lameski, P., Pires, I. M., Melero, F. J., Martinez, T. P., Garcia, N. M., Mihajlov, M., Chorbev, I., & Trajkovik, V. (2022). Technological Solutions for Sign Language Recognition: A Scoping Review of Research Trends, Challenges, and Opportunities. *IEEE Access : Practical Innovations, Open Solutions, 10*, 40979–40998. DOI: 10.1109/ACCESS.2022.3161440

Juavinett, A. L. (2022). The next generation of neuroscientists needs to learn how to code, and we need new ways to teach them. *Neuron, 110*(4), 576–578. DOI: 10.1016/j.neuron.2021.12.001 PMID: 35016038

Jung, J., Shin, Y., Chung, H., & Fanguy, M. (2024). The effects of pre-training types on cognitive load, self-efficacy, and problem-solving in computer programming. *Journal of Computing in Higher Education*. Advance online publication. DOI: 10.1007/s12528-024-09407-3

Kadar, R., Wahab, N. A., Othman, J., Shamsuddin, M., & Mahlan, S. B. (2021). A study of difficulties in teaching and learning programming: A systematic literature review. *International Journal of Academic Research in Progressive Education and Development, 10*(3). Advance online publication. DOI: 10.6007/IJARPED/v10-i3/11100

Kado, K. (2022). Teaching and learning the fundamental of calculus through python-based coding. *International Journal of Didactical Studies*. https://doi.org/ DOI: 10.33902/IJODS.202215006

Kafai, Y. B., & Proctor, C. (2021). A Revaluation of Computational Thinking in K–12 Education: Moving Toward Computational Literacies. *Educational Researcher, 51*(2), 146-151. (Original work published 2022)DOI: 10.3102/0013189X211057904

Kafai, Y. B., & Burke, Q. (2014). *Connected code: Why children need to learn programming*. MIT Press. DOI: 10.7551/mitpress/9992.001.0001

Kafai, Y. B., Proctor, C., & Lui, D. (2019, July). From theory bias to theory dialogue: Embracing cognitive, situated, and critical framings of computational thinking in k-12 cs education. *In Proceedings of the 2019 ACM Conference on International Computing Education Research* (pp. 101-109). DOI: 10.1145/3291279.3339400

Kale, U., Wang, Y., Aldebyan, A., Mann, T., & O'Brian, N. (2024, April 14). *Future teachers' interest, competence, and perception of utility value regarding computational thinking in teaching science* [Conference session]. American Educational Research Association Annual Conference, Philadelphia, PA.

Kale, U., Akcaoglu, M., Cullen, T., Goh, D., Devine, L., Calvert, N., & Grise, K. (2018). Computational what? Relating computational thinking to teaching. *TechTrends*, *62*(6), 574–58. DOI: 10.1007/s11528-018-0290-9

Kale, U., & Wang, Y. (2025). Future science educators' usage, interest, competence, and utility value for computational thinking. *Journal of Science Teacher Education*, •••, 1–28. DOI: 10.1080/1046560X.2025.2535035

Kalyuga, S., Ayres, P., Chandler, P., & Sweller, J. (2003). The expertise reversal effect. *Educational Psychologist*, *38*(1), 23–31. DOI: 10.1207/S15326985EP3801_4

Kamarudin, N. A. B., Ikram, R. R. R., Azman, F. N. B., Ahmad, S. S. S., & Zainuddin, D. B. (2022). A study of the effects of short-term ai coding course with gamification elements on students' cognitive mental health. *TEM Journal,* 1854-1862. https://doi.org/DOI: 10.18421/tem114-53

Kapucu, M. S., & Batu, A. (2022). Analysis of studies on coding education: A meta synthesis study. *The Eurasia Proceedings of Educational and Social Sciences*, *24*, 1–16. DOI: 10.55549/epess.1179319

Kapyk, I., Kolesnik, K., Kryvosheya, T., Pakhalchuk, N., & Pokhyla, S. (2024). Trends of implementation of research-experimental activities in preschool educational institutions of ukraine in today's conditions. *Society Integration Education. Proceedings of the International Scientific Conference*, 2, 16-26. https://doi.org/DOI: 10.17770/sie2024vol2.7890

Karim, M., & Cragg, C. (2016). Web development pedagogy with JavaScript. *Education and Information Technologies*, *21*(3), 679–697. DOI: 10.1007/s10639-014-9344-4

Kaszab, P., & Cserép, M. (2023). Detecting programming flaws in student submissions with static source code analysis. *Studia Universitatis Babes-Bolyai. Informatica*, *68*(1), 37–54. DOI: 10.24193/subbi.2023.1.03

Kaya, E., Newley, A., Yesilyurt, E., & Deniz, H. (2020). Measuring computational thinking teaching efficacy beliefs of preservice elementary teachers. *Journal of College Science Teaching*, *49*(6), 55–64. DOI: 10.1080/0047231X.2020.12290665

Kazakoff, E. R., Sullivan, A., & Bers, M. U. (2013). The Effect of a Classroom-Based Intensive Robotics and Programming Workshop on Sequencing Ability in Early Childhood. *Early Childhood Education Journal, 41*(4), 245–255. DOI: 10.1007/s10643-012-0554-5

Kazempour, M., Amirshokoohi, A., & Blamey, K. (2020). Putting theory to practice: Teaching the 5E learning cycle through immersive experiences for pre-service teachers. *European Journal of Science and Mathematics Education, 8*(1), 67–75. DOI: 10.30935/scimath/9547

Khalifa, S. A. M., Elshafiey, E. H., Shetaia, A. A., El-Wahed, A. A. A., Algethami, A. F., Musharraf, S. G., AlAjmi, M. F., Zhao, C., Masry, S. H. D., Abdel-Daim, M. M., Halabi, M. F., Kai, G., Al Naggar, Y., Bishr, M., Diab, M. A. M., & El-Seedi, H. R. (2021). Overview of Bee Pollination and Its Economic Value for Crop Production. *Insects, 12*(8), 688. DOI: 10.3390/insects12080688 PMID: 34442255

Khurana, A., Subramonyam, H., & Chilana, P. K. (2024). Why and when llm-based assistants can go wrong: Investigating the effectiveness of prompt-based interactions for software help-seeking. *arXiv.org*. Retrieved from /arxiv.2402.08030DOI: 10.1145/3640543.3645200

Kirschner, F., Paas, F., & Kirschner, P. A. (2009). A cognitive load approach to collaborative learning: United brains for complex tasks. *Educational Psychology Review, 21*(1), 31–42. DOI: 10.1007/s10648-008-9095-2

Kirschner, P. A., Sweller, J., & Clark, R. E. (2006). Why Minimal Guidance During Instruction Does Not Work: An Analysis of the Failure of Constructivist, Discovery, Problem-Based, Experiential, and Inquiry-Based Teaching. *Educational Psychologist, 41*(2), 75–86. DOI: 10.1207/s15326985ep4102_1

Klepsch, M., Schmitz, F., & Seufert, T. (2017). Development and validation of two instruments measuring intrinsic, extraneous, and germane cognitive load. *Frontiers in Psychology, 8*, 1997. DOI: 10.3389/fpsyg.2017.01997

Korkmaz, Ö., Çakir, R., & Özden, M. Y. (2017). A validity and reliability study of the Computational Thinking Scales (CTS). *Computers in Human Behavior, 72*, 558–569. DOI: 10.1016/j.chb.2017.01.005

Kramer, J. (2007). Is abstraction the key to computing? *Communications of the ACM, 50*(4), 36–42. DOI: 10.1145/1232743.1232745

Krueger, R., Huang, Y., Liu, X., Santander, T., Weimer, W., & Leach, K. (2020, June). Neurological divide: An fMRI study of prose and code writing. In *Proceedings of the ACM/IEEE 42nd international conference on software engineering* (pp. 678–690). https://doi.org/DOI: 10.1145/3377811.3380348

Kuhail, M. A., Mathew, S. S., Khalil, A., Khalil, A., & Shah, S. J. (2023). "Will I be replaced?" Assessing ChatGPT's effect on software development and programmer perceptions of AI tools. *arXiv.org*. Retrieved from DOI: 10.2139/ssrn.4571482

Kumar Attar, R., Goyal, V., & Goyal, L. (2023). State of the Art of Automation in Sign Language: A Systematic Review. *ACM Transactions on Asian and Low-Resource Language Information Processing*, *22*(4), 1–80. Advance online publication. DOI: 10.1145/3564769

Kunduracıoğlu, İ. (2018). Examining the interface of lego mindstorms ev3 robot programming. *Journal of Educational Technology and Online Learning*, *1*(1), 28–46. DOI: 10.31681/jetol.372826

Kutay, E., & Öner, D. (2022). Coding with minecraft: The development of middle school students' computational thinking. *ACM Transactions on Computing Education*, *22*(2), 1–19. DOI: 10.1145/3471573

Kwon, K., Brush, T. A., Kim, K., & Seo, M. (2024). Embodied Learning for Computational Thinking in a Mixed-Reality Context. *Journal of Educational Computing Research*, *62*(8), 1719–1740. DOI: 10.1177/07356331241291173

Kwon, K., Kim, K., Zhou, C., & Jeon, M. (2025). *Embodied Learning Experiences of Early Elementary Students in Computational Thinking Education*. Technology, Knowledge and Learning., DOI: 10.1007/s10758-025-09826-w

Lamichhane, B., Adhikari, B. M., & Dhamala, M. (2016). The activity in the anterior insulae is modulated by perceptual decision-making difficulty. *Neuroscience, 327*, 79–94. https://doi.org/. neuroscience.2016.04.016.DOI: 10.1016/j

Leahy, W., & Sweller, J. (2011). Cognitive load theory, modality of presentation and the transient information effect. *Applied Cognitive Psychology*, *25*(6), 943–951. DOI: 10.1002/acp.1787

Lee, C. K. M., Ng, K. K. H., Chen, C. H., Lau, H. C. W., Chung, S. Y., & Tsoi, T. (2021). American sign language recognition and training method with recurrent neural network. *Expert Systems with Applications, 167*, 114403. DOI: 10.1016/j.eswa.2020.114403

Lee, S., Matteson, A., Hooshyar, D., Kim, S., Jung, J., Nam, G., & Lim, H. (2016, October). Comparing programming language comprehension between novice and expert programmers using eeg analysis. In *2016 IEEE 16th international conference on bioinformatics and bioengineering (BIBE)* (pp. 350–355). IEEE. DOI: 10.1109/BIBE.2016.30

Lee, B. G., Chong, T. W., & Chung, W. Y. (2020). Sensor fusion of motion-based sign language interpretation with deep learning. *Sensors (Basel)*, *20*(21), 1–17. DOI: 10.3390/s20216256 PMID: 33147891

Lee, C. H., & Soep, E. (2016). None but ourselves can free our minds: Critical computational literacy as a pedagogy of resistance. *Equity & Excellence in Education*, *49*(4), 480–492. DOI: 10.1080/10665684.2016.1227157

Lee, H. S., Pallant, A., Pryputniewicz, S., Lord, T., Mulholland, M., & Liu, O. L. (2019). Automated text scoring and real-time adjustable feedback: Supporting revision of scientific arguments involving uncertainty. *Science Education*, *103*(3), 590–622. DOI: 10.1002/sce.21504

Lee, S., & Yi, S. (2021). A development of an embedded programming education platform using Python and LEGO NXT. *Journal of Engineering Education Research*, *24*(1), 45–53. DOI: 10.18108/jeer.2021.24.1.45

Leppink, J., Paas, F., Van der Vleuten, C. P. M., Van Gog, T., & Van Merriënboer, J. J. G. (2013). Development of an instrument for measuring different types of cognitive load. *Behavior Research Methods*, *45*(4), 1058–1072. DOI: 10.3758/s13428-013-0334-1

Liang, H., & Xue, Y. (2009). Avoidance of information technology threats: A theoretical perspective. *Management Information Systems Quarterly*, *33*(1), 71–90. DOI: 10.2307/20650279

Lindberg, R. S. N., Laine, T. H., & Haaranen, L. (2018). Gamifying programming education in k-12: A review of programming curricula in seven countries and programming games. *British Journal of Educational Technology*, *50*(4), 1979–1995. DOI: 10.1111/bjet.12685

Liu, Y. F., Kim, J., Wilson, C., & Bedny, M. (2020). Computer code comprehension shares neural resources with formal logical inference in the fronto-parietal network. *eLife*, *9*, e59340. DOI: 10.7554/eLife.59340 PMID: 33319745

Logothetis, N. K. (2008). What we can do and what we cannot do with fMRI. *Nature*, *453*(7197), 869–878. DOI: 10.1038/nature06976 PMID: 18548064

Lye, S. Y., & Koh, J. H. L. (2014). Review on teaching and learning of computational thinking through programming: What is next for K-12? *Computers in Human Behavior*, *41*, 51–61. DOI: 10.1016/j.chb.2014.09.012

Mah, D.-K., & Groß, N. (2024). Artificial intelligence in higher education: Exploring faculty use, self-efficacy, distinct profiles, and professional development needs. *International Journal of Educational Technology in Higher Education*, *21*(58), 58. Advance online publication. DOI: 10.1186/s41239-024-00490-1

Mahdikhanlou, K., & Ebrahimnezhad, H. (2020). Multimodal 3D American sign language recognition for static alphabet and numbers using hand joints and shape coding. *Multimedia Tools and Applications*, *79*(31–32), 22235–22259. DOI: 10.1007/s11042-020-08982-8

Maloney, J., Resnick, M., Rusk, N., Silverman, B., & Eastmond, E. (2010). The Scratch programming language and environment. *ACM Transactions on Computing Education*, *10*(4), 16. Advance online publication. DOI: 10.1145/1868358.1868363

Mangarin, R. A., & Caballes, D. O. (2024). Difficulties in learning mathematics: A systematic review. *International Journal of Innovation and Scientific Research*, *11*(9), 401–405. DOI: 10.51244/IJRSI.2024.1109037

Marevac, E., Kadušić, E., Živić, N., Buzađija, N., & Lemeš, S. (2025). Framework design for the dynamic reconfiguration of iot-enabled embedded systems and "on-the-fly" code execution. *Future Internet*, *17*(1), 23. DOI: 10.3390/fi17010023

Marín, B., Frez, J., Cruz-Lemus, J. A., & Genero, M. (2018). An empirical investigation on the benefits of gamification in programming courses. *ACM Transactions on Computing Education*, *19*(1), 1–22. DOI: 10.1145/3231709

Maulana, T. S., Setyawan, H., & Asroni, A. (2023). Web-based data information system for students and teachers at al-qur'an education parks in kasihan, bantul. *Emerging Information Science and Technology*, *2*(1), 24–29. DOI: 10.18196/eist.v2i1.16870

Mayer, R. E., & Wittrock, M. C. (2006). Problem solving. In Alexander, P. A., Winne, P. H., Alexander, P. A., & Winne, P. H. (Eds.), *Handbook of educational psychology* (pp. 287–303). Lawrence Erlbaum Associates Publishers.

McDonald, C. (2019). *England: Computer science GCSE, AS, and A levels*. British Computer Society. https://www.bcs.org/

McGinnis, J. R., Hestness, E., Mills, K., Ketelhut, D., Cabrera, L., & Jeong, H. (2020). Preservice science teachers' beliefs about computational thinking following a curricular module within an elementary science methods course. *Contemporary Issues in Technology & Teacher Education, 20*(1), 85–107.

Mecca, G., Santoro, D., Sileno, N., & Veltri, E. (2021). Diogene-ct: Tools and methodologies for teaching and learning coding. *International Journal of Educational Technology in Higher Education, 18*(1), 12. Advance online publication. DOI: 10.1186/s41239-021-00246-1

Medeiros, J., Couceiro, R., Castelhano, J., Branco, M. C., Duarte, G., Duarte, C., . . . Teixeira, C. (2019, July). Software code complexity assessment using EEG features. In *2019 41st Annual International Conference of the IEEE Engineering in Medicine and Biology Society (EMBC)* (pp. 1413-1416). IEEE. https://doi.org/ DOI: 10.1109/EMBC.2019.8856283

Meena, K. B., & Tyagi, V. (2019). Image Forgery Detection: Survey and Future Directions. In *Data, Engineering and Applications* (pp. 163–194). Springer Singapore. DOI: 10.1007/978-981-13-6351-1_14

Meena, K. B., & Tyagi, V. (2021). Distinguishing computer-generated images from photographic images using two-stream convolutional neural network. *Applied Soft Computing, 100*, 107025. Advance online publication. DOI: 10.1016/j.asoc.2020.107025

Menon, K. (2025, June 9). *Difference between coding and programming*. simplilearn. https://www.simplilearn.com/tutorials/c-tutorial/coding-vs-progrmming

Méri, L., Gaál, L., Bartók, J., Gažák, M., Gera, M., Jurašek, M., & Келемен, M. (2021). Improved radar composites and enhanced value of meteorological radar data using different quality indices. *Sustainability (Basel), 13*(9), 5285. DOI: 10.3390/su13095285

Messer, D., Thomas, L., Holliman, A., & Kucirkova, N. (2018). Evaluating the effectiveness of an educational programming intervention on children's mathematics skills, spatial awareness and working memory. *Education and Information Technologies, 23*(6), 2879–2888. DOI: 10.1007/s10639-018-9747-x

Microsoft. (2014). *Kodu Game Lab Documentation*. https://www.kodugamelab.com

Microsoft. (2020). *C# Programming Guide*. https://docs.microsoft.com/en-us/dotnet/csharp/

Ministry of Education. Culture, Sports, Science and Technology. (2020). *Programming education in elementary schools*. Government of Japan. https://www.mext.go.jp/

MIT. (2018). *MIT App Inventor – Beginner Tutorials.* Massachusetts Institute of Technology. https://appinventor.mit.edu

Molchanov, P., Gupta, S., Kim, K., & Kautz, J. (2015). Hand gesture recognition with 3D convolutional neural networks. *IEEE Computer Society Conference on Computer Vision and Pattern Recognition Workshops, 2015-October*, 1–7. DOI: 10.1109/CVPRW.2015.7301342

Monteiro, A. F., Miranda-Pinto, M. S., & Osório, A. J. (2021). Coding as literacy in preschool: A case study. *Education Sciences*, *11*(5), 198. DOI: 10.3390/educsci11050198

Montoya, J., Hernández, J., & Reyes, R. (2017). Blockly-based environments in early programming education. *International Journal of Advanced Computer Science*, *8*(10), 209–215.

Morais, C., & Araújo, J. L. (2022). An alternative experimental procedure to determine the solubility of potassium nitrate in water with automatic data acquisition using arduino for secondary school: Development and validation with pre-service chemistry teachers. *Journal of Chemical Education*, *100*(2), 774–781. DOI: 10.1021/acs.jchemed.2c00615

Morán, J. A. C., Rodas-Silva, J., & Morales, M. G. V. (2019). El uso del software alice como herramienta para el aprendizaje de programación: una revisión de literatura. Proceedings of the 17th LACCEI International Multi-Conference for Engineering, Education, and Technology: "Industry, Innovation. https://doi.org/DOI: 10.18687/LACCEI2019.1.1.161

Morrison, B. B., Dorn, B., & Guzdial, M. (2014). Measuring cognitive load in introductory CS: Adaptation of an instrument. *In Proceedings of the 10th Annual Conference on International Computing Education Research (ICER '14)* (p. 131–138). Association for Computing Machinery. https://doi.org/DOI: 10.1145/2632320.2632348

Moumoutzis, N., Xanthaki, C., Perrakis, S., Manousakas, M., & Pavlova, L. (2021). Promoting python code clubs in greece: A teacher training program and a case study. *Digital Presentation and Preservation of Cultural and Scientific Heritage*, *11*, 187–202. DOI: 10.55630/dipp.2021.11.16

Mousavi, S. Y., Low, R., & Sweller, J. (1995). Reducing cognitive load by mixing auditory and visual presentation modes. *Journal of Educational Psychology*, *87*(2), 319–334. DOI: 10.1037/0022-0663.87.2.319

Muldner, K., Jennings, J., & Chiarelli, V. (2022). A review of worked examples in programming activities. *ACM Transactions on Computing Education*, *23*(1), 1–35. DOI: 10.1145/3560266

Mumcu, F. K., Andic, B., Maricic, M., Tejera, M., & Lavicza, Z. (2025). Unpacking teachers' value beliefs about computational thinking and programming. *Journal of Educational Technology and Online Learning*, *8*(1), 41–63. DOI: 10.31681/jetol.1497284

Nardelli, E., & Ventre, G. (2015). Introducing computational thinking in Italian schools: A first report on "programma il futuro" project. In *Paper presented at the 9th international technology, education and development conference (INTED), Madrid, Spain*

National Center for Education Statistics. (2023). Teacher Openings in Elementary and Secondary Schools. *Condition of Education*. U.S. Department of Education, Institute of Education Sciences. Retrieved from https://nces.ed.gov/programs/coe/indicator/tls

National Research Council. (2010). *Report of a workshop on the scope and nature of computational thinking*. The National Academies Press., DOI: 10.17226/12840

Naveed, M. (2021). Comparison of c++ and java in implementing introductory programming algorithms. *Quaid-E-Awam University Research Journal of Engineering Science & Technology*, *19*(1), 95–103. DOI: 10.52584/QRJ.1901.14

Ndebele, M., & Mazhindu, A. N. (2023). Design and implementation of an android gis data collection application for students with non-programming experience using the mit app inventor: A case study on a tick data collection app. *Intelligent Information Management*, *15*(01), 11–23. DOI: 10.4236/iim.2023.151002

Ng, D. T. K., Leung, J. K. L., Su, J., Ng, R. C. W., & Chu, S. K. W. (2023). Teachers' AI digital competencies and twenty-first century skills in the post-pandemic world. *Educational Technology Research and Development*, *71*(1), 137–161. DOI: 10.1007/s11423-023-10203-6 PMID: 36844361

Niarman, A., Iswandi, I., & Candri, A. K. (2023). Comparative analysis of php frameworks for development of academic information system using load and stress testing. [IJSECS]. *International Journal Software Engineering and Computer Science*, *3*(3), 424–436. DOI: 10.35870/ijsecs.v3i3.1850

Nouri, J., Zhang, L., Mannila, L., & Norén, E. (2020). Development of computational thinking, digital competence and 21st century skills when learning programming in K-9. *Education Inquiry*, *11*(1), 1–17. DOI: 10.1080/20004508.2019.1627844

OECD. (2003). PISA 2003 assessment framework: Mathematics, reading, science and problem solving knowledge and skills. *OECD Publishing*. Retrieved from https://www.oecd.org/edu/school/programmeforinternationalstudentassessmentpisa/33694881.pdf

OECD. (2013). *OECD skills outlook 2013: First results from the survey of adult skills*. OECD Publishing., DOI: 10.1787/9789264204256-

OECD. (2015). OECD skills outlook 2015: Youth, skills and employability. *OECD Publishing*. Retrieved from https://www.oecd.org/edu/oecd-skills-outlook-2015-9789264234178-en.htm

OECD. (2021). *OECD Digital Education Outlook 2021: Pushing the frontiers with artificial intelligence, blockchain and robots*. OECD Publishing., DOI: 10.1787/589b283f-

OECD. (2023). *OECD digital education outlook 2023: Towards an effective digital education ecosystem*. OECD Publishing., DOI: 10.1787/c74f03de-

OECD. (2024). *Education Policy Outlook 2024: Reshaping teaching into a thriving profession from ABCs to AI*. OECD Publishing., DOI: 10.1787/dd5140e4-

Oliveira, V. F. d., Pessoa, M. A. O., Junqueira, F., & Miyagi, P. E. (2021). Sql and nosql databases in the context of industry 4.0. https://doi.org/DOI: 10.20944/preprints202111.0019.v1

Oyetade, K., Zuva, T., & Harmse, A. (2025). Integrating industry 4.0 technologies into IT education. *Cogent Education*, *12*(1), 2479195. Advance online publication. DOI: 10.1080/2331186X.2025.2479195

Oz, C., & Leu, M. C. (2011). American Sign Language word recognition with a sensory glove using artificial neural networks. *Engineering Applications of Artificial Intelligence*, *24*(7), 1204–1213. DOI: 10.1016/j.engappai.2011.06.015

Ozogul, G., Karlin, M., & Ottenbreit-Leftwich, A. (2018). Preservice teacher computer science preparation: A case study of an undergraduate computer education licensure program. *Journal of Technology and Teacher Education*, *26*(3), 375–409.

Paas, F., & Sweller, J. (2012). An evolutionary upgrade of cognitive load theory: Using the human motor system and collaboration to support the learning of complex cognitive tasks. *Educational Psychology Review*, *24*(1), 27–45. DOI: 10.1007/s10648-011-9179-2

Paas, F., & van Merriënboer, J. J. G. (1994). Variability of worked examples and transfer of geometrical problem-solving skills: A cognitive-load approach. *Journal of Educational Psychology*, *86*(1), 122–133. DOI: 10.1037/0022-0663.86.1.122

Paas, F., & van Merriënboer, J. J. G. (2020). Cognitive load theory: Methods to manage working memory load in the learning of complex tasks. *Current Directions in Psychological Science*, *29*(4), 394–398. DOI: 10.1177/0963721420922183

Paiva, J. C., Leal, J. P., & Queirós, R. (2020). Fostering programming practice through games. *Information (Basel)*, *11*(11), 498. DOI: 10.3390/info11110498

Pallavi, M. G., Indhu, N., Divya Chinni Devaki, K. S., Padmini Vasavi, P. V., & Rao, Y. N. (2024). Bridging the Communication Gap: Advanced ASL Alphabet Recognition Using VGG16. *5th International Conference on Sustainable Communication Networks and Application, ICSCNA 2024 - Proceedings, 128*, 1072–1077. DOI: 10.1109/ICSCNA63714.2024.10864239

Palop, B., Díaz, I., Rodriguez-Muniz, L. J., & Santaengracia, J. J. (2025). Redefining computational thinking: A holistic framework and its implications for K-12 education. *Education and Information Technologies*, *30*(10), 1–26. DOI: 10.1007/s10639-024-13297-4

Pangaribuan, J. J., Romindo, R., Mitra, A. R., Barus, O. P., & Prashanth, S. (2024). American Sign Language Alphabet Recognition Using Convolutional Neural Network. *Proceedings - 2024 2nd International Conference on Technology Innovation and Its Applications, ICTIIA 2024, 128*, 1–6. DOI: 10.1109/ICTIIA61827.2024.10761663

Papert, S., & Harel, I. (2016). *Constructionism: Research Reports and Essays, 1985–1990* (Reprint ed.). Routledge. https://doi.org/DOI: 10.4324/9781315045398

Papert, S. (1980). *Mindstorms: Children, computers, and powerful ideas*. Basic Books.

Park, Y., & Shin, Y. (2019). Comparing the effectiveness of scratch and app inventor with regard to learning computational thinking concepts. *Electronics (Basel)*, *8*(11), 1269. DOI: 10.3390/electronics8111269

Parnin, C. (2010). A Cognitive Neuroscience Perspective on Memory for Programming Tasks. In *PPIG* (p. 4).

Patton, E. W., Tissenbaum, M. B., & Harunani, F. (2019). Mit app inventor: objectives, design, and development. *Computational Thinking Education,* 31-49. https://doi.org/DOI: 10.1007/978-981-13-6528-7_3

Peitek, N., Siegmund, J., Apel, S., Kästner, C., Parnin, C., Bethmann, A., Leich, T., Saake, G., & Brechmann, A. (2018). A look into programmers' heads. *IEEE Transactions on Software Engineering*, *46*(4), 442–462. DOI: 10.1109/TSE.2018.2863303

Peoples, K. (2021). *How to write a phenomenological dissertation: A step-by-step guide* (Vol. 56). SAGE.

Pérez-Jorge, D., & Martínez-Murciano, M. C. (2022). Gamification with scratch or app inventor in higher education: A systematic review. *Future Internet*, *14*(12), 374. DOI: 10.3390/fi14120374

Peterson, L., & Peterson, M. J. (1959). Short-term retention of individual verbal items. *Journal of Experimental Psychology*, *58*(3), 193–198. DOI: 10.1037/h0049234

Pewkam, W., & Chamrat, S. (2022). Pre-Service Teacher Training Program of STEM-based activities in Computing Science to Develop Computational Thinking. *Informatics in Education*, *21*(2), 311–329.

Phillips, R., & Brooks, B. (2017). *The Hour of Code: Impact on attitudes towards and self-efficacy with computer science*. Code.org. https://code.org/about

Pina, E., Sá, F., & Bernardino, J. (2022). Newsql databases assessment: Cockroachdb, mariadb xpand, and voltdb. *Future Internet*, *15*(1), 10. DOI: 10.3390/fi15010010

Pollock, E., Chandler, P., & Sweller, J. (2002). Assimilating complex information. *Learning and Instruction*, *12*(1), 61–86. DOI: 10.1016/S0959-4752(01)00016-0

Popat, S., & Starkey, L. (2019). Learning to code or coding to learn? A systematic review. *Computers & Education*, *128*, 365–376. DOI: 10.1016/j.compedu.2018.10.005

Popenici, S. A. D., & Kerr, S. (2017). Exploring the impact of artificial intelligence on teaching and learning in higher education. *Research and Practice in Technology Enhanced Learning*, *12*(1), 22. DOI: 10.1186/s41039-017-0062-8 PMID: 30595727

Prather, J., Reeves, B. N., Denny, P., Becker, B. A., Leinonen, J., Luxton-Reilly, A., Powell, G., Finnie-Ansley, J., & Santos, E. A. (2023). "It's weird that it knows what I want": Usability and interactions with Copilot for novice programmers. *ACM Transactions on Computer-Human Interaction*, *31*(1), 1–31. DOI: 10.1145/3617367

Preston, L., Harvie, K., & Wallace, H. (2015). Inquiry-based learning in teacher education: A primary humanities example. *The Australian Journal of Teacher Education*, *40*(12), 73–85. DOI: 10.14221/ajte.2015v40n12.6

Psycharis, S., & Kallia, M. (2017). The effects of computer programming on high school students' reasoning skills and mathematical self-efficacy and problem solving. *Instructional Science*, *45*(5), 583–602. DOI: 10.1007/s11251-017-9421-5

Ragusa, G., & Leung, L. Y. (2023). The impact of early robotics education on students' understanding of coding, robotics design, and interest in computing careers. *Sensors (Basel), 23*(23), 9335. DOI: 10.3390/s23239335

Rahman, S. (2014). The neuroscience of musical creativity using complexity tools. PhD Thesis, Imperial College London.

Rahman, M. M., Islam, M. S., Rahman, M. H., Sassi, R., Rivolta, M. W., & Aktaruzzaman, M. (2019). A new benchmark on american sign language recognition using convolutional neural network. *2019 International Conference on Sustainable Technologies for Industry 4.0, STI 2019, 0*, 24–25. DOI: 10.1109/STI47673.2019.9067974

Rajput, K. K., Siddiqui, I. F., Saddar, S., Hussain, H., Ayaz, U., & Ruk, S. A. (2023). Mobile apps development: Towards incorporating regional and national languages in flutter app. *Sukkur IBA Journal of Emerging Technologies, 6*(1), 44–53. DOI: 10.30537/sjet.v6i1.1192

Ramadani, N. I., Surganingsih, M., & Rafee, N. N. B. M. (2023). Cultivating independent character in students at the cendekia berseri school in makassar city. *TEMATIK: Jurnal Pemikiran Dan Penelitian Pendidikan Anak Usia Dini, 9*(2), 100. DOI: 10.26858/tematik.v9i2.54728

Ramirez, G., Gunderson, E. A., Levine, S. C., & Beilock, S. L. (2013). Math anxiety, working memory, and math achievement in early elementary school. *Journal of Cognition and Development, 14*(2), 187–202. DOI: 10.1080/15248372.2012.664593

Raspberry Pi Foundation. (2021, March 15). Computer science education is a global challenge [Blog post]. https://www.raspberrypi.org/blog/

Rattan, A., Good, C., & Dweck, C. S. (2012). "It's ok—not everyone can be good at math": Instructors with an entity theory comfort (and demotivate) students. *Journal of Experimental Social Psychology, 48*(3), 731–737. DOI: 10.1016/j.jesp.2011.12.012

Remiro, M. Á., Gil-Martín, M., & San-Segundo, R. (2023). Improving Hand Pose Recognition Using Localization and Zoom Normalizations over MediaPipe Landmarks. *Engineering Proceedings, 58*(1), 69. Advance online publication. DOI: 10.3390/ecsa-10-16215

Renjith, S., & Manazhy, R. (2024). Sign language : A systematic review on classification and recognition. *Multimedia Tools and Applications, 83*(31), 77077–77127. DOI: 10.1007/s11042-024-18583-4

Renkl, A., & Atkinson, R. K. (2003). Structuring the transition from example study to problem solving in cognitive skill acquisition: A cognitive load perspective. *Educational Psychologist, 38*(1), 15–22. DOI: 10.1207/S15326985EP3801_3

Resnick, M. (2017). *Lifelong kindergarten: Cultivating creativity through projects, passion, peers, and play*. MIT Press. DOI: 10.7551/mitpress/11017.001.0001

Resnick, M., Maloney, J., Monroy-Hernández, A., Rusk, N., Eastmond, E., Brennan, K., & Kafai, Y. (2020). Scratch: Programming for all. *Communications of the ACM, 63*(11), 28–30. DOI: 10.1145/3424000

Riazi, M., Rezvani, R., & Ghanbar, H. (2023). Trustworthiness in L2 writing research: A review and analysis of qualitative articles in the Journal of Second Language Writing. *Research Methods in Applied Linguistics, 2*(3), 100065. Advance online publication. DOI: 10.1016/j.rmal.2023.100065

Rich, K. M., Yadav, A., & Schwarz, C. V. (2019). Computational thinking, mathematics, and science: Elementary teachers' perspectives on integration. *Journal of Technology and Teacher Education, 27*(2), 165–205. DOI: 10.70725/303733vqleui

Rinta-Kahila, T., Penttinen, E., Salovaara, A., Soliman, W., & Ruissalo, J. (2023). The vicious circles of skill erosion: A case study of cognitive automation. *Journal of the Association for Information Systems, 24*(5), 1378–1412. DOI: 10.17705/1jais.00829

Robins, A., Rountree, J., & Rountree, N. (2003). Learning and teaching programming: A review and discussion. *Computer Science Education, 13*(2), 137–172. DOI: 10.1076/csed.13.2.137.14200

Robotics Online Marketing Team. (2017). Robotics in agriculture: Types and applications. *Association for Advancing Automation* (blog), December 12, 2017, Retrieved from https://www.automate.org/blogs/robotics-in-agriculture-types-and-applications

Rodríguez-Ponce, R., & Mota-Muñoz, F. G. (2020). Microcontroller-based direct torque control servodrive. *Journal of Robotics, 2020*, 1–11. DOI: 10.1155/2020/9152494

Roman-Gonzalez, M., Perez-Gonzalez, J. C., & Jimenez-Fernandez, C. (2017). Which cognitive abilities underlie computational thinking? Criterion validity of the computational thinking test. *Computers in Human Behavior, 72*, 678–691. DOI: 10.1016/j.chb.2016.08.047

Roodenrys, K., Agostinho, S., Roodenrys, S., & Chandler, P. (2012). Managing one's own cognitive load when evidence of split attention is present. *Applied Cognitive Psychology, 26*(6), 878–886. DOI: 10.1002/acp.2889

Rousouliotis, M., Vasileiou, M., Manos, N., & Kavallieratou, E. (2023). Employing an underwater vehicle in education as a learning tool for python programming. *Computer Applications in Engineering Education, 32*(1), e22693. Advance online publication. DOI: 10.1002/cae.22693

Rovshenov, A., & Sarsar, F. (2023). Research trends in programming education: A systematic review of articles published between 2012–2020. *Journal of Educational Technology & Online Learning*, *6*(1), 48–81. DOI: 10.31681/jetol.1201010

Royal Society. (2017). *After the reboot: Computing education in UK schools*. https://royalsociety.org/topics-policy/projects/computing-in-schools/report/

Sabitzer, B., & Pasterk, S. (2014). Brain-based programming continued: Effective teaching in programming courses. In *Frontiers in Education Conference (FIE)*, 2014 IEEE (pp.1–6). IEEE. DOI: 10.1109/FIE.2014.7044233

Sakai, K., & Passingham, R. E. (2002). Prefrontal interactions reflect future task operations. *Nature Neuroscience*, *6*(1), 75–81. DOI: 10.1038/nn987 PMID: 12469132

Salikhov, K. M., Zaslavskiy, D. A., & Balabanov, D. (2018). C++ in robotics education. *IEEE Global Engineering Education Conference (EDUCON)*, 1079–1082. https://doi.org/DOI: 10.1109/EDUCON.2018.8363335

Sat, M., & Kadirhan, Z. (2024). Unveiling competence in the classroom: A multidimensional assessment of computer science teachers' self-efficacy in coding education. *Education and Information Technologies*, *29*, 1–29. DOI: 10.1007/s10639-024-12503-7

Scherer, R., Siddiq, F., & Sánchez Viveros, B. (2019). The cognitive benefits of learning computer programming: A meta-analysis of transfer effects. *Journal of Educational Psychology*, *111*(5), 764–792. DOI: 10.1037/edu0000314

Scherer, R., Siddiq, F., & Sánchez-Scherer, B. (2021). Some evidence on the cognitive benefits of learning to code. *Frontiers in Psychology*, *12*, 559424. Advance online publication. DOI: 10.3389/fpsyg.2021.559424

Sentance, S., & Csizmadia, A. (2017). Computing in the curriculum: Challenges and strategies from a teacher's perspective. *Education and Information Technologies*, *22*(2), 469–495. DOI: 10.1007/s10639-016-9482-0

Seo, Y. H., & Kim, J. H. (2016). Analyzing the effects of coding education through pair programming for the computational thinking and creativity of elementary school students. *Indian Journal of Science and Technology*, *9*(46), 1–5. DOI: 10.17485/ijst/2016/v9i46/107837

Sharma, S., & Kumar, K. (2021). ASL-3DCNN: American sign language recognition technique using 3-D convolutional neural networks. *Multimedia Tools and Applications*, *80*(17), 26319–26331. DOI: 10.1007/s11042-021-10768-5

Shashidhara, S., Mitchell, D. J., Erez, Y., & Duncan, J. (2019). Progressive recruitment of the frontoparietal multiple-demand system with increased task complexity, time pressure, and reward. *Journal of Cognitive Neuroscience*, *31*(11), 1617–1630. DOI: 10.1162/jocn_a_01440 PMID: 31274390

Shin, Y., Jung, J., Choi, S., & Jung, B. (2025). The influence of scaffolding for computational thinking on cognitive load and problem-solving skills in collaborative programming. *Education and Information Technologies*, *30*(1), 583–606. DOI: 10.1007/s10639-024-13104-0

Shute, V. J., Sun, C., & Asbell-Clarke, J. (2017). Demystifying computational thinking. *Educational Research Review*, *22*, 142–158. DOI: 10.1016/j.edurev.2017.09.003

Siegmund, J., Kästner, C., Apel, S., Parnin, C., Bethmann, A., Leich, T., & Brechmann, A. (2014, May). Understanding understanding source code with functional magnetic resonance imaging. In *Proceedings of the 36th International Conference on Software Engineering* (pp. 378-389). https://doi.org/DOI: 10.1145/2568225.2568252

Siegmund, J., Peitek, N., Parnin, C., Apel, S., Hofmeister, J., Kästner, C., & Brechmann, A. (2017, August). Measuring neural efficiency of program comprehension. In *Proceedings of the 2017 11th Joint Meeting on Foundations of Software Engineering* (pp. 140-150). DOI: 10.1145/3106237.3106268

Simon, S., Coelho, R., Marfisi-Schottman, I., & Pea, R. (2024). Generative ai tools in an undergraduate computer science program. Proceedings of the 18th International Conference of the Learning Sciences - ICLS 2024. https://doi.org/DOI: 10.22318/icls2024.271910

Sozio, G., Agostinho, S., Tindall-Ford, S., & Paas, F. (2024). Enhancing teaching strategies through cognitive load theory: Process vs. product worked examples. *Education Sciences*, *14*(8), 813. DOI: 10.3390/educsci14080813

Spanjers, I. A. E., Wouters, P., van Gog, T., & van Merriënboer, J. J. G. (2011). An expertise reversal effect of segmentation in learning from animated worked-out examples. *Computers in Human Behavior*, *27*(1), 46–52. DOI: 10.1016/j.chb.2010.05.011

Staacks, S., Dorsel, D., Krampe, A., Hagedorn, M., Leier, E., Heinke, H., & Stampfer, C. (2025). Bluetooth sensors in phyphox with arduino and micropython: Paving the way from an idea to an experiment for teachers and learners. *Physics Education*, *60*(3), 035014. DOI: 10.1088/1361-6552/adbf5f

Stachel, J., Marghitu, D., Brahim, T. B., Sims, R., Reynolds, L., & Czelusniak, V. (2013). Managing cognitive load in introductory programming courses: A cognitive aware scaffolding tool. *Journal of Integrated Design & Process Science, 17*(1), 37–54. DOI: 10.3233/jid-2013-0004

Starner, T., Weaver, J., & Pentland, A. (1998). Real-time american sign language recognition using desk and wearable computer based video. *IEEE Transactions on Pattern Analysis and Machine Intelligence, 20*(12), 1371–1375. DOI: 10.1109/34.735811

Stefaniak, J., & Moore, S. (2024). The Use of Generative AI to Support Inclusivity and Design Deliberation for Online Instruction. *Online Learning : the Official Journal of the Online Learning Consortium, 28*(3), 181–205. DOI: 10.24059/olj.v28i3.4458

Strange, B. A., Henson, R. N. A., Friston, K. J., & Dolan, R. J. (2001). Anterior prefrontal cortex mediates rule learning in humans. *Cerebral Cortex (New York, N.Y.), 11*(11), 1040–1046. DOI: 10.1093/cercor/11.11.1040 PMID: 11590113

Strawhacker, A., & Bers, M. U. (2019). What they learn when they learn coding: Investigating cognitive domains and computer programming knowledge in young children. *Educational Technology Research and Development, 67*(3), 541–575. DOI: 10.1007/s11423-018-9622-x

Sun, Q., Wu, J., Rong, W., & Liu, W. (2019). Formative assessment of programming language learning based on peer code review: Implementation and experience report. *Tsinghua Science and Technology, 24*(4), 423–434. DOI: 10.26599/TST.2018.9010109

Suters, L. (2021). Elementary preservice teacher coursework design for developing science and mathematics computational thinking practices. *Contemporary Issues in Technology & Teacher Education, 21*(2), 360–440.

Sweller, J. (1988). Cognitive load during problem solving: Effects on learning. *Cognitive Science, 12*(2), 257–285. DOI: 10.1207/s15516709cog1202_4

Sweller, J. (1994). Cognitive load theory, learning difficulty, and instructional design. *Learning and Instruction, 4*(4), 295–312. DOI: 10.1016/0959-4752(94)90003-5

Sweller, J. (2010). Element interactivity and intrinsic, extraneous and germane cognitive load. *Educational Psychology Review, 22*(2), 123–138. DOI: 10.1007/s10648-010-9128-5

Sweller, J. (2016). Working memory, long-term memory, and instructional design. *Journal of Applied Research in Memory and Cognition, 5*(4), 360–367. DOI: 10.1016/j.jarmac.2015.12.002

Sweller, J. (2020). Cognitive load theory and educational technology. *Educational Technology Research and Development*, *68*(1), 1–16. DOI: 10.1007/s11423-019-09701-3

Sweller, J. (2024). Cognitive load theory and individual differences. *Learning and Individual Differences*, *110*, 102423. Advance online publication. DOI: 10.1016/j.lindif.2024.102423

Sweller, J., Ayres, P., & Kalyuga, S. (2011). *Cognitive load theory*. Springer New York., DOI: 10.1007/978-1-4419-8126-4

Sweller, J., & Cooper, G. A. (1985). The use of worked examples as a substitute for problem solving in learning algebra. *Cognition and Instruction*, *2*(1), 59–89. DOI: 10.1207/s1532690xci0201_3

Sweller, J., van Merriënboer, J. J. G., & Paas, F. (1998). Cognitive architecture and instructional design. *Educational Psychology Review*, *10*(3), 251–296. DOI: 10.1023/A:1022193728205

Sweller, J., van Merriënboer, J. J. G., & Paas, F. (2019). Cognitive architecture and instructional design: 20 years later. *Educational Psychology Review*, *31*(2), 261–292. DOI: 10.1007/s10648-019-09465-5

Tagare, D. (2024). Factors That Predict K-12 Teachers' Ability to Apply Computational Thinking Skills. *ACM Transactions on Computing Education*, *24*(1), 1–26. DOI: 10.1145/3633205

Tao, W., Leu, M. C., & Yin, Z. (2018). American Sign Language alphabet recognition using Convolutional Neural Networks with multiview augmentation and inference fusion. *Engineering Applications of Artificial Intelligence*, *76*(February), 202–213. DOI: 10.1016/j.engappai.2018.09.006

Tarmizi, R., & Sweller, J. (1988). Guidance during mathematical problem solving. *Journal of Educational Psychology*, *80*(4), 424–436. DOI: 10.1037/0022-0663.80.4.424

Taya, F., Sun, Y., Babiloni, F., Thakor, N., & Bezerianos, A. (2015). Brain enhancement through cognitive training: A new insight from brain connectome. *Frontiers in Systems Neuroscience*, *9*, 44. DOI: 10.3389/fnsys.2015.00044 PMID: 25883555

Telukdarie, A., Munsamy, M., Katsumbe, T., Maphisa, X., & Philbin, S. P. (2023). Industry 4.0 technological advancement in the food and beverage manufacturing industry in south africa—Bibliometric analysis via natural language processing. *Information (Basel)*, *14*(8), 454. DOI: 10.3390/info14080454

Tissenbaum, M., Sheldon, J., & Abelson, H. (2019). From computational thinking to computational action. *Communications of the ACM*, *62*(3), 34–36. DOI: 10.1145/3265747

Tiwari, S. P., & Fahrudin, A. (2024). *Evolving school dynamics and emerging technologies in education: critical success factors*. SciFormat Publishing Books., DOI: 10.69635/978-1-0690482-0-2

Totan, H. N., & Korucu, A. T. (2023). The effect of block based coding education on the students' attitudes about the secondary school students' computational learning skills and coding learning: Blocky sample. *Participatory Educational Research*, *10*(1), 443–461. DOI: 10.17275/per.23.24.10.1

Tsarava, K., Leifheit, L., Ninaus, M., Román-González, M., Butz, M. V., Golle, J., & Moeller, K. (2019, October). Cognitive correlates of computational thinking: Evaluation of a blended unplugged/plugged-in course. In *Proceedings of the 14th workshop in primary and secondary computing education* (pp. 1-9). https://doi.org/ DOI: 10.1145/3361721.3361729

Tsarava, K., Moeller, K., Román-González, M., Golle, J., Leifheit, L., Butz, M. V., & Ninaus, M. (2022). A cognitive definition of computational thinking in primary education. *Computers & Education*, *179*, 104425. DOI: 10.1016/j.compedu.2021.104425

Tselegkaridis, S., Sapounidis, T., Tokatlidis, C., Rapti, S., & Papakostas, D. (2025). Aabc: A tool for assessing arduino basic coding skills. *Computer Applications in Engineering Education*, *33*(3), e70029. Advance online publication. DOI: 10.1002/cae.70029

Tsikalakis, G., Neofotistou, E., Kontogiannakis, E., Pau, A., Caglayan, E. M., Fernandez-Canez, R., … & Perez-Accino, M. (2023). Sustainable development as an education tool for primary school students through scratch code. E3S Web of Conferences, 436, 06007. https://doi.org/DOI: 10.1051/e3sconf/202343606007

Tuomi, P., Multisilta, J., Saarikoski, P., & Suominen, J. (2018). Coding skills as a success factor for a society. *Education and Information Technologies*, *23*(1), 419–434. DOI: 10.1007/s10639-017-9611-4

Tyagi, V. (2018). *Understanding Digital Image Processing*. CRC Press. DOI: 10.1201/9781315123905

U.S. Department of Agriculture. (n.d.a). The importance of pollinators. https://www.usda.gov/about-usda/general-information/initiatives-and-highlighted-programs/peoples-garden/importance-pollinators

U.S. Department of Agriculture. (n.d.b). National Agricultural Statistics Service. https://quickstats.nass.usda.gov/#3F7820DC-AC84-3DC9-B409-FC613BFD0EE4

Uğraş, M., Güneş, H., Uğraş, H., Papadakis, S., & Kalogiannakis, M. (2025). Coding activities in early childhood: A systematic review. *International Journal of Technology Enhanced Learning*, *17*(1), 45–80. DOI: 10.1504/IJTEL.2025.143512

UNESCO Institute for Statistics. (2025). *National education statistical capacity assessment: Global analysis based on a maturity model* (Report No. UIS/2025/ED/SD/1). UNESCO. https://unesdoc.unesco.org/ark:/48223/pf0000394897

Uwano, H., Nakamura, M., Monden, A., & Matsumoto, K. I. (2006, March). Analyzing individual performance of source code review using reviewers' eye movement. In *Proceedings of the 2006 symposium on Eye tracking research & applications* (pp. 133–140). DOI: 10.1145/1117309.1117357

Vakil, S. (2014). A critical pedagogy approach for engaging urban youth in mobile app development in an after-school program. *Equity & Excellence in Education*, *47*(1), 31–45. DOI: 10.1080/10665684.2014.866869

Valls, J., Fonseca, D., Redondo, E., & Navarro, I. (2022). Impact of educational robotics on computational thinking through project-based learning activities. *Education and Information Technologies*, *27*(1), 947–968. DOI: 10.1007/s10639-021-10644-2

van Merriënboer, J. J. G., & Kirschner, P. A. (2017). *Ten steps to complex learning: A systematic approach to four-component instructional design* (3rd ed.). Routledge., DOI: 10.4324/9781315113210

van Merriënboer, J. J. G., & Krammer, H. P. M. (1987). Instructional strategies and tactics for the design of introductory computer programming courses in high school. *Instructional Science*, *16*(3), 251–285. DOI: 10.1007/BF00120253

van Merriënboer, J. J. G., & Sweller, J. (2005). Cognitive load theory and complex learning: Recent developments and future directions. *Educational Psychology Review*, *17*(2), 147–177. DOI: 10.1007/s10648-005-3951-0

Voogt, J., Fisser, P., Good, J., Mishra, P., & Yadav, A. (2015). Computational thinking in compulsory education: Towards an agenda for research and practice. *Education and Information Technologies*, *20*(4), 715–728. DOI: 10.1007/s10639-015-9412-6

W3C. (2019). *HTML & CSS Standards*. World Wide Web Consortium. https://www.w3.org

Wadhawan, A., & Kumar, P. (2021). Sign Language Recognition Systems: A Decade Systematic Literature Review. *Archives of Computational Methods in Engineering*, *28*(3), 785–813. DOI: 10.1007/s11831-019-09384-2

Walkington, C., & Bernacki, M. L. (2019). Personalizing algebra to students' individual interests in an intelligent tutoring system: Moderators of impact. *International Journal of Artificial Intelligence in Education*, *29*(1), 58–88. DOI: 10.1007/s40593-018-0168-1

Wallis, J. D. (2007). Orbitofrontal cortex and its contribution to decision-making. *Annual Review of Neuroscience*, *30*(1), 31–56. DOI: 10.1146/annurev.neuro.30.051606.094334 PMID: 17417936

Wang, L., Geng, F., Hao, X., Shi, D., Wang, T., & Li, Y. (2023). Measuring coding ability in young children: Relations to computational thinking, creative thinking, and working memory. *Current Psychology (New Brunswick, N.J.)*, *42*(10), 8039–8050. DOI: 10.1007/s12144-021-02085-9

Weber, B., Fischer, T., & Riedl, R. (2021). Brain and autonomic nervous system activity measurement in software engineering: A systematic literature review. *Journal of Systems and Software*, *178*, 110946. DOI: 10.1016/j.jss.2021.110946

Weintrop, D., Beheshti, E., Horn, M., Orton, K., Jona, K., Trouille, L., & Wilensky, U. (2016). Defining computational thinking for mathematics and science classrooms. *Journal of Science Education and Technology*, *25*(1), 127–147. DOI: 10.1007/s10956-015-9581-5

Welling, L., & Thomson, L. (2017). *PHP and MySQL Web Development* (5th ed.). Addison-Wesley.

Werner, M. H., & Olanow, C. W. (2021). Parkinson's disease modification through abl kinase inhibition: An opportunity. *Movement Disorders*, *37*(1), 6–15. DOI: 10.1002/mds.28858

Wickham, H., & Grolemund, G. (2017). *R for Data Science: Import, Tidy, Transform, Visualize, and Model Data*. O'Reilly Media. https://r4ds.hadley.nz

Wigfield, A., & Eccles, J. S. (2000). Expectancy-value theory of achievement motivation. *Contemporary Educational Psychology*, *25*(1), 68–81. DOI: 10.1006/ceps.1999.1015 PMID: 10620382

Wigfield, A., Eccles, J. S., Roeser, R. W., & Schiefele, U. (2008). Development of achievement motivation. In Damon, W., & Lerner, R. M. (Eds.), *Child and adolescent development: An advanced course* (pp. 406–434). John Wiley and Sons.

Wilson, B., DeBruin, J., Higgins, A., Gross, T., Gum, H., & Cannon, T. (2018). *Bringing our farms into focus: Specialty food crops, farm viability and market profitability in West Virginia*. Organization Name. Retrieved from http://foodjustice.wvu.edu/wp-content/uploads/2018/12/WV-Farm-viability_study_final.pdf

Wing, J. M. (2014). *Computational thinking benefits society. 40th anniversary blog of social issues in computing*, 2014, 26. http://socialissues.cs.toronto.edu/index.html%3Fp=279.html

Wing, J. M. (2006). Computational thinking. *Communications of the ACM*, *49*(3), 33–35. DOI: 10.1145/1118178.1118215

Wing, J. M. (2008). Computational thinking and thinking about computing. *Philosophical Transactions. Series A, Mathematical, Physical, and Engineering Sciences*, *366*(1881), 3717–3725. DOI: 10.1098/rsta.2008.0118 PMID: 18672462

Wong, G. K., Cheung, H. Y., Ching, E. C., & Huen, J. M. (2015). *School perceptions of coding education in K-12: A large scale quantitative study to inform innovative practices. In 2015 IEEE international conference on teaching, Assessment, and learning for engineering (TALE)*. IEEE.

Wood, T., Milbrath, M., & Szendrei, Z. (n.d.). *Maximizing honey bee pollination in pickling cucumbers*. Michigan State University Extension. https://pollinators.msu.edu/sites/_pollinators/assets/File/PollinationPicklingCucumbers.pdf

Woodcock, T. S. (2012). *Pollination in the agricultural landscape: best management practices for crop pollination. Canadian Pollination Initiative (NSERCCANPOLIN)*. University of Guelph., https://seeds.ca/pollinator/bestpractices/images/Pollination%20in%20Agricultural%20Landscape_Woodcock_Final.pdf

Wu, J., Sun, L., & Jafari, R. (2016). A Wearable System for Recognizing American Sign Language in Real-Time Using IMU and Surface EMG Sensors. *IEEE Journal of Biomedical and Health Informatics*, *20*(5), 1281–1290. DOI: 10.1109/JBHI.2016.2598302 PMID: 27576269

Xhako, D., Hoxhaj, S., Hyka, N., & Spahiu, E. (2025). Integrating AI applications into university STEM study programs using Python. *International Journal of Innovative Research and Scientific Studies*, *8*(1), 2374–2384. DOI: 10.53894/ijirss.v8i1.4995

Yadav, A., Hong, H., & Stephenson, C. (2016). Computational thinking for all: Pedagogical approaches to embedding 21st century problem solving in K-12 classrooms. *TechTrends*, *60*(6), 565–568. DOI: 10.1007/s11528-016-0087-7

Yadav, A., Stephenson, C., & Hong, H. (2017). Computational thinking for teacher education. *Communications of the ACM*, *60*(4), 55–62. DOI: 10.1145/2994591

Yang, S. (2018). Investigation of programming education in China's primary and secondary schools. *Education and Information Technologies, 23*(5), 2005–2021. DOI: 10.1007/s10639-018-9750-x

Yao, D., & Lin, J. (2025). Cognitive enhancement through competency-based programming education: A 12-year longitudinal study. *Education and Information Technologies, 30*(14), 20347–20383. Advance online publication. DOI: 10.1007/s10639-025-13582-w

Ye, H., Liang, B., Ng, O.-L., & Chai, C. S. (2023). Integration of computational thinking in K-12 mathematics education: A systematic review on CT-based mathematics instruction and student learning. *International Journal of STEM Education, 10*(1), 3. DOI: 10.1186/s40594-023-00396-w

Yen, C.-Z., Wu, P.-H., & Lin, C.-F. (2012). Analysis of experts' and novices' thinking process in program debugging. In Li, K. C., Wang, F. L., Yuen, K. S., Cheung, S. K. S., & Kwan, R. (Eds.), *Engaging learners through emerging technologies* (Vol. 302, pp. 122–134)., DOI: 10.1007/978-3-642-31398-1_12

Yenilmez, İ. (2016). *İstatistiksel kavramların teknoloji ile öğretiminin matematik didaktiği perspektifinden incelenmesi [Evaluation of teaching statistical concepts using technology from the perspective of the didactics of mathematics]* (Unpublished master's thesis). Marmara University, İstanbul, Türkiye.

Yenilmez, İ. (2025). eduMathStatAI: An R package for math and statistics education (Version 1.0). GitHub. https://github.com/IsmailYenilmez/eduMathStatAI

Yenilmez, İ., & Yavuz, İ. (2016). Using technology in statistical education at high school level: VUstat software and a case of Eskişehir Tepebaşı. In *Proceedings of the 7th International Congress on New Trends in Education* (pp. 55). Antalya, Türkiye.

Yıldız, E., & Çengel, M. (2022). An experimental study in determining basic robotic coding skills of pre-school students with intellectual disabilities. *International Journal of Interactive Mobile Technologies (Ijim), 16*(23), 84–98. DOI: 10.3991/ijim.v16i23.36077

Yilmaz, R., & Yilmaz, F. G. K. (2023). The effect of generative artificial intelligence (AI)-based tool use on students' computational thinking skills, programming self-efficacy and motivation. *Computers and Education: Artificial Intelligence, 4*, 100147. DOI: 10.1016/j.caeai.2023.100147

Yılmaz, T., & İzmirli, S. (2023). Effect of unplugged and plugged coding activities on secondary school students' computational thinking skills. *Journal of Educational Technology and Online Learning, 6*(4), 1180–1193. DOI: 10.31681/jetol.1375335

Yousoof, M., Sapiyan, M., & Kamaluddin, K. (2007). Measuring cognitive load: A solution to ease learning of programming. *World Academy of Science, Engineering and Technology*, *26*, 216–219.

Yun, M., & Crippen, K. J. (2024). Computational Thinking Integration into Pre-Service Science Teacher Education: A Systematic Review. *Journal of Science Teacher Education*, ●●●, 1–30.

Zagalsky, A., Feliciano, J., Storey, M., Zhao, Y., & Wang, W. (2015). The emergence of github as a collaborative platform for education. *Proceedings of the 18th ACM Conference on Computer Supported Cooperative Work & Social Computing,* 1906-1917. https://doi.org/DOI: 10.1145/2675133.2675284

Zatorre, R. J., Fields, R. D., & Johansen-Berg, H. (2012). Plasticity in gray and white: Neuroimaging changes in brain structure during learning. *Nature Neuroscience*, *15*(4), 528–536. DOI: 10.1038/nn.3045 PMID: 22426254

Zawacki-Richter, O., Marín, V. I., Bond, M., & Gouverneur, F. (2019). Systematic review of research on artificial intelligence applications in higher education – where are the educators? *International Journal of Educational Technology in Higher Education*, *16*(1), 39. DOI: 10.1186/s41239-019-0171-0

Zhang, D., & Li, A. (2023). *A smart interactive and collaborative online coding platform for programming education using machine learning and web socket*. Software Engineering and Applications., DOI: 10.5121/csit.2023.131703

Zhang, I., Jia, Y. R., Cheng, X. A., Son, J. Y., & Stigler, J. W. (2025). Empowering novice programmers: Redesigning documentation for effective informal learning. *Journal of Educational Computing Research*, *63*(3), 695–727. DOI: 10.1177/07356331241311505

Zhang, L., & Nouri, J. (2019). A systematic review of learning computational thinking through Scratch in K-9. *Computers & Education*, *141*, 103607. DOI: 10.1016/j.compedu.2019.103607

Zhang, S., Wong, G. K. W., & Chan, P. C. F. (2022). Playing coding games to learn computational thinking: What motivates students to use this tool at home? *Education and Information Technologies*, *28*(1), 193–216. DOI: 10.1007/s10639-022-11181-7

Zhang, Y., & Rutherford, T. (2024). Scaffolding expertise: Evaluating scaffolds for block-based coding among experts and novices. In *ISAIE '24: Proceedings of the 2024 International Symposium on Artificial Intelligence for Education* (pp. 277-282). Association for Computing Machinery. https://doi.org/DOI: 10.1145/3700297.3700345

Zhang, Y., Wang, P., Jia, W., Zhang, A., & Chen, G. (2023). Dynamic visualization by GeoGebra for mathematics learning: A meta-analysis of 20 years of research. *Journal of Research on Technology in Education*. Advance online publication. DOI: 10.1080/15391523.2023.2250886

Zhu, M., Liu, O. L., & Lee, H. S. (2020). The effect of automated feedback on revision behavior and learning gains in formative assessment of scientific argument writing. *Computers & Education*, *143*, 103668. DOI: 10.1016/j.compedu.2019.103668

About the Contributors

Fatih Yaman earned his Ph.D. in Computer Education and Instructional Technologies from Anadolu University in 2018, following a Bachelor's degree in Computer Education and Instructional Technologies from Marmara University in 2008. Currently, he serves as a faculty member in the Department of Information Systems and Technologies at Kırşehir Ahi Evran University. Dr. Yaman has extensive teaching experience in undergraduate courses, including instructional technologies, database management systems, web design, and software engineering. His academic contributions span a variety of research areas, including digital literacy, the integration of artificial intelligence in education, and distance learning methodologies. He has previously held positions as a faculty member at Muş Alparslan University and as a research assistant at Anadolu University, where he actively engaged in both teaching and research activities. Dr. Yaman has authored numerous publications in peer-reviewed journals and presented his work at international conferences, significantly contributing to the academic discourse in educational technology. Dr. Yaman is committed to leveraging technology to enhance educational practices and to fostering innovative solutions that address the challenges of modern learning environments.

Nihal Dulkadir Yaman earned her Ph.D. in Computer Education and Instructional Technologies from Anadolu University in 2019, following a Master's degree in Distance Education (2018) and a Bachelor's degree in Computer Education and Instructional Technologies (2008) from the same institution. Currently, she serves as a faculty member in the Department of Management Information Systems at Kırşehir Ahi Evran University. Her academic journey includes faculty positions at Muş Alparslan University and Burdur Mehmet Akif Ersoy University, as well as research assistant roles at Anadolu University and Muş Alparslan University. Throughout her career, Dr. Yaman has made significant contributions to integrating technology into education, focusing on digital literacy, distance education, and the application of artificial intelligence in learning environments. Her research interests span educational technology, database management systems, and computer networks. Dr. Yaman has an extensive teaching portfolio, offering undergraduate courses such as instructional technologies, database management systems, computer networks, programming languages, and web design. She has authored numerous publications in respected journals and conferences, contributing to the academic discourse in her areas of expertise. Dr. Yaman's work is dedicated to advancing educational practices through technology, bridging the gap between theoretical knowledge and practical application in modern learning environments.

***

Onur Dönmez is an Associate Professor and currently works at the Department of Computer Education and Instructional Technology, Ege University. Onur does research in Teacher Education, e-Learning, Multimedia Learning and Children's Safe Internet Use.

Ugur Kale an Associate Professor in Indiana University's Learning, Design, and Adult Education Department, teaching and researching issues and potentials that emerging technologies bring to computational thinking, online learning, and teacher education.

Kyungbin Kwon is an Associate Professor in the Department of Learning, Design, and Adult Education at Indiana University Bloomington. Dr. Kwon's research focuses on fostering positive student interactions within Computer-Supported Collaborative Learning (CSCL) contexts and designing effective instruction for computational thinking and AI literacy.

Hanh Le is a passionate researcher and accomplished Full Stack Software Developer with deep expertise in software development, data analytics, data science, and cloud computing. She holds a Ph.D. in Information Technology and a Master's in Computer Science, bringing both academic rigor and a solution-driven mindset to her work. With extensive experience in front-end and back-end development, she specializes in scalable, database-driven applications that support evidence-based decision-making. Dr. Le has led transformative tech initiatives across healthcare, law enforcement, and retail, translating complex needs into high-performing systems. She values interdisciplinary collaboration, believing that impactful innovation often arises at the intersection of fields. Her blend of technical skill, research excellence, and collaborative spirit continues to drive progress in academia and industry alike.

Kunj Bihari Meena is an Assistant Professor in the Department of Computer Science and Engineering at Jaypee University of Engineering and Technology, Guna. He received his M.Tech. from IIT Kharagpur in 2013 and completed his Ph.D. from JUET, Guna. With over 12 years of teaching experience, he has guided numerous UG and PG students and taught subjects including Data Structures, OOP, Machine Learning, and Microprocessors. He has published several research papers in SCI and Scopus-indexed journals and is a lifetime member of the Computer Society of India (CSI). His research interests include machine learning, deep learning, digital image forensics, and blockchain technology.

Özgür Örün obtained his Ph.D. degree with an interdisciplinary thesis from the Department of Computer Education and Instructional Technology at Anadolu University in 2019. As of 2024, he has started a second graduate program in Neuroscience at the Graduate School of Health Sciences, Ege University, Türkiye. In 2013, he was an Erasmus visiting academic staff for a short term at Adam Mickiewicz University in Poznan, Poland. In 2018, as a researcher focusing on the physiological measurement of learning processes with Electroencephalogram (EEG), he attended the EEGLAB at the Swartz Center for Computational Neuroscience, University of California, San Diego, USA. Since 2021, Dr. Özgür ÖRÜN has been working at the Izmir Institute of Technology, contributing as a researcher and consultant to various projects supported by different institutions, including the Development Agency and the Scientific and Technological Research Council of Türkiye. His interdisciplinary research interests include educational neuroscience, cognitive science, (multimedia) learning, working memory, multitasking, instructional design and technology. He publishes and continues his academic production within this scope.

Gamze Ozogul is a Professor of Instructional Systems Technology and serves as the Department Chair of Learning Design and Adult Education at Indiana University.. Her research centers on instructional design and instructional strategies for emerging learning environments, with a particular emphasis on feedback design and artificial intelligence in higher education.

Juhyun Park is currently pursuing her PhD in Instructional Systems Technology at Indiana University Bloomington. She previously worked as an elementary school teacher in Korea, designing learner-centered and project-based learning experiences. Her current research focuses on integrating computational thinking and artificial intelligence education into K-12 learning environments.

Fırat Hayyam Sabuncu is currently getting PhD at the Department of Computer Education and Instructional Technology (CEIT), Graduate School of Educational Sciences at Ege University. He has been working as an ICT Teacher in public schools since 2006. He does research in educational technology, cognitive load theory and computer assisted education. He teaches computer algorithms, programming, robotics and 3D design.

Anushka Samaiya is a BTech (Computer Science and Engineering) student at Jaypee University of Engineering and Technology, Guna MP . She is interested in technology and love building useful projects.

İsmail Tonbuloğlu is an assistant professor at Marmara University, Department of Computer Education and Instructional Technologies. He completed his master's degree on usability evaluation of educational software and his PhD on pre-service teachers' acceptance of mobile technologies for instructional purposes. His research interests are computer science education, educational technology integration, distance education, e-learning, technology acceptance, usability evaluation.

Vipin Tyagi is a distinguished academician, researcher and author, currently serving as Dean (Academics and Research) at Jaypee University of Engineering and Technology in Guna, Madhya Pradesh. Prof. Tyagi joined JUET, Guna in July 2005. His expertise spans across Image Processing, Cyber Forensics, and Speech Recognition. He is also Director – IQAC of JUET Guna and NEP 2020 UGC University coordinator. Prof. Tyagi has a prolific publication record, contributing significantly to his fields of interest. His scholarly work includes numerous journal articles, conference papers, and books. Some of his notable publications are in the areas of image forgery detection, image denoising, and content-based image retrieval. He has authored and edited several books and papers in the field of computing and data sciences, such as "Predictive Computing and Information Security" and "Content-Based Image Retrieval: Ideas, Influences, and Current Trends" published by Springer Singapore. His scholarly work has earned him a respectable h-index and numerous citations in the academic community. In addition to his academic pursuits, Prof. Tyagi has been actively involved in professional societies. Prof. Tyagi is a senior life member of the Computer Society of India, a Fellow of the IETE, Senior Member - IEEE and a member of the Indian Science Congress Association, ACM, and the Remote Sensing Society of India. He was elected as President and Recorder of Engineering Science Section of Indian Science Congress Association. He also worked as member of management committee of Computer Society of India-Bhopal Chapter, executive committee member of IETE-Bhopal center for year 2010-12. He was also MP State Student Coordinator of Computer Society of India. He has also served as Vice-President for the regions of Madhya Pradesh, Rajasthan, and Gujarat and Hon. National Secretary of the Computer Society of India. Prof. Tyagi is elected as member Board of Governors of Engineering Council of India third time consecutively for 2 years (2020-2022, 2022-2024, 2024-26). He also served as Regional Coordinator of the AICTE National Coordination Committee-Induction Program (Central Region).

Abhinav Varshney is a final-year Bachelor of Technology student with specialization in Computer Science and Engineering at Jaypee University of Engineering and Technology, Guna, Madhya Pradesh, India. His professional and study interests are mainly in the fields of Data Science, Artificial Intelligence, and Web Automation. With a keen interest in applied machine learning and intelligent system design, he is deeply involved in developing AI-based solutions that connect the divide between automation and analytics. He wants to be a Data Scientist and contribute meaningfully toward the development of intelligent technologies and data applications in the real world.

Shrinu Varshney is a B.Tech Computer Science and Engineering student at Jaypee University of Engineering and Technology, Guna. He is passionate about Data Science, Artificial Intelligence, and inclusive technology. With a strong interest in applying data-driven solutions to real-world challenges, Shrinu actively engages in research and projects that promote accessibility and innovation in education.

Index

Symbols

A

C

D

E

G

I

J

M

N

P

R

S

T

U

V

W

www.ingramcontent.com/pod-product-compliance
Lightning Source LLC
LaVergne TN
LVHW080905300926
849162LV00003B/555